The Making of
Political Identities

V

PHRONESIS

A series from Verso edited by
Ernesto Laclau and Chantal Mouffe

There is today wide agreement that the left-wing project
is in crisis. New antagonisms have emerged – not only in
advanced capitalist societies but also in the Eastern bloc
and in the Third World – that require the reformulation
of the socialist ideal in terms of an extension and
deepening of democracy. However, serious disagreements exist as to the theoretical strategy needed to
carry out such a task. There are those for whom the
current critique of rationalism and universalism puts
into jeopardy the very basis of the democratic project.
Others argue that the critique of essentialism – a point of
convergence of the most important trends in contemporary theory: post-structuralism, philosophy of language
after the later Wittgenstein, post-Heideggerian her-
meneutics – is the necessary condition for understanding the widening of the field of social struggles
characteristic of the present stage of democratic politics.
Phronesis clearly locates itself among the latter. Our
objective is to establish a dialogue between these
theoretical developments and left-wing politics. We
believe that an anti-essentialist theoretical stand is the
sine qua non of a new vision for the Left conceived in
terms of a radical and plural democracy.

The Making of Political Identities

Edited by

ERNESTO LACLAU

VERSO

London · New York

First published by Verso 1994
© Individual contributors 1994
All rights reserved

Verso
UK: 6 Meard Street, London W1V 3HR
USA: 29 West 35th Street, New York, NY 10001–2291

Verso is the imprint of New Left Books

ISBN 0–86091–409–7
ISBN 0–86091–663–4 (pbk)

British Library Cataloguing in Publication Data
A catalogue record for this book is available from the British Library

Library of Congress Cataloging-in-Publication Data
The Making of political identities/edited by Ernesto Laclau.
p.   cm. – (Phronesis)
Includes bibliographical references and index.
ISBN 0–86091–409–7 – ISBN 0–86091–663–4 (pbk.)
1. Political science – Philosophy.   2. Group identity.   3. Post-communism.
I. Laclau, Ernesto.   II. Series: Phronesis (London, England)
JA71.M115   1994
320′.01′1 – dc20   93–50722
CIP

Typeset by Type Study, Scarborough
Printed and bound in Great Britain by
Biddles Ltd, Guildford and Kings Lynn

Contents

Acknowledgements

We want to thank the Department of Government, University of Essex, and the Political Studies Association of Great Britain for their financial support which made possible our initial workshop. We also want to thank Sue Golding, senior research Associate at the Centre for Theoretical Studies, University of Essex, for her thorough analytic editing of this volume; Patrick Camiller for his translations of the German and Spanish texts; and Noreen Harburt for her administrative efficiency.

Introduction

Few people would today question that we are living at the epicentre of a major historical mutation. The sense of the change, however, is difficult to determine, and one wonders to what extent the problems found in defining it are not in themselves major indicators of what is changing. In a certain sense, giving an external account of the mutation is rather simple. It amounts to something like this: the end of the Cold War has also been the end of the globalizing ideologies that had dominated the political arena since 1945. These ideologies, however, have not been replaced by others that play the same structural function; instead, their collapse has been accompanied by a general decline of ideological politics. The discourse of both camps in the Cold War has been, in this sense, a last version of the political ideology of modernity: that is, the attempt to legitimate one's own ideology by presenting it as a fulfilment of a universal task (whatever that might be). In a post-Cold War world, on the contrary, we are witnessing a proliferation of particularistic political identities, none of which tries to ground its legitimacy and its action in a mission predetermined by universal history – whether that be the mission of a universal class, or the notion of a privileged race, or an abstract principle. Quite the opposite. Any kind of universal grounding is contemplated with deep suspicion.

Two points are especially worth making in connection with this change. The first is that the crisis of universalism does not simply rule the latter out of existence, but opens the way to the very tangible emergence of its void, of what we could call *the presence of its absence*. A History without ultimate meanings, without Absolute Spirit, shows itself *in a first way* as a consciousness of the contingent, precarious, limited character of what remains. And this leads to a new awareness of the complex mechanisms through which all identity – and all social reality – is constructed; indeed, it leads to an awareness of its deeply ambiguous conditions of existence. If we live in an era of deconstruction, it is

1

because the crisis of essentialist universalism as a self-asserted ground has led our attention to the contingent *grounds* (in the plural) of its emergence and to the complex processes of its construction. This operation is, *sensu stricto*, *transcendental*: it involves a retreat from an object to its conditions of possibility.

Our second point is that this move – which can be called a radical constructivism – widens and diversifies the strategies that it is possible to develop within the social. It is, in that sense, at the root of an intellectual thaw. Let us consider a theoretical orientation such as pragmatism. It involves both a movement away from essentialist universalism and an 'instrumental' use of theoretical categories. But the 'uses' to which it can be put depend entirely on the horizon of possibilities that define a context. If such a context is defined in a rigidly institutional way, the pragmatic turn can only give way to a very limited 'piecemeal engineering'. But, if the transcendental retreat goes far enough, the institutions themselves will be seen as the actualization of merely contingent possibilities, and more risky strategic movements will become possible. A radicalized pragmatism will thus join forces with a historicist deconstructivism.

It is in a similar sense that I see the transformation today of the discourses informing both political theory and political practice (in fact, the separation between the two is largely an artificial operation). Theoretical categories which in the past were considered as bearers of a univocal sense become deeply ambiguous once that sense is seen as the actualization of only *some* of the possibilities opened by their internal structure. Once this is realized, once the deconstruction of those categories fully reveals the power games that govern their actual structuration, new and more complex hegemonico-political moves become possible within them. And, as theoretico-political categories do not only exist in books but are also part of discourses actually informing institutions and social relations, these deconstructive operations are an integral part of the making of political life.

The essays in this volume attempt to contribute to this task through the analysis of 'political identities'. Let us consider what is involved in these two terms by first taking up the issue of identities. Paradoxically, this issue acquired paramount importance in political theory, once the obviousness of social identities was put into question. If agents were to have an always already defined location in the social structure, the problem of their identity, considered in a radical way, would not arise – or, at most, would be seen as a matter of people *discovering* or *recognizing* their own identity, not of *constructing* it. Problems of social dislocation would thus be seen in terms of the contradictory locations of the social agents, not in terms of a radical lack threatening the very identity of those agents. If, however, the basic question of the social were to be posed at this last level, all social conflict would have to be considered not only from the viewpoint of the contradictory claims, but also from that of the destructuration of the social identities that the conflict would bring about. For if all social conflict were, necessarily, to provoke a certain destructuration of social identities, and if a conflict-free situation were, now, incompatible with any form of society, it would follow that any social identity would necessarily entail, as one of its dimensions, construction, and not simply recognition. The key term for understanding this process of construction is the psychoanalytic category of *identification*, with its explicit assertion of a lack at the root of any identity: one needs to identify with something because there is an originary and insurmountable lack of identity. In a variety of ways, all the contributions to this volume address this process.

An important consequence of this distinction between identity and identification is that it introduces a constitutive split in *all* social identity. If the lack is truly constitutive, the act of identification that tries to fill it cannot have a source of justification external to itself, since the order with which we identify is accepted, not because it is considered as valuable in terms of the criteria of goodness or rationality which operate at its bases, but because it brings about the possibility of *an* order, of a certain regularity. As we argue in one of the essays of this volume, one approves of the Law because it is Law, not because it is rational. In a situation of radical disorganization there is a need for *an* order, and its actual contents become a secondary consideration. This means that, between the ability of a certain order to become a principle of identification and the actual contents of that order, there is no necessary link. This, as we will see, has considerable consequences for the understanding of the functioning of political logics.

The same conclusion we reached regarding the relationship identity/ identification is obtained if we concentrate on the *political* dimension of social identities. As I have argued elsewhere, our time period is one of an increasing awareness of the political character embedded in the institution of all social identity. The social world presents itself to us, primarily, as a sedimented ensemble of social practices accepted at face value, without questioning the founding acts of their institution. If the social world, however, is not entirely defined in terms of repetitive, sedimented practices, it is because the social always overflows the institutionalized frameworks of 'society', and because social antagonisms show the inherent contingency of those frameworks. Thus a dimension of construction and creation is inherent in all social practice. The latter do not involve only repetition, but also reconstruction.

Now, the crucial question is how to conceive this constructive moment which exceeds the repetitive possibilities opened by a sedimented social framework. Does the latter provide the criteria to carry out acts of social inno-vation? If this were the case, if, that is to say, the solution of all social problems were an algorithmic solution provided by the social itself, sedimented social practices would have as something inherent to themselves the principle of their own transformations. But if this were not the case, if historical innovation were *radical* innovation, then historical discontinuities would also be radical, and history could not appeal to any underlying logic or cunning of reason to explain social change. Radical innovation, however, means radical *institution*, and it is this instituting dimension – constitutive of social practices – that we call 'the *political*'. But if the political involves radical institution, and if the latter cannot appeal to anything in the social order that would operate as its ground (otherwise it would not be radical), the act of institution can only have its foundation in itself. Now, isn't this self-founding character (which is, as we have seen, constitutive of the political as opposed to sedimented social practices), not precisely the same as that of 'identification' (as opposed to mere identity)? If this is so, all *political* identity requires the *visibility* of the acts of identification (that is, of the *instituting* acts).

This visibility is only obtained in so far as opposite forms of institution (of the social) are possible, and this possibility is revealed when those forms are actually postulated and fought for in the historical arena. For it is only in their antagonistic relation to other projects that the contingency of particular acts of institution is shown, and it is this contingency that gives them their political character. (Sedimented social practices are unchallenged and, as such, they conceal the political moment of their institution.)

Now, the more the 'foundation' of the social is put into question, the less the sedimented social practices are able to ensure social reproduction, and the more new acts of political intervention and identification are socially required. This necessarily leads to a politicization of social identities, which we see as a main feature of social life in the societies of the end of the twentieth century. We find here a double movement: in the so-called post-modern societies there is a decline both of the great historical actors and of those central public spaces where decisions meaningful for society as a whole had been taken in the past. But, at the same time, there is a politicization of vast areas of social life that opens the way for a proliferation of particularistic political identities. The emergence of a plurality of new subjects that have escaped the classical political frameworks and, in this way, have put new challenges to political practice and political theory, constitute the main theme of this volume.

Two final remarks. The first concerns the question of the relation between proliferation of particularisms and decline of universal values. Is it true that the emergent plurality of political identities dangerously challenges the universalistic tradition that started with the Enlightenment? The answer cannot be unambiguous. In one sense, it is true that the idea of a subject which, in its own particularity, incarnates the universal as such – as, for instance, the 'universal class' in Marx – is definitely on the wane. And, in actual fact, there is little to regret in that loss. The notion of a subject that is, by itself, pure and universal human essence, is profoundly anti-democratic and can only be accompanied by a disrespect for all forms of particularism. Does this mean that the only alternative is a particularism which disregards all universal values and opens the way to various kinds of xenophobic exclusivism? That this is a real possibility is convincing enough, if only by taking a general look over the current international scene. But I do not think that these are the only alternatives. For the very emergence of highly particularistic identities means that the particular groups will have to coexist with other groups in larger communities, and this coexistence will be impossible without the assertion of values that transcend the identities of all of them. The defence, for instance, of the right of national minorities to self-determination involves the assertion of a universal principle grounded in universal values. These are not the values of a 'universal' group, as was the case with the universalism of the past but, rather, of a universality that is the very result of particularism. It is, in this sense, far more democratic. Whether this new relationship between universality and particularism – grounded in the notion of *rights* – will prevail or, on the contrary, be submerged by rampant xenophobia, is something that cannot be predicted. But, clearly, it is something worth fighting for.

My last remark concerns also the question of the democratic possibilities opened by the emergence of new particularisms. Let me go back to my previous argument concerning the constitutive split of all political identity. On the one hand, any political order is a *concrete* form of organization of the community; on the other, it incarnates, against radical disorganization, the principle of order and organization as such. Now, if the split between these two dimensions is constitutive, does this not mean that no ultimate order of the community is achievable, and that we will only have a succession of failed attempts at reaching that impossible aim? Again, this is true in one sense, but its consequences are not necessarily negative: because in the case that the split *could* be superseded, this would only mean that society would have reached its *true* order, and that all dissent would thereupon have come to an end. Obviously no social division or democratic competition between groups is possible in such conditions, since the very condition of democracy is that there is an insurmountable gap between what the social groups attempt to achieve and their abilities to succeed in such attempts. It is only if there is a plurality of political forces substituting for each other in power – as the attempt to hegemonize the very principle of 'order' and 'organization' – that democracy is possible. Whether the proliferation of political identities in the contemporary world will lead to a deepening of the logic inherent in the democratic process, or whether it will lead, as some predict, to an implosion of the social and to a radically deregulated society that will create the terrain for authoritarian solutions, remains to be seen. But, whatever the outcome, this is the question that sets the agenda for democratic politics in the decades to come.

This volume has its origin in a workshop on 'Identities and Political Identification', which took place in January 1989, in the Department of Government,

University of Essex, and which was sponsored by the Political Studies Association of Great Britain. Most of the contributors to the volume participated in it and their papers are re-elaborations of their presentations to that meeting.

The first part of the volume focuses mainly on theoretical issues concerning the notion of 'identity' and its relation to politics. In their essay on 'Minding the Gap: The Subject of Politics', Ernesto Laclau and Lilian Zac start from the constitutive split of all political identity and try to ground, on that basis, both the notion of an original lack and that of 'identification' as the central categories for politics. They elaborate their theoretical approach through the discussion of four discursive bodies: the debates on power and legitimacy in modern political philosophy; the critique of violence by Walter Benjamin; the Heideggerian distinction between 'presencing' and 'presence'; and the Lacanian conception of the 'logic of the signifier'.

The chapter by Slavoj Žižek, 'Identity and its Vicissitudes: Hegel's "Logic of Essence" as a Theory of Ideology', and the one by Rodolphe Gasché, 'Yes Absolutely: Unlike Any Writing Pen', try to reach a concept of identity through two different, though largely opposed, intellectual operations. Žižek delimits his approach from deconstruction by grounding it in the Lacanian 'Real' as the gap separating the universal from the particular, and then attempts to link Lacanian categories to those of Hegel's 'logic of essence'. Gasché considers this attempt misleading because it seems to forget that the categories of the 'logic of essence' in Hegel are sublated by those of the Notion. Consequently he presents his deconstructive critique of identity as operating at the higher level of 'Absolute reflection'. This leads to a presentation of Derrida's thought as an 'infrastructural account' attempting, through the isolation of 'undecidables', to go beyond the constitutive categories of 'reflection'. It could be discussed to what extent Žižek's 'Real' and Gasché's 'undecidables' offer some points of comparison – or even convergence – that (beyond their disagreement concerning the interpretation of Hegel) would supersede a strict opposition between deconstruction and Lacanian theory.

The chapter by Claudia Hilb, 'Equality at the Limit of Liberty', addresses the question of political identities through a discussion of some of the basic categories in Political Philosophy. She takes as her starting point the categories of 'liberty' and 'equality', categories both necessary for modern political discourse, though, at the same time, as she argues, only able to produce their effects by limiting each other. By so arguing, she paves the way for a consideration of modern politics as an emergence of the individual through the production of its limits, thus also underscoring its radical historicity.

The second part of the volume includes pieces which, although reaching general theoretical conclusions, take as their starting point concrete historical experiences of identity construction.

A central issue in any contemporary theory of political identities is the ambiguity of the key signifiers stabilizing them and the various hegemonic and counter-hegemonic movements to which they are submitted. Three essays in the volume address particular aspects of that question. In her chapter, 'Social Ambiguity and the Crisis of Apartheid', Aletta J. Norval discusses the basic instability that the political frontier of racism has undergone, an instability which has led to the decline of apartheid as a hegemonic social imaginary. She shows through concrete examples how this is far from being a merely 'superstructural' phenomenon, given that the very social processes involved in the circulation of the black population between homelands and urban centres are also those involved in the logic of the signifier structuring the identities of social agents. Glenn Bowman's '"A Country of Words": Conceiving the Palestinian Nation from the Position of Exile', concentrates on an even more radical process of emptying of the signifiers constituting the marks of national identities: those of the Palestinian diaspora. His chapter shows the difficulties of nation-building in a situation where many of the projects and experiences, developed in totally different cultural contexts, find serious obstacles in constructing an even relatively unified political culture. Anna Marie Smith, in 'Rastafari as Resistance and the Ambiguities of Essentialism in the "New Social Movements"', addresses the problem of 'essentialism' in relation to the question of identity construction. Taking the Rastafarians as her reference point, she shows how the need to create a social and cultural identity for the West Indian migrants to Great Britain has led to a strong segregationist assertion of their own specificity. At the same time, though, she also shows how the need for political efficacy has led to forms of participation that move in the opposite direction. This is an ambiguity very much inscribed in the process of identity construction of various social movements in advanced industrial contexts.

The three remaining chapters deal mainly with the question of the diversity of identity construction in different historical situations. Renata Salecl, in 'The Crisis of Identity and the Struggle for New Hegemony in the Former Yugoslavia', attempts to define the specificity of the new forms of political identity in the former Communist bloc, vis-à-vis those which are characteristic of the West. She discusses the hegemonic crisis at the root of the current civil wars in ex-Yugoslavia – the decline of self-management as a dominant political discourse and the emergence of nationalism – and shows, through an argument formulated in terms of Lacanian categories, the mechanisms in Eastern European societies which block the formation of a democratic imaginary. The chapter by Zoltán Szankay, 'The Green Threshold', argues that some contemporary political experiences (Solidarnosc in Poland, the Green movement in Germany) constitute a threshold which put into question the basic European parameters structuring political spaces, and indicate a radical new tension affecting the representability of the political in the West.

Bobby Sayyid, in 'Sign O' Times: Kaffirs and Infidels Fighting the Ninth Crusade', attempts to link Islamic revivalism to the general discussion concerning the relationship modernity/post-modernity. He claims there is a close link between modernity, as a discourse of closure, and the dominant position of the West and tries to link various aspects of the post-modern critique to the political experience of Third World countries.

PART I

Minding the Gap: The Subject
of Politics

Ernesto Laclau and *Lilian Zac*

It was in Buchel in September 1910. The visit of the devil lay still far away in the future. Adrian Leverkühn took his friend Serenus Zeitblom for a walk. The conversation turned around the relationship between the archaic and the revolutionary in music. At some point Zeitblom started the following exchange:

> 'It would be tragic,' I said, 'if unfruitfulness should be ever the result of freedom. But there is always the hope of the release of the productive powers, for the sake of which freedom is achieved.' 'True,' he responded. 'And she does for a while achieve what she promised. But freedom is of course another word for subjectivity, and some fine day she does not hold out any longer, some time or other she despairs of the possibility of being creative out of herself and seeks shelter and security in the objective. Freedom always inclines to dialectical reversals. She realizes herself very soon in constraint, fulfils itself in the subordination to law, rule, coercion, system – but to fulfil herself therein does not mean that she therefore ceases to be freedom.'

> 'In your opinion,' I laughed: 'So far as she knows. But actually, she is no longer freedom as little as dictatorship born out of revolution is still freedom.'

> 'Are you sure of it?' he asked. 'But anyhow that is talking politics. In art, at least, the subjective and the objective intertwine to the point of being indistinguishable, one proceeds from the other and takes the character of the other, the subjective precipitates as objective and by genius is again awakened to spontaneity, "dynamized", as we say; it speaks all at once the language of the subjective. The musical conventions today destroyed were not always so objective, so objectively imposed. They were crystallizations of living experiences and, as such, long performed an office of vital importance: the task of organization. Organization is everything. Without it, there is nothing, least of all, art. And it was aesthetic subjectivity that took on the task, it undertook to organize the work out of itself, in freedom.'

> 'You are thinking of Beethoven.'[1]

This sequence contains all the points relevant for our argument: (i) the identification of freedom with the subject; (ii) the idea of freedom as not only unable to provide its own forms of self-determination ('she despairs of the possibility of being creative'), but as searching for such determination in something external to itself – a 'something' which will operate as both 'shelter' and source of 'security'; (iii) the principle of organization as the realization of freedom. If freedom can only be realized through its alienation to an external content, thereby providing the determination that freedom lacks, and if such a content is the principle of organization, the latter can neither be something merely objective nor, for that matter, merely subjective. Why? Because the principle of organization is the point of crystallization of a tension, of an undecidable alternative *between* subject and object; it expresses itself *through* the objective and can only manage to do so by its dialectical reversal. Not surprisingly, the exploration of this tension will lead us to the very centre of the problematic of the subject – which, as we will see, is precisely the subject *as the subject of the lack*. The starting point of the analysis, then, will be to consider these three oppositions: freedom/identity; subjectivity/objectivity; organization and its lack.

First relation: freedom/identity

As we have seen in the foregoing quote, Thomas Mann poses the question of the subject in terms of *creativity*. Creativity requires as its *sine qua non* – no, more than that, as a definition of itself – that the subject is the origin of 'her' expressive forms, and that these forms do not emerge from any source other than subjectivity as such. Subjectivity and creativity in this case require each other; the realization of subjectivity is freedom conceived as self-determination. To pose the question in Kantian terms one would say: it is only the autonomy of the will that creates the possibility of a self-determined subject. And yet, if we take this as given, the content of that autonomous will starts immediately to blur the strict frontier between autonomy and heteronomy. Let us accept for a moment the central maxim of a rigorous ethical formalism: 'behave in such a way that your actions can become a universal norm of conduct'. Let us also accept, for the sake of argument, that this is a rational criterion. A question, however, remains unanswered: what is the source of the principle of rationality as a basis for action? It is clear that such a principle does not logically follow from the notion of a free subjectivity, and that the link between the two requires an act of identification of the latter to the former. But if the condition of pure subjectivity is self-determination, and if no determinate content follows *a priori* from the form of subjectivity as such, two necessary conclusions emerge: (i) that the condition of freedom – and, as a result, of subjectivity – is indeterminacy; and (ii) that all determinate content (even the most formal, in the Kantian sense) is objective rather than subjective and, as a result, must be heteronomous from the point of view of a pure subjectivity.

Second relation: the contraposition between the subjective and the objective

Mann presents this relation in terms of 'dialectical reversals'. It is clear why: if subjectivity, as such, is indeterminacy, there is no possibility that we can derive from it any determinate content. Determination can only be the result of the 'alienation' of subjectivity, of its becoming the opposite of itself. There is a subtle movement of significations on which the very meaning of the relation between the subjective and the objective depends. Let us assume for a moment that we are in the field of 'determinate negation' in the Hegelian sense: in that case indeterminacy would be superseded by a specific content, by a concrete determination. Thus we would conclude that indeterminacy is indeterminacy-for-the-determination; determination would be hegemonic and indeterminacy would be only one of its internal moments. So, let us modify the assumption: let us suppose that by 'dialectical reversal' we do not understand an indeterminacy that just anticipates its overcoming by specific forms of determination, but, rather, a passage from the indeterminate to the determination as such – a certain indifference or distance of the indeterminate vis-à-vis the forms of determination that supersede it. In that case the relation between the indeterminate and the determinate, between the subjective and the objective, will be dramatically different: there will never be real supersession, nor peace, between the two. The subjective will only acquire a content by alienating itself in an objectivity which is its opposite (though this, as we will later see, is what is involved with the notion of *identification*, as different from mere identity). But the objective cannot be reduced to its specific content either, as it only functions as a surface for identification. Indeed, given that the latter is not a *necessary* identification – for, to assume otherwise would lead right back to the hypothesis of a determinate negation – this concrete content will represent the opposite of subjective indeterminacy. That is, it will represent the principle of *determinability* as such. In saying this, it becomes clear that what is at stake in Thomas Mann's 'dialectical reversals' is not a determinate freedom which realizes itself in a determinate content, but *determinability* as the condition of the realization of freedom. 'She [freedom] realizes herself in the subordination to law, rule, coercion, system,' Mann reminds us, 'but to fulfil herself therein does not mean she therefore ceases to be freedom.'

Third relation: organization and its lack

It remains to be explained why the freedom that fulfils itself in coercion is still freedom. This point is crucial for our argument, and its elaboration leads us to our third relation. Leverkühn's response to the question concerning a freedom that realizes itself in coercion turns on the principle of 'organization', which is, as he puts it, 'an office of vital importance' without which 'there is nothing, least of all art'. Two intertwined dimensions can clearly be read from this response, the first being that the centrality of the principle of organization is derived from the staunch assertion: without organization 'there is nothing'. For even though Leverkühn is speaking about art – in spite of his tantalizing hint about politics – Hobbes would not have presented differently his opposition between Leviathan and the state of nature. The decisive point is that this 'nothing', set in opposition to 'organization', is not the nothing of a logical impossibility that would simply collapse into the nonexistent: it is a *real* nothing, an empty place that 'organization' would come to fill. What makes that 'nothing' possible? The answer is: the subject, as freedom and indeterminacy. This leads us to the second dimension. We have seen that dialectical reversals imply a freedom only able to realize itself through its identification with something that is its opposite – that is, with an objectivity that can only fulfil its identificatory role as far as it accomplishes the alienation of the subject. But in that case, why is it that freedom does not simply annul itself through this act of alienation? Why is it 'still freedom'? A preliminary answer, upon which we will elaborate later, could be formulated in the following terms: an active identification is not a purely submissive act on the part of the subject, who would passively incorporate all the determinations of the object. The act of identification, on the contrary, destabilizes the identity of the object. Let us suppose, for example, that in the context of extreme social disorganization the identities of the social agents are subverted, and that this anomic situation leads to the identification of those agents with a certain political discourse – which thus plays the role of the principle of organization in Leverkühn's sense. The contents of that discourse will appear necessarily split as a result of the identificatory act. For, on the one hand, these contents will be a set of proposals for social organization; but, on the other, as they will appear as the symmetrically opposed alternative to the possibility of 'nothingness', they would incarnate the very possibility of *a* social organization – that is, the principle of social organization as such. If we draw the point out to its full conclusion, what we have here, then, is that the lack (that is, indeterminacy) of the subject will constitute the object of identification as *split* object.

The ultimate incompatibility of the two poles of the 'dialectical reversal' is thus maintained and reproduced throughout all its stages. The structure of the identificatory act preserves, without superseding, the constitutive nothingness of the subject; and the representation of the latter takes place through the subversion of the surface of identification. Moreover, the alienating character of the act of identification is also maintained, in so far as there is no supersession of the subject/object duality. Two basic consequences follow:

(1) If the objective 'fills' my originary lack, this filling can only take place in so far as what is objective is external to me. Through the act of filling my

lack, the objective does not lose its externality; it is not assimilated to an identity that was *already* mine. On the contrary, its alien character is precisely what allows it to function as a filler. Its 'magic' filling can operate because the subject is originary lack of being. But if the subject is originary and *ineradicable* lack, any identification will have to represent, as well, the lack itself. This can only be done by reproducing the external character of that with which the subject identifies itself, that is, its incommensurability vis-à-vis itself. It is because of this that the acceptance of the Law – that is, the principle of organization as opposed to 'nothingness' – is the acceptance of the Law because it is Law, not because it is rational. If the acceptance of the Law had resulted from its rationality, in that case, the Law would be a prolongation of the subject as a positive identity and could not fulfil its filling role. But if the Law can fulfil this role, it necessarily follows that this role has to be its own justification, and that the latter cannot be granted by any *a priori* tribunal of reason.

(2) The filling function requires an empty place, and the latter is, to some extent, indifferent to the content of the filling, though this filling function has to be incarnated in *some* concrete contents, whatever those contents might be. This is the originary split constitutive of all representation, to which we referred before. Now, this means that between the filling function and the concrete content that actualizes it, there is a constitutive incommensurability. This incommensurability would only be eliminated if a concrete content qua concrete could exhaust and become identical with the filling function. But in that case, we would be back to the reabsorption of the indeterminate within the determinate, and the radical character of the opposition between 'organization' and 'nothingness' would have been lost. So let us return to our previous example. Suppose somebody is confronted with a deep anomic situation – what would be required would be the introduction of *an* order, the concrete contents of which would become quite secondary. Thomas Mann perceived this clearly. In his *Lotte in Weimar*, one of the characters describes the successive occupation of the city by the French and the Prussians at the end of the Napoleonic period:

> We peered through the curtains at the tumult in the streets, we heard the crashing gunfire and the braying of horns. The fighting soon passed from the streets to the park and presently beyond the city limits. The enemy, alas, won his accustomed victory. And actually, against our wills, it seemed to us like a triumph of order over rebellion – a childish and foolish rebellion, as the event had proved. 'Order and quiet are good – no matter what one owes them.' We had to provide for the billeting of the French troops, and the town was straightaway burdened to the utmost limit of its capacity. Not only heavy but long was the burden laid upon it. Still, there was peace; the streets were open till sundown, and the citizen might go about his business under the oppressive protection of the victors.[2]

However, when the forces of the anti-Napoleonic coalition approached the city, a clear change in the public attitude took place:

> The nearer they drew, the less were they called barbarians, the more the sympathies and hopes of society veered towards them and away from the French. That of course was partly because we began to see in them the victors one might hope to placate – even from a distance. But even more, it was because we human beings are by nature submissive. We need to live in harmony with outward events and situations. We need to come to terms with power – and now fate itself seemed to be giving the signal for the change. In the space of a few days the barbarians, the rebels against civilization, turned into liberators. Their successful advance brought to a bursting point the general enthusiasm for folk and fatherland.[3]

It would be a mistake to think that what is involved in this rapid change of position is sheer opportunism. As Mann himself says, that would be neither the only, nor the main, reason. For if the objective of national independence was to prevail, it had to show something more than a spontaneous attractiveness or moral superiority. It had to show its ability to become a realistic alternative for the organization and management of the community (in Gramscian terms, it had to show it was an alternative that could become hegemonic). The dislocation created by the war had autonomized the general need for a continuity of the communitarian order from the alternative political projects that attempted to guarantee such a continuity. The possibility of identification with a certain political order depended not only on its political virtues or attractiveness abstractly considered, but on its ability to guarantee the continuity of the community. But this continuity, precisely because it did not coincide with any of the political forms that would make it possible at particular moments in time – precisely because it would have no content of its own – would be nothing other than the name of an absent plenitude that could not be exhausted by any of the concrete forms that would attempt to realize it.

Now, if this incommensurability is *constitutive* – because the gap between indetermination and determination is utterly unbridgeable; and if no concrete content is, in its concreteness, destined *a priori* to fulfil the filling function, this also means, then, that all concrete content will be constitutively *inadequate* to carry out that function, and the place of the subject will be perpetuated on the basis of the reproduction of this inadequacy. This means that there is not a unique act of identification whose effects would fulfil unchallenged its filling function. As any identification takes place through contents which are essentially inadequate to this fulfilment, the identification will be constitutively incomplete and will have to be always re-created through new identification acts. Thus there is an originary short circuit in any social logic: on the one hand, the objective content has its own principles of rationality and of differentiation; on the other, these principles are constantly interrupted and subverted. This logic of the 'subversion of the rationality of the determinate' is what we have called *overdetermination* – and it is crucial for understanding the formation of political identities.

Before we delve into the intricacies of overdetermination, let us first turn to the various dimensions of this constitutive split of all social identities – which, as we have noted, is at the very basis of the emergence of the duality subject/identification. We will discuss these dimensions by exploring four theoretical avenues: (i) the approaches to power and legitimacy in Political Philosophy; (ii) the critique of violence by Walter Benjamin; (iii) the distinction between 'presencing' and 'presence' in Heidegger; and (iv) the logic of the signifier in Lacan.

Power and Legitimacy

What are the presuppositions of a theory of power as variously developed in modern political thought? The first is that power is located at some point *within* society, from where its effects would in some way spread over and around the social structure as a whole; indeed, that there is a structure at all is, to a large extent, the result of power. Power is, in a sense, the *source* of the social, though one could equally say in another (and related) sense, that it is the very condition of intelligibility of the social (given that the possibility of representing the latter as a coherent entity depends on a set of orderly effects emanating from power). There is no difference, from this point of view, between holistic and pluralistic conceptions of power. For, whether the social effect comes from a 'power elite' or is, instead, conceived as the pure and simple result of competitive interactions between a plurality of groups, that effect will always be there, as an actual consequence of power – or of power struggle – and, at the same time, the source of its justification.

However, as soon as we attempt to explore the logic of this imbrication between power and 'society effect', we find a contradictory movement in which power can engage itself but cannot really supersede. What would be a fully achieved 'society effect'? Clearly, it would have to be one in which the relationship between the effect and its cause would be entirely undisturbed, in which the fullness of the effect would entirely be derived from the fullness of the cause. Power would then be the absolute origin of whatever order there is in society. The more absolute is the origin, the more complete is power. There is, however, a problem: to what extent can an absolute origin be conceptualized in terms of power? If, for example, A has absolute power in society, then its effects over B, C and D will fully constitute the identity of the latter. (This total identification is a requisite of total power, otherwise, B, C and D would suffer from the effects of power and that would mean that from some point – even if that point meant simply their solitary consciousness – they would be able *to resist* A's power. Ergo, A's power could not reach that point and the power could not be absolute.) But from this, it would follow that a situation of absolute power must be one where the concept of power entirely loses its meaning. A cause qua cause can only exist in its effects; a cause is nothing but the sequence of its effects, the latter being part of the cause's identity. If an individual or group had absolute power in society, this would mean – as we have seen – that the other groups would have no other identity than the effects deriving from that power and, as a result, they would also be part of the identity of the dominant group. A feudal lord, for instance, is feudal lord only in so far as there are serfs; and in the hypothetical case that the identity of the serfs is exhausted in their relationship with the lord, it is evident that both lord and serfs would be internal positions or differentiations within a unique identity, and that no relation of power could exist between the two. Whatever decision the lord takes as a result of his status, it will express not only his identity but also that of the serf.

That is, the 'society effect' can only take place in so far as power is eliminated. But this also shows clearly that certain conditions must be met in order that a relation of power exists: there has to be a conflict of wills in which one of them would prevail. And yet, as we know, the very possibility of a conflict requires the partial efficacy of the conflicting forces (for, in order to resist a dominant power there has to be a point in society where the dominated forces can organize and initiate their resistance). This means that the very condition of existence of power is that it is not absolute. It is only if Power is impossible that actual powers can exist in the social terrain. But if there is a plurality of powers, then the 'society effect' is also impossible. For, as we have seen, the society effect is the constitution and representation of the social totality as a coherent object resulting from the combination of orderly effects that unfold from a unique centre of power. To put this point differently: if the very condition of actual powers is conflict, and conflict presupposes the irreducibility of the social to a unique source of effects, there would have to be a limit to the representability of the social – since representability presupposes compatibility – and, as a consequence, no society effect.

Is not this logical conclusion, however, a bit excessive? Can we purely and simply just do away with the 'society effect'? Let us consider the matter carefully. What would such a 'doing away' logically imply? Clearly, that the forces in conflict would be unable to hegemonize the social totality, and they would thus be limited to their own particularities. But that limitation would not necessarily close them in on themselves, for if a force is threatened by another force external to it, neither of the two forces could be fully constituted. As a result, they could not close themselves within their own being. Only by going beyond themselves – only by realizing their own being in terms of a 'society effect' that transcends their own particularities – could those particularities become fully constituted. This transcendence, as we have seen, would involve the elimination of power. But the important point is precisely that, as power makes that transcendence impossible, the society effect does not simply disappear: it remains present as that which is absent, as the empty place which prevents the full being of each of the opposing forces being achieved. The reality of power constructs the irreality of society as a structural lack accompanying and distorting all social identities.

This becomes clearer if we consider another dimension closely associated with the conceptualization of power; namely, the one connected to the relationship between power and legitimacy.[4] What is the theoretical possibility of such a distinction? If by power we just understand the ability of producing a society effect, the distinction would be impossible. For to distinguish between legitimacy and power involves the possibility that an actual system of power is illegitimate. But if the totality of 'social effects' can be referred to power as its sole source, there would be no place in society from which to put that power into question. Let us not forget that the initial theory of power was a theological one: it dealt with the omnipotence of God as creator of the world. It is clear that if God were the only source of all created things, there would be no way in which his power, or even a part of the actions in which that power would be expressed, could be illegitimate. Power and legitimacy would be one and the same. In fact, it would not even enter as a question whether God's power would be legitimate, because God Himself would represent absolute goodness. To assert otherwise would be to erect a tribunal to judge God's actions that would have to be independent of Him. God's power is legitimate because it is *His* power. If the question of legitimacy were not to be reduced, even in those early theological discussions, to that of power per se, it is because of the problem of the existence of evil in the world and the resulting possibility that man acts in a way that is illegitimate in God's eyes. (This poses, of course, the well-known theological problem of how, if God is both omnipotent and the expression of absolute goodness, He allows for the existence of evil in the world.) But the important point for our discussion is that this disjunction between power and legitimacy raised the question that was to become central in the modern theorization of politics: what are the sources of legitimacy once there are 'social effects' that conflict with each other and that cannot be referred back to a single generating force?

While God operated as a source of legitimacy external to the world, the gap between power and legitimacy could conceptually be contained – more or less – within manageable limits. But when, in modern times, the search began for a source of legitimacy from which to judge the world, and yet one that was, however, internal to the world, the aporias implicit in the very terms of the question became fully visible. For if legitimacy qua legitimacy were not endowed with power, it would have had to create its own power; but in that case it would itself be mere power – mere contingency – and could only ground its claims in the power that it could obtain. As in the theological case, we find the concept of legitimacy indistinguishable from power, with the difference that there was now a power that could always be reversed. Machiavelli happily accepted these conclusions – in as much as they grounded legitimacy both in power and in what concerns the contingent character of that power. But even theories that attempted to legitimate absolute power – as did Hobbes's – accepted a purely secular perspective and a unidirectional relation of causality; power was the root of legitimacy, albeit with the reservations that we will consider momentarily.

The problem, however, is this: to what extent could we say that a legitimacy purely derivative from power remains legitimate? Is not a factually based legitimacy a contradictory concept, one that entirely does away with the distinction between fact and value? At this point we are struck by the structural parallelism between the duality 'power/society effect' and the duality 'power/legitimacy'. Our conclusion concerning the first was that a fully fledged 'society effect' was impossible as far as there is power; but that, on the other hand, power logically *requires* the fullness of society as that which is absent, as the place of a structural lack. In the present case we have concluded that power makes impossible a fully fledged legitimacy. Should we conclude as well, then, that power requires its other – legitimacy – as absent filler of its impossible fullness? A brief consideration of Hobbes will help clarify matters. The logical conclusions Hobbes drew, which follow directly from a secularized conception of power, entail a rigour never reached before him and few times after. In asking the question, 'Is there any hope of having an ordered society quite apart from power relations?', Hobbes's answer, as is well known, was emphatically negative. Civil society, left to itself, can only reproduce the chaos of the state of nature. But having said that, would it be possible to institute an absolute power that could generate a 'society effect'? Hobbes thought that it was possible; and he invoked the social covenant as a way to achieve it. But there are two consequences that necessarily follow from this way of addressing the problem. The first is that, as in all absolute power, including the case of God in medieval theology, the distinction between power and legitimacy cannot emerge. It is not the case that there is only a relation of causality between power and legitimacy; it is, rather, that power and legitimacy are one and the same. To call a power illegitimate would presuppose another social order whose content would be the basis to judge the existing power. But if outside power there were only the chaos of the state of nature, then that basis would simply not exist. The only way in which a power could, thereby, become illegitimate would be if it were incapable of guaranteeing the life and security of the subjects – that is, if it ceased to be the basis of a viable Commonwealth. This would mean that power would have to be, at the very least, partially justified by an instance external to itself; if it were incapable of providing that guarantee of life and security, it would cease to be legitimate. Clearly, then, this would mean that the *conditions* of its legitimacy must be external to itself. The split between power and the condition of its legitimacy would have a dual effect. On the one hand, if power were to be justified by an instance different from itself, the latter could not be a derivative of power. This is the basis for postulating a distinction between a public and private sphere, a seminal split introduced by Hobbes which now marks his work as one of the starting points of modern liberalism. On the other hand – and this is our second consequence – because that guarantee of power was to be both the necessary and sufficient condition of its legitimacy, then, *as far as that condition were to be met, power would become legitimate independently of its forms and contents*. Why? Because given that the 'other' of power was simply the disorganization of society, whatever political order exists would be legitimate not as a result of the value of its own contents, but due to its ability to incarnate the abstract principle of social order as such.

Hobbes's theory consists in a well-knit argument wherein (i) power and legitimacy cannot – in the case of a successful political order – be differentiated from each other; though, (ii) a potential split exists between the general function of the guaranteeing of a social order and the concrete political arrangements capable of fulfilling such a function. If this split is only potential, it is because – if a political order is to be successful – it is impossible to distinguish a concrete form from its general function. The concrete form would still incarnate the general function, but the incarnation would be so perfect that the split would not show itself. To put the matter in a slightly different way: legitimacy and power would collapse into each other *only* under the condition that the split between the general function and the concrete social arrangement remains concealed. For what would happen if this split shows itself? Purely and simply, the concrete social arrangement would appear as *merely* concrete, and this could only happen when that arrangement loses its ability to incarnate the general function; that is, when it shows itself as mere, unjustified power. The crisis of a system of power, therefore, consists in the disarticulation of its internal dimensions, each of which runs wild and develops its own internal logic, once the latter is not limited in its effects by their precise location within the model of the Hobbesian Commonwealth.

It is worthwhile unknotting this model and following the wild logic of its liberated dimensions, for this exercise will lead us directly to the question of the subject. In order to do so, we do not need to move an inch from the grammar of Hobbes's theory. What is shown in the crisis of a system of power is that the general function is no longer attached to the concrete social organization that has ensured it thus far. But what happens in that case? Is it that an old organization is automatically substituted by a new one, so that the whole crisis and its resolution take place entirely in the terrain of the concrete? Certainly not, because the first manifestation of a crisis is the emergence of a threat that always haunts the social order: the return to the state of nature. It is this threat that presents the social order as something which is present through its absence, as structural lack. And as this absent social order acquires its meaning only as the alternative to radical disorganization, it can only be order in general, order as such, dispossessed of any concrete attribute. Now, we have seen that it is precisely this crisis that re-creates the potential split between power and legitimacy. Power loses its legitimacy when it is unable to ensure the social order; in that case it shows itself as *mere* power. But if the perception of legitimacy as separated from power coincides with the perception of the general function as different from the social arrangements guaranteeing it, the principle of legitimacy can equally only be an abstract and general principle, which has to be differentiated from the concrete historical forms incarnating it. A discourse on legitimacy, therefore, is only possible when illegitimate outcomes are possible as well. It is only in the context of a failure in the achievement of fully fledged identities that calling something 'illegitimate' makes sense. We can now see why there is a parallelism between the duality power/'society effect' and the duality power/legitimacy: in both cases the second term of the alternative points to an absolute fullness whose total realization would make the first term meaningless.

At this point, we can return to Mann's 'dialectical reversals' and ask what Hobbes would have made of them. Hobbes's ruler presents himself in terms that amount to a total and final elimination of such reversals. There is no longer a freedom that realizes itself in subjection, but, rather, an absolute coincidence between the subjective and the objective in the case of the ruler, and the absolute lack of objectivity in the case of the individual wills of the state of nature. It would appear that the will of the ruler represents the triumph of the subjective principle, given that the source of objectivity is pure will, and neither an objective order escaping human decisions nor a transcendent being. In actual fact, what happens is the opposite. For a will which is automatically – as a result of the covenant – the source of social objectivity, becomes indistinguishable from the latter. The ruler has abolished the split between his individuality and the universality of the community, and in this sense, far from representing the introduction of a subjective principle, he is just the point in which the distinction between subject and object, between individuality and universality, collapses. This first modern resolution of the tension between power and 'society effect' takes place on the basis of asserting the latter through the emptying of the former of its particularity – or rather, through the making of this particularity the very form of universality.

Yet, we have only to modify slightly some of Hobbes's assumptions to be able, without going beyond the rules of Hobbesian grammar, to develop a set of different possibilities. For what actually happens if the two sides of Hobbes's picture contaminate each other; that is, if we have a situation in which the ruler is less than omnipotent, and the state of nature less than totally unstructured? This is the point at which the various dimensions of the Hobbesian model start running wild. The perfect balance which had concealed the split between the individuality and the universality of the ruler, between power and legitimacy, between concrete social arrangement and universal function, no longer obtain. The individual will of the ruler does not become automatically the universal law of the community, and so the gap between the two becomes unbridgeable. Power, not being absolute, cannot ensure the conditions of its own legitimacy; and, as no concrete social arrangement is entirely capable of guaranteeing social order, the general need for the latter is emancipated from any necessary link with the former. Why, however, does such a situation not inexorably drift towards the state of nature? Because we have interrupted Hobbes's algorithms with a possibility not contemplated by him, but one which can theoretically be constructed in terms of his own system of categories. The ruler is still the only source of social order, and the individual wills are still fully structured by the latter. But as the ruler is no longer capable of *entirely* fulfilling his or her function, the individual wills will be partially unstructured. Precisely because order in society can only be constructed along Hobbesian lines, the partial failure of the ruler creates a fissure in the structure. But as the individual wills are only partially destructured by that fissure, they will be forced to engage in a succession of partial covenants. Only a total collapse of order would return society to the state of nature. Short of that extreme situation, there are only dialectical reversals between objectivity and freedom. This means that whatever social objectivity exists, it will not reach the closing point of a 'society effect' but instead will be, constitutively, power. And as individual wills cannot be reduced to objective differences or identities within a fully fledged social order, they will only be *subjects*, places of a constitutive lack whose only identity can be reached by acts of identification (dialectical reversals, submission to the externality of the Law as the sole source of social objectivity).

Walter Benjamin and the Politics of Pure Mediacy

A similar conclusion can be reached if we move to our second theoretical discussion: namely, Benjamin's analysis of violence. Benjamin starts by asserting that a critique of violence belongs to the moral sphere, and counterposes two apparently opposite approaches: natural law, for which just ends justify violent means; and positive law, for which legal means justify ends. In spite of this opposition, however, both share the dogma of the possibility of reaching – although in opposite ways – a point of non-conflict between means and ends. As Benjamin puts it:

> [B]oth schools meet in their common basic dogma; just ends can be obtained by justified means, justified means used for just ends. Natural law attempts, by the justness of the ends to 'justify' the means, positive law to 'guarantee' the justness of the ends through the justification of the means. This antinomy would prove

insoluble if the common dogmatic assumption were false, if justified means, on the one hand, and just ends, on the other, were in irreconcilable conflict.[5]

It is this latter hypothesis that Benjamin's whole critique of violence tries to explore. Putting aside the realm of ends, Benjamin poses the question of the 'justification of certain means that constitute violence', and takes as his starting point the distinction between sanctioned and unsanctioned violence. The latter presents an ambiguity, noticed by Benjamin, which is crucial for our argument: to *what* does unsanctioned violence pose a threat? To legal ends in their concreteness? Certainly not – or at least, not only. Instead, what is put into question is the principle of legality as such:

> [O]ne might perhaps consider the surprising possibility that the law's interest in a monopoly of violence vis-à-vis individuals is not explained by the intention of preserving legal ends but, rather, by that of preserving the law itself; that violence, when not in the hands of the law threatens it not by the ends that it may pursue but by its mere existence outside the law. The same may be more drastically suggested if one reflects how often the figure of the 'great' criminal, however repellant his ends may have been, has aroused the secret admiration of the public. This cannot result from his deed, but only from the violence to which it bears witness. In this case, therefore, the violence of which present-day law is seeking in all areas of activity to deprive the individual appears really threatening, and arouses even in defeat the sympathy of the masses against law.[6]

Now, here we are on the same terrain as in Hobbes: as something 'outside', the law is a real alternative threatening concrete legal ends. The latter are constitutively split because – beyond their concreteness – they incarnate the principle of 'lawfulness' or 'legality' as such. But this means that between *means* and *ends* an insurmountable caesura has been introduced. If the ends, in their concreteness, were the only thing that counted, the means would be transparent and the entirety subordinated to the ends. If, on the contrary, the legality of the means is what is at stake, the ends would become indeterminate, but within the concrete limits established by the means. But if legal means are subverted in their concreteness because they incarnate the principle of lawfulness as such, a more radical possibility emerges: a politics of pure mediacy which, by its passage through concrete, and transient, means and ends, attempts to enact or to subvert legality as such. The whole distinction by Benjamin between law-making and law-preserving attempts to show the constitutive character of this possibility, its inherence in any legal system.

Benjamin illustrates his argument about pure mediacy with two examples: language, and the distinction in Sorel between political and proletarian strike. Let us concentrate on the latter. A political strike is entirely dominated by particularistic aims. It tries to abolish concrete forms of state power, not state power as such. The proletarian strike, on the other hand, does not attempt to substitute one form of power from another or one form of legal organization from a different one, and so on; but, whatever are its concrete aims, it tries to put into question the very principle of legality and state organization.

> In contrast to this political general strike (which incidentally seems to have been summed up by the abortive German revolution), the proletarian general strike sets itself the sole task of destroying state power. It 'nullifies all the ideological consequences of every possible social policy; its partisans see even the most popular reforms as bourgeois'. . . While the first form of interruption of work is violent since it causes only an external modification of labour conditions, the second, as pure means, is non-violent. For it takes place not in readiness to resume work following external concessions and this or that modification to working conditions, but in determination to resume only a wholly transformed work, no longer enforced by the state, an upheaval that this kind of strike not so much causes as consummates. For this reason, the first of these undertakings is law-making, but the second anarchistic.[7]

This, however, immediately raises a problem: to what extent is the proletarian strike an actually possible historical event? And if it is actual, under what conditions? For a politics of pure violence, of pure mediacy, is, strictly speaking, directed against nothing; however, if it is going to succeed, it requires some content. Benjamin, in the above quotation, seems to point to such a content: the determination to resume 'only a wholly transformed work'. Let us remember that what was at stake in both law imposition and law violation was not only the content of a particular law but the principle of lawfulness as such. So, if the proletarian strike is directed against the latter, its consummation can only be a post-legal history, a history that breaks with the dialectics imposition/violation. Benjamin's text seems to point in this direction when he speaks of the emergence and reversal of the various legal systems as dominated by the dialectical law of their succession, and when he thinks of the overthrow of legal state power by the proletarian strike as an actual event which is the beginning of a new history. This looks like a rather traditional Marxist view, according to which the content of a post-legal history can only be a reconciled society that supersedes the opposition subject/object. For, as we have seen, we have in such a case a pure 'society effect' which abolishes power while, at the same time, abolishing also the possibility of a subject.

Things, however, are not so clear cut, even for Sorel. It is rather doubtful that Sorel conceived the revolutionary strike as an actual, possible, historical occurrence. On the contrary, its efficacy as a myth was independent of the actual possibility of its arrival; it lay, instead, in the possibility that it opened for reconstructing a revolutionary will not integrated into decadent bourgeois society. Sorel's support of the aims of the proletariat resulted not so much from his approval of those aims, but from the revolutionary will which was constructed in their persecution. That is the way in which Sorel conceived a politics of pure mediacy: whatever the concrete aims of the proletarian struggles, the workers, in struggling, would construct a subjectivity capable of arresting the corruption and decline of European civilization. All emphasis is put on the exercise of the means, not in the achievement of the ends. So, in that case, the general strike is not so much an actual event, as a historical horizon that gives sense and direction to the particular struggles and prevents their closure within their own concreteness. The counterposition political strike/proletarian strike is not so much the opposition of two types of event, as two dimensions which, in different proportions, are combined in any particular struggle (they are the metaphorical embodiment of the constitutive split of all social identity).

The difference between Sorel and Benjamin can be reduced to the following point: while for Benjamin the elimination of legal and State violence is an *event* which closes a historical cycle and opens a new one, for Sorel it is a dimension constitutive of all political experience – it is for this reason that a politics of pure mediacy can be formulated more in Sorelian than in Benjaminian terms. This becomes even clearer if we turn to Werner Hamacher's analysis of Benjamin's text.[8] In his attempt to radicalize the pure mediacy of the *Critique of Violence*, Hamacher is led to blurring the separation between political and proletarian strikes:

> [F]or cognitive purposes, any strike must take place in the border region between political and anarchist general strikes, between negotiation or, rather, extortion and acts of positing new law on the one hand, and the pure violence of deposition on the other. For cognitive purposes, there can be no more a pure anarchism than there can be absolute afformatives. Afformatives can have unforeseen effects, precisely insofar as they 'strike' the cognition directed toward them with powerlessness. The more the event of afformation becomes possible and thus unpredictable in its effects for constative or thetic consciousness, the less the question of its actuality becomes cognitively decidable. Pure violence 'shows' itself precisely in the fact that it never appears *as such*. 'For only mythical violence, not divine [violence], will be recognizable as such with certainty, unless it be in incomparable effects. . .' The strike is not a matter of theory; it can be the object neither of prognosis nor of programmes; it belongs to the order of events that break through the continuum of history, as they do the incommensurability of cognition. Whoever speaks of the strike cannot be sure that he is not affected by it, that he is not already participating in it.[9]

Hamacher links pure violence, as an act not of *posing* but of *deposing*, to what he calls *afformatives*, which are the condition of any performative act. They are not acts *separated* from the performatives per se, but are, in a special way, internal to the latter:

> [A]fformative, or pure, violence is a 'condition' for any instrumental, performative violence, and, at the same time, a condition which suspends their fulfilment in

principle. But while afformations do not belong to the class of acts – that is, to the class of positing or founding operations – they are, nevertheless, never simply outside the sphere of acts or without relation to that sphere. The fact that afformations allow something to happen without making it happen has a dual significance: first, that they let this thing enter into the realm of positings, from which they themselves are excluded; and, second, that they are not what shows up in the realm of positings, so that the field of phenomenality, as the field of positive manifestation, can only indicate the effects of the afformative as ellipses, pauses, interruptions, displacements, etc., but can never contain or include them.[10]

That is, pure violence, pure deposing, cannot be performative and can never acquire, accordingly, the character of an independent event. But this leaves us with a constitutive split that can never be overcome: we will combat violence, as such, through its incarnation in a concrete system of violence, but the moment of pure deposing of violence never arrives. The destruction of a system of power can only mean the construction of a different power. There is going to be an ineradicable asymmetry in all social identity: the forces attempting to depose violence are going to be hopelessly inadequate to carry out the task that they assume. The pure deposing circulates among bodies which have an unbridgeable distance from it. Paraphrasing Lacan, we could speak of 'a subject supposed to liberate'. And we would find ourselves again with the place of the subject as the place of a constitutive lack. If the pure deposing – a violence as pure mediacy (a non-violent violence because it is not directed against any particular object) – were possible as an independent act, that would mean, then, the death of the subject because the duality subject/object would have been entirely eliminated. But if the relation posing/deposing is one of mutual contamination, then pure deposing can only inhabit the historical acts of the posing/deposing as that which is absent, as something required by the structure of the act, but, at the same time, as something that is made impossible by that very structure. The relation political strike/proletarian strike will be constitutively undecidable. This space of undecidability, of unrepresentability, is the locus of the subject. There are subjects (in the plural) because the Subject (or the Object, which amounts to the same) is impossible.

Presencing and Presence

Let us move now to the distinction between 'presence' and 'presencing' in Heidegger – the so-called ontological distinction. Let us approach it with reference to the plurality of senses of the notion of 'origin' – *arché*, *principium*, *Ursprung* – in Heidegger, as discussed, in particular, by Reiner Schürmann.[11] The Aristotelian notion of *arché* combines for the first time two different meanings: inception and domination. It is the fusion between the two, with the increasing subordination of the first to the second, that is going to constitute the central discourse of Western metaphysics. Moreover, it is the *concealment* involved in this subordination that the Heideggerian intervention will try to deconstruct in an attempt to launch a new beginning. But that fusion of meanings is only possible with the advent of a causalist type of explanation. Indeed, a causalist explanation is the first step in the subordination of inception to domination:

> The alliance between the notions of inception and domination is possible only *once the metaphysics of the causes is constituted*. Once it is understood that phenomena as a whole are knowable from the viewpoint of causality, then it can be said that a true cause is only that which begins its action 'and never ceases to begin it', that is, a cause that also commands. In this way Heidegger links the fate of the concept of *arché* to the constitution of the metaphysics of causes.[12]

Now this causalist explanation – which is the first step in the subordination of inception to domination – is linked to the paradigmatic character, which the fabrication of tools or works of art is going to assume in the explanation of any kind of change or movement. As far as the distinction between things that have the origin of their movement in themselves and those moved by another is concerned, the latter are the model that is going to be metaphorically extended to the understanding of the former. If the efficient cause takes precedence, the final cause, the *telos* of the process of change, has to be active from the beginning: it is only as a result of this teleological orientation of action that 'becoming' acquires a being which it lacks. Becoming is intelligible only as far as it is *dominated* by its *telos*. And this domination-oriented conception of origin is generalized to all human action.

> The teleocratic frame of reference applies to action to the extent that action is still seen as becoming: magistrates 'move' the city because they are themselves 'moved' by the idea that is its end. This is why architecture is the paradigmatic art: the anticipation of end through which Aristotle comprehends the origin is observed most clearly in construction. . . . How, then, does *arché* dominate? In anticipating *telos*.[13]

The turn towards a total concealment of the distinction between presencing and presence – between inception and domination – is not complete in Aristotle because, as Heidegger says, he speaks Greek and cannot be entirely blind to the original sense of *physis* as presencing, as coming forth. But all the essential preconditions for the turn are already there:

> [W]e glimpse how the reversal of history sets in which will place first a divine, then a human constructor, in the position of origin. What anticipates onto-theological and

onto-anthropological doctrines, in which the origin figures as the predicate of one entity, is the novel concept – if not the word – *arché* in Aristotle.[14]

A first hardening of the subordination of inception to domination takes place with the transition from the Greek *arché* to the Latin *principium*: the latter is not a neutral translation by Cicero from one language to the other, but one that reinforces the dimension of ruling (*principium, princeps*). This move reaches its climax first, when, in the Middle Ages, the *Principium* becomes divine and is conceived as the supreme cause of everything; and second, when this supreme principle is transferred to the logical order and it is thus identified with the universal representation for a subject.

The concept of *ordo dependentiae* in Scotus privileges in the *principium* the dimension of hierarchy over that of source. With this, the temporal dimension that was still present in Aristotle as a result of the insufficiency of being shown by becoming, is replaced by pure *presence* in an entirely dominated order. God, rather than a Creator, assumes the figure of *Pantocrator*. The process comes to a close with Leibniz's principle of sufficient reason, by which reason rules even over God. With this transition from an ontological to a logical principle, the latter becomes a law of the mind, and assumes a function of universal representation grounded in human subjectivity. Thus it becomes a subjective rule for 'enframing' things. According to Heidegger, this hardening of the dimension of domination that sanctions the concealment of Being as inception, finds its highest point in contemporary technology.

The deconstruction of Western metaphysics is conceived by Heidegger as the attempt to undo this hardening and to restore the lost dimension of inception. It is this restoration which makes visible the ontological difference between Being and beings as a temporal difference. This leads to a different type of origin, what Heidegger calls *Ursprung* (literally, 'primal leap'). Now, the important point for our argument is that the possibility of access to this more radical origin – which shows itself as temporal difference and thus splits the unity of the principle, depends on a passage through nothingness. As Schürmann cogently asserts:

Phuein has no history, no destiny. But this is not to say that it is atemporal. If it were, how could acting ever be *kata phusin*, following the coming about of presence? The temporality of this coming-about may be understood through the corresponding notion of nothingness. The 'original', i.e., an epochal beginning, is a rise out of *ontic* nothingness, out of all those (possible) entities that remain absent for an age. The 'originary' is a rise out of *ontological* nothingness, out of the pull towards absence that permeates presencing to its very heart. The presencing–absencing is originary time: both approaching (*Angang*) and departing (*Abgang*); genesis and *pthora*, rising and declining; being and not being. The mutual emergence of phenomena, in which non-being temporalizes being is the 'originary' origin, *Ursprung*.[15]

The structure of the argument is clear enough: nothingness is the very condition of access to Being. For, if something were mere, unchallenged actuality, no ontological difference would be possible: the ontic and the ontological would exactly overlap and we would simply have pure presence. In that case, Being would only be accessible as that which is the most universal of all predicates, as that which is beyond all *differentia specifica*. And that would mean it would not be accessible at all, for reasons Heidegger discusses at the beginning of *Sein und Zeit*. But if nothingness were there as an actual possibility, any being which presents itself would also be, to its very roots, mere possibility, and would show, beyond its ontic specificity, Being as such. *Possibility*, as opposite to pure *presence*, temporalizes Being and splits, from its very ground, all identity. Presencing (*Ursprung*) and what is present, the ontological and the ontic, are irremediably split, but this has a double consequence: the first is that the ontic can never be closed in itself; the second, that the ontological can only show itself through the ontic. The same movement creating the split, condemns its two sides (as in all splits) to mutual dependence. Being cannot inhabit a 'beyond' all actual beings, because in that case, it would only be one more being. Being *shows* itself in the entities as that which they are lacking and as that which derives from their ontological status as mere possibility. Being and nothingness, presence and absence, are the mutually required terms of a ground constitutively split by difference.

This allows us to link Heidegger's argument with our previous discussions – though moving in a direction which Heidegger did not take and of which, most likely, he would not have approved. As we have seen, the split between political and proletarian strike is, for Sorel, ineradicable, because any concrete struggle will put into question both an actual system of violence and the principle of violence as such. But now, if pure violence, violence as such, cannot be something which has an actual existence of its own, the 'beyond violence' cannot be an actual event either. The impossible, the 'beyond violence', would certainly eliminate the split: in a fully reconciled society we would have total and undisturbed presence, absolute domination by a pure *principium*. But if violence *is* constitutive, it becomes the nothingness which shows the character of mere possibility of itself and of that which it opposes. It is this effect of unconcealment that splits the opposing forces between their 'ontic' contents and the character of mere possibility – that is, inception, pure Being – of those contents. In the same way, we have seen Hobbes's state of nature as a 'nothingness' which splits the identity of the order imposed by the ruler: on the one hand, the ruler imposes a *particular* order; on the other, and as the alternative to this particular order is chaos (nothingness), it has also to incarnate order as such, whose indifference to the particularity of its contents likens it to pure Being. Heidegger's ontological difference clears the way to think the various structural dimensions of this constitutive split of all identity.

But now, is it not precisely this subject that we have found in our various explorations – the subject of the lack of being – which is made possible by this difference? This is not the subject of onto-theology or onto-anthropology (a *cogito*, an *ousia* conceived as mere presence), but exactly the opposite: a subject whose lack of being is the precondition for its access to Being.

Subject of the Lack and Logic of the Signifier

It is time now to move from these various theoretico-discursive surfaces, which have shown us the emergence of the subject as lack, to a fuller theorization of the latter. We will do this through a consideration of Lacanian theory and its approach to the question of the relation between subject (lack) and identity (objectivity), mediated through the mechanism of identification. We will argue that the act of identification is precisely what performs the function of filling as a 'dialectical reversal': a movement involving a function of determination triggered by the failure in the constitution of an objective unity.

Following Freud, Lacan argues that the ego is an ensemble of successive imaginary identifications (historical and contingent).[16] The world of the ego is enjoyed as a reflection, where relationships amongst egos are dual and fixed (fascination, hostility, love). The ego has the function of misrecognizing the impossibility of fullness: the illusion of closure is the illusion of the ego. Throughout its life the ego will be transformed by means of a series of identifications which will involve two main mechanisms: projection and introjection of the features of an 'object' of identification.[17] This points precisely to the double incidence of the imaginary and the symbolic, where the 'mediator' or hinge is the ego ideal. The structure – that is to say, the Other – is also the field of the ego's projections, whereas the mechanism of introjection is crucial for the articulation of the symbolic. The structure does not return our image, otherwise the ego would only be that which I can see myself being in the structure. But I am also that *Other* who sees what I see: the one who, when I look at it, looks also at itself through me and in me. It sees itself in the place that I occupy in it.[18]

All imaginary identifications constituting the ego can only be assumed if ratified by the Other as symbolic referent. Here we have an ego, then, that while misrecognizing the Law, nevertheless must submit to it. The symbolic identification involves the interplay of signifiers and the structure of intersubjective relations that is dominated by the Law: proper names, syntactic rules of language – and the assumption of the place of the Other as the third term which sanctions truth and guarantees stability. What we thus have is an operation of alienation and internalization: a subject is alienated in an identity-as-objectivity which is part of an objective system of differences, that is, the Law, which is internalized in the same movement.

However, there is another element in any act of identification: the failure in the constitution of any identity. Every signifier fails to represent the subject and leaves a residue: something fails to be reflected in the mirror-world of reflections. There is an essential asymmetry, between projection and introjection, for although the image is brought in, it remains outside; the inside 'starts' outside. In other words, not everything is reflected in the image-mirror, and what remains on the other side is the impossible, the primarily repressed. This asymmetry points to the faults that instal uncertainty and trigger identifications. The moment of failure marks the emergence of the subject of lack through the fissures of the discursive chain. This moment has destructuring effects: the subversion of objectivity (identity) becomes ineradicable. The construction of any unity instals also something of the order of the impossible in that reality: a void which has 'unwelcome effects' – distortions and excesses that point at its precarious and contingent constitution.

This inevitability of failure of any identity, and the anxiety involved with the emergence of that moment with respect to uncertainty, can be shown to be at work in the logic of Borges's poem 'The Golem'. Borges confronts us with the anxiety of the rabbi of Prague in the face of his creation: the Golem. After complicated permutations of letters, the rabbi has achieved the act of Creation by pronouncing 'the Name which is the Key'. But his creation can never become more than just a clumsy and crude simulacrum of a man, one who could never learn to speak ('perhaps there was a faulty text?'). Looking at the Golem the rabbi wondered with terror:

> How (he asked) could it be done
> That I engendered this distressing son?
> To an infinite series why was it for me
> To add another integer?[19]

The anxiety of the rabbi is no more than a mere distortion or even the imperfect repetition of divine anxiety itself:

> Who can tell us the feelings in His breast
> As God gazed on His rabbi there in Prague?[20]

In each inscription something is lost: there is a discordance, a failure which triggers anxiety – the failure of the rabbi vis-à-vis the Golem, and the failure of God vis-à-vis the rabbi – an anxiety which points at the place of emergence of the subject.

It is the ineradicable character of this failure that instals the very possibility of the lack in the structure – a lack which is, as we have seen, the very condition of power relations. Failure will trigger new acts of identification – new 'partial covenants', as referenced in our discussion on Hobbes – which attempt (vainly) to master those destructuring effects. It is in these interruptions that the subject of lack will emerge and disrupt that imaginary-symbolic universe. This constitutive duality between the lack (as the domain – or non-place – of the subject) and the structure or Law (as an objective system of differences as identities) is the terrain where identification takes place as a 'dialectical reversal' between the two.[21]

The dynamic relation between lack and structure is shown by several logics of Lacanian theory: (a) the logic of suture; (b) the logic of repression; and (c) the logic of the subject. The logic of suture focuses on the point of maximum tension ('point of suture') in the relation between lack (subject) and structure (object), as the place of least resistance. It involves the articulation of the signifier which, in circulating beneath the discursive chain, acts as a 'stand-in' for the lack, and thus later appears as an element of the structure (for example, Death, Sexuality). But this operation is misrecognized and, as it is represented through a stand-in, the lack cancels itself out. This is why there is a permanent and alternating movement whereby the lack is rejected and invoked, articulated and annulled, included and excluded. In this way the lack triggers the metonymic chain in an endless process of differentiation. This is the process that determines the appearance of the successor in the series of natural numbers $(n + 1)$, the classic example that J.A. Miller draws upon from the work of Frege. Here the lack is articulated as a unity in so far as the zero names the lack, and is counted as a unity, that is, as 1, while the zero circulates as an element beneath the series of numbers which fixes and produces the 1. The zero thus comprises three logical moments: (i) the zero as lack: the non-concept, the Real, the blank; (ii) the zero as a number: as a stand-in concept of the impossible which evokes and annuls the lack; (iii) the zero number as 1: that is, as a unity and as identity.

We could say, similarly, that there are signifiers occupying this point of suture in a particular political field. Let us take the case of the policy of disappearances put into effect by many Latin American dictatorships. The signifier '*desaparecidos*' occupies a central place in the political field, where various discursive threads are knotted. On the one hand, the authorities tend to deny the existence of any *desaparecidos*: all government arrests have been executed according to the legal framework. Thus, the *desaparecidos* as a category are excluded from the world of objects. On the other hand, the authorities recognize their existence but deny responsibility for their disappearance, saying that they are abroad, or have been killed by 'subversive' organizations, and so on. Then again, there are times when the government officials may assume responsibility but try to minimize it along the lines that these disappearances are inevitable 'consequences' of war, excesses, abuses, and so forth. As a result of these two operations, these *desaparecidos* inhabit a space where they are neither dead nor alive; they can reappear, they can also be killed. Their death and their life is suspended, deferred. And by means of this operation fear is installed into that context: the *desaparecidos* point to the existence of another space, a space of suspension, which is both part of, and excluded from, the realm of 'society', and, in this way, it becomes necessary to define its limits.[22]

A similar logic is at work in repression, where the primarily repressed (irreducible to discourse) insists on being represented in the discursive chain via a stand-in. By means of primary repression 'something' (that real impossible Thing that escapes the signifier) is excluded and is relatively fixed on to something else: the *Vorstellung Representanz*. But what is excluded exerts a certain force of attraction and insists on emerging in the signifying chain. It is the function of secondary repression to prevent such eruption. However, that which is excluded manages to emerge, even if through a remote derivative: this is the moment of dislocation.[23] A function analogous to that of the 'point of suture' is assigned here to the *Vorstellung Representanz*, which Lacan also calls 'binary signifier';[24] that is, the condition of possibility of representation and of subversion. This is the paradoxical signifier which marks the limit to any totality because something will always be lost . . . until it erupts.

It is in this fundamental division where the dialectic of the split subject is established: in so far as 'when the subject appears somewhere as meaning, he [sic] is manifested elsewhere as "fading", as disappearance'.[25] The articulation of the 'point of suture' and of the *Vorstellung Representanz* follow the same logic as the subject vis-à-vis the structure or the Law-as-Other. On the one hand, the subject is excluded from the field of the Other: the subject 'is' lack – that is, pure indeterminacy which cannot be reduced to the structure or constituted discursively. On the other hand, the subject is counted also as a unity in the field of the Other, by means of the signifier of identity, resulting from the process of identification. This is the fictional 'self' and the subject of the *énoncé*.[26] Finally, this dual articulation and the exteriority/interiority of the relation between the subject and the Other establishes both the unconscious ('the core of our being') and the subject as an excess of the *énonciation* – as a cut in the chain, as the permanent possibility of one more signifier operating from within the chain, as a stand-in for the subject of lack.[27] Through this stand-in the subject of lack is inscribed in the text, but only as a residue, via, for example, the loss of a signifier (parapraxis) and certain 'particles' (like the 'not' in denegation), and so on.[28] The subject, then, appears and disappears in the interstices of the structure, by way of, at least, a 'pair of signifiers', one of which is eclipsed by the ascendancy and return of the other. This triggers the movement of the chain: a signifier represents the subject for another signifier. The movement is founded in a process of permanent differentiation in so far as the signifier fails and constantly defers in representing the subject. This is also why the subject of lack is an 'active or productive' impossibility rather than 'just' an impossibility. For while it constantly re-marks the moment of impossibility of constituting a full identity – a re-marking that becomes, also, the moment of power and of the emergence of the subject in the structure itself – it also triggers action, that is, the act of identification and the struggle to re-suture the political field. In this sense it is important to bear in mind that the logic of the subject not only involves three terms – the subject of lack, identity and the stand-in; it also involves a move towards Being, a 'want to be'. 'Man is the subject of the lack because he [sic] emerged from a certain relation to discourse, and he [sic] can only fill that lack by means of . . . action. . . . But such action is not a solution.'[29]

The failure of any identification or filling triggers the movement leading to 'dialectical reversals'; reversals which, as we have seen, are inherent in any act of identification. When Lacoue-Labarthe asks, 'Why, after all, should the problem of identification not be, in general, the essential problem of politics?',[30] we could add that the problem of politics is not identification, but identification *and its failure*.

Politics and the Subject

Let us draw from the previous developments some conclusions relevant for political analysis. Identification presupposes the constitutive split of all social identity, between the *content* which provides the surface of identification and the *function* of identification as such – the latter being independent of any content and linked to the former only in a contingent way. The recognition of this split involves a whole historical mutation. As we have seen, the concealment of this split is deeply rooted in the tradition of Western metaphysics and in the political philosophy deriving from it. In the movement from *arché* to *principium* the dimension of domination prevails over that of inception and, as a result, the distinction between presencing and what is present tends to be cancelled out. The notion of a political order, as a result, was not open to any differentiation between 'political ordering' and the actual order which was implemented.

This is what gives to Hobbes's discourse its crucial role in the constitution of the political discourse of modernity. On the one hand, God is no longer there to determine the content of a good communitarian order; on the other, the state of nature poses a threat not to this or that particular social order but to social order as such, and this makes visible, perhaps for the first time, the function of 'political ordering' as different from the various concrete political orders which could historically fulfil it. For even if God were no longer there as a *Pantocrator*, as *principium* of the cosmic order as a whole, the need for His presence cannot be eradicated – the unicity of the *principium* remains as a requirement for society not to dissolve into the chaos of the state of nature.

This explains the need for a ruler whose omnipotence should reproduce, in a secularized version, as many as possible of the divine attributes. But a secularized God is different from God *sensu stricto* in one crucial respect: while in God the ruling function and the contents which actualize the latter cannot properly be differentiated, secular rulers have to justify themselves by proving themselves capable of properly fulfilling the ruling function. There is, in this way, an initial split between the empty place of a function which is not necessarily linked to any particular content, and the plurality of the contents which can actualize it.

Modern political theory has been, to a large extent, the development and deepening of this initial split. Democracy, in the modern sense, is going to be the institution of a space whose social function has had to emancipate itself from any concrete content, precisely because, as we have seen, *any* content is able occupy that space. It is a mistake to oppose a conception of democracy as having a particular content, to that which is merely procedural. What is at stake is more than mere procedures: it is the institution of signifiers of a social lack resulting from the absence of God as fullness of Being. The Hobbesian ruler, as we have seen, cannot avoid having to justify his rule, and this justification requires, as a necessary prerequisite, that those who are ruled can *judge* the extent to which the ruling function is fulfilled by the ruling order – something not possible in the case of God. The fissure through which this judgement can operate is minimal in the case of Hobbes (those ruled cannot be the source of the social order, and their protagonism is only required when the ordering function of the ruler is not fulfilled), but it is already there and its widening will open the way to the discourses of modern democracy. While previous forms of social organization led to the concealment of this difference by presenting concrete forms of political organization as the only possible ones that fulfil the function of political organization as such, modern democracy makes that difference fully visible.

But it would be a mistake to think that the ordering function is linked to the idea of an order which has to be *maintained* and is, in that sense, essentially stabilizing and conservative. Revolutionary violence, as described by Sorel and Benjamin, plays exactly the same role. The subversion of an existing order is the search for a fullness that the latter is preventing. And, as we have seen, there is no alternative order that can achieve that fullness. The politics of pure mediation – of a violence which is addressed to no particular targets, although particular targets are always the occasions which trigger it off – would be impossible without the split between the fullness that pure violence is searching for and the constitutively inadequate objectives of the actual struggles that attempt to incarnate it. The objectives of revolutionary violence – in the same way as the function of social ordering – are deprived of any content and are, in this sense, the empty places of an absent fullness.

Now, two important corollaries follow from this. The first is that a series of signifiers of the lack, of the absent fullness, have to be constantly produced if politics – as different from sedimented social forms – is going to be possible. Politics presupposes the – peaceful or violent – competition between social forces and the essential instability of the relation between ruling order and ruling function. Terms such as 'the *unity* of the *people*', the '*welfare* of the *country*', and so forth, as something that antagonistic political forces claim to ensure through totally different political means, have to be necessarily empty in order to constitute the aims of a political competition. They are alternative terms to refer to the plenitude of a fully fledged communitarian order as something which is absent and which has to be achieved. The second corollary is this: that in a *politically* managed society, whatever identity the political agents have can only result from precarious and transient forms of identification. It is easy to see why. If the relation between the ordering function and the actual order is going to be always an unstable one, this is only possible in so far as the identity of the political agents will change by means of successive acts of identification; acts that will sustain, modify, resist or reject that concrete order – an identification that will always ultimately fail to achieve a fully fledged identity.

If we maintained – which we do not – that the fullness of society is something that can finally be achieved (be it the communist society, the harmonic organic society, or whatever), we would imply that, in this order, the agents will finally achieve their true identity. There is no need and no place for identification in this perspective, and there is no longer a place for political ordering, due to the radical elimination of all splitting and decentring. This elimination would be equivalent to the 'death of the subject', given that it presupposes the abolition of the distinction between subject and object. Neither do we want to suggest, however, that the subject can be reduced to an effect of a non-subjective process that constitutes the identities of the political agents. The latter would be more in line with those types of analyses concerned simply with the study of relative subject positions in social networks, disciplinary techniques, hierarchies, and so on; that is, the relative subject positions that empower, denigrate, subordinate, exclude. This is only part of the story since it does not contemplate the interruptions and dislocations through which the subject will emerge and will disrupt the imaginary-symbolic universe.

If, on the contrary, the split between ordering and order is constitutive, the subject, as the subject of lack and identification, cannot be superseded by any fully fledged identity, whether of an objectivist or a transcendental character. In that sense, the death of the subject and the unstable character of all identity are conditions of that management of the incompletion of society that we call politics.

Notes

1. Thomas Mann, *Dr Faustus* (London: Penguin, 1968) pp. 184–5.
2. Thomas Mann, *Lotte in Weimar* (London: Penguin, 1968), pp. 130–31.
3. Ibid., p. 138.
4. We have profited in this section from the work of Törben Dyrberg, *Power and the Subject: A Presuppositionless Conception of Power* (Ph.D. thesis, University of Essex, 1989).
5. W. Benjamin, *Reflections, Essays, Aphorisms, Autobiographical Writings*, trans. Edmund Jephcott (New York: Schocken Books) p. 278.
6. Ibid., p. 281.
7. Ibid., p. 291.
8. W. Hamacher, 'Afformative Strike', *Cardozo Law Review*, vol. 13, no.4, December 1991, pp. 1133–57.
9. Ibid., pp. 1154–7.
10. Ibid., p. 1139 n. 12.
11. Reiner Schürmann, *Heidegger; On Being and Acting: From Principles to Anarchy*, trans. Christine-Marie Gros (Bloomington: Indiana University Press, 1990) especially pp. 97–154.
12. Ibid., p. 99.
13. Ibid., pp. 103–4.
14. Ibid., p. 105.
15. Ibid., pp. 141–2.
16. For Freud identification, the endless processes of identification involve the transformation of the ego; or, as he writes, 'the character of the Ego is a precipitate of abandoned object-cathexes and . . . it contains the history of those object-choices . . . accepted or resisted . . .' (Sigmund Freud, 'The Ego and the Id', *The Standard Edition [SE] of the Complete Psychological Works of Sigmund Freud*, trans. James Strachey in collaboration with Anna Freud, and with Alix Strachey and Alan Tyson [London: Hogarth Press, 1923] Volume XIX, p. 29). We should remember that for Freud the ego is produced rather than always being there: 'a unity comparable to the ego cannot exist in the individual from the start; the ego has to be developed . . . so there must be something added to auto-erotism – a new psychical action – in order to bring about narcissism' (Freud, 'On Narcissism: an Introduction,' *SE*, 1914, Volume XIV, p. 77).
17. Ideal formations are created by projective processes; i.e. they are thrown 'outside' to be recuperated by means of identification. In this process, therefore, a certain outside is created as projection of the inside. The ego ideal functions as a source of introjection, whereas the Ideal ego functions as a source of projection. The latter is a function of the imaginary.
18. J. Lacan, 'La Identificación', in *Imago: Revista de Psicoanálisis, Psiquiatría y Psicología* (Buenos Aires, 1979) p. 66.
19. J.L. Borges, 'The Golem', *Selected Poems. 1923–1967*, edited with introduction and notes by Norman Di Giovanni, trans. John Hollander (Harmondsworth: Penguin), p. 127.
20. Borges, 'The Golem', p. 127.
21. That is, there is a decentred and incomplete structure (a relatively stable terrain of meaning) that in- and ex-cludes moments of subversion. The structure is organized around the gaps that disorganize it. There is production of meaning because something is lost and something else occupies its place, and this is what makes possible differential relations between signifiers and the production of a signified. The lack enables productivity and multiplicity of meaning, the play of signification, overdetermination, and it also triggers determination. But the lack will always escape this demand for presence and it will be eternally postponed.
22. Of course, this logic on its own cannot define the limits of the social. Other logics are in operation and are articulated to this one in several ways. For instance, the logic of equivalences defines the antagonistic other, many times in very vague terms, and in this way contributes to the installing of fear among the population since anyone can cross the limit: nobody is certain where the limit lies.
23. We could think of, for instance, the classical Freudian example of parapraxis: his forgetting of the name of the painter of the Orvieto fresco, 'Signorelli'. His forgetting caused Freud an 'inner torment' and only after a few days could he come up with two names: 'Botticelli and Boltraffio'. When he finally remembered the name 'Signorelli', he attempted to explain the parapraxis by examining the overdetermined character of the forgotten signifier. Freud's analysis weaves a

chain of signifiers: Bosnia, Herzegovina, Traffoi. These are the 'metonymic ruins' of other rejected signifiers of impossibility: death, the 'Herr' of sexuality. Freud concluded that, by means of condensation and displacement, this signifier became a substitute for something else, 'some-Thing' that crossed the bar of signification and which Freud would link to Death and Sexuality. This lost something was rejected from the chain but remained within it via the distortion of that chain ('The Psycho-pathology of Everyday Life', *SE*, 1901, Volume III, p. 332).

24. Jacques Lacan, *The Four Fundamental Concepts of Pyscho-Analysis*, edited by Jacques-Alain Miller, trans. Alan Sheridan (Harmondsworth: Penguin, 1977) p. 219.

25. Ibid., p. 218.

26. This does not mean that the distance between the self and the Other disappears. Quite the contrary; the Other is external to the unity of the ego (of the narcissistic contract) in so far as the Other exists in the tri-dimensional spaciality of the ego, where there is an inside and an outside.

27. Discontinuity is the form in which the unconscious appears. For Lacan, what strikes us from the phenomena of the unconscious is 'the sense of impediment to be found in all of them. Impediment, failure, split. . . . What occurs, what is *produced*, in this gap, is presented as the *discovery* [of psychoanalysis].' *The Four Fundamental Concepts*, p. 25. These moments of rupture of meaning 'mark and re-mark the text' and leave traces (ibid.). The formations of the unconscious, in this context, are the traces that appear and disappear: they are produced in the (symbolic) order but point at something which is *outside* its signifying dialectic.

28. This is not a split subject that is secondary to a primary unity. The subject emerges as a split subject and therefore is non-subject before this moment.

29. Lacan, 'La Identificación', p. 61.

30. Philippe Lacoue-Labarthe, 'Transcendence Ends in Politics', *Typography: Mimesis, Philosophy, Politics* (Cambridge, Mass.: Harvard University Press, 1989) p. 300.

2

Identity and Its Vicissitudes: Hegel's 'Logic of Essence' as a Theory of Ideology

Slavoj Žižek

The Principle of the Insufficient Ground

Love lets us view imperfections as tolerable, if not adorable. *But it's a choice.* We can bristle at quirks, or we can cherish them. A friend who married a hot-shot lawyer remembers, 'On the first date, I learned that he could ride out rough hours and stiff client demands. On the second, I learned that what he couldn't ride was a bicycle. *That's* when I decided to give him a chance.'

The lesson of the so-called 'endearing foibles' referred to in this quote from *Reader's Digest* is that a choice is an act which *retroactively grounds its own reasons*. Between the causal chain of reasons provided by knowledge (S_2, in Lacanian mathemes) and the act of choice (that is, the decision that by way of its unconditional character concludes the chain, S_1), there is always a gap, a leap that cannot be accounted for by the preceding chain.[1] Let us recall what is perhaps the most sublime moment in melodramas: a plotter or a well-meaning friend tries to convince the hero to leave his sexual partner by way of enumerating the latter's weak points; yet, unknowingly, he thereby provides reasons for continued loyalty, that is, his very counter-arguments function as arguments for commitment (*'for that very reason* she needs me even more').[2] This gap between reasons and their effect is the very foundation of what we call transference, the transferential relationship, epitomized by love. Even our sense of common decency finds it repulsive to enumerate the reasons we love somebody: the moment I can say 'I love this person for the following reasons . . .', it is clear beyond any doubt that this is not love properly speaking.[3] In the case of true love, apropos of some feature which is in itself negative, that is, which offers itself as reason against love, we say 'For this very reason I love this person even more!' *Le trait unaire*, the unitary feature which triggers love, is always an *index of an imperfection*.

This circle within which we are determined by reasons, but only by those which, retroactively, we recognize as such, is what Hegel has in mind when he talks about the 'positing of presuppositions'. The same retroactive logic is at work in Kant's philosophy, in the guise of what, in the Anglo-Saxon literature on Kant, is usually referred to as the 'Incorporation Thesis'.[4] There is always an element of autonomous 'spontaneity' which pertains to the subject, making him irreducible to a link in the causal chain. True, one can conceive of the subject as submitted to the chain of causes which determine his or her conduct in accordance with 'pathological' interests; and, indeed, therein consists the wager of utilitarianism (since the subject's conduct is wholly determined by seeking the maximum of pleasure and the minimum of pain, it would be possible to govern the subject, to predict his or her steps, by controlling the external conditions which influence his or her decisions). But what eludes utilitarianism is precisely the element of 'spontaneity' (in the sense of German Idealism) – the very opposite of the everyday meaning of 'spontaneity', that is, surrendering oneself to the immediacy of emotional impulses, and so on. According to German Idealism, when we act 'spontaneously' in the everyday meaning of the word, we are not free from, but prisoners of, our immediate nature, determined by the causal link which chains us to the external world. True spontaneity, on the contrary, is characterized by the moment of reflexivity; reasons ultimately count only in so far as I 'incorporate' them, 'accept them as mine' – in other words, the determination of the subject by the other is always the subject's self-determination. A decision is thus simultaneously dependent on, and independent of, its conditions: it 'independently' posits its own dependence. In this precise sense, the subject in German Idealism is always the subject of self-consciousness: any immediate reference to my nature ('What can I do, I was made like this!') is false; my relationship to the impulses in me is always a mediated one, that is, my impulses determine me only in so far as I recognize them, which is why I am fully responsible for them.[5]

Another way to exemplify this logic of 'positing the presuppositions' is the spontaneous ideological narrativization of our experience and activity: whatever we do, we always situate it in a larger symbolic context charged with conferring meaning upon our acts. A Serbian fighting the Muslim Albanians and Bosnians in today's ex-Yugoslavia conceives of their fight as the last act in the centuries-old defence of Christian Europe against Turkish penetration; the Bolsheviks conceived of the October Revolution as the continuation and successful conclusion of all previous radical popular uprisings from Spartacus in ancient Rome to the Jacobins in the French Revolution (this narrativization is tacitly assumed even by some critics of Bolshevism who, for example, speak of the 'Stalinist Thermidor'); the Khmer Rouge in Cambodia or Sendero Luminoso in Peru conceive of their movement as a return to the old glory of an ancient empire (the Inca empire in Peru, the old Khmer kingdom in

Cambodia); and so on. The Hegelian point to be made is that such narratives are always retroactive reconstructions for which we are in some way responsible; they are never simple given facts. We can never refer to them as a found condition, context or presupposition of our activity precisely because as presuppositions such narratives are always-already 'posited' by us. Tradition is tradition in so far as we constitute it as such.

These paradoxes enable us to specify the nature of 'self-consciousness' in German Idealism. In his critical remarks on Hegel, Lacan as a rule equates self-consciousness with self-transparency, dismissing it as the most blatant case of a philosophical illusion bent on denying the subject's constitutive decentring. However, 'self-consciousness' in German Idealism has nothing whatsoever to do with any kind of transparent self-identity of the subject; it is rather another name for what Lacan himself has in mind when he points out how every desire is by definition the 'desire of a desire'. The subject never simply finds in itself a multitude of desires; he or she always entertains towards them a reflected relationship. By way of actual desiring, the subject implicitly answers the question, 'which of your desires do you desire (have you chosen)?'[6] As we have already seen apropos of Kant, self-consciousness is positively founded upon the non-transparency of the subject to itself: the Kantian transcendental apperception (that is, the self-consciousness of pure I) is possible only in so far as I am unattainable to myself in my noumenal dimension, qua the 'Thing which thinks'.[7]

There is, of course, a point at which this circular 'positing of the presuppositions' reaches a deadlock – the key to which is provided by the Lacanian logic of the non-all [pas-tout].[8] Although 'nothing is presupposed that was not previously posited'; that is, although, for every particular presupposition, it can be demonstrated that it is 'posited' (that is to say that it is not 'natural' but naturalized), it would be wrong to draw the seemingly obvious universal conclusion that 'everything presupposed is posited'. The presupposed X which is 'nothing in particular', that is, totally substanceless, is, nevertheless, resistant to retroactive 'positing'; it is what Lacan calls the real, the unattainable, elusive je ne sais quoi. In Gender Trouble, Judith Butler demonstrates how the difference between sex and gender – the difference between a biological fact and a cultural-symbolic construction (which, a decade ago, was widely used by feminists in order to show that 'anatomy is not destiny', that is, that 'woman' as a cultural product is not determined by her biological status) can never be unambiguously fixed or presupposed as a positive fact. It is always-already 'posited': how we draw the line separating 'culture' from 'nature' is always determined by a specific cultural context. This cultural overdetermination of the dividing line between gender and sex should not, however, push us into accepting the Foucauldian notion of sex as the effect of 'sexuality' (the heterogeneous texture of discursive practices), for what gets lost is, thereby, precisely the deadlock of the real.[9] Here we see the thin, but crucial, line that separates Lacan from 'deconstruction': by granting the opposition between nature and culture as always-already culturally overdetermined, that is, that no particular element can be isolated as 'pure nature', does not mean that 'everything is culture'. 'Nature' qua Real remains the unfathomable X that resists cultural 'gentrification'. Or, to put it another way: the Lacanian Real is the gap which separates the Particular from the Universal, the gap that prevents us from completing the gesture of universalization, blocking our jump from the premiss (that every particular element is P), to the conclusion (that all elements are P).

Consequently there is no logic of Prohibition involved in the notion of the Real qua the impossible-nonsymbolizable. In Lacan, the Real is not surreptitiously consecrated, envisioned as the domain of the inviolable. When Lacan defines the 'rock of castration' as real, this in no way implies that castration is excepted from the discursive field as a kind of untouchable sacrifice. Every demarcation between the Symbolic and the Real, every exclusion of the Real qua the prohibited-inviolable, is a symbolic act *par excellence*. Such an inversion of impossibility into prohibition-exclusion *occults the inherent deadlock of the Real*. In other words, Lacan's strategy is to prevent any tabooing of the Real; one can 'touch the real' only by applying oneself to its symbolization, up to the very failure of this endeavour. In Kant's *Critique of Pure Reason*, the only proofs that there are Things beyond phenomena are paralogisms – inconsistencies in which reason gets entangled the moment it extends the application of categories beyond the limits of experience. In exactly the same way, *'le réel'* – the real of *jouissance* – *'ne saurait s'inscrire que d'une impasse de la formalisation'* in Lacan can be discerned only by way of the deadlocks of its formalization.[10] In short, *the status of the Real is thoroughly non-substantial*. It is a product of failed attempts to integrate it into the Symbolic.

The impasse, then, of 'presupposing' (that is, of enumerating the presuppositions – the chain of external causes/conditions – of some posited entity) is the reverse of these 'troubles with the non-all'. An entity can easily be reduced to the totality of its presuppositions. What is missing from the series of presuppositions, however, is simply the performative act of formal conversion which retroactively posits these presuppositions and makes them into what they are: that is, into the presuppositions *of* . . . (such as the above-mentioned act which retroactively 'posits' its reasons). This is the 'dotting of the i', the tautological gesture of the Master-Signifier that constitutes the entity in question as One. Here we see the asymmetry between positing and presupposing: *the positing of presuppositions chances upon its limit in the 'feminine' non-all; what eludes it is the real; whereas the enumeration of the presuppositions of the posited content is made into a closed series by means of the 'masculine' performative.*

Hegel endeavours to resolve this impasse of positing the presuppositions ('positing reflection') and of the presuppositions of every positing activity ('external reflection') by way of determining reflection. This logic of the three modalities of reflection (positing, external, determining reflection)[11] renders the matrix of the entire logic of essence, that is, of the triads which follow it: identity, difference, contradiction; essence/form, form/matter, content/ form; formal, real, complete ground; and so on.[12] The aim of the ensuing brief examination of Hegel's logic of essence is thus double: to articulate the successive, and ever more concrete, forms of 'determining reflection' (the Hegelian counterpart of what Kant calls 'transcendental synthesis') and, simultaneously, to discern in them the same pattern of an elementary ideological operation.

Identity, Difference, Contradiction

When dealing with the theme 'Hegel and identity', one should never forget that identity emerges only in the logic of essence, as a 'determination-of-reflection': what Hegel calls 'identity' is not a simple self-equality of any notional determination (red is red, winter is winter . . .); it is the identity of an essence which 'stays the same' beyond the ever-changing flow of appearances. But how are we to determine this identity? If we try to seize the thing as it is 'in itself', irrespective of its relation to other things, its specific identity eludes us and we cannot say anything about it; the thing coincides with all other things. Rather, we must say that *identity hinges upon what makes a difference*. But the moment we grasp that the 'identity' of an entity consists of the cluster of its differential features, we pass from identity to difference. The social identity of a person X, for example, is composed of the cluster of its social mandates which are all by definition differential: a person is 'father' only in relation to 'mother' and 'son'; in another relation, he is himself 'son', and so on. Here is the crucial passage from Hegel's *Logic* in which he brings about the passage from difference to contradiction apropos of the symbolic determination 'father':

> Father is the other of son, and son the other of father, and each only *is* as this other of the other; and at the same time, the one determination only is, in relation to the other . . . The father also has an existence of his own apart from the son-relationship; but then he is not father but simply man . . . Opposites, therefore, contain contradiction in so far as they are, in the same respect, negatively related to one another or *sublate each other* and are *indifferent* to one another.[13]

The inattentive reader may easily miss the key accent of this passage, the feature which belies the standard notion of the Hegelian contradiction. 'Contradiction' does *not* take place between 'father' and 'son' (here, we have a case of simple opposition between two co-dependent terms); but neither does it turn on the fact that in one relation (to my son) I am 'father' and in another (to my own father) I am myself 'son', that is, I am 'simultaneously father and son'. If this were all there were to the Hegelian contradiction, Hegel would effectively be guilty of logical confusion, since it is clear that I cannot be both in the same respect. The last phrase in the quoted passage from Hegel's *Logic* locates the contradiction clearly *inside 'father' himself*: 'contradiction' designates the antagonistic relationship between what I am 'for the others' – my symbolic determination – and what I am 'in myself', abstractedly, from my relations with others. It is the contradiction between the void of the subject's pure 'being-for-himself' and the signifying feature which represents him for the others; in Lacanian terms: between S and S_1. More precisely, 'contradiction' means that it is my very alienation in the symbolic mandate, in S_1, which retroactively makes S (the void that eludes the hold of the mandate) out of my brute reality. I am not only 'father', not only this particular determination; but beyond these symbolic mandates, I am nothing but the void that eludes them. As such, I am their own retroactive product.[14] It is the very symbolic representation in the differential network which evacuates my 'pathological' content; that is, which makes out of S, the substantial fullness of the 'pathological' subject, the barred \$, the void of pure self-relating.

What I am 'for the others' is condensed in the signifier which then represents me for other signifiers (for the 'son' I am 'father', and so on). Outside of my relations to the others I am nothing. I am only the cluster of these relations (or as Marx would have said: 'the human essence is the entirety of social relations'), but this very 'nothing' is the nothing of pure self-relating: I am only what I am for the others, yet simultaneously I am the one who self-determines myself, that is, I am the one who determines which network of relations to others will determine me. In other words, I am determined by the network of (symbolic) relations precisely and only in so far as I, qua void of self-relating, self-determine myself this way.

We encounter here again spontaneity qua self-determination: in my very relating to the other, I relate myself to myself, since I determine the concrete form of my relating to the other. Or, to put it in the terms of Lacan's scheme of discourse:[15]

$$\frac{S_1}{\$} \text{------} S_2$$

We must be careful not to miss the logic of this passing of opposition into contradiction: it has nothing to do with coincidence or co-dependence of the opposites, with one pole passing into its opposite, and so forth. Let us take the case of man and woman: one can endlessly vary the motif of their co-dependence (each is only as the other of the other, its being is mediated by the being of its opposite, and so on), but as long as we continue to set this opposition against the background of some neutral universality (the human genus with its two species, male and female), we are far from contradiction. In male-chauvinist terms, we arrive at contradiction only when 'man' appears as the immediate embodiment of the universal-human dimension, and 'woman' as 'truncated man'. Here the relationship of the two poles ceases to be symmetrical, since man stands for the genus itself, whereas woman stands for specific difference as such. (Or, to put it in the language of structural linguistics: we enter contradiction proper when one of the terms of the opposition starts to function as 'marked', and the other as 'non-marked').

Consequently, we only pass from opposition to contradiction through the logic of what Hegel called 'oppositional determination': when the universal, common ground, of the two opposites 'encounters itself' in its oppositional determination, that is, in one of the terms of the opposition. Let us recall Marx's *Capital*, in which the supreme case of 'oppositional determination' is capital itself. The multitude of capital (invested in particular companies, that is, productive units) necessarily contains 'finance capital', the immediate embodiment of capital in general as opposed to other particular capitals. 'Contradiction' designates, therefore, the relationship between capital in general and the species of capital that embody capital in general (finance capital). A more obvious example appears in the Introduction to *Grundrisse*; here, production as the structuring principle of the whole of production, distribution, exchange and consumption 'encounters itself' in its oppositional determination; the contradiction is thus one between production, as the encompassing totality of the four moments, and production as one of these four moments.[16]

In this precise sense, contradiction is also the contradiction between the position of enunciation and the enunciated content. It occurs when the enunciator himself, by way of the illocutionary force of his speech, accomplishes what, at the level of locution, is the object of his denunciation. A text-book case from political life: when a political agent criticizes rival parties for considering only their narrow party interests, he thereby offers his own party as a neutral force working for the benefit of the whole nation. Consequently, he does what he charges the other with, that is, he promotes, in the strongest way possible, the interest of his own party; the dividing line that structures his speech runs between his own party and all the rest. What is at work here is again the logic of 'oppositional determination': the alleged universality beyond petty party interests encounters itself in a particular party – *that* is 'contradiction'.

At the end of the credits of *The Great Dictator*, Chaplin revises the standard disclaimer concerning the relationship between diegetic reality and 'true' reality ('any resemblance is purely coincidental') to read: 'Any resemblance between the dictator Hynkel and the Jewish barber is purely coincidental.' *The Great Dictator* is ultimately a film about this coincidental *identity*: Hynkel-Hitler, this all-pervasive Voice, is the 'oppositional determination', the shadowy double, of the poor Jewish barber. Suffice to recall the scene in the ghetto where loudspeakers transmit the ferocious anti-Semitic speech by Hynkel, while the barber runs down the street, as if persecuted by the multiplied echoes of his own voice, as if running away from his own shadow. Therein lies a deeper insight than might at first seem: the Jewish barber in *The Great Dictator* is not depicted primarily as a Jew, but rather as the epitome of 'a little man who wants to live his modest, peaceful everyday life outside of political turmoil'; whereas Nazism is precisely the enraged reverse of this 'little man', erupting when its customary world is thrown off the rails. In the ideological universe of the film, the same paradoxical equation is articulated in another implicit identity of opposites: Austria = Germany. Which country in the film plays the role of the victim and at the same time the idyllic counterpart of 'Tomania'? It is Germany, which embodies at the same time an 'Austerlic'-Austria, the small wine-growing country of happy innocent people living together like a large family. In short, it is the land of 'fascism with a human face'.[17] The fact that the same music (the Prelude to Wagner's *Lohengrin*) accompanies both the barber's final speech and Hynkel's famous playing with the globe-balloon acquires thereby an unexpected ominous dimension: at the end, the barber's words about the need for love and peace correspond perfectly to what Hitler-Hynkel himself would say in his sentimental *petit bourgeois* mood.

Form/Essence, Form/Matter, Form/Content

As we start losing ground in an argument, our last recourse is usually to insist that 'despite what has been said, things are essentially what we think them to be'. This is precisely what Hegel has in mind when he speaks of the essence in its immediacy: essence designates here the immediate inwardness, the 'essence of things', that persists irrespective of the external form. Cases of such an attitude, best exemplified by the stupidity of the proverb 'a leopard cannot change his spots', abound in politics. Suffice it to recall the usual right-wing treatment of ex-Communists in the East: irrespective of what they actually do, their democratic 'form' should in no way deceive us, it is mere form; 'essentially' they remain the same old totalitarians, and so on.[18] A recent example of such a logic of 'inner essence' that stuck to its point notwithstanding the changes of the external form, was the judgement of the distrustful on Gorbachov in 1985: nothing will change, Gorbachov is even more dangerous than ordinary hard-line Communists, since he provides the totalitarian system with a seductive 'open', 'democratic' front, whose ultimate aim is to strengthen the system, not to change it radically. The Hegelian point to be made here is that this statement is probably true: in all likelihood, Gorbachov 'really' did want only to improve the existing system; however, and notwithstanding his intentions, his acts set in motion a process which transformed the system from top to bottom. The 'truth' resided in what not only Gorbachov's distrustful critics took to be, but also what Gorbachov himself took to be, a mere external form.

'Essence', thus conceived, remains an empty determination whose adequacy can be tested only by verifying the extent to which it is expressed, rendered manifest, in the external form. We thus obtain the subsequent couple 'form/matter' in which the relationship is inverted. Form ceases to be a passive expression-effect, behind which one has to look for some hidden 'true essence', and becomes instead the agency which individuates the otherwise passive-formless matter, conferring on it some particular determination. In other words, the moment we become aware of how the entire determinatedness of the essence resides in its form, essence, conceived abstractly from its form, changes into a formless substratum of the form; that is, into *matter*. As Hegel concisely puts it: the moment of determination and the moment of subsistence thereby fall apart, are posited as distinct; where a thing is concerned, 'matter' is the passive moment of subsistence (its substantial substratum-ground), whereas 'form' is what provides for its specific determination, what makes this thing what it is.

The dialectic which hampers this seemingly straight opposition is not limited to the fact that we never encounter 'pure' matter devoid of any form (the clay out of which a pot is made must already possess properties which make it appropriate for some form and not for another – for a pot, not for a needle, for example), so that 'pure' formless matter passes into its opposite, into an empty form-receptacle bereft of any concrete, positive, substantial determination, and vice versa, of course. But what Hegel has in mind here is something more radical: the inherent contradiction of the notion of form which designates both the principle of universalization and the principle of individuation. Form is what makes out of some formless matter a particular, determinate, thing (say, a cup out of clay); but it is at the same time the abstract Universal, common to different things (paper cups, glass cups, china cups and metal cups are all 'cups' on account of their common *form*). The only way out of this deadlock is to conceive matter not as something passive-formless, but as something which already in itself possesses an inherent structure, that is, something which stands opposite form and, at the same time, is furnished with its own *content*. But to avoid regression into the initial abstract counterposition of inner essence and externally imposed form, one has to keep in mind that *the couple content/form (or, more pointedly, content as such) is just another name for the tautological relationship by which form is related to itself.* For what is 'content' if not, precisely, *formed matter*? One can thus define 'form' as the way some content is actualized, realized, in matter (by means of the latter's adequate *formation*): 'the same content' – the story of Caesar's murder, for example – can be told in different forms, from Plutarch's historiographical report, through Shakespeare's play, to a Hollywood movie. Alternatively, one can define form as the universality which unites the multitude of diverse contents (the form of the classical detective novel, for example, functions as the skeleton of codified genre rules which set a common seal on the works of authors as different as Agatha Christie, E.S. Gardner, and so on). In other words, and in so far as matter stands for the abstract Other of the form, 'content' is the way matter is mediated by form, and inversely, 'form' is the way content finds its expression in matter. In both cases, the relationship content/ form, in contrast to the relationship matter/form, is *tautological*: 'content' is form itself in its oppositional determination.

With a view to the totality of this movement from essence/form to content/form, it is easy to perceive how its logic announces, in a condensed way, the triad of notion, judgement and syllogism, from that of the 'subjective logic', the third part of Hegel's *Logic*. The couple essence/form remains on the level of notion, that is, essence is the simple in-itself of the notion, of the substantial determination of an entity. The next step literally brings about the *Ur-Teilung*, judgement qua 'original division', the falling apart of the essence into its two constitutive moments that are thus 'posited' as such; that is to say, explicated, but in the mode of externality, that is, as external, indifferent to each other: the moment of subsistence (matter qua substratum) and the moment of determination (form). A substratum acquires determination when a form is predicated to it. The third step, finally, renders manifest the ternary structure of mediation, the distinguishing mark of syllogism, with form as its middle term.

Formal, Real, Complete Ground

There is something almost uncanny about the 'prophetic' dimensions of this apparently modest subdivision in Hegel's *Logic*; it is as if we can truly comprehend it only if we know the history of philosophy, and especially the crucial Hegel-critiques, of the next 150 years, inclusive of Althusser. Among other things, this subdivision anticipates both the young Marx's critique of Hegel and the concept of overdetermination which was developed by Althusser precisely as an alternative to the allegedly Hegelian notion of 'expressive causality'.

Formal ground repeats the tautological gesture of the immediate reference to 'true essence': it does not add any new content to the phenomenon to be explained, it just translates, transposes, the found empirical content into the form of ground. To comprehend this process, one need only recall how doctors sometimes respond when we describe our symptoms: 'Aha, clearly a case of . . .'. What then follows is a long, incomprehensible Latin term which simply translates the content of our complaints into medicalese, adding no new knowledge. Psychoanalytic theory itself offers one of the clearest examples of what Hegel has in mind with 'formal ground', in the way it sometimes uses the notion of death-drive. Explaining the so-called 'negative therapeutic reaction' (more generally, of the phenomena of aggressivity, destructive rage, war, and so on) by invoking *Todestrieb* is a tautological gesture that only confers upon the same empirical content the universal form of law: people kill each other because they are driven to it by the death-drive. The principal target of Hegel himself is here a certain simplified version of Newtonian physics: this stone is heavy – why? On account of the force of gravity, and so on. But the bountiful sneers in Hegel's comments on formal ground should not blind us to its positive side for the necessary, constitutive, function of this formal gesture of converting contingent content that was simply found into the form of ground. It is easy to deride the tautological emptiness of this gesture, but Hegel's point lies elsewhere: by means of its very formal character, this gesture renders possible the search for the real ground. Formal causality qua empty gesture opens up the field of the analysis of content, as with Marx's *Capital*, wherein the formal subsumption of the process of production under capital precedes (comes before and opens up the way for) the material organization of production in accordance with the requirements of capital. (That is, first, the pre-capitalist material organization of production which was simply found – individual artisans, and so on – is formally subsumed under capital [for example, the capitalist provides the artisan with raw materials, etc.]; then, gradually, production is materially restructured into a collective manufacturing process directly run by the capitalist.)

Hegel further demonstrates how such tautological explanations, in order to conceal their true nature and to create an appearance of positive content, fill out again the empty form of ground with some fantasized, imaginary content, conceived as a new, special kind of actual empirical content: we thus obtain ether, magnetism, phlogiston, and other similar mysterious 'natural forces', where empty determinations-of-thought assume the form of positive, determinate content. In short, we obtain the inverted 'topsy-turvy world' in which the determinations-of-thought appear under the guise of their opposite, that is, the guise of positive empirical objects. (An exemplary case within philosophy itself, of course, is Descartes' placing of the link connecting body and soul within the pineal gland: this gland is nothing but a quasi-empirical positivization of the fact that Descartes was unable to *grasp conceptually* the mediation of thinking and extended substance in man.) For Hegel, the inverted 'topsy-turvy world' does not consist in presupposing, beyond the actual, empirical world, the kingdom of supra-sensible ideas. Rather, and in a kind of double inversion by means of which these supra-sensible ideas themselves assume again sensible form, the very sensible world is redoubled: as if, by the side of our ordinary sensible world, there exists another world of 'spiritual materiality' (of ether qua fine stuff, and so on). Why are Hegel's considerations of such interest? They articulate, in advance, the motive that Feuerbach, the young Marx and Althusser proclaim as the 'critique of speculative idealism': that the hidden obverse and 'truth' of speculative idealism is positivism, an enslavement to contingent empirical content, that is, idealism only confers speculative form on the empirical content simply found there.[19]

The supreme case of such a quasi-empirical object that positivizes the subject's inability to think a purely conceptual relationship is provided by Kant himself, who, in his *Opus Posthumum*, proposes the hypothesis of ether.[20] If space is full, Kant reasoned, movement from one place in space to another is not possible since 'all places are already taken'. If, however, space is empty, no contact, no interaction can occur between two bodies separated by space since no force can be transmitted via pure void. From this paradox, Kant drew the conclusion that space is possible only if sustained by 'ether' qua all-pervasive, all-penetrating world-stuff which is practically the same as space itself hypostatically conceived: an all-present element which is space itself, which continuously fills it out and is as such the medium of the interaction of all other 'ordinary' positive forces and/or objects in space. This is what Hegel has in mind apropos of the 'topsy-turvy world': Kant solves the opposition of empty space and the objects filling it out by way of presupposing a 'matter' which is its opposite, that is, thoroughly transparent, homogeneous and continuous – similar to primitive religions with their notion of the Supra-sensible as an etherial-material Beyond. (The need for this hypothesis evaporates, of course, as soon as one accepts the post-Newtonian notion of non-homogeneous space.)[21]

Consequently, formal ground is followed by real ground: the difference between ground and grounded ceases to be purely formal. It is displaced into content itself and is conceived as the distinction between two of its constituents; in the very content of the phenomenon to be explained, one has to isolate some moment and to conceive of it as the 'ground' of all other moments which thereby appear as what is 'grounded'. In traditional Marxism, for example, the so-called 'economical basis' (that is, the structure of the process of production), is the moment that, notwithstanding the inconveniences of the notorious 'last instance', determines all other moments (political and ideological superstructure). Here, of course, the question emerges immediately: Why *this* moment and not some other? That is to say, as soon as we isolate some moment from the whole and conceive of it as its 'ground', we must also take into account the way ground itself is determined by the totality of relations within which it functions as ground: 'ground' can only exert its grounding function within a precisely defined network of conditions. In short, we can only ever answer the question 'Why *this* moment and not some other?' through the detailed analysis of the entire network of relations between the ground and the grounded. And that explains why it is precisely this element of the network that plays the role of ground; for what is thus accomplished is the step to the next, final, modality of ground, in order to complete the ground. It is crucial to grasp the precise nature of Hegel's accomplishment: he does *not* put forward another, even 'deeper' supra-Ground which would ground the ground itself; he simply grounds the ground in the totality of its relations to the grounded content. In this precise sense, complete ground is the unity of formal and real ground: it is the real ground whose grounding relationship to the remaining content is again grounded. But in what is it grounded? *In itself; that is, in the totality of its relations to the grounded.* The ground grounds the grounded, but this grounding role must itself be grounded in the relationship of the ground to the grounded. Thus, we again arrive at the tautology (the moment of formal ground), but not at the empty tautology, as in the case of formal ground. Now, the tautology contains the moment of contradiction in the precise above-mentioned Hegelian sense. It designates the identity of the Whole with its 'oppositional determination': the identity of a moment of the Whole – the real ground – with the Whole itself.

In *Reading Capital*,[22] Louis Althusser sought to illuminate the epistemological break of Marxism by means of a new concept of causality, that of 'over-determination'. Rather than posing an oppositional determination, he held that the very determining instance is overdetermined by the total network of relations within which it plays the determining role. Althusser contrasted this notion of causality to that of both mechanical transitive causality (the linear chain of causes and effects whose paradigmatic case is classical, pre-Einsteinian physics) and expressive causality (the inner essence which expresses itself in the multitude of its forms-of-appearance). 'Expressive causality', of course, targets Hegel in whose philosophy the same spiritual essence – *zeitgeist* – allegedly expresses itself at the different levels of society; for example, in religion as Protestantism, in politics as the liberation of civil society from the chains of medieval corporatism, in law as the rule of private property and the emergence of free individuals as its bearers. This triad of expressive-transitive-overdeterminant causality parallels the Lacanian triad Imaginary-Real-Symbolic. Expressive causality belongs to the level of the Imaginary; it designates the logic of an identical imago which leaves its imprint at different levels of material content. Overdetermination implies a symbolic totality, since such retroactive determination of the ground by the totality of the grounded is possible only within a symbolic universe. And, finally, transitive causality designates the senseless collisions of the real. Today, in the midst of ecological catastrophe, it is especially important that we conceive this catastrophe as a meaningless real *tusche*; that is, that we do not 'read meanings into things', as is done by those who interpret the ecological crisis as a 'deeper sign' of punishment for our merciless exploitation of nature, and so on. (Suffice it to recall the theories on the homology between the soul's inner world and the outer world of the universe which are again fashionable within the so-called

'New Age consciousness' – the exemplary case of a new rise of 'expressive causality').

It should be clear, now, that the Althusserian critical attribution to Hegel of 'expressive causality' misses the target: Hegel himself articulated, in advance, the conceptual framework of Althusser's critique. This is particularly clear given his triad of formal, real and complete ground, each of which corresponds perfectly to the triad of expressive, transitive and overdetermined causality. For, what is 'complete ground' if not the name for a 'complex structure' in which the determining instance itself is (over)determined by the network of relations within which it exerts its determining role?[23] In *Hegel ou Spinoza?*,[24] Pierre Macherey rhetorically maintains that Spinoza's philosophy must be read as a critique of Hegel – as if Spinoza read Hegel and was able in advance to answer the latter's critique of 'Spinozism'. The same could be said of Hegel in relation to Althusser: Hegel outlines in advance the contours of the Althusserian critique of (what Althusser presents as) 'Hegelianism'. Moreover, Hegel develops the element that is missing in Althusser (the one that had prevented him from thinking through the notion of overdetermination); that is, the element of subjectivity that cannot be reduced to imaginary (mis)recognition qua effect of interpellation – that is to say, the subject as $; the 'empty', barred subject.

From 'In-itself' to 'For-itself'

Let us stop at this point and abstain from delineating the same matrix up to the final section of the second part of *Logic*. Suffice it to say that the fundamental antagonism of the entire logic of essence is the antagonism between *ground* and *conditions*; that is, between the inner essence ('true nature') of a thing and the external circumstances which render possible the realization of this essence – that is, the impossibility of reaching a common measure between these two dimensions, of coordinating them in a 'higher-order synthesis'. (It is only in the third part of *Logic*, with the 'subjective logic' of Notion, that this incommensurability is surpassed.) Therein consists the alternative between positing and external reflection: do people create the world they live in from within themselves, autonomously, or do their activities result from external circumstances? Philosophical commonsense would impose the compromise of a 'proper measure'; and true, we have the possibility of choice, for we can realize our freely conceived projects. But that recognition can only happen within the framework of tradition, that is, of the inherited circumstances which delineate our field of choices. Or, as Marx put it in his 'Eighteenth Brumaire of Louis Bonaparte': 'Men make their own history; but they do not make it just as they please; they do not make it under circumstances chosen by themselves, but under circumstances directly encountered, given and trans-mitted from the past.'[25]

And yet, it is precisely such a 'dialectical synthesis' that Hegel declines. For the whole point of his argument is that we have no way of drawing a line between the two aspects: every inner potential can be translated (its form can be converted) into an external condition, and vice versa. In short, what Hegel does here is something very exact: he undermines the usual notion of the relationship between the inner potentials of a thing and the external conditions that render (im)possible the realization of these potentials *by positing between these two sides the sign of equality*. The consequences are far more radical than they appear. They concern, above all, the radically anti-evolutionary character of Hegel's philosophy, as exemplified in the notional couple *in-itself/for-itself*. This couple is usually taken as the supreme proof of Hegel's trust in evolutionary progress (the development from 'in-itself' into 'for-itself'), but a closer look dispels this phantom of Evolution. For the 'in-itself' in its opposition to the 'for-itself' means at one and the same time: (i) that what exists only potentially, as an inner possibility, contrary to the actuality wherein a possibility has externalized and realized itself; *and* that (ii) actuality itself, in the sense of external, immediate, 'raw' objectivity which is still opposed to subjective mediation, which is not yet internalized, rendered conscious. In this sense, the 'in-itself' is actuality in so far as it has not yet reached its Notion.

The simultaneous reading of these two aspects undermines the usual idea of dialectical progress as a gradual realization of the object's inner potentials, as its spontaneous self-development. Hegel is here quite outspoken and explicit: the inner potentials of the self-development of an object and the pressure exerted on it by an external force are *strictly correlative*, they form the two parts of the same conjunction. In other words, the potentiality of the object must also be present in its external actuality, under the form of heteronomous coercion. For example (and the example here comes from Hegel himself), to say that a pupil at the beginning of the process of education is somebody who potentially knows, somebody who, in the course of his development, will realize his or her creative potentials, *equals saying* that these inner potentials must be present from the very beginning in external actuality as the authority of the Master who exerts pressure upon his or her pupil. Today, one can add to this the sadly-famous case of the working class qua revolutionary subject: to affirm that the working class is 'in itself', potentially, a revolutionary subject, equals the assertion that this potentiality must already be actualized in the Party which knows in advance about the revolutionary mission and therefore exerts pressure upon the working class, guiding it towards the realization of its potential. Thus the 'leading role' of the Party is legitimized, that is, its right to 'educate' the working class in accordance with its potential, to 'implant' in this class its historical mission, and so forth.

We can see, now, why Hegel is as far as is possible from the evolutionist notion of the progressive development of in-itself into for-itself: the category of 'in-itself' is strictly correlative to 'for us', that is, for some consciousness external to the thing-in-itself. To say that a clump of clay is 'in itself' a pot means the same thing as saying that this pot is already present in the mind of the craftsman who will impose the form of pot on the clay. The current way of saying 'under the right conditions the pupil will realize his or her potential' is thus deceptive. When, for example, in excuse for the pupil's *failure* to realize his potential, we insist that 'he would have realized it, if only the conditions had been right', we thereby commit an error of cynicism worthy of Brecht's famous lines from the *Threepenny Opera*: 'We would be good instead of being so rude, if only the circumstances were not of this kind!' For Hegel, then, external circumstances are not an impediment to realizing inner potentials, but on the contrary *the very arena in which the true nature of these inner potentials is to be tested*. But are such potentials true potentials or just vain illusions about what might have happened? Or, to put it in Spinozian terms, 'positing reflection' observes things as they are in their eternal essence, *sub specie aeternitatis*, whereas 'external reflection' observes them *sub specie durationis*, in their dependence on a series of contingent external circumstances. Here everything hinges on *how* Hegel overcomes 'external reflection'. If his aim were simply to reduce the externality of contingent conditions to the self-mediation of the inner essence-ground (the usual notion of 'Hegel's idealism'), then Hegel's philosophy would truly be a mere 'dynamized Spinozism'. But what does Hegel actually do?

Let us approach this problem via Lacan: in what precise sense can we maintain that Lacan of the late forties and early fifties was a Hegelian? In order to get a clear idea of his Hegelianism, it is sufficient to take a closer look at how he conceives of the analyst's 'passivity' in the psychoanalytical cure. Since 'the actual is rational', the analyst does not have to force her interpretations upon the analysand; all she has to do is clear the way for the analysand to arrive at his own truth by means of a mere punctuation of his speech. This is what Hegel has in mind when he speaks of the 'cunning of reason': the analyst does not seek to undermine the analysand's self-deceit, his attitude of the 'Beautiful Soul', by directly confronting him with the 'true state of things', but rather by giving him a free rein, of removing all obstacles that may serve as an excuse, thus compelling him to reveal 'the stuff he is actually made of'. In this precise sense 'the actual is rational'. And our – that is, the Hegelian philosopher's – trust in the inherent rationality of the actual means that actuality provides the only testing ground for the reasonableness of the subject's claims. Or, to put it slightly differently, the moment the subject is bereft of external obstacles which can be blamed for his failure, his subjective position will collapse on account of its inherent inauthenticity. What we have here is a kind of cynicized Heideggerianism: since the object is in itself inconsistent, since what allows it to retain the appearance of consistency is the very external hindrance which allegedly restrains its inner potentials, then the most effective way to destroy it, to bring about its collapse, is precisely to renounce any claims of domination, to remove all hindrances and to 'let it be', that is, to leave the field open for the free deployment of its potentials.[26]

However, does the Hegelian notion of the 'cunning of reason' not entail a 'regression' to pre-Kantian rationalist metaphysics? It is a philosophical commonplace to oppose here Kant's critique of the ontological proof of God's existence to Hegel's reaffirmation of it, and to quote Hegel's reaffirmation as the supreme proof of Hegel's return to the domain of classical metaphysics, but the story goes somewhat like this. Kant demonstrates that existence is not a predicate, since, at the level of predicates (which defines the notional content of a thing), there is absolutely no difference between 100 actual dollars and a mere notion of 100 dollars, and, *mutatis mutandis*, the same holds for the notion of God. Furthermore, one is even tempted to see in Kant's position a kind of prefiguration of the Lacanian eccentricity of the real with reference to the symbolic: existence is real in so far as it is irreducible to the network of notional-symbolic determinations. Nevertheless, this commonplace has to be rejected thoroughly.

Kant's actual line of argumentation is far more refined. He proceeds in two basic steps.[27] First, he demonstrates that there is still a hidden if-clause at work in the ontological proof of God's existence. True, God does designate a being whose existence is implied in its very notion, but we still must presuppose that such a being exists (that is, all that the ontological proof actually demonstrates is that, *if* God exists, he exists necessarily); so it remains possible that there is simply no such being whose notion would entail existence. An atheist would cite such a notion of God's nature as an argument *against* His existence: there is no God precisely because one cannot imagine in a consistent way a being whose notion would entail existence. Here Kant's next step aims at the same point: the only legitimate use of the term 'existence' is to designate the phenomenal reality of the objects of possible experience; and yet, *the difference between Reason and Intuition is constitutive of reality*. In other words, the subject accepts that something 'exists in reality' only in so far as its representation is filled out by the contingent, empirical content provided by intuition, that is, only in so far as the subject is passively affected by senses. Existence is not a predicate, that is, part of the notion of an object, precisely because, in order to pass from the notion to actual existence, one has to add the passive element of intuition. For that reason, the notion of 'necessary existence' is self-contradictory; *every existence is by definition contingent*.[28]

What, then, is Hegel's answer to all this? Hegel in no way returns to traditional metaphysics. Instead, he refutes Kant within the horizon opened up by Kant himself. He, so to speak, approaches the problem from the opposite end: first by asking how does the 'coming-to-notion [*zum-Begriff-kommen*]' affect the existence of the object in question; and, more to the point, when a thing 'reaches its notion', what impact does this have on its existence? To clarify this question, let us recall an example confirming Lacan's thesis that Marxism is not a 'world view';[29] namely, the idea that the proletariat becomes an *actual* revolutionary subject by way of integrating the *knowledge* of its historical role.[30] Historical materialism, then, is not a neutral 'objective knowledge' of historical development, since it is an act of self-knowledge of a historical subject – an act that, as such, implies the proletarian subjective position. In other words, the 'knowledge' proper to historical materialism is self-referential; it changes its 'object'. Indeed, it is only via the act of knowledge that the object becomes what it truly 'is'. So, the rise of 'class-consciousness' produces the effect in the existence of its 'object' (the proletariat) by way of changing it into an actual revolutionary subject. Is it not the same with psychoanalysis? Doesn't the interpretation of a symptom constitute a direct intervention of the Symbolic in the Real; doesn't it offer an example of how the word can affect the Real of the symptom? And, on the other hand, doesn't such an efficacy of the Symbolic presuppose entities whose existence literally hinges on a certain non-knowledge? For, the moment knowledge is assumed (through interpretation), existence disintegrates. Here, existence is not one of the predicates of a Thing, but designates the way the Thing relates to its predicates; or, rather, the way the Thing *is related to itself* by means of (through the detour of) its predicates-properties.[31] When a proletarian becomes aware of his or her 'historical role', *none of their actual predicates change*. What changes is just the way he or she relates to them, and this change in the relationship to predicates radically affects their existence.

To designate this awareness of 'historical role', traditional Marxism makes use of the Hegelian couple 'in-itself/ for-itself'. Hence, by way of arriving at its 'class-consciousness', the proletariat changes from a 'class-in-itself' to a 'class-for-itself'. The dialectic at work here is that of a *failed encounter*: the passage to 'for itself', to the Notion, involves the loss of existence. Nowhere is this failed encounter more obvious than in a passionate love affair: its 'in itself' occurs when I simply yield to the passion, unaware of what is happening to me; afterwards, when the affair is over, *aufgehoben* in my recollection, it becomes 'for itself' – I retroactively become aware of what I had, of what I lost. This awareness of what I lost gives birth to the fantasy of the impossible conjunction of being and knowledge ('if only I would have known how happy I was . . .'). But is the Hegelian 'in-and-for-itself [*An-und-Fuer-sich*]' really such an impossible conjunction, the fantasy of a moment when I am happy and I know it? Is it not rather the unmasking of the illusion of the 'external reflection' that still pertains to 'for-itself'; that is, to the illusion that, in the past, I actually *was* happy without knowing it? Is it not precisely the insight into how 'happiness' by definition comes to be, retroactively, by means of the experience of its loss?

This illusion of the external reflection can be further exemplified by *Billy*

Bathgate, the film based on E.L. Doctorow's novel. The film is fundamentally a failed version of the novel and the impression it arouses is that what we see is a pale, distorted reflection of its, far superior, literary source. There is, however, an unpleasant surprise in store for those who, after seeing the film, set about to read the novel: the novel is far closer to the insipid happy end (wherein, Billy pockets the hidden wealth of Dutch Schultz). Moreover, numerous delicate details that the spectator unacquainted with the novel experiences as fragments happily not lost in the impoverishing process of transposition to cinema – fragments that miraculously survived the shipwreck – actually turn out to be added by the scriptwriter. In short, the 'superior' novel evoked by the film's failure is not the pre-existent actual novel upon which the film is based, but a retroactive chimera aroused by the film itself.[32]

Ground versus Conditions

This conceptual background allows us to reformulate the vicious circle of ground and conditions. Let us recall the usual mode of explaining outbreaks of racism, which invokes the categorial couple of ground and conditions-circumstances: one conceives of racism (or, more generally, so-called 'outbreaks of irrational mass-sadism') as a latent psychic disposition, a kind of Jungian archetype which comes forth under certain conditions (social instability and crisis, and so on). From this point of view, the racist disposition is the 'ground' and current political struggles the 'circumstances', the conditions of its effectuation. However, what counts as ground and what counts as conditions is ultimately contingent and exchangeable, so that one can easily accomplish the Marxist reversal of the above-mentioned psychologist perspective and conceive the present political struggle as the only true determining ground. In the present civil war in ex-Yugoslavia, for example, the 'ground' of Serbian aggression is not to be sought in any primitive Balkan warrior archetype, but in the struggle for power in post-Communist Serbia (the survival of the old Communist state apparatus). Indeed, the status of eventual Serbian bellicose dispositions and other similar archetypes (the 'Croatian genocidal character', the 'centennial tradition of ethnic hatreds in the Balkans', and so on) is precisely that of the conditions/circumstances in which the power-struggle realizes itself. The 'bellicose dispositions' are precisely that – latent dispositions which are actualized, drawn forth from their shadowy half-existence by the recent political struggle qua their determining ground. One is thus fully justified in saying that 'what is at stake in the Yugoslav civil war are not archaic ethnic conflicts: these centennial hatreds are inflamed only on account of their function in the recent political struggle'.[33]

How, then, are we to eschew this mess, this exchangeability of ground and circumstance? Let us take another example: *renaissance*, that is, the redis-covery ('rebirth') of antiquity which exerted a crucial influence on the break with the medieval way of life in the fifteenth century. The first, obvious explanation is that the influence of the newly discovered antique tradition brought about the dissolution of the medieval 'paradigm'. Here, however, a question immediately arises: why did antiquity begin to exert its influence at precisely that moment and not earlier or later? The answer that offers itself, of course, is that due to the dissolution of medieval social links, a new '*zeitgeist*' emerged which made us responsive to antiquity – something must have changed in 'us' so that we became able to perceive antiquity not as a pagan kingdom of sin but as the model to be adopted. That's all very well, but we still remain locked in a vicious circle, since this new '*zeitgeist*' itself took shape precisely through the discovery of antique texts as well as fragments of classical architecture and sculpture. In a way, everything was already there, in the external circumstances; the new '*zeitgeist*' formed itself through the influence of antiquity which enabled renaissance thought to shatter the medieval chains. And yet, for this influence of antiquity to be felt, the new '*zeitgeist*' must already have been active. The only way out of this impasse is thus the intervention, at a certain point, of a tautological gesture: the new '*zeitgeist*' had to constitute itself by literally *presupposing itself in its exteriority*, in its external conditions (in antiquity). In other words, it was not sufficient for the new '*zeitgeist*' retroactively to posit these external conditions (the antique tradition) as 'its own', it had to (presup)pose itself as already-present in these conditions. Or, to put it directly, *the return to external conditions (to antiquity) had to coincide with the return to the foundation, to the 'thing itself', to the ground.* (This is precisely how the 'renaissance' conceived itself: as the return to the Greek and Roman foundations of our Western civilization.) We do not, as a consequence, have an inner ground, the actualization of which depends on external circumstance. Instead, the external relation of presupposing (ground presupposes conditions and vice versa) is surpassed in a pure tautological gesture by means of which the thing *presupposes itself*. This tautological gesture is 'empty' in the precise sense that it does not contribute anything new; it only retroactively ascertains that the thing in question *is already present in its conditions*, that is, that the totality of these conditions *is* the actuality of the thing. Such an empty gesture provides us with the most elementary definition of the *symbolic* act.

Here we see the fundamental paradox of 'rediscovering tradition' at work in the constitution of national identity: a nation finds its sense of self-identity by means of such a tautological gesture, that is, by way of discovering itself as already present in its tradition. Consequently, the mechanism of the 'rediscovery of national tradition' cannot be reduced to the 'positing of presuppositions' in the sense of the retroactive positing of conditions as 'ours'. The point is rather that, in the very act of returning to its (external) conditions, *the (national) thing returns to itself*, the return to conditions is experienced as the 'return to our true roots'.

The Tautological 'Return of the Thing to Itself'

Now, although 'actually existing socialism' has already receded into a distance which confers upon it the nostalgic magic of a post-modern lost object, some of us still recall a well-known joke about what socialism is: a social system that is the dialectical synthesis of all previous history. From the prehistoric classless society, it took primitivism; from antiquity, slave labour; from medieval feudalism, ruthless domination; from capitalism, exploitation; *and from socialism, the name*. This is what the Hegelian tautological gesture of the 'return of the thing to itself' is all about: one must include along with the definition of the object its name. That is to say, after we decompose an object into its ingredients, we look in vain in them for some specific feature which holds together this multitude and makes of it a unique, self-identical thing. But as to its properties and ingredients, a thing is wholly 'outside itself', in its external conditions, every positive feature is already present in the circum-stances which are not yet this thing. The supplementary operation which produces from this bundle a unique, self-identical thing is the purely symbolic, tautological gesture of positing these external conditions as the conditions-components of the thing and, simultaneously, of presupposing the existence of ground which holds together this multitude of conditions.

And, to throw our Lacanian cards on the table, this tautological 'return of the thing to itself' (which renders forth the concrete structure of self-identity) is what Lacan designates as the '*point de capiton*', the 'quilting point', at which the signifier 'falls into' the signified (as in the above-mentioned joke on socialism, where the name itself functions as part of the designated thing). Let us recall an example from popular film culture: the killer shark in Spielberg's *Jaws*. A direct search for the shark's ideological meaning evokes nothing but misguided questions: does it symbolize the threat of the Third World to America epitomized by the archetypal small town? Is it the symbol of the exploitative nature of capitalism itself (Fidel Castro's interpretation)? Does it stand for the untamed nature which threatens to disrupt the routine of our daily lives? In order to avoid this lure, we have to shift our perspective radically: the daily life of the common man is dominated by an inconsistent multitude of fears (he can become the victim of big business manipulations; Third World immigrants seem to intrude into his small orderly universe; unruly nature can destroy his home; and so forth), and the accomplishment of *Jaws* consists in an act of purely formal conversion which provides a common 'container' for all these free-floating, inconsistent fears by way of anchoring them, 'reifying' them, in the figure of the shark.[34] Consequently, the function of the fascinating presence of the shark is precisely to *block* any further inquiry into the social meaning (social mediation) of those phenomena that arouse fear in the common man. But to say that the murderous shark 'symbolizes' the above-mentioned series of fears is to say both too much and not enough at the same time. It does not symbolize them, since it literally annuls them by occupying itself the place of the object of fear. It is therefore 'more' than a symbol; it becomes the feared 'thing itself'. Yet, the shark is decidedly less than a symbol, since it does not point towards the symbolized content but rather blocks access to it, renders it invisible. In this way, it is homologous with the anti-Semitic figure of the Jew: 'Jew' is the explanation offered by anti-Semitism for the multiple fears experienced by the 'common man' in an epoch of dissolving social links (inflation, unemployment, corruption, moral degradation); behind all these phenomena lies the invisible hand of the 'Jewish plot'. However, the crucial point here, again, is that the designation 'Jew' *does not add any new content*: the entire content is already present in the external conditions (crisis, moral degeneration, and so on); the name 'Jew' is only the supplementary feature which accomplishes a kind of transubstantiation, changing all these elements into so many manifestations of the same *ground*, the 'Jewish plot'. Paraphrasing the joke on socialism, one could say that anti-Semitism takes from the economy, unemployment and inflation; from politics, parliamentary corruption and intrigue; from morality, its own degeneration; from art, 'incomprehensible' avant-gardism; *and from the Jew, the name*. This name enables us to recognize behind the multitude of external conditions the activity of the same *ground*.

Here we also find at work the dialectic of contingency and necessity. As to their content, they fully coincide (in both cases, the only positive content is the series of conditions that form part of our actual life-experience: economic crisis, political chaos, the dissolution of ethical links, and so on); the passage of contingency into necessity is an act of purely formal conversion, the gesture of adding a *name* which confers upon the contingent series the mark of necessity, thereby transforming it into the expression of some hidden ground (the 'Jewish plot'). This is also how later – at the very end of the 'logic of essence' – we pass from absolute necessity to freedom. To comprehend properly this passage, one has to renounce thoroughly the standard notion of 'freedom as comprehended necessity' (after getting rid of the illusions of free will, one can recognize and freely accept one's place in the network of causes and their effects). But Hegel's point, on the contrary, is that *it is only the subject's (free) act of 'dotting the i' which retroactively instals necessity*, so that the very act by means of which the subject recognizes (and thus constitutes) necessity is the supreme act of freedom and, as such, the self-suppression of necessity. *Voilà pourquoi Hegel n'est pas spinoziste*: on account of this tautological gesture of retroactive performativity. So 'performativity' in no way designates the power of freely 'creating' the designated content ('words mean what we want them to mean', and so forth); the 'quilting' only structures the material which is found, externally imposed. The act of naming is 'performative' only and precisely in so far as *it is always-already part of the definition of the signified content.*[35]

This is how Hegel resolves the deadlock of positing and external reflection, the vicious circle of positing the presuppositions and of enumerating the presuppositions of the posited content: by means of the tautological return-upon-itself of the thing in its very external presuppositions. And the same tautological gesture is already at work in Kant's analytic of pure reason: the synthesis of the multitude of sensations in the representation of the object which belongs to 'reality' implies an empty surplus, that is, the positing of an X as the unknown substratum of the perceived phenomenal sensations. Suffice it to quote Findlay's precise formulation:

> [W]e always refer appearances to a Transcendental Object, an X, of which we, however, know nothing, but which is nonetheless the objective correlate of the synthetic acts inseparable from thinking self-consciousness. The Transcendental Object, thus conceived, can be called a Noumenon or thing of thought [*Gedankending*]. But the reference to such a thing of thought does not, strictly speaking, use the categories, but is something like *an empty synthetic gesture* in which nothing objective is really put before us.[36]

The transcendental object is thus the very opposite of the *Ding-an-sich*: it is 'empty' in so far as it is devoid of any 'objective' content. That is to say, to obtain its notion, one has to abstract from the sensible object its entire sensible content, that is, all sensations by of which the subject is affected by *Ding*. The empty X which remains is *the pure objective correlate/effect of the subject's autonomous-spontaneous synthetic activity.* Or, to put it paradoxically, the transcendental object is the 'in-itself' in so far as it is for the subject, posited by it; it is pure 'positedness' of an indeterminate X. This 'empty synthetic gesture' – which adds to the thing nothing positive, no new sensible feature, and yet, in its very capacity of an empty gesture, constitutes it, makes it into an object – is the act of *symbolization* in its most elementary form, at its zero-level. On the first page of his book, Findlay points out that the transcendental object:

> *is not for Kant different* from the object or objects which appear to the senses and which we can judge about and know . . . but it is the *same* object or objects conceived in respect of certain intrinsically unapparent features, and which is in such respects incapable of being judged about or known.[37]

This X, this unrepresentable surplus which adds itself to the series of sensible features, is precisely the 'thing-of-thought [*Gedankending*]': it bears witness to the fact that the object's unity does not reside within it, but is the result of the subject's synthetic activity. (As with Hegel, where the act of formal conversion inverts the chain of conditions into the unconditional Thing, founded in itself.) Let us briefly return to anti-Semitism, to the 'synthetic act of apperception' which, out of the multitude of (imagined) features of Jews, constructs the anti-Semitic figure of 'Jew'. To pass for a true anti-Semite, it is not enough to claim that we oppose Jews because they are exploitative, greedy intriguers; that is, it is not sufficient for the signifier 'Jew' to designate this series of specific, positive features. One has to accomplish the crucial step further by saying 'they are like that (exploitative, greedy, and so forth) *because they are Jews*'. The 'transcendental object' of Jewishness is precisely that elusive X which 'makes a Jew into a Jew' and for which we look in vain among his or her positive properties. This act of pure formal conversion, that is, the 'synthetic act' of uniting the series of positive features in the signifier 'Jew' and thereby transforming them into so many manifestations of the 'Jewishness' qua their hidden ground, *brings about the appearance of an objective surplus*, of a mysterious X which is 'in Jew more than Jew'; in other words, of the transcendental object.[38] In the very text of Kant's *Critique of Pure Reason*, this void of the synthetic gesture is indicated by an exception in the use of the pair constitutive/regulative:[39] in general, 'constitutive' principles serve to construct objective reality, whereas 'regulative' principles are merely subjective maxims which guide reason without giving access to positive knowledge. However, when Kant speaks of existence [*Dasein*], he makes use of the pair constitutive/regulative in the midst of the very domain of the constitutive, by way of linking it to the couple mathematical/dynamical:

> In the application of pure conceptions of understanding to possible experience, the employment of their synthesis is either *mathematical* or *dynamical*; for it is concerned partly with the mere *intuition* of an appearance in general, partly with its *existence*.[40]

In what precise sense, then, are dynamical principles 'merely regulative principles, and distinguished from the mathematical, which are constitutive'?[41] The principles of the mathematical use of categories refer to the intuited phenomenal content (to phenomenal properties of the thing); it is only the dynamical principles of synthesis which guarantee that the content of our representations refers to some objective existence, independent of the flux of perceiving consciousness. How, then, are we to explain the paradox of making objective existence dependent not on 'constitutive' but on 'regulative' principles? Let us return, for the last time, to the anti-Semitic figure of the Jew: mathematical synthesis can only gather together phenomenal properties attributed to the Jew (greediness, intriguing spirit, and so forth). But then dynamical synthesis accomplishes the reversal by means of which this series of properties is posited as the manifestation of an inaccessible X, 'Jewishness'; that is to say, of something *real*, really existing. At work here are regulative principles, since dynamical synthesis is not limited to phenomenal features, but refers them to their underlying-unknowable substratum, to the transcendental object. In this precise sense, the existence of 'Jew' as irreducible to the series of predicates, that is, his existence as pure positing [*Setzung*] of the transcendental object qua substratum of phenomenal predicates, hinges on dynamical synthesis. In Lacanian terms, dynamical synthesis posits the existence of an X as the trans-phenomenal 'hard kernel of being' beyond predicates (which is why the hatred of Jews does not concern their phenomenal properties but aims at their hidden 'kernel of being') – a new proof of how 'reason' is at work in the very heart of 'understanding' in the most elementary positing of an object as 'really existing'. It is therefore deeply significant that, throughout the subdivision on the second analogy of experience, Kant consistently uses the word *Objekt* (designating an intelligible entity) and not *Gegenstand* (designating a simple phenomenal entity): the external, objective existence achieved by the synthetic use of dynamic regulative principles is 'intelligible', not empirical-intuitive; that is, it adds to the intuitive-sensible features of the object an intelligible, non-sensible X and thus makes an object out of it.

In this precise sense Hegel remains within Kant's fundamental framework. But, then, in what resides the fundamental paradox of Kant's transcendentalism? For Kant's initial problem is that given, for example, my senses bombard me with a confused multitude of representations, how am I to distinguish, in this flux, between mere 'subjective' representations and objects that exist independently of the flux of representations? The answer: my representations acquire 'objective status' via transcendental synthesis which changes them into the objects of experience. What I experience as 'objective' existence, the very 'hard kernel' of the object beneath the ever-changing phenomenal fluctuations, independent of the flux of my consciousness, thus results from my (the subject's) own 'spontaneous' synthetic activity. And, *mutatis mutandis*, Hegel says the same thing: the establishment of absolute necessity equals its self-cancellation, that is, it designates the act of freedom which retroactively 'posits' something as necessary.

The 'Absolute Unrest of Becoming'

The trouble with contingency resides in its uncertain status. Is it ontological, that is, are things *in themselves* contingent, or is it epistemological, that is, is contingency merely an expression of the fact that *we do not know* the complete chain of causes which brought about the allegedly 'contingent' phenomenon? Hegel undermines the common supposition of this alternative, namely the external relationship of being and knowledge: the notion of 'reality' as something that is simply given, that exists 'out there', prior and external to the process of knowledge. The difference between the ontological and the epistemological version is only that, in the first case, contingency is part of this reality itself, whereas in the second case, reality is wholly determined by necessity. In contrast to both these versions, Hegel affirms the basic thesis of speculative idealism: the process of knowledge (that is, our comprehending the object) is not something external to the object but inherently determines its status. As Kant puts it, the conditions of possibility of our experience are also the conditions of possibility of the objects of experience. In other words, while contingency does express the incompleteness of our knowledge, *this incompleteness also ontologically defines the object of knowledge itself*. It bears witness to the fact that the object itself is not yet ontologically 'realized', fully actual. The merely epistemological status of contingency is thus invalidated, without us falling back into ontological naivety: behind the appearance of contingency there is no hidden, not-yet-known necessity, but *only the necessity of the very appearance that, behind superficial contingency, there is an underlying substantial necessity*. And this is similar to the case of anti-Semitism, where the ultimate appearance is the very appearance of the underlying necessity, that is, the appearance that, behind the series of actual features (unemployment, moral disintegration, and so on), there is the hidden necessity of the 'Jewish plot'. Therein consists the Hegelian inversion of 'external' into 'absolute' reflection: in external reflection, appearance is the elusive surface concealing its hidden necessity, whereas in absolute reflection, appearance is the appearance of this very (unknown) Necessity behind contingency. Or, to make use of an even more 'Hegelian' speculative formulation, if contingency is an appearance concealing some hidden necessity, then this necessity is *stricto sensu an appearance of itself*.

This inherent antagonism of the relationship between contingency and necessity offers an exemplary case of the Hegelian triad: first the 'naive' ontological conception which locates the difference in things themselves (some events are in themselves contingent, others necessary), and then the attitude of 'external reflection' which conceives of this difference as purely epistemological, that is, dependent upon the incompleteness of our knowledge (we experience as 'contingent' an event when the complete causal chain that produced it remains beyond our grasp). But what, then, what exactly would be the third choice – other than the seemingly exhaustive one between ontology and epistemology? Answer: *the very relationship between possibility (qua subjective seizing of actuality) and actuality (qua the object of conceptual seizing)*. Here we find, then, that both contingency and necessity are categories which express the dialectical unity of the actual and possible. They are to be distinguished only in so far as contingency designates this unity conceived in the mode of subjectivity, of the 'absolute unrest' of becoming, of the split between subject and object, and 'necessity' of this same content conceived in the mode of objectivity, of determinate being, of the identity of subject and object, of the rest of the Result.[42] In short, we are again at the category of pure *formal conversion*, the change concerns only the modality of form:

> This *absolute unrest* of the *becoming* of these two determinations is *contingency*. But just because each immediately turns into its opposite, equally in this other it simply *unites with itself*, and this identity of both, of one in the other, is *necessity*.[43]

Hegel's counter position here was adopted by Kierkegaard, with his notion of the two different modalities of observing a process: from the standpoint of 'becoming' and from the standpoint of 'being'.[44] 'After the fact', history can always be read as a process governed by laws; that is, as a meaningful succession of stages. However, in so far as we are history's agents, caught, indeed embedded, in the process, the situation appears – at least at the turning points when 'something is happening' – open, undecidable, far from the exposition of an underlying necessity. We must bear in mind here the lesson on the mediation of the subjective attitude with objectivity: we cannot reduce one perspective to another by claiming, for example, that the 'true' picture is that of necessity discovered by the 'backward view', that freedom is just an illusion of the immediate agents who overlook how their activity is a small wheel within the large causal mechanism. Or, conversely, we cannot reduce one to another by embracing a kind of Sartrean existentialist perspective, affirming, in so doing, the subject's ultimate autonomy and freedom, and conceiving the appearance of determinism as the later 'pratico-inert' objectivization of the subject's spontaneous *praxis*. In both cases, the ontological unity of the universe is saved, whether in the form of substantial necessity pulling the strings behind the subject's back or in the form of the subject's autonomous activity 'objectivizing' itself in substantial unity. But what gets lost is the ontological scandal of the ultimate *undecidability* between the two choices. Here Hegel is far more subversive than Kierkegaard, since the latter escapes the deadlock only by giving preference to possibility over actuality – an escape that ends up announcing the Bergsonian notion of actuality qua mechanical congelation of the life-process.[45]

In this undecidability lies the ultimate ambiguity of Hegel's philosophy, the index of an impossibility by way of which it 'touches the real': how are we to conceive of the dialectical re-collection?[46] Is it a retroactive glance enabling us to discern the contours of inner necessity where the view immersed in the events can only perceive an interplay of accidents, that is, as the 'sublation [*Aufhebung*]' of this interplay of accidents in underlying logical necessity? Or is it, on the contrary, a glance enabling us to resuscitate the openness of the situation, its 'possibility', its irreducible contingency, in what afterwards, from objective distance, appears as a necessary objective process? And does not this undecidability bring us back to our starting point: is not this ambiguity again the way sexual difference is inscribed into the very core of Hegel's logic?

Actuality of the Possible

The ontological background of this ambiguity is a kind of 'trading of places' between possibility and actuality: possibility itself, in its very opposition to actuality, possesses an actuality of its own. In what precise sense do we mean this? Hegel always insists on the absolute primacy of actuality: true, the search for the 'conditions of possibility' abstracts from the actual, calls it in question, in order to (re)constitute it on a rational basis; yet in all these ruminations actuality is presupposed as something given. In other words, nothing is stranger to Hegel than Leibnizian speculation about the multitude of possible worlds out of which the Creator picks out the best; speculation on possible universes always takes place against the background of the hard fact of actual existence. On the other hand, there is always something traumatic about the raw factuality of what we encounter as 'actual', since actuality is always marked by an indelible brand of the (real as) 'impossible'. The shift from actuality to possibility, the suspension of actuality through inquiry into its possibility, is therefore ultimately an endeavour to avoid the trauma of the real, that is, to integrate the real by means of conceiving it as something that is meaningful within our symbolic universe.[47]

Of course, this squaring of the circle of the possible and the actual (that is, first the suspension of actuality and then its derivation from the conceptual possibility), never works out, as proven by the very category of contingency. For 'contingency' designates an actual content in so far as it cannot be wholly grounded in its conceptual conditions of possibility. According to philosophical common sense, contingency and necessity are the two modalities of actuality: something actual is necessary in so far as its contrary is not possible; it is contingent in so far as its contrary is also possible (in so far as things could also have turned out otherwise). The problem, however, resides in the inherent antagonism that pertains to the notion of possibility: possibility designates something 'possible' in the sense of being able to actualize itself, as well as something 'merely possible' as opposed to being actual. This inner split finds its clearest expression, perhaps, in the diametrically opposed roles played by the notion of possibility in moral argumentation. On the one hand, we have the 'empty possibility', the eternal excuse of the weak: 'If I really wanted to, I could have . . . [stopped smoking, or whatever]'. In challenging this claim, Hegel again and again points out how the true nature of a possibility (is it a true possibility or a mere empty presumption?) is confirmed only by way of its actualization: the only effective proof that you really can do something is simply to do it. On the other hand, the possibility of acting differently exerts pressure on us in the guise of the 'voice of conscience': when I offer the usual excuses ('I did all that was possible, there was no choice'), the superego-voice keeps gnawing at me, 'No, you could have done more!' This is what Kant has in mind when he insists that freedom is actual already as possibility: when I gave way to pathological impulses and did not carry out my duty, the *actuality* of my freedom is attested to by my awareness of how I *could have* acted otherwise.[48] This is also what Hegel aims at when maintaining that the actual [*das Wirkliche*] is not the same as that which simply exists [*das Bestehende*]: my conscience pricks me when my act (of giving way to pathological impulses) was not 'actual', did not express my true moral nature – this difference exerts pressure on me in the guise of 'conscience'.

One can discern the same logic behind the recent revival of the conspiracy theory (Oliver Stone's *JFK*): who was behind Kennedy's murder? The ideological cathexis of this revival is clear: Kennedy's murder acquired such traumatic dimensions retroactively, from the later experience of the Vietnam War, of the Nixon administration's cynical corruption, and of the revolt of the sixties that opened up the gap between the young generation and the establishment. This later experience transformed Kennedy into a person who, had he remained alive, would have spared us Vietnam, the gap separating the sixties generation from the establishment, and so on. (What the conspiracy theory 'represses', of course, is the painful fact of Kennedy's *impotence*: Kennedy himself would not have been able to prevent the emergence of this gap.) The conspiracy theory thus keeps alive the dream of another America, different from the one we came to know in the seventies and eighties.[49]

Hegel's position with regard to the relationship of possibility and actuality is thus very refined and precise: possibility is simultaneously less and more than what its notion implies. Conceived in its abstract opposition to actuality, it is a 'mere possibility' and, as such, coincides with its opposite, impossibility. On another level, however, possibility already possesses a certain actuality *in its very capacity of possibility*, which is why any further demand for its actualization is superfluous. In this sense, Hegel points out that the idea of freedom realizes itself through a series of failures: every particular attempt to realize freedom may fail; from its point of view, freedom remains an empty possibility – but the very continuous striving of freedom to realize itself bears witness to its 'actuality', that is, to the fact that freedom is not a 'mere notion', but manifests a tendency that pertains to the very essence of reality. On the other hand, the supreme case of 'mere possibility' is the Hegelian 'abstract universal'. What we have in mind here is the well-known paradox of the relationship between universal judgement and judgement of existence in the classical Aristotelian syllogism: judgement of existence implies the existence of its subject, whereas universal judgement can also be true even if its subject does not exist, since it concerns only the notion of the subject. If, for example, one says 'At least one man is (or: some men are) mortal', this judgement is true only if at least one man exists. If, on the contrary, one says 'A unicorn has only one horn', this judgement remains true even if there are no unicorns, since it concerns solely the immanent determination of the notion of 'unicorn'. Far from its relevance being limited to pure theoretical ruminations, this gap between the universal and the particular has palpable material effects – in politics, for example. According to the results of a public-opinion poll in the autumn of 1991, in the choice between Bush and a non-specified Democratic candidate, the non-specified Democrat would win easily. However, in the choice between Bush and any concrete, individual Democrat, provided with face and name (Kerrey, Cuomo, or whatever), Bush would have an easy win. In short, the Democrat in general wins over Bush, whereas Bush wins over any concrete Democrat. To the misfortune of the Democrats, there is no 'Democrat in general'.[50]

The status of possibility, while different from that of actuality, is thus not simply deficient with regard to it. Rather, *possibility, as such, exerts actual effects which disappear as soon as it 'actualizes' itself.* Such a 'short-circuit' between possibility and actuality is at work in the Lacanian notion of 'symbolic castration': the so-called 'castration-anxiety' cannot be reduced to the psychological fact that, upon perceiving the absence of the penis in woman, man becomes afraid that 'he also might lose it'.[51] Rather, 'castration anxiety' designates the precise moment at which the possibility of castration takes precedence over its actuality, that is, the moment at which the very possibility of castration, its mere threat, produces actual effects in our psychic economy. This threat, as it were, 'castrates' us, branding us with an irreducible loss. And it is this same 'short-circuit' between possibility and actuality which defines the very notion of power: power is *actually* exerted only in the guise of a *potential* threat, that is, only in so far as it does not strike fully but 'keeps itself in reserve'.[52] Suffice it to recall the logic of paternal authority: the moment a father loses control and displays his full power (starts to shout, to beat a child), we necessarily perceive this display as impotent rage – as an index of its very opposite. In this precise sense symbolic authority always, by definition, hinges on an irreducible potentiality-possibility, on the actuality-effectivity that pertains to possibility qua possibility: we leave behind the 'raw', pre-symbolic real and enter the symbolic universe the moment possibility acquires actuality of its own. This paradox is at work in the Hegelian struggle for recognition between the [future] Lord and Bondsman: to say that the impasse of their struggle is resolved by way of the Lord's *symbolic* victory and the Bondsman's *symbolic* death equals saying that the mere *possibility* of victory is sufficient; the symbolic pact at work in their struggle enables them to stop before the actual physical destruction and to accept the possibility of victory as its actuality. In this sense, too, then, the Master's potential threat is far worse than his or her actual display of power. This is what Bentham counts on in his fantasy-matrix of Panopticon: the fact that the Other – the gaze in the central observing tower

– *can* watch me, that is, my radical uncertainty as to whether I am being observed or not at any precise moment gives rise to an anxiety far greater than that aroused by the awareness that I am actually observed. This surplus of what is 'in the possibility more than a mere possibility' and which gets lost in its actualization is *the real qua impossible*.

Notes

1. Perspicuous theologians know very well this paradox of a decision that retroactively posits its own reasons: of course there are good reasons to believe in Jesus Christ, *but these reasons are fully comprehensible only to those who already believe in Him.*

2. It was the same with Ronald Reagan's presidency: the more liberal journalists enumerated his slips of tongue and other *faux pas*, the more they (unknowingly) strengthened his popularity – reasons against functioned as reasons for. As to Reagan's 'teflon presidency', see Joan Copjec, 'The *unervmoegender* Other: Hysteria and Democracy in America', *New Formations*, 14 (London: Routledge 1991). On another level, an exemplary case of this gap separating S_1 from S_2 (i.e., the act of decision from the chain of knowledge) is provided by the institution of jury. The jury performs the formal act of decision, it delivers the verdict of 'guilt' or 'innocence'; then it is up to the judge to ground this decision in knowledge, to translate it into an appropriate punishment. Why can't these two instances coincide, i.e. why can't the judge himself decide the verdict? Is he not better qualified than an average citizen? Why is it repulsive to our sense of justice to leave the decision to the judge? For Hegel, the jury embodies the principle of free subjectivity: the crucial fact about the jury is that it comprises a group of citizens who allegedly are peers of the accused and who are selected by a lottery system – they stand for 'anybody'. The point is that I can be judged only by my equals, not by a superior agency speaking in the name of some inaccessible Knowledge beyond my reach and comprehension. At the same time, the jury implies an aspect of contingency which suspends the principle of sufficient ground. If the concern of justice were only to be the correct application of law, it would be far more appropriate for the judge to decide on guilt or innocence. By entrusting the jury with the verdict, the moment of uncertainty is preserved; up to the end we cannot be sure what the judgment will be, so its actual pronouncement always affects us as a surprise.

3. The paradox, of course, consists precisely in the fact that, there is *nothing* behind the series of positive, observable features: the status of that mysterious *je ne sais quoi* which makes me fall in love is ultimately that of a pure semblance. This way, we can see how a 'sincere' feeling is necessarily based upon an illusion (I am 'really', 'sincerely', in love only in so far as I believe in your secret *agalma*; i.e. in so far as I believe that there is something behind the series of observable features).

4. As for this 'Incorporation Thesis', see Henry E. Allison's *Kant's Theory of Freedom* (Cambridge: Cambridge University Press 1990).

5. The adverse procedure is also false, that is, the attribution of personal responsibility and guilt which relieves us of the task of probing into the concrete circumstances of the act in question. Suffice it to recall the moral-majority practice of attributing a moral character to the higher crime rate among African Americans ('criminal dispositions', 'moral insensitivity', etc.): this attribution precludes any analysis of the concrete social, economic and political conditions of African Americans.

6. When we desire X, we always identify ourselves with a certain self-image ('ideal ego') of ourselves as desiring X. For example, when we are enraptured by an old melodrama and are moved to tears by the events on the screen, we do not do it immediately; we first identify ourselves with the image of a 'naive' viewer moved to tears by this type of film. In this precise sense, our ideal-ego image is our symptom; it is the tool by means of which we organize our desire: *the subject desires by means of his or her ego-symptom*. What we have here is thus another example of the Hegelian rhetorical inversion in Lacan: we can identify with the other's desire since our desire as such is already the desire of the other (in all its meanings: our desire is a desire to be desired by the

other, i.e. a desire for another's desire; what we experience as our innermost desire is structured by the decentred Other; etc). In order to desire, the subject has to identify with the desire of the other.

7. The ultimate proof of how this reflectivity of desire that constitutes 'self-consciousness' not only has nothing whatsoever to do with the subject's self-transparency but is its very opposite; i.e., involves the subject's radical splitting, which is provided by the paradoxes of love-hate. The Hollywood publicity-machinery used to describe Erich von Stroheim who, in the thirties and forties, regularly played sadistic German officers, as 'a man you'll love to hate'; to 'love to hate' somebody means that this person fits perfectly the scapegoat role of attracting our hatred. At the opposite end of the spectrum, the *femme fatale* in the *noir* universe is clearly a woman one 'hates to love': we know she means evil; it is against our will that we are forced to love her, and we hate ourselves and her for it. This hate-love clearly registers a certain radical split within ourselves, the split between the side of us that cannot resist love and the side which finds this love abominable. On the other hand, tautological cases of this reflectivity of love-hate are no less paradoxical. When, for example, I say to somebody that I 'hate to hate you', this again points towards a splitting: I really love you, but for certain reasons I am forced to hate you, and I hate myself for it. Even the positive tautology 'love to love' conceals its opposite: when I use it, it must usually be read as 'I (would) love to love you . . . (but I cannot any more)'; i.e., as expressing a willingness to go on, although the thing is already over. In short, when a husband or a wife tells his or her conjugal partner 'I love to love you', one can be sure that divorce is round the corner.

8. As to this logic of the 'non-all', see Slavoj Žižek, *For They Know Not What They Do* (London: Verso 1991), especially Chapter 3.

9. See Judith Butler, *Gender Trouble* (New York: Routledge, 1990), the hitherto most radical attempt to demonstrate how every 'presupposed' support of sexual difference (in biology, in symbolic order, etc.) is ultimately a contingent, retroactive performative effect; that is, it is already 'posited'. One is tempted to summarize its result in the ironic conclusion that women are men masked as women, and men are women who escape into manhood to conceal their own femininity. As long as Butler unfolds the impasses of the standard ways to substantiate sexual difference, one can only admire her ingenuity; problems arise in the last, 'programmatic' part of the book, which unfolds a positive project of an unbounded performative game of constructing multiple subject-positions which subvert every fixed identity. What is lost thereby is the dimension designated by the very title of the book – gender *trouble*: the fact that sexuality is defined by a constitutive 'trouble', a traumatic deadlock, and that every performative formation is nothing but an endeavour to patch up this trauma. What one has to accomplish here is therefore a simple self-reflexive reversal of the negative into the positive: there is always trouble with gender. Why? *Because gender as such is a response to a fundamental 'trouble'*: 'normal' sexual difference constitutes itself in an attempt to avoid an impasse.

10. Jacques Lacan, *Le séminaire, livre XX: Encore* (Paris: *Editions du Seuil*, 1975) p. 85. Consequently, Lacan's statement that 'there is no sexual relationship' does not contain a hidden normativity, an implicit norm of 'mature' heterosexuality impossible to attain – in the eyes of which the subject is always, by definition, guilty. Quite the contrary, Lacan's point is that in the domain of sexuality, *it is not possible to formulate any norm that should guide us with a legitimate claim to universal validity*. Every attempt to formulate such a norm is a secondary endeavour to mend an 'original' impasse. In other words, Lacan does not fall into the trap of invoking a cruel superego agency that 'knows' the subject is not able to meet its demands (thereby branding the subject's very being with a constitutive guilt). The relationship of the Lacanian subject to the symbolic Law is *not* a relationship to an agency whose demand the subject can never fully satisfy. Such a relationship to the Other of the Law, usually associated with the God of the Old Testament or with the Jansenist *Dieu obscur*, implies that the Other *knows* what it wants from us and that it is only we who cannot discern the Other's inscrutable will. With Lacan, however, *the Other of the Law itself does not know what it wants*.

11. For a detailed reading of the Hegelian logic of reflection, see Slavoj Žižek, *The Sublime Object of Ideology* (London: Verso Books 1989) Chapter 6.

12. Therein consists the crucial weakness of Robert Pippin's *Hegel's Idealism* (Cambridge: Cambridge University Press, 1988), a book that otherwise announces a new epoch in Hegelian studies. Its fundamental intention is not only to reaffirm the continued relevance of Hegel's dialectical logic, against the prevalent 'historicist' approach (which dismisses Hegel's 'metaphysics' –

read: dialectical logic – as a hopelessly outdated mastodon, and argues instead that the only thing 'still alive' in Hegel is to be found in the concrete socio-historical analyses of the *Phenomenology*, *Philosophy of Right, Aesthetics*, etc.), but demonstrates, also, how the only way to grasp this relevance leads back through to Kant. For even though Hegel's position in no way entails a regression to the 'precritical' metaphysical ontology of the Absolute, it remains thoroughly confined to the Kantian criticism: Hegel's speculative idealism is Kantian criticism brought to a close. In this sense, Pippin's project deserves full support. And yet, Pippin fails at the crucial place: in his treatment of the logic of reflection. The final result of his analysis is that we are ultimately condemned to the antinomy of positing and external reflection, and, as a result, he repudiates 'determining reflection' as an empty metaphoric formula, a failed attempt to break out of this antinomy.

13. *Hegel's Science of Logic* (Atlantic Highlands: Humanities Press International, 1989) p. 441. Since our concern here is limited to the paradoxical structure of the notion of contradiction, we leave aside the difference between difference and opposition, i.e. the mediating role of opposition between difference and contradiction.

14. Hegel's choice of example – father, the symbolic function *par excellence* – is, of course, no way accidental or neutral. It was already Thomas Aquinas who evoked paternity when arguing that in order to survive, we must accept another's word for things we ourselves do not witness: 'if man refused to believe anything unless he knew it himself, then it would be quite impossible to live in this world. How could a person live, if he did not believe someone? How could he even accept the fact that a certain man is his father?' (*The Pocket Thomas* [New York: Washington Square Press, 1960] p. 286). This, in contrast to maternity (as pointed out by Freud in his *Moses and Monotheism*), establishes paternity, from the very outset, as a matter of belief, i.e. a symbolic fact. As such, the Name-of-the-Father exerts its authority only against the background of trusting the Other's word.

15. And what about the fourth term of the Lacanian algebra, *a*? The *object small a* designates precisely the endeavour to procure for the subject a positive support of his being beyond the signifying representation: by way of the fantasy-relation to *a*, the subject ($) acquires an imaginary sense of his 'fullness of being', of what he 'truly is' independently of what he is for others, i.e. notwithstanding his place in the intersubjective symbolic network.

16. *Marx's Grundrisse*, selected and edited by David McLellan (London: Macmillan, 1980) p. 99.

17. Was Chaplin aware of the irony of the fact that Austria, Hitler's first victim, was from 1934 (i.e., from Dolfuss's right-wing coup) a proto-Fascist corporatist state? And does not the same hold for *The Sound of Music* in which the force opposed to Fascism assumes the form of self-sufficient Austrian provincialism, i.e. in which the politico-ideological struggle between Fascism and democracy is ultimately reduced to the struggle between two Fascisms, the one overtly barbarian and the one which still maintains a 'human face'?

18. So whatever ex-Communists do, they are lost: if they behave aggressively, they display their true nature; if they behave properly and follow democratic rules, they are even more dangerous since they conceal their true nature.

19. The science-fiction film *Hidden* provides, in its very naivety, one of the most poignant *mises-en-scène* of such a materialization of a notional relationship: everyday life goes on in today's California, until the main character puts on special green glasses and sees the true state of things – the ideological injunctions, invisible to the ordinary, conscious gaze, i.e. the inscriptions 'do this, buy that . . .' which bombard the subject from all around. The fantasy of the film thus provides us with glasses which literally enable us to 'see ideology' qua voluntary servitude, to perceive the hidden injunctions we follow when we experience ourselves as free individuals. The 'error' of the film, of course, is to hypothesize the ordinary material existence of ideological injunctions: their status is actually that of pure symbolic relations – it is only their effects which have material existence. (In other words, *Hidden* realizes in a slightly modified form the classical Enlightenment fantasy of ideology as the plot of the clerical caste which, in the interests of those in power, consciously deceives people.)

20. See J.N. Findlay, *Kant and the Transcendental Object* (Oxford: Clarendon Press 1981) pp. 261–7.

21. What we must bear in mind here is that Kant is compelled to hypothesize the existence of ether by the fundamental fantasmatic frame of his philosophy, namely the logic of 'real

opposition'; ether is thus deduced as the necessary positive opposite of the 'ordinary' ponderable-compressible-cohesible-exhaustible stuff.

22. See Louis Althusser et al., *Reading Capital* (London: New Left Books, 1970) pp. 186–9.

23. This point was first made by Beatrice Longuenesse in her excellent *Hegel et la critique de la métaphysique* (Paris: Vrin, 1981).

24. See Pierre Macherey, *Hegel ou Spinoza?* (Paris: Maspero, 1975).

25. Karl Marx, 'Eighteenth Brumaire of Louis Bonaparte', in Karl Marx, Frederick Engels, *Collected Works*, Volume 11 (London: Lawrence and Wishart, 1979) p. 103.

26. In his reference to the Hegelian 'Beautiful Soul', Lacan makes a deeply significant mistake by condensing two different 'figures of consciousness'. He speaks of the *Beautiful Soul* who, in the name of her *Law of the Heart*, rebels against the injustices of the world (see, for example, *Écrits: A Selection*, translated by A. Sheridan [London: Tavistock, 1977] p. 80). With Hegel, however, the 'Beautiful Soul' and the 'Law of the Heart' are two quite distinct figures: the first designates *the hysterical* attitude of deploring the wicked ways of the world while actively participating in their reproduction (Lacan is quite justified to apply it to Dora, Freud's exemplary case of hysteria). The 'Law of the Heart and the Frenzy of Self-Conceit', on the other hand, clearly refer to a *psychotic* attitude, i.e., to a self-proclaimed Saviour who imagines his inner Law to be the Law of everybody and is therefore compelled, in order to explain why the 'world' (his social environs) is not following his precepts, to resort to paranoiac constructions – to some plot of dark forces (like the Enlightened rebel who blames the reactionary clergy's propagating of superstitions for the failure of his efforts to win the support of the people). Lacan's slip is all the more mysterious for the fact that this difference between the Beautiful Soul and the Law of the Heart can be formulated perfectly by means of the categories elaborated by Lacan himself: the hysterical Beautiful Soul clearly locates itself within the big Other, it functions as a demand to the Other within an intersubjective field; whereas the psychotic, clinging to the Law of one's Heart, involves precisely a rejection, a suspension, of what Hegel referred to as the 'spiritual substance'.

27. See I. Kant, *The Critique of Pure Reason*, trans. Norman Kemp Smith (New York: St. Martin's Press, 1965) A, 584–603.

28. Existence in the sense of empirical reality is thus the very opposite of the Lacanian Real: precisely in so far as God does not 'exist' qua part of experiential, empirical reality, He belongs to the Real.

29. Jacques Lacan, *Le séminaire, livre XX: Encore* (Paris: Editions du Seuil, 1975) p. 32.

30. This point was articulated in all its philosophical weight by Georg Lukács in his *History and Class Consciousness* (London: NLB 1969).

31. That Kant himself already had a premonition of this link between existence and self-relating is attested to by the fact that in the *Critique of Pure Reason* he conferred on dynamical synthesis (which concerns also existence, not only predicates) regulative character.

32. The role of fantasy in perversion and in neurosis offers an exemplary case of this passage of in-itself into for-itself at work in the psychoanalytic clinic. A pervert immediately 'lives' his/her fantasy, stages it, which is why he or she does not entertain towards it a 'reflected' relationship. S/he does not relate towards it qua fantasy. In Hegelian terms: fantasy is not 'posited' as such, it is simply his or her in-itself. The fantasy of a hysteric, on the other hand, is also a perverse fantasy, but the difference consists not only in the fact that a hysteric relates to it in a reflected, 'mediated', way – *vulgari eloquentia* – but that he or she 'only fantasizes about what a pervert is actually doing'. The crucial point is that, within the hysterical economy, fantasy acquires a different function, becomes part of a delicate intersubjective game; by means of fantasy, a hysteric conceals his or her anxiety, while at the same time offering it as a lure to the other for whom the hysterical theatre is staged.

33. This exchangeability could be further exemplified by the ambiguity as to the precise causal status of trauma in psychoanalytic theory: on the one hand, one is fully justified in isolating the 'original trauma' as the ultimate ground which triggered the chain-reaction the final result of which is the pathological formation (the symptom); on the other hand, in order for event X to function as 'traumatic' in the first place, the subject's symbolic universe has had (already) to have been structured in a certain way.

34. See Fredric Jameson, 'Reification and Utopia in Mass Culture', in *Signatures of the Visible* (New York: Routledge, 1991).

35. In this precise sense Lacan conceives Master-Signifier as an 'empty' signifier, a signifier

without signified: an empty container which rearranges the previously given content. The signifier 'Jew' does not add any new signified – all its positive signified content is derived from the previously given elements which have nothing whatsoever to do with Jews as such. It just 'converts' them into an expression of Jewishness qua ground. One of the consequences to be drawn from it is that, in endeavouring to provide an answer to the question 'Why precisely were Jews picked out to play the scapegoat-role in anti-Semitic ideology?', we might easily succumb to the very trap of anti-Semitism, looking for some mysterious feature in them that, as it were, predestined them for that role: the fact that Jews were chosen for the role of the 'Jew' ultimately *is* contingent. As is pointed out by the well-known anti-anti-Semitic joke: 'Jews and cyclists are responsible for all our troubles. Why cyclists? WHY JEWS?'

36. Findlay, *Kant and the Transcendental Object*, p. 187.

37. Ibid., p. 1.

38. Here we must be attentive to how a simple symmetrical inversion brings about an asymmetrical, irreversible, non-specular result. That is to say, when the statement 'the Jew is exploitative, intriguing, dirty, lascivious . . .' is reversed into 'he is exploitative, intriguing, dirty, lascivious . . . *because he is Jewish*', we do not state the same content in another way. Something new is produced thereby, the *objet petit a*, that which is 'in Jew more than the Jew himself' and on account of which the Jew is what he phenomenally is. This is what the Hegelian 'return of the thing to itself in its conditions' amounts to: the thing returns to itself when we recognize in its conditions (properties) the effects of a transcendent Ground.

39. As to this exception, see Monique David-Menard, *La folie dans la raison pure* (Paris: Vrin, 1991) pp. 154–5.

40. Kant, *Critique of Pure Reason*, B, 199.

41. Ibid., B, 223.

42. This irreducible antagonism of being and becoming thus also provides the matrix for Hegel's solution of the Kantian enigma of the Thing-in-itself: *the Thing-in-itself is in the modality of 'being' what the subject is in the modality of 'becoming'*.

43. *Hegel's Science of Logic*, p. 545. What we encounter in the tetrad *actuality – possibility – contingency – necessity* is thus the repetition, on a higher, more concrete, level, of the initial tetrad of *being – nothing – becoming – determinate being*: contingency is the 'passing' of possibility into actuality, whereas necessity designates their stable unity.

44. See Žižek, *For They Know Not What They Do*, Chapter 5; and also Slavoj Žižek, *Enjoy Your Symptom* (New York: Routledge, 1992) Chapter III.

45. This Kierkegaardian opposition of 'becoming' and 'being' perhaps lurks in the background of Heidegger's recurrent figure apropos of the ontological difference, namely the tautological verbalization of the substantive: 'worlding of the world', etc. 'Worlding of the world' designates precisely 'world in its becoming', in its possibility, which is not to be conceived as a deficient mode of actuality: ontological difference is the difference between (ontic) actuality and its (ontological) possibility, i.e. that surplus of possibility which gets lost the moment possibility actualizes itself. On another level, the 'ordering of the [political] order' could be said to designate the 'open' process of the formation of a new order, the 'unrest of becoming' (epitomized, in the case of Rumania, by the hole in the centre of the flag, previously occupied by the red star, the Communist symbol) which disappears, becomes invisible, the moment a new order is established via the emergence of a new Master-Signifier.

46. This undecidability also pertains to Hegel's *Phenomenology of Spirit*, (Oxford: OUP, 1977): one has only to bear in mind that its close, absolute knowledge, coincides with the starting point of *Logic*, the point without presuppositions, the point of absolute *non-knowledge* in which all one is capable of expressing is the empty being, the form of nothingness. The path of *Phenomenology* thus appears as what it is: a *process of forgetting*, i.e. the very opposite of the gradual, progressive 'remembering' of the Spirit's entire history. *Phenomenology* functions as the 'introduction' to the 'system' proper in so far as, and by way of it, the subject has to learn to obliterate the false fullness of the non-notional (representational) content – all non-reflected presuppositions – in order to be able, finally, to begin from (being which is) nothing. It is against this background that one has to conceive the re-emergence of the term 'skull' on the last page of *Phenomenology*, where Hegel designates its itinerary as 'the Calvary of absolute Spirit', (*Phenomenology of Spirit*, p. 493). For the literal meaning of the German term for Calvary, *Schaedelstaette*, is 'the site of skulls'. The infinite judgement 'spirit is a bone (a skull)' acquires thereby a somewhat unexpected dimension: what is

revealed to the Spirit in the backwards-gaze of its *Er-Innerung*, inwardizing memory, are the scattered skulls of the past 'figures of consciousness'. The worn-out Hegelian formula according to which the Result, in its abstraction from the path leading to it, is a corpse, has to be inverted once again: this 'path' itself is punctuated by scattered skulls.

47. Is not the computer-generated *virtual reality* an exemplary case of reality conceived through the detour of its virtualization, i.e. of a reality wholly generated from its conditions of possibility?

48. Suffice it to recall here Kant's reflections on the meaning of the French Revolution: the very belief in the *possibility* of a free rational social order, attested to by the enthusiastic response of the enlightened public to the French Revolution, witnesses to the *actuality* of freedom, of a tendency towards freedom as an anthropological fact. See I. Kant, *The Conflict of the Faculties* (Lincoln and London: University of Nebraska Press, 1992) p. 153.

49. This, of course, is a leftist reading of the Kennedy murder conspiracy theory; the reverse of it is that the trauma of Kennedy's death expresses a conservative longing for an authority which is not an imposture; or, to quote one of the commentaries on the anniversary of the Vietnam War: 'Somewhere within the generation now taking power, Vietnam may have installed the suspicion that leadership and authority are a fraud. That view may have subtle stunting effects upon moral growth. If sons don't learn to become fathers, a nation may breed politicians who behave less like full-grown leaders than like inadequate siblings, stepbrothers with problems of their own.' Against this background, it is easy to discern in the Kennedy myth the belief that he was the last 'full-grown leader', the last figure of authority which was not a fraud.

50. Another exemplary case of this paradoxical nature of the relationship between possible and actual is Senator Edward Kennedy's candidacy for presidential nomination in 1980: as long as his candidacy was still in the air, all polls showed him easily winning over any Democratic rival; yet the moment he publicly announced his decision to run for the nomination, his popularity plummeted.

51. What this notion of feminine castration ultimately amounts to is a variation on the notorious old Greek sophism, 'What you don't have, you have lost; you don't have horns, so you have lost them.' To avoid the conclusion that this sophism could be dismissed as inconsequential false reasoning – that is, to get a presentiment of the existential anxiety that may pertain to its logic – suffice it to recall the Wolf-Man, Freud's Russian analysand, who was suffering from a hypochondriacal *idée fixe*. He complained that he was the victim of a nasal injury caused by electrolysis; however, when the thorough dermatological examinations established that absolutely nothing was wrong with his nose, this triggered an unbearable anxiety in him: 'Having been told that nothing could be done for his nose because nothing was wrong with it, he felt unable to go on living in what he considered his irreparably mutilated state' (Muriel Gardiner, *The Wolf-Man and Sigmund Freud* [Harmondsworth: Penguin, 1973] p. 287). The logic is here exactly the same as that of the old Greek sophism: if you do not have horns, you lost them; if nothing can be done, then the loss is irreparable. Within the Lacanian perspective, of course, this sophism points towards the fundamental feature of a structural/differential order: the unbearable absolute lack emerges at the very point when the lack itself is lacking.

52. As to this potentiality that pertains to the very actuality of power, see Žižek, *For They Know Not What They Do*, Chapter 5.

3

Yes Absolutely: Unlike Any Writing Pen

Rodolphe Gasché

In Hegel's *Phenomenology of Spirit*, the smooth and flawless dialectical run of the Spirit through the various moments that constitute its itinerary comes to a stop while still in advance of its final fulfilment. This provisional point of closure is the *yes* that, at the end of the section on 'Religion', on the verge of 'Absolute Knowing', resounds and bursts forth as spontaneously and unpredictably as any genuine response. Yet this *yes*, reverberating at the crucial transition point between 'Spirit' and 'Absolute Knowing', is a moment on the Spirit's trajectory. With this *yes*, Spirit says *yes* to itself. It answers its own call for a response to its dialectical progression – for a response that would complete it. Indeed, the *yes* in question is an *affirming* yes. But although this *yes* erupts with all the suddenness and unexpectedness of a genuine response, it coincides with the eruption and surpassing of the idea of the whole or the Absolute, where all the Spirit's elements let go their antithetical existence. For the *yes* of the *Phenomenology* affirms only the totality of that which, up to and including 'Spirit', develops in dialectical oppositions and reversals. It is thus 'the reconciling yes' of *ta panta* which, as is well known, is also released in a burst – the burst of philosophical wonder.[1] It shares with the *yes* of genuine response the suddenness of the event, and yet, this suddenness itself circles back into that which called for completion, that to which it would genuinely respond. This *yes*, through which the reconciling whole – the absolute identity of all that is in the mode of opposition – imposes itself to religious consciousness, is not yet the full affirmation of absolute knowing itself. Hegel writes:

> The Notion of Spirit which had emerged for us as we entered the sphere of religion ... as the movement in which what is in absolute antithesis recognizes itself as the same as its opposite, this recognition bursting forth as the *affirmative* (*als das Ja*) between these extremes ... this Notion is *intuitively apprehended* by the religious consciousness to which the absolute Being is revealed, and which overcomes the

difference between its Self and what it intuitively apprehends; just as it is Subject, so also it is substance, and hence it *is* itself Spirit just because and in so far as it is this movement.[2]

As Hegel has argued in his analysis of tragedy in the chapter 'Religion in the Form of Art', the very exclusiveness of the two principles or powers of the upper and the nether law that are in conflict in tragedy results from the ethical substance's actualization in limiting self-consciousness. In the downfall of the two heroes who incarnate this same substance in particular but opposite ways, both being thus equally right and wrong, the 'unitary being of Zeus (*der einfache Zeus*)', prevails in whom Apollo and the Erynnies become reconciled.[3] In short, what bursts forth at the moment when that which is in a relation of antithetical opposition manifests itself as the same as its opposite is the idea of the whole as the truth of the finite and antithetical moments. Yet this reconciling *yes*, or the Notion of Spirit, is *only* intuitively apprehended in the sphere of religion. Moreover, religious consciousness, or the ethical, moral and cultural substance of a people in the mode of self-consciousness, continues to apprehend its spirit in the form of representation (*Vorstellung*). Of religious consciousness, Hegel remarks:

> This unity of essence and the Self having been *implicitly* achieved, consciousness, too, still has this *picture-thought* [*Vorstellung*] of its reconciliation, but as picture-thought. It obtains satisfaction by *externally* attaching to its pure negativity the positive meaning of the unity of itself with the essential Being; its satisfaction thus itself remains burdened with the antithesis of a beyond.[4]

Affirmative reconciliation, the *yes* between the extremes, will only be fully realized in a sphere beyond representation, that is, in the figureless sphere of absolute knowing, in which thought itself has become its own 'figure'. In absolute knowing, the *yes* that simply burst forth in the sphere of religion develops into the self-affirming *yes* of the Notion (*Begriff*), into an affirmation that is no longer separated from what is affirmed. Here, in the Notion, the unpredictable, and at the limit, improbable surge of the *yes* as a response to those moments and movements that are still other to the Spirit has turned into the affirmative response of the Spirit to itself. Rather than a response to the Other, the Notion recognizes itself not only in the elements and movements of the Spirit, but as that movement itself. With this, even the *eruption* of the resounding *yes* toward the end of 'Religion', appears in fact to have been anticipated and calculated in advance by the *yes* of the Notion in which all relation to Other has become relation to self in absolute identity. In the absolute *yes* of the Notion, the burst, in all its abruptness and suddenness of the *yes*, has become contingent, and hence necessary.

How is one to respond to Hegel's all-inclusive *yes*; a yes, that by sublating up to the finite event of its eruption, has also forgone its nature as a response?

More precisely, how is one to relate to a *yes* that is not only all-encompassing but, by virtue of its all-inclusiveness, seems no longer in need of any response? Moreover, how is one to handle, in general, a Hegel whose uniqueness consists in having attempted to demonstrate that all finitude sublates *itself*, and that, in so doing, the reconciling *yes* – the *yes* between the extremes – is nothing but the self-sublating suddenness with which each of the extremes erupts into a relation of Otherness to self? Evidently, whatever such a response may prove to be, in order that it be a response – both responsive and responsible – it must respond to the absolute *yes*. Yet, to make such a response, one must first read and hear Hegel to the end – to the eruption of the resounding *yes*. There can be no responsible debate with Hegel without the recognition that all the Hegelian developments take place in view of, and are always already predetermined by, the telos of absolute knowing or the Notion; that is, by the thought of a figureless and non-representational thinking in which thought can say *yes* to itself in a mode in which even saying is no longer different from what is said. In other words, any genuine response to Hegel must say *yes* – and not in the mode of parrot-like repetitive affirmation – to the call to Other by the speculative *yes* itself which, as the event of the positive assimilation of all Otherness, addresses itself as a whole to Other. The *yes* of genuine response is, at its most elementary, a *yes* to the very singularity of the Hegelian enterprise, to the call to say *yes* to it in its all-embracing affirmation of self and Other in absolute identity. But such a response, precisely because it is presupposed and requested by the *yes* of Hegel's thought, falls out of its range and power. For while the responding *yes* comes to meet the demand for recognition, it necessarily escapes what it thus lets come into its own: the speculative *yes*. Indeed, any genuine response to the Hegelian *yes* implies not only that it be formulated in its most powerful and demanding articulation – as exemplified at the end of *Phenomenology of Spirit* and within the entirety of the *Greater Logic* (rather than in disembodied or decapitated versions) – but also that it resist *corresponding* to the demand and the call of the all-encompassing *yes*. For the *yes* must stand up to the demand to respond to the speculative yes in all its affirmative power; but it must also *stand it up*. That is, at the very moment it meets the speculative yes, it must fail to keep the appointment. Only thus is it a genuine response.

On the last page of *Glas* – in the Genet column that faces the exposition of Hegel's developments on the family – Derrida evokes the Nietzschean moment or instant of 'the vast and boundless . . . Yes (*das ungeheure unbegrenzte Ja*)' from *Zarathustra*.[5] Although this yes 'common to you and me' appears in a column that accompanies another one largely celebrating the assimilative power of the Hegelian system in the mode of a doubling and contradictory band, or double bind), it does not stand in a simple relation of contradiction to the Hegelian reconciling and speculative *yes*. By contrast, 'the vast and boundless . . . Yes', is a *yes* to speculative thought, that at the same time gives it and its Other the slip. It 'sneaks away' in its response, precisely because it is both a response in the strict sense (that is, from the affirmative account of all Otherness) *and* the doubling band in which Genet is largely shown to disband, break up and reject what Hegel had wrapped up in the tight bands of the speculative bond. In '*Ja, ou le faux-bond*', an interview given some time after the publication of *Glas*, Derrida remarks thus:

> Beyond the indefatigable contradiction of the *double bind*, an affirmative, innocent, intact, cheerful difference must *in the end* [*bien*] come to give the slip, escape in one leap, and sign in laughing what it lets happen and pass by in a double band. Standing up the contradiction of the double bind in one blow, and having it suddenly no longer out with the double band. This is, what I love, this stand-up [*faux-bond*] . . . [For in spite of the ineluctable nature of the double band] *it is necessary* [*il faut*] – an altogether other *it is necessary* – that somehow the double band not be the last word. Otherwise it all would come to a stop . . .[6]

This affirmative difference is a *yes* that, as the title of the interview suggests, not only 'stands up' and rebuffs the speculative yes, but also rebuffs the inescapable questioning of it that, as its Other, cannot fail to accompany it. For although this *yes* sneaks away from the speculative bond and its negating other, it also affirms it, letting it unfold (from it) in a double procession. This *yes*, then, to Hegel (*and* to what in Hegel, or outside him, fails to fall in line with his yes-saying), is also a *yes* to what Derrida calls 'the neither-swallowed-nor-rejected, what remains in the throat as Other, neither-taken-in-nor-expelled'.[7] A response that lives up to its concept, and hence must be responsive to an invitation to respond, can only take its possibility from what in the Other remains open to an Other. This openness – which is the place of the Other – is not the other of the speculative *yes*. The latter, as *Glas* shows, is always taken in as that which cannot be taken in 'off the beat', so to speak. The openness from which a response becomes possible – possible only as always unpredictable, incalculable and improbable – can only be the *faux-bond* in the Other itself; that, which in the Other, stands up its (his or her) self or identity and gives it the slip. For this openness, a response is responsible, and to it, it responds, responsibly. The speculative *yes* permits no yes to itself but a preprogrammed and repetitive *yes* that cannot be the *yes* of a response. What is excluded by the system, what claims to be the excluded Other, the non-identical, is what it is only in secret harmony, in an inextricable double bind with the system. Blindly it affirms what it negates; surreptitiously it mimics the speculative yes-saying. The *yes* that gives the reconciling *yes* and its Other the slip, as we have said – and, only thus, meets the condition under which a genuine response and encounter can take place – is consequently no longer the *yes* of truth. The *faux-bond*, the *yes* that makes the speculative *yes* stand up,

> betrays itself, *it stands itself up*, which means it lacks truth, strays from its truth even so – in betraying itself and becoming after all, in spite of the consciousness or

representation of the one who responds or hears, an exact response, punctual and true – it keeps the appointment.[8]

At the end of *Glas*, then, an 'other end'[9] is affirmed, that of a *yes* that responds to, and is thus different from the speculative *yes* that it addresses, but which it runs the risk of becoming as it arrives to meet the latter.

The foregoing developments about a responsive and responsible *yes* to Hegelian affirmation synoptically describe the problematic of deconstruction. And even though Derrida's writings from *Glas* onward cannot *simply* be subsumed under one unifying and univocal title like 'deconstruction', deconstruction and the 'operations' characteristic of Derrida's works after *Glas* are indeed *responses* to texts. Deconstruction is 'affirmative', in that, in its debate with positions or texts – a debate not rooted in a critical relation – it seeks its legitimate possibility from what in (philosophical or literary) thinking *remains* as an appeal to the Other to respond to thinking's attempt to coil upon itself in a gesture of auto-affective self-positioning. Deconstruction affirms this constitutive relation to outside, this call upon Other, which the most foundationalist, self-comprehensive, and encyclopaedic, text or thought – any text or thought that successfully includes *its* Other – *must*, for structural reasons, contain within itself. Deconstruction affirms this Necessity which constitutes it, in essence, as a response. But as a response, deconstruction *must* for equally essential, structural reasons, constantly risk failing to re-spond, risk becoming a merely acquiescing and repetitive *yes*. It is only by running this risk that deconstruction can be a response. Derrida has pointed to the near-perfect coincidence between deconstruction and Hegelian *Aufhebung*: 'it is most similar to it', nearly, almost identical, he writes.[10] Indeed, the very concern with Other, in deconstruction (and speculative thought), does not only expose deconstruction to the risk of being mistaken for, covered up, and recovered by speculative dialectics, but also explains why it itself is never safe from the possibility of effectively sliding back into a speculative reappropriation of the Other. If this is so, it is not merely because in giving a philosophical account of deconstruction, Derrida or his interpreters (myself included) may themselves have resorted to Hegelian categories and moves that ultimately fall short of capturing the very 'radicality' of deconstruction. In contrast to these empirical considerations, there remains the essential risk of failing genuinely to respond to the call by the Other which renders a genuine response possible at all. Indeed, in the same way as the *place* of the Other in a text or work of thought is nothing but a referential vector, a gesturing, pointing toward and calling upon the Other – one that cannot avoid determining itself as for-itself, and hence must give itself a self, or identity, a genuine response that is at first nothing but a *yes*-saying to the Other as Other – it cannot altogether escape the risk of saying *yes* to itself, and hence opening the annulation of its own identity. Now, the very 'fact' that a response can always slip from a repetitive *yes* to, in our case, a philosophy of absolute identity or a self-positioning responding I; or, the very 'fact' that such a slippage comes with the possibility itself of managing a place for the Other and of responsibly responding to the Other, is, of course, no excuse for overlooking the difference in question. Indeed, the very 'fact' that deconstruction, on occasion, has all the allures of dialectical thought is no licence to identify them. However, utterly irresponsive, if not irresponsible, is the claim that the Derridean approach to the Hegelian yes of reconciliation would systematically overlook the Hegelian character of its own way of responding. The levelling of difference between the two *yeses* and between each *yes* and *itself* would mean nothing less than to do injustice to *both* Hegel and Derrida.

Rather than opposing it, what deconstruction sets forth in response to the speculative *yes* is thus a *yes* to what in Hegel remains as an address to Other; one on whose confirming response the very possibility of closure depends, but which also infinitely transcends it. The speculative, affirmative, reconciling *yes* of Hegelian thought, is the yes of absolute knowing, of the Notion or Concept, of absolute identity. From his early writings to those of the *Greater Logic*, Hegel has conceived of the unity achieved in the absolute as 'the unity of differentiatedness and non-differentiatedness, or the identity of identity and non-identity'. The concept of this unity is, as Hegel notes, to 'be regarded as the first, purest, that is, most abstract definition of the absolute', one that will ultimately have to make room for 'more specific and richer definitions of it'.[11] Indeed, the unity achieved in the absolute as Spirit – the richest and final conceptualization of absolute identity – is a unity in which all external conditions that may have seemed necessary to conceive it show themselves not only to be the instances in which the Absolute is present, in that they sublate *themselves by themselves*, but also as the Other in which the Absolute *relates to itself*. The Absolute, in relating to the Other, consequently relates to itself. The absolute identity and equality with itself achieved by Spirit is thus that of self-relation and relation to Other, as that in which self also relates to itself. As self-consciousness, the absolute achieves absolute identity, which is also the all-inclusive One or totality.[12]

Considering the fact that the term 'identity' has most recently become a common, if not hackneyed term often used without further qualification in many contexts (especially in discourses more or less loosely derivative upon psychoanalysis and sociology), it is necessary at this point to recall, briefly, the meaning of 'identity' in philosophy. The logical and philosophical concept of identity designates the relation in which any object (or any objective realm as well) stands all by itself to itself. Identity, thus linked in elemental fashion to the thought of the singular, is a predicate that serves to distinguish one thing from another of the same kind. Since identity pertains, here, to mere *being itself*, it applies to any object as object, however protean or erratic it may prove to be. Although logical identity (that is, where a thing is identical with itself and thus implies itself) also takes on, in Leibniz's law on indiscernibles, a metaphysical or ontological form (according to which no two things in the universe are exactly alike and hence identical, and thus must differ numerically), the strictly logical definition of identity remains prevalent up to Kant, for whom identity is only a conceptual tool for establishing differences, and not an ontological principle. And yet, as the *Critique of Pure Reason* shows, Kant's insight (that the unity characteristic of objectivity must in the last resort be retraceable to the unity that the thinking subject has of itself) also reveals a meaning of identity that is, formally, thoroughly different from the logical identity constitutive of things. This meaning of identity, which applies exclusively to the consciousness of the thinking subject, has motivated idealist philosophers, in the wake of Kantian thought, to experiment, in Dieter Henrich's words, 'first with the subject as principle of identity, and then with the meaning of identity that had been attributed to the subject, even without connection to self-consciousness, thus disregarding the Kantian fundamental distinctions'.[13] In question is Schelling's philosophy of identity. Taking Spinoza as a model, Schelling's philosophy indeed conceives of the Absolute as the One, wherein nature and spirit, necessity and freedom, Being and intellectual intuition, are identical. Absolute identity, beyond and removed from the problematic of both substance and subject, names here the universe itself. Although the young Hegel sympathizes with Schelling's attempt to transcend in his philosophy of identity the limits of Fichte's subjective idealism, as early as the *Phenomenology of Spirit* he criticizes Fichte's concept of identity and the Absolute for their abstraction. By recasting the Absolute in terms of Spirit (that is, as a relational identity of self-consciousness in which absolute subjectivity and *its* [absolute] Other become unified), Hegel's dynamic, processual, and relational concept of absolute identity is thus to be regarded as the elaborate attempt to realize, philosophically, the idea of the universal One; that is, of a metaphysical and ontological conception of identity, while at the same time avoiding the difficulties of Schelling's monism.

Although Derrida has on several occasions discussed the possibility and the limits of the philosophical and logical concept of identity (most explicitly in *Limited, Inc.*), the concept of identity deconstructed in 'affirmative' response is the Hegelian concept of absolute identity, the *yes* between the extremes of which the *Phenomenology* speaks, and the one that gains its fullest development in the final chapters of the *Greater Logic*. The concept of identity under deconstruction is a concept that testifies to Hegel's impressive efforts to overcome the difficulties in articulating a philosophical monism freed of both subject and substance – difficulties that have haunted the history of philosophy from Parmenides to Schelling.[14] But to comprehend correctly what deconstruction achieves with respect to absolute identity, it is crucial that the latter be understood on its own terms, and not as (or mixed with) concepts originating in the sociopsychological and psychoanalytical notions of identity. Bringing the empirical (and logically, very different) concepts of identity relating specifically to the structure of personality to bear on an analysis of the speculative concept of identity (and the way in which deconstruction relates to it) only produces utter confusion. In short, without a clear grasp of the Hegelian concept of the absolute identity of Spirit as an epistemic self-relation in which self and Other have been successfully reconciled – of Spirit as the Yes between the extremes – all possible assessment on how the deconstructive *yes* relates to the identity of Spirit, on the difference and similarity between deconstruction and speculative dialectic, and especially on the 'status' of the deconstructive *yes* itself (and hence, on the specific kind of heterogeneity from which it proceeds), is simply out of question.

And yet, in this essay, I shall not engage in a systematic elaboration on the speculative concept of identity as it emerges from the chapter of *Phenomenology* or the final part of *Science of Logic*. All such elaboration presupposes a thorough familiarity with Hegel's speculative criticism, in particular in the *Greater Logic*, of the concept of identity itself. It is to this criticism that I shall limit myself here. Indeed, rather than being Hegel's last word on identity, the explicit thematization of identity in *Science of Logic* as a reflective determination is a critical and speculative evaluation of it. It only paves the way for the considerably richer understanding of it as the absolute identity of Spirit. To take Hegel's treatment of identity as a reflective determination for Hegel's positive theory of identity, is not only to get his theory of identity wrong, but to misconstrue the whole of the Hegelian philosophical enterprise in the first place.

I

With this in mind, I want to turn to Hegel's treatment of the question of identity in Book II of *Science of Logic*, entitled 'The Doctrine of Essence'. In the first section, 'Essence as Reflection Within Itself', in a chapter on 'Illusory Being', Hegel introduces the notion of identity, and shows it to be coextensive with essence and reflection. Before embarking on an analysis of how identity is to be understood here, some preliminary remarks as to the precise context in which this term is situated are inevitable. Since identity will be defined as a reflective determination, it is especially important to grasp clearly what 'reflection' means here. Let me first advance the following: reflection as it appears in *Science of Logic* is no longer the philosophical reflection whose shortcomings Hegel had stigmatized in his earlier work, but a *rectified reflection* that, while not yet absolute or speculative reflection, has been stripped of everything improper to that sphere and is thus a moment on the way to absolute reflection itself. In *Science of Logic*, Hegel has put reflection into its proper place, as it were. To assess correctly the modifications bestowed on reflection so as to assign it a positive but limited place within the self-knowing Absolute, a word, first, on *Science of Logic* itself, on its goal and scope.

Hegel's logic is not based on judgement as the vehicle of truth. For Hegel, formal logic is a dead body compared to which speculative logic represents the living movement of thinking. It is a genuinely philosophical logic in that it explores a field of rationality beyond the logical axioms from which formal logic deduces its logical forms and elements of form. It is an inquiry into the principles of thinking in general and into Thinking as a principle itself, into Thinking as the absolute ground of thought. According to Hegel's logic, this absolute ground is the Notion, or Concept. Hegel writes:

> The Notion is the most concrete and richest determination because it is the ground and the *totality* of the preceding determinations, of the categories of being and of the determinations of reflections; these, therefore, are certainly also present in it. (*SL*, 617)

In the Notion, or the absolute Idea, the idea that has itself for its object, all the possible logical determinations of that one and same Notion – as being, as essence, and finally *as* Notion, that is, as including itself – have been sublated, overcome and preserved. Since all these determinations of the Notion are figures of thinking, Hegel can claim to have shown how, with the absolute Idea, thinking engenders itself and becomes its own ground, the absolute ground of thinking.

The *Science of Logic* divides in two parts: 'The Objective Logic', and 'Subjective Logic or the Doctrine of the Notion'. The first part, which contains the development of the categories and the reflective determinations of thinking up to the point where the concept of the Notion begins to impose itself, further comprises the two books on 'The Doctrine of Being', and 'The Doctrine of Essence'. Compared to these first two books that make up objective logic, the subjective logic represents the true exposition of the logic of the free Notion, or absolute Idea, that is, of logic as a formal ontology. Now, the speculative unfolding of reflection occurs right after the exposition of the doctrine of being; in other words, as part of the developments that ultimately will give rise to the idea of the Notion. The dialectical exposition of the problem of reflection is entirely mediated by its relation to the doctrine of being, and is intelligible only on the basis of the continual cross-references to that preceding realm. But in addition, it must be read in terms of what will issue from, and thus limit, the sphere of reflection – that is, the Notion, or the unfolded positive totality of all determinations of thought itself. It is not possible to broach here the difficult question of how exactly the Logic of being and the Logic of Essence (in which reflection is discussed) relate. The following schematic outline of what both parts and both books seek to achieve, and how they relate, must suffice.

In the logic of being, Hegel can be said to have rehearsed the great systems of the metaphysics of being. In this part he discusses the various modes of the sensuous in so far as they are contained in the *logos*. It is an investigation into the meaning of being, or of the immediate, which reinterprets Kant's *transcendental aesthetics*, that is, of objectifying thought and the traditional logic implied by this kind of thinking. The thrust of this whole inquiry is to demonstrate that being, as the immediate and abstract, shows itself as something Other, and has its truth in its essence, in something universal presupposing a reflective distance. The logic of essence is the counterweight to being's self-negation. 'The truth of being is essence', Hegel notes (*SL*, 389). This truth follows upon the negation of the immediate presence of being as being's eternal past: *to ti en einai*. The doctrine of essence, consequently, amounts to a reinterpretation by Hegel of the various historical metaphysics of the intelligible, including Kant's *transcendental analytics*. Yet, this logic of essence serves also as a stage for a speculative critique of the philosophy of understanding, or reflection, in that the concept of essence presupposes precisely the (seemingly) irreducible doubling of the world characteristic of a metaphysics of reflection. Indeed, this metaphysics explains immediate and sensuous being by flanking it with explanation itself, understanding, or essence. A *mundus intelligibilis*, as Saint Augustine termed it, arches up in reflection over and against the phenomenal world, irreconcilably distinct from it. The point that Hegel makes in the 'Logic of Essence', is that essence, as an internal negation of the whole sphere of being, lacks the stability that it promised. Although the negation by essence of being allows being to turn upon itself – to reflect itself – essence, for its part, fails to reflect itself, and thus to achieve the foothold in itself that would have made the intelligible the deciding truth of being. Essence remains unable to comprehend itself. As a result, the movement characteristic of this part of the *Greater Logic* is bound to reintroduce the immediacy of being. But, since the immediate that is thus reinstituted is the immediacy of the being of essence, it reappears on a higher level. The relapse in question, indeed, opens up the new sphere of the Concept, or Notion. Hegel writes: 'The movement of essence is in general the becoming of the Notion' (*SL*, 526). The logic of the Notion corresponds to a recast version of Kant's *transcendental dialectics*, since it radically exceeds Kant's limitation of the idea to a merely regulative role. Differently put, the Hegelian Concept or Notion, that is, the major category of the subjective logic, is nothing but the expounded transcendental unity of apperception – the originary unity that Kant had acknowledged as having to accompany all synthesis of the manifold. In this part of the logic, then, Hegel surmounts the reflective dualism of being and essence, being and appearance, that characterized Part I. In the absolute reflection of the Notion, thinking thinks itself. It becomes the all-encompassing totality that leaves reflective dualism behind. This is the end of the process in which substance finally grasps itself as subject. The three parts of this process correspond, as Hyppolite has suggested, to the three moments contained in the German word *Selbstbe-wusstsein* – being, appearing, self.[15] This process, as it is expounded by the *Science of Logic*, culminates in the self-consciousness of the Notion, or Concept, as the unity of all determinations of thinking.

In this extremely broad, and most schematic outline of how the *Science of Logic* is organized, I have made repeated reference to Kant's critical philosophy. As I will now begin to discuss the notion of reflection which dominates the 'Logic of Essence' it must, however, be emphasized that although this second part of Book I corresponds to Kant's transcendental analytics in the same way as the 'Logic of Being' corresponds to formal or objective logic, Hegel does not simply replay Kant's developments. The two parts of Book I do not merely reproduce the types of reflection characteristic of formal or transcendental logic. In themselves they are indefensible modes of thinking, according to Hegel. Instead, what we encounter in the two parts of Book I are only two different ways of synthetic constitution that are *already* moments of true absolute reflection. Indeed, the movement of reflection outlined in the 'Logic of Essence' has only a faint resemblance to Kant's corresponding notion. It has already been thoroughly reinterpreted in the perspective of the specular reflexivity of the Notion. It is a kind of reflection that can be called rectified, since its reflective falsifications have been corrected in the perspective of the absolute; it is thus distinct from philosophical reflection on the one hand, while on the other, from absolute reflection.[16] In the following, I will limit myself to a description of what Hegel calls 'the movement of reflection' and what characterizes this notion of reflection itself, leaving aside, however, a detailed discussion of the various phases that reflection must pass through before turning into the specularity of the Notion.

Essence is the main topic of the, at times rather difficult if not obscure, 'Logic of Essence'. 'Essence stands between *being* and *Notion*: it constitutes their mean, and its movement is the *transition* from being into the Notion', Hegel writes (*SL*, 391). Essence issues from being. It is a negation brought about not from the outside of Being, but by being itself. Hegel holds that essence in 'its self-movement is reflection' (*SL*, 399). How does Hegel want us to understand this intrinsic relation between essence and reflection? Essence is the negation of being as pure immediacy. For essence, being is secondary and derivative. It is, compared to essence, nothingness, or 'illusory being', essenceless being; that is, mere *Schein*, mere semblance. Yet, the non-essence that in the sphere of essence is thus attributed to being, shows itself to be essence's own illusory being. 'The illusory being . . . is essence's own positing', Hegel remarks (*SL*, 393). However, if illusory being is the result of essence positing itself, then this means that 'essence *shines* or *shows within itself*'. This doubling of essence within itself by which it takes on the illusory appearance of being is what Hegel calls *reflection* in the *Greater Logic*. 'The showing of this illusory being within essence itself *is reflection*', he concludes (*SL*, 394).

There are three aspects to this movement of reflection and they need to be distinguished: (i) that reflection takes place *within* the sphere of essence; (ii) that it coincides with the establishment of an Other to essence in the sphere of essence itself; and (iii) that this establishment is nothing but the shining, or showing of essence in that very sphere. Consequently, essence as reflection is the whole itself, including itself as its own moment. But although the positing in essence's shining within itself of an Other in opposition to self and the self-positing of self are identical movements, reflection, because it opens the difference of the Other in the totality of essence, is also negation. However, this very negativity of reflection that results from the showing-in-itself of essence – a showing supposed to establish the identity of essence – is illusory as well, Hegel holds. In any case, reflection, negativity (or Otherness) and identity, are found in profound unison in the sphere in question. This difficult synthesis needs some further clarification.

What remains of being in the sphere of essence – illusory being – 'is not the illusory being of an Other, but is illusory being per se, the *illusory being* of essence itself', because '*essence* is the reflection of itself within itself', we are told (*SL*, 398). The equality of essence with itself is, thus, speculatively speaking, identical with the negativity of essence since it is the relation to the Other (the non-being of being); that is, it is the relation to essence's illusory being. In the sphere under consideration, reflection of an Other and self-reflection are identical. Hegel writes: 'The movement of reflection . . . is the other as the *negation in itself*, which has a being only as self-related negation' (*SL*, 399). Indeed, in this sphere – which consists of immediate being's self-negation, in which being returns into itself, and consequently has become essence – the Other to which reflection relates is only an illusory Other, since it is an Other that negates itself as Other. Reflection amounts to a movement in which a relation to an Other is achieved, but this Other is itself characterized by reflection in that it is negation in itself and of itself. Therefore Hegel can claim that reflection is self-related negation, that is, a negation of negation, and can conclude his analysis of the movement of reflection with the following formula: 'Consequently, becoming in essence, its reflective move-ment, is the *movement of nothing to nothing, and so back to itself*' (*SL*, 400). But if it is true that reflection in the sphere of essence knows the Other exclusively as the Other of essence, that is, as illusory being, essence is also its own negation because in shining within itself it shows to have this Other within itself. In Hegel's words, reflection is an 'interchange of the negative with itself' (*SL*, 400). *Pure* absolute reflection leads only to the very identity of negation with itself. Reflection as pure absolute reflection, or still abstract reflection, is merely 'the *illusory being of the one in the other*', the mere shining of one into the other (*SL*, 622). Hegel notes:

> The former, the movement of nothing through nothing back to itself, is the reflection of *itself* in the other; but because the opposition in the reflection has not yet any self-subsistence, the one that reflects is not a positive, nor is the *other* in which it is reflected a negative. (*SL*, 445)

There is something extremely farcical about reflection. It is a movement incapable of securing any self-subsistence for the terms between which it takes place. The Other that reflection posits negates itself as Other, and thus lacks what must characterize an Other as Other: negativity. By contrast, the essence from which reflection takes off achieves at best illusory being. Reflection is a ghostly movement between a bloodless self and an Other reduced to a lifeless husk. In it, no distinction of substance takes place, and hence neither does movement, strictly speaking. It is a shadow play between nothing and nothing, in which even the movement from nothing to nothing, on the one hand, and, on the other, back into itself, is hardly distinguishable. In this analysis of the sad spectacle of reflection, whose humour escapes at best the totally insensitive reader, Hegel has given a final deathblow to the metaphysics of understanding and reflection. Needless to say, it would of course be terribly wrong if one were to isolate and hypostatize this analysis by conceiving of it as *the* model of Hegelian dialectic and of what Hegel understands by identity. It would mean arresting the development of the Hegelian treatment of both reflection and identity in what, in Hegel's eyes, are the most devastating arguments against these concepts.[17]

Yet, in spite of Hegel's critique of essential reflection, his account of essence and reflection is a dialectical one. Apart from the fact that the shadow play of the ghostly movement between nothings within nothing sets forth only the formal, and, hence still empty, moments that will acquire their substantive content only in the logic of the Notion, pure absolute, or abstract reflection – before all further determination and concretion – it *is* the matrix of the (logically) most elementary idea of a 'coincidence with itself [*mit sich selbst zusammengehen*]' and with what it is not (*SL*, 400). In one single unity, reflection achieves a (however illusory) coinciding of being-self and Other. It is necessary to recall here, that if reflection, by which the essence shines in itself, happens in the sphere of essence to begin with, it is because essence is *already* identity. But it is identity in the most elementary way. Indeed, as Hegel puts it, 'essence is at first, simple self-relation, pure *identity*' (*SL*, 409). It is 'pure equality-with-self', 'simple identity-with-self', in which 'otherness and relation-to-other has vanished' (*SL*, 4ll). Conversely, 'identity is, in the first instance, essence itself, not yet a determination of it, reflection in its entirety, not a distinct moment of it' (*SL*, 412). '*Essential* identity' is thus 'in general the same as essence' (*SL*, 411–12). But this identity of essence, which is reflection in its entirety, achieves its equality-with-self not through 'a restoration of itself from another', but in 'this pure origination from and within itself' (*SL*, 411). In other words, essential identity, by knowing no Other and relation-to-Other, is nothing in itself but Otherness sublated, or simple negativity of being-in-itself. But since this identity 'contains nothing of its other but only itself, that is, in so far as it is absolute identity with itself', it is also '*in its own self* absolute non-identity', Hegel concludes (*SL*, 413). It follows from this that the idea of a coincidence which accomplishes its concept only if it is the coincidence with self and Other must develop further. This happens through the various modes that reflection takes on in the sphere of essence, and which can, in view of the foregoing developments on reflection, be described as an illusory dialectic, but a dialectic, notwithstanding, of self and other. This dialectic comes to an end with the emergence from the sphere of essence and reflection, of the ground (*Grund*). In it, reflection as pure mediation has made room for the real mediation of the ground with itself and thus for an identity in which essence has returned from its non-being into positing itself. But ultimately, the dialectic of identity that arises with essential identity comes only *to a rest* in the full mediation of self and Other in the Notion. Hegel writes: '*truth is complete only in the unity of identity with difference*, and hence consists only in this unity' (*SL*, 414).

One must not lose sight of the fact that the 'Logic of Essence' is not only a debate, then, about reflective, as opposed to and as distinct from the objectifying, thinking deliberated throughout the 'Logic of Being'. Essence is nothing but the 'pure, *absolute difference*' (*SL*, 413) which is also being sublated in itself. Therefore essence is tied up from the start with thinking the unity of identity and difference. The 'Logic of Essence' comes to a halt, indeed, after the two modes of thinking (that is, of being and essence) have been united in the Notion. Only in the Notion does Hegel believe he has achieved both a logically and ontologically satisfactory reconciliation between the relation-to-self and relation-to-Other demanded in the name of reflection.

With the unfolding of the initially abstract notion of absolute reflection, the results of mediation become, of course, more concrete. It now becomes equally evident that the various specific forms that reflection takes on fail to achieve unity. This failure, constitutive of reflection as analysed in the realm of essence, thus calls for its sublation in the speculative movements of the Notion by which absolute identity finally comes into its own. This essential failure of identity in the sphere of reflection is a consequence of the reflective mode by which it is supposed to be brought about. The illegitimacy of tearing what Hegel says about identity and its relation to reflection from its context, and heralding these statements as the final truth of the Hegelian concept of identity, likewise follows. If the increasingly more concrete forms of reflection that Hegel distinguishes fail to establish the sought-for identity, it is because, *as forms of reflection*, they cannot but give unequal treatment to what is to be united. Either they subordinate self-relation to Other, or the other way around. What, then, are the different forms of reflection that Hegel distinguishes in the *Greater Logic?* Pure absolute reflection, which differentiates into *positing*, external, and determining reflection.

Positing and external reflection stress opposite features in the still abstract notion of reflection examined until now, making it logically richer. Only in determining reflection does the notion of reflection acquire its full conceptual concretion. Determining reflection, Hegel tells us, is 'the completed . . . reflection' (*SL*, 406). Since this final mode of reflection pretends to unite what had remained separate in the two previous forms of reflection, it needs to be examined more closely. Determining reflection 'is in general the unity of *positing* and *external* reflection' (*SL*, 405). If, as Hegel holds, determinatedness is relation to Other, it is essential to review first how positing and external reflection achieve such determinatedness. Indeed, whereas 'external reflection, when it determines, posits an other . . . in the place of the sublated being', namely essence, positing reflection 'starts from nothing'; the determination that it posits

> is not put in the place of an other; the positing has no presupposition. But that is why it is not the completed, determining reflection; the determination that it posits is consequently *only* something posited; it is immediate, not as equal to itself, but as negating itself; it has an absolute relation to the return-into-self; it *is* only in reflection-into-self, but it is not this reflection itself. (*SL*, 405–6)

In positing reflection, an Other is posited, but since this posited Other relates to itself as sublated Other (it is *only* posited), 'the equality of reflection is completely preserved' (*SL*, 406). It is as if nothing had happened (except for putting into place the formal relations constitutive of reflection-into-self). Now, in determining reflection, such determination, by positing reflection, becomes united with external reflection. External reflection, as Hegel has previously shown, starts from something immediately given. It is thus presupposing (*voraussetzende*) reflection. Whatever determinations are posited 'by external reflection in the immediate are to that extent external to the latter' (*SL*, 403). It stands over against its own starting point. But, says Hegel, a closer consideration reveals that it is 'a positing of the immediate, which consequently becomes the negative or the determinate'; hence, 'this immediate from which it seemed to start as from something alien, *is* only in this its beginning' (*SL*, 403–4). In exterior reflection, the immediate that is presupposed thus becomes determined as the Other of reflection. Therefore Hegel can conclude: 'the externality of reflection over against the immediate is sublated; its positing in which it negates itself is the union of itself with its negative, with the immediate, and this union is the immediacy of essence itself' (*SL*, 404). This return to positing reflection in exterior reflection is thus not a simple return. By being the immanent reflection of the immediate that it at first presupposed, reflection has become determined by this very immediate, whereas the immediate itself has become fully transparent to reflection. In this unity of positing and exterior reflection, the latter has become an 'absolute presupposing, that is, the repelling of reflection from itself, or the positing of the determinatedness as *determinatedness of itself*' (*SL*, 406). Simply put, in the unity in question, the exteriority of reflection makes reflection coil upon itself, whereas positing becomes determination of reflection by itself. Being posited, in other words, now means being reflectively determined. 'Positedness is thus a *determination of reflection*' (*SL*, 406) Hegel writes. The relation to other characteristics of positing has turned into relation to reflectedness-into-self. In determining reflection, reflection is equal to itself. Or differently put, with determinate reflection 'essence is determinate essence, or it is *an essentiality*' (*SL*, 409). It has persistence, since it is no longer unequal to itself. In determinate reflection, reflection has achieved a unity with itself and its other which, compared to all previous forms of transitional determination, is stable self-determination.

However, this stability of determining reflection does not last. It disintegrates instantly into *reflective determinations*. Indeed, although essence is infinite return-into-self, a movement of absolute self-mediation through distinct moments, essence as essence can achieve this unity with self in Other only by *shining* 'into these its moments which consequently are themselves determinations reflected into themselves' (*SL*, 409). Consequently, the essentialities, or reflective determinations, into which determining reflection divides 'appear as free essentialities floating in the void without attracting or repelling one another. In them, the determinateness has established and infinitely fixed itself through relation-to-itself' (*SL*, 403). The stable essence has thus fallen apart into determinations that have lost all commerce with one another. And Hegel can conclude that in determining reflection, reflection has become exterior to itself, beside itself (*ausser sich gekommene Reflexion*). Indeed, 'the equality of essence with itself has perished in the negation, which is the dominant factor', of determining reflection.

Identity is the first of these reflective determinations into which the unity and equality with self and Other diffracts. The others are difference, contradiction and ground. As a reflective determination, identity marks the fixation of the stability sought by determining reflection into relation-to-self. It thematizes the determinate's bending 'back [of] its reflection-into-other into reflection-into-self' (*SL*, 407). Remembering that, as stated earlier, essence, reflection-into-self, is the first moment of its shining into itself (as Hegel remarks: 'Essence is *at first* simple self-relation, pure *identity*. This is its determination, but as such it is rather the absence of any determination' (SL,

409). Identity, consequently, is not only the first moment of essence's reflecting itself into a stable relation to itself and its other; in this sphere, it is merely pure, that is, simple, abstract identity. This is an identity that ultimately is not one since – to refer to Hegel's analysis of the *law* of identity – the reflective movement that constitutes it is 'a beginning that hints at something different to which an advance is to be made; but this different something does not materialize . . . the difference is only a vanishing; the movement returns into itself' (*SL*, 415–16). This is further proof, if any should still be needed, that what Hegel develops with respect to identity in this part of *Science of Logic* cannot be construed as *the* final word on identity (or on reflection, for that matter). Everything Hegel says about the so-called laws of thinking – in this case: the law of identity – is valid for the concept of identity outlined up to this point: 'these laws contain *more* than is *meant* by them, to wit, this opposite, absolute difference itself' (*SL*, 416). The concept of identity, indeed, is haunted by absolute inequality, or contradiction per se, and as such is a dialectical concept in anticipation of its fulfilment.

It would be too time-consuming to expand here on Hegel's speculative critique of the four reflective determinations, or essentialities. The thrust of his analysis is to demonstrate that the first three reflective determinations – identity, difference and contradiction, become sublated by mutually putting their self-subsistant autonomy into question. In brief: the determination of essence as pure *identity* achieves only simply self-relation. It is, therefore, the absence of any determination. Although *difference* is a proper determination of essence, difference is either *diversity* (that is, external or indifferent difference to essence), or operates within identical essence as unmediated *opposition*. In the reflective determination of contradiction, the indifferent sides of opposition become mutually relating sides, or moments, of difference. Thus reflected into itself, opposition become contradiction withdraws into its *ground* (*SL*, 409). With this, essence has become the *ground* into which all three reflective determinations have returned. Yet, as the last of the reflective determinations, the ground is also sublated determination as such. Hegel writes: '*ground is itself one of the reflected determinations of essence*; but it is the last of them, or rather, the meaning of this determination is merely that it is a sublated determination' (*SL*, 444). The ground appears as that determination of reflection from which identity, difference and opposition draw their origin and to which they return. Assuming this function of a ground, the fourth reflective determination signifies the end of reflection. But in the same stroke, all the immanent presuppositions and implications of reflection, and those which it was unable to realize in its different shapes, come into full view. In Hegel's own words:

Ground . . . is real mediation because it contains reflection as sublated reflection; it is essence that, through its non-being, *returns* into and *posits itself*. In accordance with this moment of sublated reflection, the posited receives the determination of *immediacy*, of an immediate that, apart from the relation, or its illusory being, is self-identical. This immediate is *being* which has been restored by essence, the non-being of reflection through which essence mediates itself. (*SL*, 445)

In the 'Logic of Essence', this idea of totality and absolute identity, in which identity and reflection are sublated, starts off with the reflective determination of the ground which therefore is also the end of determining reflection. But this idea gains full concretion in the notion of Actuality (*Wirklichkeit*) in which the fundamental contradictions of reflection are welded into a successful kind of identity. This last stage in the process of the sublation of reflection and the becoming of the all-encompassing and absolute identity corresponds to the end of objective logic. It makes the transition to the logic of the Notion the richest category of dialectical thinking. If Hegel speaks of absolute reflection and identity in this final part of the *Greater Logic*, he clearly refers to something for which pure absolute reflection and identity as a reflective determination were at best the blueprint.

II

Having argued that deconstruction's response to speculative thought is a response to the strong concept of identity, it is now necessary to say a word about the deconstructive 'operation' on identity itself. First, however, it has to be established, and in no uncertain terms, that deconstruction is not a critique of identity in the name of the non-identical. Undoubtedly, Derrida has, at times, made recourse to the concept of non-identity to describe the limits of identity. In 'Before the Law', for example, he speaks of the 'non-identity in itself' of the sense or destination of a text such as Kafka's parable, whose 'personal identity' – 'the identity with itself of a bequeathed corpus' – passes on nothing but 'non-identity with itself'; yet, the identity of Kafka's text that 'does not tell or describe anything but itself as text', is not, Derrida charges, achieved

> within an assured specular reflection of some self-referential transparency – and I must stress this point – but in the unreadability of the text, if one understands by this the impossibility of acceding to its proper significance and its possibly inconsistent content, which it jealously keeps back.[18]

Not only is this identity of 'Before the Law', then, not speculatively constituted; more importantly for our concerns here neither is the non-identity that it is said to pronounce and to pass on of speculative origin. It shares only the wording with what is called non-identity in speculative thinking, as well as in the critique of speculative thought. Derrida holds: 'The text guards itself, maintains itself – like the law, speaking only of itself, that is to say, of its non-identity with itself [*Il ne parle que de lui-même, mais alors de sa non-identité à soi*]. It neither arrives nor lets anyone arrive.'[19] If a text such as Kafka's parable 'Before the Law' can be said to close upon itself, it is in non-identity. But the statement of such non-identity comes with a conditional clause: *If* the text can be said to speak only of itself, *then* (*alors*) it is at best about its non-identity with itself. If one uses a language akin to that of speculative thought to describe what happens in Kafka's parable, that of which this text speaks when it is said to speak only of itself, it must then invariably be cast in terms of non-identity. The reference to non-identity is clearly a tribute paid to a particular way of phrasing the fact that a text such as Kafka's guards and maintains itself. The non-identity that a deconstructive reading of a text such as 'Before the Law' points to, however, shares only the name with the speculative concept of non-identity. Indeed deconstruction does not object to the idea of an all-encompassing identity on the basis that such a concept does not come without remainders. Since all identifying thinking, as well as the thinking of absolute identity, considers what it is to be identified (or taken up into the all-embracing and identical whole) from the perspective of identity, such thought, its critics claim, looks away from the 'what of the to be identified' as not identical. Ineluctable non-identity, they hold, is the remainder that drops through the otherwise tight nets of identifying, or speculative thought.

Adorno, from such a position, has opposed Hegelian thought and its attempt to conceptualize the relation of identity between subject and object as the identity of identity and non-identity. To counter identifying thought, he has suggested to start off by thinking of the non-identity of identity and non-identity. Yet, as Ute Guzzoni has convincingly shown, any attempt to think toward a thinking that would no longer be guided by the principle of identity must acknowledge that Adorno's concept of the non-identical is essentially something other than what Hegel designates by that term. Guzzoni remarks:

> Although Hegelian dialectic lives, undoubtedly, from the tension between identity and non-identity, identity has never here the meaning of something that is simply in opposition to the identical, precisely because of the tension in question.[20]

Indeed, the non-identical in Hegel is a *moment*, and does thus lack any 'fundamental heterogeneity with respect to the universal'.[21] Non-identity for Hegel is a relational concept, whose meaning is determined by *its* other – identity – and, thus, is part of a movement in which the dialectically different achieves unity. From the outset, the non-identical stands in a relation of opposition to the identical – it is the non-identical *of* the identical – and is viewed as constituted from the start (in the same way as the identical) by the absolute identity toward which it unfolds. Consequently, the non-identical in Hegel (and this is the case with the identical as well) is non-identical only when it is no longer itself, but already beyond itself; that is, tied into the whole of which it is a positive moment. The Hegelian concept of the non-identical, therefore, cannot serve in any way to challenge the speculative conception of absolute identity. Rather than something that falls through the meshes of the absolute, it is part of the net itself that constitutes the re-lational whole in question. What follows from this is that the totalizing and unifying thrust of absolute identity cannot be thwarted by any singularity, in particular, by the sensible, or merely brute being before any conceptualization has occurred. Hegel has made this point with all the necessary clarity in his rebuttal of one Mr. Krug, who had challenged transcendental idealism to 'deduce each particular cat and dog, as well as Mr. Krug's own pen'.[22] In the context of his criticism of Krug, Hegel notes that to object to transcendental idealism because it would have neglected 'facts' such as 'having been born at a very determined time, of dying at a specific time, of receiving daily news through the newspaper about things that happen in the world, and in places where we are not present',[23] simply shows that Krug has no idea whatsoever of 'philosophical construction'. He writes:

> If Krug had had an inkling however slight of the greatness of this task, or of what currently constitutes the prime interest of philosophy, namely to once again put God absolutely at the top of philosophy as the sole ground of everything, as the only *principium essendi* and *cognoscendi*, after He had been put long enough next to other finite things, or entirely at the end as a postulate that proceeds from an absolute finitude, how could he have come up with the idea to demand that philosophy deduce his writing pen?[24]

Apart from the fact that such items as those to which Krug refers are trivial (Hegel challenges Krug to confront, by contrast, the *organization* of a dog or cat, the *life* of a rose, the *individuality* of a Moses or Alexander), they are not even characterized, strictly speaking, by independence, singularity, or finite being. As Hegel's emphasis on thinking the organization, the life and the individuality of things, animals or persons demonstrates, singular items have an independent singularity and are philosophically significant only on the basis of what makes them intelligible in the first place. Yet, with this, they are, for Hegel, always already, moments of the absolute as the unity of the intelligible. In short, if anything can make absolute identity tremble, it is certainly not the non-identical in the Hegelian sense, nor, as is now to be seen, in the sense that Adorno gives to this term.

For Adorno, 'the non-identical negates identity, it is something negative compared to the identical, that is, something that refuses to be identified, and to be taken together with Other in a common unity . . . insofar as it is always more than what it could have in common with Other'.[25] In other words, the non-identical in Adorno's sense is never a *moment*, and, as Guzzoni has argued, 'Adorno's dialectic is a *dialectic without moments*, as it were, precisely because for him the non-identical is not sublated in the movement of an all-embracing and all penetrating whole.'[26] The starting point for his conception of the non-identical lies with the assumption that every object that is encountered, whether in the mode of experience or conceptualization, harbours a kernel resistant to experience and thought. Guzzoni notes that 'for Adorno what is, is there first before Other – the thinking subject – can direct itself upon it'.[27] The non-identical, in Adorno's sense, escapes identifying thought and absolute identification, because, in essence, it has an altogether different ontological character, and is heterogeneous to experience, thought and conceptual arrangement. This remainder would, in principle, have to be distinguished from what Hegel calls immediacy, or mere being. The latter does not escape the logic of the concept; it is, on the contrary, its first moment. As Hegel recalls toward the end of the *Greater Logic*,

> at each stage of its further determination . . . [the universal] raises the entire mass of its preceding content, and by its dialectical advance it not only does not lose anything or leave anything behind, but carries along with it all it has gained, and inwardly enriches and consolidates itself.[28]

Not only does the idealizing process by which absolute identity enriches itself have no remainder, but to speak of a remainder to the process as a whole is nonsensical, since the Absolute *is* sublated remainder, the remaining totality of all remains. What Adorno calls the non-identical, and which is said to be heterogeneous and incommensurable to the concept, would here be radically different from what Hegel terms the immediate, or simple, being. Yet, such a non-identical, which precedes the speculative logic of identity and non-identity as the heterogeneous and incommensurable, is ultimately without relation to the Concept. To the Concept and absolute identity, it is an insignificant non-identical which has no bearing whatsoever on the process through which the Absolute achieves completion in absolute identity. Whereas Hegel's 'immediate' (mere being, sensible immediacy) is part of the whole, the non-identical in Adorno's sense remains outside speculative identity, occupying the place that the latter has assigned to the meaningless. Indeed, in its utter exteriority to absolute identity, the non-identical lacks up to the negativity of the most minute moment. But by slipping through the so-called meshes of totalizing thought, this non-identity (which is thus clearly understood to be non-relational, and hence of the order of substance) acquires no enabling status, however ephemeral, with respect to such thought. Neither does it make that thought possible by escaping it, nor does it represent the limit of absolute identity. It is, strictly speaking, meaningless. But the meaningless is, as we have said, determined as such by speculative thought.

Paradoxically, then, even Adorno's non-identical remains, as the always already anticipated, and hence sublated remainder of speculative thought.

It would thus seem that the very absence of relation to the Concept robs even Adorno's notion of the non-identical of any (significant) critical thrust. Absolute identity can only be questioned from a 'position' that is *neither* inside *nor* outside of it, and which entertains a relation to it that is without relation to it at the same time. This is a direct consequence of the relational nature of the speculative Absolute.

The point to be made is that the deconstruction of speculative identity does not consist in opposing a non-identical (either in a Hegelian sense, or one determined by a critique of identifying thought and of the thought of absolute identity) to identity. However, before such a point can be made, a persistent confusion must be addressed: by virtue of its relational nature, nothing of the order of a substantial remainder can in principle be held against absolute identity. Only something of the order of the relational could escape the Absolute. Yet, as absolute totality, this relational whole includes all relations, even that to itself. Consequently, for essential reasons, only a *relation without relation* to absolute identity can escape or resist it. As a *response* to absolute identity, that is, to its strongest claim of all-inclusiveness and absolute identity, deconstruction cannot, for equally essential reasons, conceive of what absolute identity must exclude, or of what resists it as a remainder, residue, refuge, or rest. Occasionally Derrida has spoken of *rests*, but its italicization or suspension between quotation marks are clear indications that the term is not to be taken in its usual sense. Rather than a rigorously identifiable and decidable residue, like the Adornean non-identical, the remainder that a deconstruction discerns *in* a speculative totality and identical whole is 'a remainder that is both quasi-transcendental and supplementary'. Such a remainder is characterized by its *resistance* to a speculative, absolute identity in that it 'adds itself to . . . [it] without allowing itself to be added in or totalized', Derrida writes.[29] This remainder, by re-traversing all the moments of the absolute totality, re-marks these moments and hence escapes participation in their organization. It is thus neither of the order of the speculative, nor transcendent to it. By virtue of its structure, such a remainder cannot therefore be properly determined. It is neither an identity, nor strictly speaking, something non-identical. As Derrida remarks with respect to *text* as remainder,

> dialectical happiness will never account for a text. If there is text, if the hymen constitutes itself as a textual trace, if it always leaves something behind, it is because its undecidability cuts it off from (prevents it from depending on) every – and hence *any* – signified, whether antithetic or synthetic.[30]

A remainder such as the one in question *resists* the meanings of both the identical and the non-identical, and cannot be questioned within their horizon. This undecidability of the remainder with respect to a totality of meaning, or to a speculative totalization as the identity of identity and non-identity, has prompted Derrida to speak of it in terms of remaining (*restance*). Rather than a positive or negative remainder, the supplementary and quasi-transcendental – hence, undecidable limit of a speculative totality – resists it by *remaining*. *Remaining* is the structure of that which simultaneously adds itself to, and withdraws itself from, a self-identical and self-present totalization. As Derrida has noted in *Spurs*, the structure of *remaining* prevents all essential identification, in other words it escapes the 'assured horizon of a hermeneutic question'.[31]

> Such *remaining* is not caught up in any circular trajectory. It knows of no proper itinerary which would lead from its beginning to its end and back again, nor does its movement admit of any center. Because it is structurally liberated from any living meaning, it is always possible that it means nothing at all or that it has no decidable meaning. There is no end to its parodying play with meaning, grafted here and there, beyond any contextual body of finite code.[32]

However, from the undecidability of this structure, discussed by Derrida in *Spurs* – where his example is the Nietzschean fragment 'I have forgotten my umbrella' – and from the impossibility of determining it within the horizon of the totality to which it adds itself while subtracting itself from that totality's meaning, it does not follow that all attempts to determine the structural traits of *remaining* should be abandoned. On the contrary, such an effort 'must be carried to the furthest lengths possible', Derrida concludes.[33] *The Tain of the Mirror* has investigated and analysed instances of such *remaining* with respect to the structures that determine their undecidability, under the title of infrastructures; consequently, there is no need to take this issue up again here. Nor is there any reason to demonstrate that infrastructures characterized by *remaining* are not the speculative Other of, and thus within, absolute identity. Infrastructural *remaining* does not stand in a relation of opposition and contradiction to a speculatively identical. Hence, no reflective reappropriation of *remaining as such*, or in general, is possible. Yet, it is always possible that *remaining* be understood in terms of a remainder, initiating the dialectical process of totalization with the opposition of the non-identical to the identical. But what such a becoming 'opposite' and 'Other' of *remaining* leaves behind is, precisely, *remaining*. To this I would add: that the very undecidability of infrastructural *remaining* allows it to play the role of a condition of possibility *and* impossibility for absolute identity. The dialectical non-identical, or Other, can, of course, never acquire such status or position. The non-identical, or the Other, is a moment, and a moment is not a condition of possibility, not to mention impossibility. If the non-identical and Other inaugurate a series of dialectical inversions that ultimately culminates in the identity of identity and non-identity, infrastructural *remaining* is 'anterior' to all dialectical reversal or inversion. It is 'anterior' to it in that it will always have resisted, even in failing, having become a remainder.

Yes as a response to the call upon the Other to say *yes* to the speculative *yes* of reconciliation is one such instance of undecidable infrastructural *remaining*. It is a response demanded by the very fact that even the most absolute, that is self-inclusive, totalization involves, as a performative event, the Other and, hence, the request to say *yes*. Analysing with respect to Joyce's work what in classical philosophical terminology would be called a 'transcendental condition of all performative dimension', Derrida remarks: 'We are in an area which is *not yet* the space where the large questions of the origin of negation, of affirmation or of denegation, can and must be unfolded . . . The *yes* to which we now refer is "anterior" to all these reversible alternatives, to all these dialectics. They assume it and envelop it.'[34] Without this *yes* of the Other to whom the speculative *yes* addresses itself – and with it the entirety of the moments and movements that it comprises – speculative totalization and absolute identity would not get off the ground as an event. Yet this *yes* that the speculative and reconciling *yes* requires is not part of speculative affirmation and negation. It adds itself to all affirmations and negations that the *yes* between the extremes embraces into a whole, yet resists being added to the organization of the movements of positing and reversal. It is neither inside nor outside in any decidable manner and, for that very reason, not of the order of a non-identical Other *of* the system of identity. As such, it enables the speculative *yes* to *embrace* and reconcile the totality of what is, but it also represents the limit of such affirmation, in that it must necessarily remain excluded from what it makes possible. But, precisely because of its undecidability – of the involved *yes*'s status as neither a moment nor strictly speaking a transcendental, as neither identity nor non-identity, self nor Other – this *yes* can always slip, turning into the affirmative *yes* itself or into mere repetitive affirmation of Hegelian reconciliation. Without the possibility of slippage, no response to the call to say *yes* to *yes* is even thinkable at all. In addition, genuine response to the call to say *yes* to *yes*, and thus to a mode of thinking that is both encyclopaedic and self-inclusive, is genuine only if it remains different, even when, by respecting the force of Hegelian thought, *yes* may seem nearly identical to *yes*.

Unlike Krug's writing pen whose very insignificance makes it easy prey for dialectical reappropriation, but also unlike all the versions of Hegelian, or Adornean non-identity which either propel the system of absolute identity forward or entirely fall away from it, the *yes* of response, by answering the call, *remains* and, while enabling the system of identity, resists its own identification by it. The singularity of the *yes* of response is not that of the raw singularity that Krug's writing pen is supposed to exemplify, as opposed to what sort of pen it is, how it is constructed, who fabricated it, and so forth. It is intelligible, but of an intelligibility that includes undecidability. The *yes* of response must be a *yes* that can always be denied. Its singularity is constituted both by the possibility that it might not occur and that, if it does, its response recedes out of the reach of that to which it consents. These intelligible structural traits of the deconstructive *yes*, all by themselves and alone, explain why and how such a *yes* makes absolute identity tremble. In answering the call to say *yes* to absolute identity, *yes* has, indeed, deconstructed it. In responding to the call, the *yes* of deconstruction opens the space of Other without whose consent absolute identity as event could not spiral upwards, encircling itself and Other, and redescend into itself. By the same token, however, an outside of absolute identity has become marked, and *remains*.

Notes

1. G.W.F. Hegel, *Phenomenology of Spirit*, trans. A.V. Miller (New York: Oxford University Press, 1979) p. 409.

2. Ibid., p. 477.

3. Ibid., p. 448.

4. Ibid., p. 478.

5. Jacques Derrida, *Glas*, trans. J.P. Leavey and R. Rand (Lincoln: University of Nebraska Press, 1986) p. 291.

6. Jacques Derrida, 'Ja, ou le faux-bond', *Digraphe*, 11 (1977) p. 111 [bracketed remarks, RG].

7. Ibid., p. 94.

8. Ibid., p. 88.

9. Ibid., p. 100.

10. Jacques Derrida, *Dissemination*, trans. B. Johnson (Chicago: University of Chicago Press, 1981) p. 248.

11. G.W.F. Hegel, *Science of Logic*, trans. A.V. Miller (New York: Humanities Press, 1969) p. 74. Hereafter abbreviated in the text as *SL*.

12. For a more detailed account of absolute identity and, in particular, of how it is different from Schelling's conception of the absolute, see Dieter Henrich, 'Andersheit und Absolutheit des Geistes. Sieben Schritte auf dem Wege von Schelling zu Hegel', in *Selbstverhaltnisse* (Stuttgart: Reclam, 1982) pp. 142–72.

13. Dieter Henrich, '"Identität" – Begriffe, Probleme, Grenzen', in *Identität, Poetik und Hermeneutik*, VIII, edited by O. Marquard and K. Stierle (Munich: Fink, 1979) p. 138.

14. Ibid., p. 138.

15. Jean Hyppolite, *Logique et Existence* (Paris: Presses Universitaires de France, 1953) p. 221.

16. Such a distinction, however, encounters some difficulties that arise from Hegel's inconsistent use of the term 'absolute reflection' in *Science of Logic*. It signifies 'the domain of the Notion', i.e. 'the region of free infinitude and truth' (*SL*, 673), and is therefore sometimes called 'infinite reflection-into-self' (*SL*, 580). But absolute reflection, at times, also simply means 'reflection as such' (*SL*, 622), or 'abstract reflection' (*SL*, 499).

17. Yet, it is precisely on such a misconception of Hegel's treatment of identity in the *Greater Logic* that Slavoj Žižek bases what he deems to be a refutation of the deconstructive approach to absolute identity. In 'The Wanton Identity', a chapter from *For They Know Not What They Do. Enjoyment as a Political Factor* (London: Verso, 1991), he seeks to formulate 'a Hegelian criticism of Derrida', as well as 'a symptomatic impasse of the Derridean reading of Hegel'. Not only does this project presuppose the reductionist interpretation of Hegel alluded to, but it looks for its evidence not in Derrida's writings themselves, but in secondary sources. In a gesture reminiscent of Habermas's recourse, in *The Philosophical Discourse of Modernity*, to Jonathan Culler's interpretation of deconstructive thought and of his monological discourse of which Heinz

Kimmerle notes that in it 'the Other does not truly appear as Other, but only as supplier of additional reasonable arguments' (Heinz Kimmerle, 'Ist Derridas Denken Ursprungsphilo-sophie? Zu Habermas' Deutung der philosophischen "Postmoderne", in *Die Frage nach dem Subjekt*, edited by M. Frank, et al. [Frankfurt/Main: Suhrkamp, 1988] p. 275), Žižek uses my *The Tain of the Mirror* as the primary (if not sole) source for his understanding of Derrida's thinking. (R. Gasché, *The Tain of the Mirror: Derrida and the Philosophy of Reflection* [Cambridge, Mass.: Harvard University Press, 1986].) In the piece in question, he claims that 'although the Derridean reading misses the crucial dimension of Hegelian dialectics, the very form of its criticism of Hegel is often uncannily "Hegelian"'. First, then, Derrida (not to mention myself) is dead wrong about Hegelian dialectics because he has a common-sensical and non-sensically simplified version of absolute identity, one that resumes 'worn-out textbook platitudes'. While pretending to crack many a hard nut, nuts too hard 'to crack even for those followers of Hegel who remain fascinated by the "power of the Negative"', Žižek opposes a nondoxical, if not exotic, interpretation of Hegelian identity to such a simplistic and academic rendering of this important issue. This more Hegelian version of Hegelian identity takes off in Žižek's own words, from 'the fact that identity as such is a "reflective determination", an inverted presentation of its opposite'. Paying little attention to the minimal conditions of reasoning spelled out in Hegel's discussion of the law of identity in the very chapters of the *Greater Logic* to which Žižek turns in order to make his point, he takes Hegel's discussion of identity in 'Logic of Essence' for the latter's definite and final conception, thus creating the deceptive impression that Hegel's concept of identity is always already bereft of its absolute telos. With this thoroughly botched-up notion of identity, Žižek tries to argue that all Derridean attempts to 'set free heterogeneity from the constraints of identity' are pointless and self-defeating, since all such heterogeneities are always only inverted Others of identity itself. They have, consequently, always already 'been *taken into account*' by it. Without bothering in the least to explain how it is still possible, to begin with, that after having radically overcome all the misguided text-book platitudes about absolute identity as the One, or whole, as well as the 'notorious formulas' that define identity as the identity of identity and non-identity, he can still speak of relations of opposition, of inversions between identity and *its* Others, and especially of a coincidence of identity with *its* space of inscription, Žižek limits all possible Otherness with respect to identity to Otherness *in opposition to* identity, and hence to the Other *of* identity. Second, all the while Derrida is said to be wrong about Hegel's understanding of identity, and profoundly misled in thinking that a space of conditions of possibility and impossibility 'exterior' to absolute identity can be made out, Žižek also claims that the Derridean approach 'systematically overlooks the Hegelian character of its own basic operation'. The problem, according to Žižek, is that Derrida 'is . . . thoroughly "Hegelian"'. Indeed, he asserts that what Derrida supposedly unearthed 'through the hard work of deconstructive reading' as conditions of possibility and impossibility, is nothing other than the 'empty place of its [identity's, R.G.] "inscription"', with which identity, in a movement of reversal, coincides. Consequently, what is wrong with deconstruction is that it 'seems unable to accomplish . . . the step' of recognizing that there is no escape from the logic of binary opposition. Rather than joyfully espousing the dialectic of opposition and inversion as an iron law, as Žižek does, deconstruction fools itself by believing in the possibility that the limits of dialectical mediation can be thought. This is the delusion of deconstruction that Žižek has set out to unground. For the champion of dialectics, any such attempt falls flat on its face in that it merely confirms the logic of opposition that it sought to delimit. It is here that the high price for having overlooked the dynamics of Hegel's critical treatment of identity, and especially its retake in a non-representational mode toward the end of *Phenomenology*, or in *Science of Logic*, become evident. It is a price indicative of the extent to which, in Žižek's theory of identity, sociopsychological and psychoanalytical concepts of identity have become mixed up with its philosophical concept. The sphere beyond representation is, indeed, that of thinking. If thinking, as philosophical thinking, is the thinking of limits, then the step that Žižek's cheerful embrace of the logic of opposition is unable to accomplish is the step toward philosophical thinking.

18. Jacques Derrida, 'Before the Law', *Acts of Literature*, edited by D. Attridge (New York: Routledge, 1992) p. 211.

19. Ibid.

20. Ute Guzzoni, *Identität oder nicht. Zur kritischen Theorie der Ontologie* (Freiburg: Alber,

1981) p. 45; bracketed remarks, RG. For an excellent discussion of what Hegel calls 'moment', see pp. 38–41.

21. Ibid., p. 45.

22. G.W.F. Hegel, 'Wie der gemeine Menschenverstand die Philosophie nehme, dargestellt an den Werken des Herrn Krug', *Werke in zwanzig Banden*, Volume 2 (Frankfurt/Main: Suhrkamp, 1970), p. 194.

23. Ibid., p. 196.

24. Ibid., p. 195.

25. Guzzoni, *Identität oder nicht*, p. 105.

26. Ibid., p. 39.

27. Ibid., pp. 44–5.

28. Hegel, *Science of Logic*, p. 840.

29. Jacques Derrida, 'Ulysses Gramophone: Hear Say Yes in Joyce', *Acts of Literature*, p. 291.

30. Derrida, *Dissemination*, p. 261.

31. Jacques Derrida, *Spurs: Nietzsche's Styles*, trans. B. Harlow (Chicago: University of Chicago Press, 1978) p. 127.

32. Ibid., pp. 131–3, modified translation (RG).

33. Ibid., p. 133.

34. Derrida, 'Ulysses Gramophone', p. 298.

4

Equality at the Limit of Liberty
Claudia Hilb

Our epoch, as is well known, has presented us with a poisoned gift for the handling of our perplexities. It appears that modern political thought constantly struggles with the paradoxical structure of its questions, as if modernity itself – or more precisely, democratic modernity – were permanently inscribing its interrogations in the tension of a contradictory formulation, and in such a way that it simply cannot answer them. This article will try once more to probe these perplexities. A first version was drafted on the occasion of a conference on the relationship between liberty and equality. There I had intended to tackle head-on the theme of my particular session, 'How should equality be conceived between liberty and egalitarianism?', but whenever I focused on a strategy to follow, I suddenly had to face an unexpected fact: I imagined I was thinking about equality, though in reality I was thinking of liberty. I started from their joint possibility but found myself thinking of their impossible conjunction. I was discovering for myself the various paradoxical conundrums toward which this question inevitably led.

Making a virtue of necessity, I then set out to make my difficulties into the object of my investigation, in the hope that this would also allow me to probe a paradox which seemed to me irreducible. I was not unaware that there was something extremely banal in the statement of this paradox, but I believed – and still believe – that in and through it we can find the keys to many contemporary debates.

The Paradox

It seems banal to insist on the paradoxical relation of liberty to equality. Certainly, we have a rich legacy of texts (some of them already classics) which have illuminated this tension. Isaiah Berlin's 'Two Concepts of Liberty' is one of the prime references: few texts have stated so clearly that liberty and equality (and justice, and order) are equally basic principles, and that to coexist they have to limit each other.[1] 'No', Berlin would say to de Tocqueville, a maximum of liberty is not compatible with a maximum of equality; 'that we cannot have everything is a necessary, not a contingent, truth'.[2] Human ends are many and they come into conflict: this fits the tragic condition of human life. But it also fits human freedom. And yet, can we be satisfied with an answer that poses this necessary limitation in terms of *values*? Is this value conflict, even for Berlin, not perhaps a distinctively modern problem, derived from a world in which values are ascribed, not to a transcendent order, but to the individual?[3] May we not therefore ask in what way these tentatively related principles are inscribed in the very horizon of political modernity so that they appear as limits of each other?

Paul de Man once referred to Rousseau's *Social Contract* as an 'allegory of illegibility', a figure that deconstructs the very thing it figures; for in the illegibility of the contract the paradoxes upon which modern democracy is constructed become visible.[4] In what follows, I shall try to approach this illegibility from the point of view of the difficulty which modern political theory has in combining the two terms – liberty and equality – terms which modernity has placed on its horizon of legitimacy. The idea that a truth peculiar to modernity becomes visible in the contradictory combination of liberty and equality is thus the starting point of this survey, whose three steps may be briefly summarized with the following three questions: (i) If we conceptualize liberty as individual liberty, can we conceive equality as anything other than a limit to liberty? (ii) If we conceive liberty as individual liberty, so that we concern ourselves with the liberal individual, are we recognizing a truth of that individual? And if so, what is this truth that emerges through the liberty-bearing individual? Finally, (iii) how can we conceptualize, at one and the same time, both this truth of the liberal individual and the construction of equality as the limit of liberty? For perhaps the liberal individual only becomes legible on the horizon of an equality that figures its own limit; perhaps equality is the form in which community presents itself within modernity. I want to say yes to both those formulations. The rest of this essay will explore why that must be the case.

Let us reframe the first question in the following way: can liberty be conceived politically as an individual attribute if its limit is not thought together with this property of liberty? Or, to repeat the previous formulation: if we conceive liberty as individual liberty, can we conceive equality as anything other than a limit to liberty? In the conjunction of liberty and equality, modernity brings human coexistence into play; and, indeed, that is how we may speak of conceiving liberty politically. Already in the formulation 'equal liberty for all', which appears in classical descriptions of the state of nature, *equal* liberty appears to mark the need to institute political society, or to institute liberty, politically. In the state of nature, liberty is equal because it is unlimited, and because it is unlimited its expansion leads to war and the endangering of liberty. But liberty may be limited by the mediation of Natural Law, as it is in Locke: reason, in agreement with Natural Law, teaches that since everyone is equal and independent they should not harm one another; therefore I can do anything – but only anything which I also allow to my equals.[5] On the other hand, liberty may also be limited by reason of fear. In Hobbes, for example, liberty is unlimited in the state of nature, and only a pact among equals whereby they submit to a third force can limit it for the purposes of security. Or in Rousseau, the re-establishment of natural equality may require a pact in which natural liberty, being incapable of sustaining equality, has to transmute into conventional liberty. The same natural right of all to unlimited liberty appears to demand in every case the *political* institution of liberty that is at once guaranteed and limited by rivalry through the pact among equals. Without ignoring the differences between Hobbes and Rousseau, I want simply to emphasize here that the political institution of individual liberty entails the institution of equality – of the community of equals – as its limit. Only a state of total harmony, where unlimited liberty would go together with unfailing equality, would be able to escape this situation.

But a state of natural and lasting harmony could never explain the necessity of passing from the state of nature to the political institution of the community; if the pact is necessary it is because such harmony is always destroyed. 'Any doctrine of the state of nature and the social contract,' Pierre Manent rightly insists, 'necessarily has a Hobbesian element.'[6] I would add that this moment of conflict appears at the limit both of an individual principle of liberty and of a social principle of equality. The pact signals the impossibility of natural harmony: it is necessary because there is conflict; it is possible because it is inscribed as limit, because it inscribes equality as limit.[7]

For the moment, let us stay with the idea that, in establishing individual liberty and equality on its horizon, modernity does so in such a way that the one appears as the limit of the other. It simultaneously combines an individual natural principle (liberty) and a shared natural condition (equality). So far I have taken it for granted that liberty, as an individual attribute, is a specifically modern conception, or at least that modernity can be read, among other ways, as establishing the principle of an individual who bears individual liberty as a right. Modernity has been defined precisely as the shift from one teleological order – which assigns duties and locations to an individual who is supposed to fit into this transcending order by means of virtue – to another order whose essential moral category is not duty but right. This new order has replaced the notion of end with that of principle, which in turn coincides with the individual.[8] Or as Daniel Bell puts it:

> The fundamental assessment of modernity, the thread that has run through Western civilization since the sixteenth century, is that the social unit of society is not the group, the guild, the tribe, or the city, but the person. The Western ideal was the autonomous man who, in becoming self-determining, would achieve freedom.[9]

Political modernity and the individual go hand in hand, and the rights-bearing individual emerges in the space opened up by a political order which leaves the question of legitimacy without a substantive answer. This symbolic shift involves a break with any given meaning, with the naturalness of a tradition. 'The modern age,' writes Jean-Luc Nancy, 'was access to meaning qua will to produce meaning, whereas the age of antiquity had acceded to meaning qua disposition of the world.'[10] Political modernity – that which bears 1776 and 1789 as its inaugural dates – inscribes free and equal individuals on its horizon of legitimacy. But it hardly seems necessary to dwell on this point; I think there is sufficient agreement about it, both among those who hold by the negative liberty peculiar to this modern individual, and among those who, while criticizing the reduction of the idea of liberty to an individual attribute vis-à-vis political power, nevertheless recognize that this image is the one that modernity projects of itself. To put it somewhat differently: the liberty-bearing modern individual is not a natural figure but is politically instituted by democratic modernity; we may consider the anthropological premisses underlying this individual to be true or false, but even if we consider them to be false we cannot deny that in some way they signal a truth of our contemporary society.

This brings us to the second question. How can we say that these anthropological premisses of the liberal individual signal a truth if, at the same time, we base ourselves on the historicity of the modern conception of the individual? It seems to me that this question may be approached in two ways. First, we may think that in its historicity the establishment of the rights-bearing individual on the horizon of modernity helps to force that same individual to extend its rights and to assert its prerogatives. According to this view, then, the individual is an invention of the modernity that has imposed itself as our contemporary reality and, in this realm of the individual, there is a fundamental truth that we might call epochal: the individual as self-realization, as self-production, emerges as the centre of the modern world. This self-understanding of modernity – that of an individual producing its world – may be read in an optimistic or a pessimistic key. The optimistic version grasps this self-understanding as an inescapable and incontrovertible fact, makes it the starting point for thought about the political problems of our age, and therefore bases its conception of liberty and equality upon the fact of the individual. Among contemporary thinkers, we might again mention Isaiah Berlin and John Rawls who, though otherwise quite distinct, resemble each other in their suggestive treatment of this problem. Unlike Nozick,[11] for example, neither denies the historical character of the individual from which they start. The more pessimistic attitude to this self-understanding of modernity as self-production of the individual, and one much more critical with regard to its future, considers that the erection of the individual into an unconditioned centre is essentially a loss and, at times, an almost monstrous aberration of the human condition. In various ways we can recognize here communitarian theorists; but as well, we can recognize Hannah Arendt, with her dark vision of the subordination of action to the realm of production and labour, or Leo Strauss with his attempt to recover a natural law that will resist the advance of the realm of the conquering individual.[12]

On the other hand, and as a second point, it could be argued that there is another way of conceiving a truth inherent in modernity, a way which does not simply take the individual for granted as a fact of modernity. This involves asking whether, in the emergence of the modern individual, there is not a truth that transcends its mere facticity; whether, in modernity and the institution of the modern individual, there is not something that becomes visible to us even at the cost of making other things obscure; something which was not visible in that way before. If this is so, then modernity confronts us with a truth whose appearance illuminates with a new light our understanding of the past – that is, a truth which reveals itself in its historicity while transcending it.

Is the emergence of this modern individual, or, rephrased, is it not perhaps the very movement of emerging, that makes itself visible to us? 'Being in its history has released [*délivré*] the historicity or historiality of Being', says Jean-Luc Nancy in *L'Expérience de la liberté*; we have reached 'the end of any kind of grounding relationship between Being and history'.[13] This is echoed by Claude Lefort: 'Democracy shows itself to be the historical society *par excellence*, the society whose form admits and preserves indeterminateness';[14] it is that preserving of indeterminateness which is new in our political modernity, in our modern democracy. It is a 'historical society *par excellence*'; but it is so in two senses: (i) given that its legitimacy always hinges upon human enunciation, it does not succeed in covering the traces of its institution or advent *in* history; (ii) because it preserves this defect in its form, and because the instance of law is separated from that of power, it does not succeed in solidifying the fusion between form and content, which continues *to write its history*. Our epoch reveals and preserves in its form the lack of an ultimate foundation for all order, all identity, all happening; what our history reveals to us is historicity.

Preserving this lack of foundation, it only half obscures it in a meta-principle: people are born free and equal by right. This principle, whereby men and women assign to themselves that which is at once their own nature and the foundation of order, reveals at the same time the hanging of legitimacy upon its enunciation, its debt of plenitude. The legitimacy of the institution of the political is made to hang, but the reign of pure positivity is not thereby installed. In hanging the legitimacy of order upon this 'self-assignation of the natural',[15] political modernity establishes as its horizon the possibility – or even more, the legitimacy – of the question concerning the humanly natural, concerning the legitimate order. In this sense, there is a truth of modernity which can be read in the impossibility of concealing the instituted character of every order and every identity, its non-naturalness, its lack of an ultimate foundation. But there is another side to this truth: the lack of an ultimate foundation cannot be reduced to mere facticity; any order, any society has to face up to the question of its origin and legitimacy. The lack of an ultimate foundation does not do away with the question, nor does it answer it. Rather, it instals the question as a question, rendering it manifest. And what is heard in this question is the enigma of an institution which does not allow itself to be reduced to empirical existence or to transcendence – the enigma of a form of human coexistence which is not welded together outside human beings but which does transcend them and is not identical with their immediate existence.

What is it in human coexistence, then, that takes shape this side of transcendence and the other side of immanence? What is the truth that reveals itself to us in its historicity? Answer: what modernity makes visible to us is the enigma of institution displayed in the dual movement of the institution of an institutor, the advent of an actor, the acquisition of freedom by a free being. The individual arrives, and arrives as producer of itself and of its world. Modernity is the flashing of the limit; it is display of the limit of the institution and the instituted. Hannah Arendt, who is justifiably often considered anti- or pre-modern, is perhaps more than that. At the end of the preface to her *Between Past and Future*, in which the gap between the two is described as the space where liberty appears, she asserts that as the thread of tradition weakened and finally snapped,

> the gap between past and future ceased to be a condition peculiar only to the activity of thought and restricted as an experience to those few who made thinking their primary business. It became a tangible reality and perplexity for all; that is, it became a fact of political relevance. [Modernity displays the limit:] the gap becomes a fact of political relevance.[16]

From this rift – within this limit – emerges the figure of the individual, at once institutor and instituted. Modernity establishes individual liberty and equality on its horizon, and it does so in such a way that the one appears as limit of the other. For it supports the enigma of institution, of community, over free and equal human beings; and there, in its figuration of free and equal human beings, it shelters both indeterminacy and permanence, individual and community, motion and stability.

Within the conception of the liberty-bearing individual, community is given in the figure of equality. The modern, liberty-bearing individual is inscribed in community through the limit of his or her liberty, through equality. The individual appears as an instituting of community, so that equality stands out as a limit to the liberty of the individual. If to think politics is to think coexistence, we can say that it is *in* and *through* this limit that politics is thinkable within the world of the liberal individual. On the other hand, if we must think of the individual as *emerging* as well *from a specific form of the manifestation of coexistence*; if, in thinking of the individual, we do not have hidden from us the movement whereby the political is instituted in this form of singularity; clearly then, individual liberty must be thought together with its limit – it must be thought together with the equality that inscribes singularized liberty as a partition or division between human beings. If the community as coexistence has to appear desubstantivized and fragmented in singularity – that is, as always incapable of being represented as essence or transcendence – it will be able to appear only as a limit of the individual and of individual liberty. Individual liberty is an irreducible break in the (non-substantial) web of community. And community – in the figure of equality – becomes, at once, the space of irruption and limit, at once the condition of possibility and the condition of impossibility for the deployment of liberty. Plurality – and what term other than plurality would express an equality that does not cancel singularity? – cannot be represented except as limit. It is the temporal flashing of liberty which irrupts and interrupts the space of equality. It is equality, the stage-presentation of plurality, which never ceases to constitute itself as limit.

The institution of the political in the realm of the liberal individual is thinkable – no, *politics* in the realm of the liberal individual is thinkable – only if the erection of liberty as an individual attribute is understood as a break on the ground of a desubstantivized community, as that which only irrupts *among* men and presents itself as singularization. This, in my view, is precisely how we should understand Hannah Arendt when, with reference to action (and we know how for her, action and liberty combine in the same harmonics), she says that people recognize one another on the public stage as equal and distinct; or when she makes of individual liberty a late resultant of original liberty, which is appearance on a public stage of equals. And perhaps it is also one of the forms in which we can read Carl Schmitt's statement that only theories which assume a people to be 'evil' are capable of thinking politics. This might be reformulated as follows: any political theory in order that it be *political* must think coexistence, community and otherness. *If we start from individual liberty we will be able to think politics only if we simultaneously think a limit to that liberty*, a limit figured by the other or others. Perhaps not necessarily taking 'man as evil', but certainly taking as a given thought focused on limits, does seem to be a condition for thinking politics in the realm of the individual.[17] To return to Nozick, it seems to me that the irresolvable difficulties blocking the path in *Anarchy, State and Utopia* are bound up with the impossibility of deriving the state from individual liberty, politics from the individual, and of making community a product. What Nozick finds impossible is to pass from individual to community through an extension of the individual; what is inaccessible is thought of the collective which is not at the same time thought of the limit.[18]

Now, I mentioned earlier that plurality cannot be represented except as the limiting of liberty by equality, and of equality by liberty. But in the movement that institutes the free individual, the revelation of singularity may conceal the institution of the individual as equality. The modern individual may thus remain in the grip of his or her image, leaving in oblivion the movement by which he or she is generated. It is in this movement – which imposes the individual as centre, as self-creation – that one side of what we are shown is actually concealed from us. Not to see the conditions of the political grounding of the individual, not to see equality as the constitutive limit of individual liberty can involve a twin-track subjection: either to the naturalness of the market or to the logic of conspiracy – a subjection either conceived as utterly external and natural, or entirely self-constituted as will. For if the grounding dimension of equality as community is left out of the first account, this original limit is naturalized and replaced by the invisible hand of the market; or, to take the other track, all people are evil, only tainted interests exist, power is the law of the strongest, and so forth, as the only alternative vision available. Cynicism is the realism of the isolated individual of mass society: it is impossible to conceive of plurality; and the only common space is a battlefield.[19] Both forms, in their different ways, are a cancellation of the distance between the individual and his or her world: the first with respect to the absolute exteriority of the individual; the second, with respect to interiority without a plural dimension. Both therefore represent the will to cancel – to reduce to one of its terms – the founding paradox of democratic modernity.

Equality, Liberty, Memory

We have, then, a final rupturing of community, one which marks, un-reservedly, the death of individual singularity; for only on the ground of plurality can the individual stand out as unique. 'We have abolished the real world: what world is left? the apparent world, perhaps? . . . But no! *with the real world we have also abolished the apparent world.*'[20] There is no choice to be made between individual and community, between the liberty of the ancients and the liberty of the moderns, between equality and liberty. As we have learnt from those who thought about such things earlier and better than ourselves, we can do nothing other than continue to ruminate over this paradox itself so as to keep illuminated the limits of its possibility.

Today, in my view, we cannot turn backward beyond the modern individual, nor, to be frank, would it be desirable. But we may perhaps rediscover in individual liberty the marks of the political grounding of the individual on equality. To rediscover the marks of equality in the institution of liberty means to remember the space in which liberty opens out as irruption. Memory of this space is equality qua locus of liberty. It is the memory of the advent of liberty which always presents itself in men and women as *among* fellow-humans; that is, it always presents itself as a singularization of a shared condition.

Notes

1. Isaiah Berlin, 'Two Concepts of Liberty', in *Four Essays on Liberty* (Oxford: OUP, 1969).

2. Ibid., p. 170.

3. 'In other words, it seems to me that the issue of individual freedom had not clearly emerged at this stage [in ancient Greece] . . .; the central value attached to it may, perhaps . . . be the late product of a capitalist civilization, an element in a network of values that includes such notions as personal rights, civil liberties, the sanctity of the individual personality, the importance of privacy, personal relations and the like'. Berlin, 'Introduction' to ibid., p. xli.

4. Paul de Man, *Allegories of Reading: Figural Language in Rousseau, Nietzsche, Rilke and Proust* (New Haven: Yale University Press, 1979), ch. 11. Although it is in Rousseau that this illegibility is inscribed with the greatest force at each point in the text, I agree with J.-P. Dupuy that 'nearly all the great thinkers of modernity have given us two opposing and disconnected visions of the individual, whose articulation within their work has posed serious problems for them'. ('L'Individu libéral, cet inconnu: d'Adam Smith à Friedrich Hayek', in John Rawls, ed., *Individu et justice sociale* [Paris: 1988] p. 75.) As Dupuy also points out, this duality coincides with the one identified by Gauchet in modern conceptions of equality: M. Gauchet, 'L'École à l'école d'elle-même', *Le Débat*, 37, November 1985.

5. C.B. Macpherson has shown how the limitations based on equality that Locke sets to the natural right to property are overcome with the introduction of money. I think that, far from solving the question, Locke here explicitly reintroduces the duality to which Dupuy refers (see n. 4 above). *The Political Theory of Possessive Individualism* (Oxford: OUP, 1962), esp. pp. 203–20.

6. P. Manent, *Histoire intellectuelle du libéralisme* (Paris: 1987). In my view, one of the sublime formulations of this passage is that which Leo Strauss offers in his comments on Carl Schmitt's 'concept of the political': 'Hobbes differs from full-grown liberalism only by what he regards as the obstacle against which the liberal ideal of civilization is to be established in a determined fight: the obstacle is not corrupt institutions or the ill will of a ruling stratum, but man's natural malice. Hobbes established liberalism in an illiberal world against the (*sit venia verbo*) illiberal nature of man, whereas his successors, ignoring their presuppositions and goals, trust in the original goodness of human nature . . .'. Strauss, 'Comments on Carl Schmitt's *Der Begriff des Politischen*', in Carl Schmitt, *The Concept of the Political*, trans. and notes by George Schwab, with comments by Leo Strauss (New Brunswick: Rutgers University Press, 1976) pp. 89–90.

7. It is true that equality, in its institution as limit, may absorb or cancel individual liberty: that is, absorb it into the General Will, through cancellation of the particular interest and fusion within a single will. Or it may be an equality of submission to the only free one, the Leviathan. It is also true that individual liberty may be conceived in some other way than as limited by equality, in an effort to break the modern inheritance from Natural Law. It may be conceived, for instance, as limited not by an original equality but by a constitutive difference or irreducible otherness, as in Carl Schmitt. Or it may be unlimited – and for that very reason, incapable of being articulated politically – as in a number of modern ultraliberal writers. But I shall return to this later.

8. See Leo Strauss, *Political Philosophy: Six Essays*, edited with introduction by Hilail Gildin (Indianapolis: Pegasus, 1975), and also, of course, his *Natural Right and History* (Chicago: University of Chicago Press, 1965) esp. ch. 5a.

9. Daniel Bell, *The Cultural Contradictions of Capitalism*, 2nd edn (London: Heinemann Educational, 1979) p. 16.

10. Jean-Luc Nancy, *L'Oubli de la philosophie* (Paris: Galilée, 1986) p. 39.

11. Nozick begins his *Anarchy, State and Utopia* (New York: Basic Books, 1974) by affirming the following: 'Individuals have rights, and there are things no person or group may do to them (without violating their rights)' (p. ix). I shall return below to the inescapable problems that seem to face Nozick as a result of certain theoretical-historical anachronisms.

12. I agree with Albrecht Wellmer when he says that for communitarian theorists, 'the anthropological premisses of individualist conceptions are profoundly false and have *not proved true* in any sense within modern bourgeois society'. (Wellmer, 'Modèles de la liberté dans le monde moderne', *Critique*, 505–506, June/July 1989, p. 510.) This 'pessimistic' view of the modern individual often leads to the theme of a 'return' to the natural law of antiquity, to Machiavelli, to the republican tradition, and so on.

13. Jean Luc Nancy, *L'Expérience de la liberté* (Paris: Galilée, 1988) p. 20.

14. Claude Lefort, *Essais sur le politique (XIXe–XXe siècles)* (Paris: Seuil, 1986) p. 25.

15. I take this expression from Lefort, ibid., p. 51. My whole development of this point is deeply indebted to the work of Lefort. With regard to this self-assignation of a right which enunciates itself as prior to its enunciation, see also the lecture by Jacques Derrida published under the title *Otobiographies: l'enseignement de Nietzsche et la politique du nom propre* (Paris: Galilée, 1984): 'In signing, the people says, and does what it says it does, but by deferring it through its representatives whose signature is fully legitimized only by the signature, therefore after the event: henceforth I have the right to sign, and in fact I will already have had it because I was able to give it to myself. . . . There was no signatory, *de jure*, before the text of the Declaration, which itself remains the producer and guarantor of its own signature. Through this fabulous event, through this fable which implies traces and is in reality possible only because a present does not correspond to itself, a signature gives itself a name' (pp. 22–3).

16. Hannah Arendt, *Between Past and Future* (Harmondsworth: Penguin, 1977) p. 14. It may seem contradictory that Hannah Arendt is located amongst those who see in the modern individual an 'almost monstrous' aberration of the human condition (see above) and amongst those who read in the break of modernity the *mise-en-scène* of a formerly invisible truth. This dual location is not fortuitous; it reflects the ambivalent, or even contradictory, position with regard to modernity that runs throughout Arendt's work.

17. Leo Strauss's well-known accusation against Schmitt in the above-mentioned commentary on 'the concept of the political' is precisely that, in failing to propose a substantive definition of 'the natural', Schmitt remains immersed in liberal thought and its characteristic inability to escape from a polemical definition of its concepts. Personally, I consider that it is here – where Schmitt shows himself to be an eminently modern thinker – that his greatest interest lies for political thought.

18. The first difficulty is to justify the process of appropriation according to the right of the first occupier – given that, for this process to be legitimate, there must always exist the possibility that others will appropriate similar goods. As Locke already knew, this makes illegitimate the appropriation of the last piece of ground or the last good (since it would leave other people without an equal possibility), and logically this should also apply to the next-to-last appropriation, and so on, until one returns to the first. Finding this problem impossible to solve, Nozick eventually appeals to the status quo. The second difficulty is with the theoretical legitimacy (within Nozick's framework) of passing from the ultra-minimal to the minimal state – that is, from voluntary to obligatory association. Here the break implied by the obligation of submitting to the state appears unjustifiable on the basis of Nozick's premisses.

19. This is what Sloterdijk affirms: 'anonymity . . . is becoming the great open space of cynical deviation. The modern cynic is unintegrated and non-social.' Quoted and translated from the French edition: P. Sloterdijk, *Critique of Cynical Reason*, trans. Michael Eldred (Minneapolis: University of Minnesota Press, 1987).

20. Friedrich Nietzsche, 'How the "Real World" At Last Became a Myth', *Twilight of the Idols* (Harmondsworth: Penguin, 1968) section IV, p. 41. Emphases in the original.

PART II

5

Social Ambiguity and the Crisis of Apartheid

Aletta J. Norval

[I]f 'it is a long time since there were so many grounds for hoping that everything will turn out well', at the same time 'there have never been so many reasons for us to fear that, if everything went wrong, the catastrophe would be final'.

VACLAV HAVEL[1]

The significance of Havel's remarks on the situation in Eastern Europe, made in the context of a speech condemning the totalizing nature of the discourses shaping those societies, certainly extends beyond its specific context of utterance. His condemnation of the artificial gods of modernity who, on Sayer's reading, have 'stolen, by divine right of ideology, decades of people's lives, hopes and dreams',[2] finds a wider resonance today – both in the theoretical arena where the crisis of grand narratives has been at the centre of interpretative controversies, and in the specific context of discussions surrounding the crisis of apartheid and the nature of a possible post-apartheid settlement. This article attempts to bring together these two areas of concern, since, as is clear from the events in Eastern Europe and now in Southern Africa, the crisis of grand narratives has produced effects within – which have also continued to reverberate throughout – the political imaginaries ordering our everyday existence.

In contrast to the almost triumphalist optimism of commentators such as Fukuyama, my reading of the current crisis of the dominant political imaginaries and its implications for apartheid society leave room only for a cautious optimism. This is the result of the continued presence of a certain enduring logic, a logic that, arguably, forms one of the most disturbing aspects of the legacy of apartheid. Apartheid, one may say, is its highest expression; and yet it is a logic which draws on and feeds off much wider metaphysical discourses. Thus it will be suggested that while in one sense we are witnessing the 'end' of apartheid, in another the very logic of apartheid continues to exercise a destructive hold over society. We are not yet, and might not for some time to come, be in what may properly be called a 'post-apartheid' situation. The latter would require a break with the more general logics of apartheid, and this is not easily effected.

Thoughts on the Crisis

It has often been observed by commentators on the crisis in South Africa that the past decade witnessed the burgeoning of what is undoubtedly the most pronounced political crisis in recent South African history. By now it is a commonplace to argue that since the late 1970s the apartheid state has faced a sustained and deepening crisis of legitimation. However, events in South Africa since then have been subject to a bewildering diversity of interpretations. One of the aims of this article is to suggest a principle of reading that might facilitate not only an alternative interpretation of the crisis itself, but also a means of moving beyond the signs of an impasse present on a theoretical level.

One possible way into (and perhaps out of) the labyrinth of explanations and interpretations, is to disaggregate the issues involved into two broadly related sets of questions. The first concerns the nature of the crisis itself, that is, whether it is an organic or merely a cyclical crisis; the other, the nature of the 'system' perceived to be in crisis. With respect to the first criterion, accounts have tended to divide into two groups, either suggesting that the crisis is of a generalized nature, permeating most domains of the social or, alternatively, that the crisis is strictly limited to one region of the social, namely the economy.[3] Most accounts, however, share the view that the crisis is *not* of a partial, cyclical nature, and therefore not simply a regular feature of the capitalist system. Rather, it is regarded as a generalized, highly overdetermined *organic crisis* characterized by its extreme duration, and involving a collapse of hegemony in both the political and economic spheres. With respect to the second criterion – wherein the nature of the system is deemed to be in crisis – closer scrutiny reveals remarkable differences: the crisis has been depicted as a crisis of the *apartheid system*, or of the system of *racial domination*, or of *racial capitalism*, or of a specific *mode of accumulation*, and so on.[4]

Most of these accounts, while rich in historical and empirical detail, seemed to be marred by an inability to provide a consistent theoretical principle of reading. This could be ascribed to a number of factors, of which I would like to consider two. First, as I have indicated, any attempt to come to terms with the nature of the crisis is complicated by the fact that the character of the system considered to be in crisis is the subject of a particularly acute conflict of interpretations. In this sense, accounts of the crisis have tended to reproduce problems inherent in the theoretical traditions utilized in the analysis of the nature of social division in South Africa. These problems are *not* specific to explanations of the crisis, but are the effects of the broader theoretical traditions from which they are drawn.

Second, it has to be said that there is often a serious omission in these accounts having to do with the absence of investigating and theorizing the phenomenon of *crisis* as such. For what is it that one refers to when one speaks of a crisis? Some have depicted a situation of crisis as an extraordinary or abnormal situation, characterized by acute tension, great uncertainty, an element of surprise or a feeling that a watershed has been reached. But what I want to suggest is that the element of uncertainty has a specific importance for our discussion, for it marks a context that is defined by its own undecidability, a turning-point, as it were – but one where the outcome is not predetermined.[5] One could say that the situation of crisis marks an *undecidable* terrain, one that accounts not only for the immediate eruptions of antagonisms and the attempts of the forces of resistance to turn events in their favour, but also marks the terrain in which persistent efforts will be made to conserve and defend the existing order of things.[6]

Many of the accounts based on a Gramscian perspective have highlighted one or more of these aspects. Yet, the notion of crisis as such, as well as the relation between the event of crisis (and the discursive responses to it), have not been addressed.[7] In most cases Gramsci is cited as an authority on organic crisis, without any further discussion of the matter at hand. This is obviously not a satisfactory way of proceeding, since the process of citation covers over a silence in the meta-discourse at this point. While a proliferation of explanations of the crisis is offered, these explanations remain of the order of *enumeration*, listing symptoms and effects of the crisis, but being unable to construct a coherence between them on the grounds of a theoretical narrative. One of the commentators, Murray, has addressed the radical insufficiency of explanation by enumeration, arguing that the 'inventory of observable symptoms' (for him, meagre growth-rates, recession, bankruptcies, un-employment and so forth) merely signifies the 'physiognomy of the organic crisis', and that '... a catalogue of social indicators cannot substitute a rigorous analysis of the anatomical nature of the crisis'.[8]

While agreeing with the sentiment (that a listing of indicators cannot fulfil the function of providing an explanation), I would differ from Murray by offering a possible solution based on a distinction *other than* the one proposed between the general appearance or 'physiognomy' of the crisis and a deeper structural or 'anatomical' analysis. The reason a different set of distinctions is necessary is because it is not only the theorization of the crisis, but the manner in which one thinks about the nature of the system that becomes relevant. At this point, then, it is necessary to turn to the question of the *logic* of apartheid discourse, though it might immediately be asked whether, if by focusing on the logic of the *apartheid* discourse, the question at stake is not prejudged. In answering that question – why we must focus on *apartheid* discourse – I would simply suggest that, rather than closing off discussion, it will pave the way for a series of important issues to be raised directly and addressed.

The Logic of Apartheid

APARTHEID: by itself the word occupies the terrain like a concentration camp. Systems of partition, barbed wire, crowds of mapped out solitudes. Within the limits of the mark, the glaring harshness of the abstract essence (*heid*) seems to speculate in another realm of abstraction, that of confined separation. The word concentrates on separation. It institutes, declares, writes, inscribes . . . A system of marks, it outlines in space in order to assign residence or close off borders. It does not discern, it discriminates.[9]

DERRIDA

To classify means to set apart, to segregate. It means first to postulate that the world consists of discrete and distinctive entities; then to postulate that each entity has a group of similar or adjacent entities with which it belongs, and with which – together – it is opposed to some entities . . . To classify is to give the world a structure.[10]

BAUMAN

It has been argued by Sayer that the revolution in Prague could be seen as a revolution against modernity in so far as it was based on a rejection of the totalizing representations (of categories such as class, nation and so forth) fostered by modernity.[11] He argues, furthermore and precisely in the context of modernity, that the revolutions of 1989 are not to be considered as a 'return to the fold of "the West" [as] hailed by politicians from Thatcher to Bush, but [as] something quite new: a "post-modern revolution" . . .'[12]

In a recent response, commenting on Derrida's article in *Critical Inquiry*, Fynsk addresses a series of very similar issues with regard to the relation between apartheid and 'the West'.[13] In so doing, he opens up space for discussion around the analytic ways one may come to terms with the phenomenon of apartheid or to think through and imagine the nature of a post-apartheid society. Fynsk's argument leads to the heart of the question at stake: namely the logic of the discourse of apartheid. He suggests that the existence of apartheid raises significant questions for Western political thought in that it speaks to something already existing in the political discourse of the West.[14] The resonance between apartheid and certain European discourses on race, he argues, 'speaks the essence of a racism that is Western in its provenance and final form'.[15] Apartheid, in this account, is an exemplary discourse in two senses: first, because it is 'the most racist of racisms'; it is racism *par excellence*; and second, because the very form this racism takes exemplifies an extreme identitary logic, at least inasmuch as it can portray itself, in its essence, as 'self-sufficient, separate, intact, independent', identical to itself, and uncontaminated by any relation to alterity.[16] It is this aspect of the apartheid discourse that contains the seeds of the problem to be located at the heart of the discourse of Western metaphysics, and it is here that its wider importance lies. While I will not pursue the question of essentiality and its relation to Western metaphysics at length, some remarks in this respect, nevertheless, are crucial for an understanding of the nature and character of apartheid discourse.

In brief, then, the argument is one that attempts to link apartheid to 'a certain European discourse on race' – as well as to the wider domain of Western metaphysics – by drawing out the logic inherent in its construction. This is what I have called the *identitary logic*: the logic of what is involved in the process of identity construction, in its broadest sense, wherein the impossibility of bridging the gap between identification and the reaching of a fully fledged identity, is denied. Against such an identitary logic, the possibility of developing a more democratic logic of identity construction, one that recognizes the peculiar logic of a 'never-sutured identity', will be held out. Identitary logic, I would suggest, is precisely what Sayer is referring to in his discussion of the totalizing representations of modernity – and it is also where much of Derrida's critique of Western metaphysics is aimed.[17] What is important at this point is to draw out the political implications for thinking the logic of apartheid discourse from within this terrain of theoretical critique. In this respect, there are two issues which are of particular relevance and which deserve more detailed comment. The first concerns the way in which apartheid has constituted itself as a discourse; and here it is important to look at its relation to otherness.[18] The second concerns the more mundane (but nevertheless crucial) question as to whether it is at all possible to delimit the 'essence' of apartheid. These two questions come together for me in discussions of the logic of apartheid.

Let us start with the latter of the two, namely whether it is possible and desirable to delimit the 'essence' of apartheid discourse. It is here that I would like to return to Derrida's intervention and to Fynsk's response. In a text accompanying an art exhibition destined to find its place in a post-apartheid society, Derrida states that apartheid can be thought of as a system of marks that outlines space in order to 'assign forced residence or closed off borders'.[19] Though these themes, particularly around the notion of place and the borders drawn to assign people to their rightful 'locations', will be taken up later, the particular point Derrida wants to make, however, concludes with the following statement: 'It [apartheid] does not discern, it discriminates.'[20]

'It does not discern, it discriminates.' Most commentators on apartheid society would agree with this description without any hesitation. And in that sense, the undeniably discriminatory and repressive nature of apartheid is directly affirmed as its essence. However, as I have indicated, the nature of apartheid has been the object of long and bitter contestation, not least since the very determination of its essence has prefigured, in some way, the appropriate response to it. The specificity of characterizations of apartheid society is therefore of essential importance, for it is in and through them that the division of social and political spaces and the emergence of antagonisms are accounted for. The extent to which the widely divergent literature on South African history and politics has displayed an inattention to questions such as the delimitation of apartheid from other social practices, its periodization and so forth, is all the more curious in this light. Its 'essential' nature has been portrayed by some as racial, while others have contended that the racial definition is a mere facade for more profound class differentials. Even the more sophisticated attempts to think the nature of apartheid in terms of an interrelation between race and class have been less than successful in their endeavours to construct coherent theoretical accounts.[21] The proliferation of discourses on apartheid does not therefore necessarily indicate an increasing understanding of this phenomenon. On the contrary, 'apartheid' may have become so naturalized, what we mean by it so obvious, that it has become an empty signifier, signifying everything and yet nothing.[22]

There is a certain danger inherent in this emptying out of our understanding of apartheid, for in the context of the organic crisis of the past decade, the more recent prospects of a negotiated settlement, and the dismantling of apartheid itself, the question as to the 'nature' of 'the system' is raised once more. In the midst of discussions on the form of post-apartheid society, the need for a retroactive understanding of apartheid, and the division of the social accompanying it, have emerged with renewed urgency. It is in this sense that I would argue that the nature and history of apartheid discourse can best be understood in and through an investigation of the precise manner in which it has drawn political frontiers.[23] However, the possibility of thinking the division of the social in terms of political frontiers emerges only once social division is no longer thought of as determined by a pre-existing objective space. Two possibilities are therefore logically ruled out. The first is a situation in which social division is theorized with reference to an empirical distribution of individuals in the process of production. The second is where social division is thought to correspond to pre-existing political units such as, for instance, the nation-state. Thinking social division in terms of political frontiers thus becomes increasingly important in situations where the political identities, emerging as a result of the division of the social, do not correspond naturalistically to predesignated elements, but can clearly be seen to emerge as a result of a particular project's attempt to construct social and political identities in a specific manner. Political and social identities, on this reading, are subject to *political* contestation and construction.

Here is the claim I want to advance in terms of this process of identity construction: that all identity is constituted through an *externalization* of the other via the drawing of political frontiers. This can be formalized in theoretical terms. Briefly, it involves the assertion that the process of identity formation cannot be thought merely in terms of an elaboration of a set of features characteristic of a certain identity. As has been remarked already, an enumeration of positive characteristics will not suffice in individuating an identity, or in delineating its essence.[24] In order to achieve that, an additional element is needed; namely, the positing of an 'other' which is constituted as opposed to the identity in the process of construction.[25] This positing of an other is what allows for the closure that facilitates the individuation; or in Smith's terms, the 'cerning' of a particular identity.[26]

This focus on the process of identity formation via the construction of political frontiers must play the role assigned by Foucault to 'effective history'; that is, its purpose is not to 'discover the roots of our identity but to commit ourselves to its dissipation'.[27] Therefore one needs to follow a double strategy in a Derridean sense; one needs to 'feign obedience to the tyrannical system of rules, while simultaneously laying traps for it in the form of problems that it is at a loss to settle'.[28] It is in this respect that Fynsk's remark that apartheid portrays itself as 'self-sufficient, separate, intact and independent', takes on its full significance. For the presumed innocence of this discourse has to be unmasked. The process of unmasking, however, cannot simply take place by rejecting identitary logic constitutive of apartheid discourse. Neither can the solution be found by moving to a so-called 'deeper' level. Rather, since we need to employ strategies which will weaken its effects, one way to achieve this is by showing how the moment of institution of discursive formations – such as that of apartheid – always involves a reference to the other. We need to show how the possibility of creating any identity at all is related to the exclusion, and in many cases the silencing of the other. Indeed it can be said that the contradiction between the pretence to self-containedness and the fact that the self could only be constructed by the exclusion of an other, lies at the heart of apartheid discourse. It is in this logic that I would wish to locate the 'essence of apartheid' as an identitary discourse centrally concerned with a certain constitution and affirmation of social and political identities.

It is important, though, not to oversimplify the issue. The political frontiers of apartheid discourse, constituting political identities and dividing the social, correspond simply neither to racial nor to class divisions. Rather, the division of the social, which has taken the form of a *dichotomization* of political spaces, cuts across these boundaries in a fashion that forces us to go beyond any notion of objectively given divisions. This characteristic of apartheid discourse is perhaps the reason for many of the difficulties in accounting for it, since the construction of frontiers is always an ambiguous process in which the logics of inclusion and exclusion do not operate along clear-cut lines. Thus, it would be a mistake to think of frontiers in terms of a stark and absolute inside–outside division. The model of a simple 'friend–enemy' or 'us–them' division is wholly inadequate to thinking the complex strategies involved in the creation of social division. This is particularly clear in the case of apartheid discourse where much of its effectivity has relied upon a series of strategies fashioning sophisticated distinctions such that the same 'empirical' subject could be regarded as both forming a part of the systems of differences making up the dominant bloc, and as being excluded as 'other', as the 'enemy'.

It is thus not simply the case that political frontiers change over time, but that they may be differentially constructed with reference to a singular set of subjects at one particular point in time. This possibility emphasizes, once more, the importance of not relying on so-called 'natural' or 'objectively given' divisions in doing political analysis – for political frontiers do not exist as the internal and closed moments of a particular discourse. The establishment of and changes in political frontiers result from complex processes of interaction of different and opposing discourses; in Gramscian terms, from wars of position. Moreover, then, if any identity is necessarily constructed with reference to another, that other cannot be regarded as merely passive – otherwise our reading could only reproduce the type of silencing of the other for which liberal histories written in the South African context have been criticized.[29] Rather, the constitutive outside – brought into being through the drawing of boundaries – functions as both a condition of possibility and as a condition of impossibility of identity and objectivity. That is to say, the constitutive outside of any order has the capacity to put into question the very identity which is constituted through its externalization.

This can be illustrated with reference to the transformist project initiated by the National Party in the early 1980s. Following Gramsci's analytic remarks, it could be argued that the transformist action of this period, which aimed at creating an ever more extensive dominant bloc, consisted in efforts to expand the systems of difference defining that dominant bloc.[30] This project, in a nutshell, initially involved two clear-cut elements: (i) the co-optation of the so-called coloured and Indian sectors of the population into a tricameral parliamentary political system, and (ii) a series of strategies aimed at the co-optation of sections of the urban black population. The miserable failure of this strategy can only be understood in terms of resistances produced by the attempted redrawing of the political frontiers defining the identity of the dominant bloc. Instead of resulting in a lessening of the antagonistic potential of the excluded elements, the transformist project opened up new spaces of opposition, and – rather than limiting the development of antagonisms – led to a proliferation and deepening of antagonistic relations and ultimately to a series of important changes in the construction of political frontiers.

How, then, does this proliferation and deepening of these antagonistic relations bear on our remarks concerning the logic of apartheid discourse? Let me summarize by returning to a few of my opening remarks. First, that it is impossible in principle to define and delimit the 'essence' of apartheid in any final, objective sense. As I have proposed, instead, we direct our attention to the precise manner in which boundaries or political frontiers constitutive of apartheid are drawn in the discourse itself, where it will become clearer that social divisions do not naturally inhere in one or another facet of the system we are studying. Consequently, it becomes impossible to give one correct definition of apartheid. Not only does this mean that we must not be compelled to accept as natural or inevitable the manner in which the dominant discourse divides the social. It also means that we need to investigate the functioning and political efficacy of the construction of these divisions as well as the fashioning of social and political identities. In this manner one may attempt to overcome the anatomy–physiognomy or surface–depth structure dualism characteristic, not only of the work on the nature of apartheid but, as I have indicated, also of the current crisis.

One need only think here of the most prominent facets of the South African political landscape during 1990: the violence between Inkatha and ANC supporters which raises important questions for our understanding of the centrality of the process of identity construction. Andrew Mapheto, commenting on this, has argued that the South African media have divested the violence of any political meaning by calling it 'black on black' violence. Much the same could be said about media coverage in Britain as well. 'It is disturbing,' writes Mapheto, 'that in some areas the "ethnic conflict" view almost gained acceptance.'[31] I am in full agreement with his analysis – in so far as it constitutes a rejection of the 'ethnic conflict' view dominant in liberal discourses which tend to trace the existence of so-called 'tribal' identities back to some mythical past from which these 'natural' identities are supposed to have emerged. Rather than putting the blame at the door of so-called 'natural ethnic ties', it is necessary to investigate the historical emergence of these antagonisms which should not be seen in isolation from the whole apartheid project. Indeed, as Mapheto suggests, 'We may be justified in asking ourselves how the formulation that this violence is a Xhosa–Zulu war feeds into the politics of apartheid.'[32]

It is precisely in this respect that the argument put forward by Derrida, and indeed by most commentators on apartheid, has been lacking in a serious consideration of the power of the apartheid discourse in creating 'positive' identities of one kind or another. Contrary to Derrida's assertion, I would argue that much of the effectivity of the discourse in its construction of consent could be located in the fact that it did *not* merely discriminate; but that it aimed, and succeeded to a certain extent, in creating so-called ethnic identities and allegiances. The element of the apartheid discourse aiming at the constitution of different identities is thus crucial both for understanding the process through which it became hegemonic, as well as for understanding the present crisis. It is in this identitary logic at the heart of apartheid discourse that I would want to locate the 'essence' of apartheid. The boundary around apartheid can be *drawn* in terms of what I have called at the outset its most disturbing feature: its peculiar logic of identity construction.

Finally, it has to be emphasized that it is important to take into account the fact that the logic of apartheid cannot simply be reduced *either* to a discriminatory *or* a discerning one; it is *both* one *and* the other, and yet not reducible to either. This characteristic is what makes it unrealistic to analyse apartheid discourse in terms of its overt classificatory logics: for the latter do not succeed in capturing the ambiguity and undecidability inherent in, and at the heart of, the discourse of apartheid – an ambiguity characteristic, not only of apartheid discourse, but of modernity itself.

Reform and Crisis: State Strategies and Resistances

The ambiguities constitutive of the discourse of apartheid became ever more prominent as the very logic of the discourse was put into question during the 1980s. The extent to which this has occurred is clear from the developments to which we have been witness over the past few years. Events in Eastern Europe have not failed to make their mark on the discursive context in which resistance and dominant strategies have been articulated. As was the case in Europe, where these events have been portrayed as a return to the fold of the West, the revolutions in Eastern Europe, perhaps paradoxically, have been articulated to the discourse of the dominant bloc. In his speech to parliament in February 1990, F.W. de Klerk argued that one of the key conditions facilitating the 'unbanning' of the African National Congress (ANC), the South African Communist Party (SACP), and other proscribed organizations, stemmed directly from the economic and political upheavals in Eastern Europe. In particular, the demise of Stalinism and the collapse of the 'economic system in Eastern Europe' were utilized to warn against forcing 'this failure of a system on South Africa'.[33]

Justifying the unbannings, de Klerk stressed two factors which influenced the government in its decision. They were the 'weakened capability of organizations which were previously strongly supportive of those quarters', and the fact that these organizations 'no longer entail[ed] the same degree of threat to internal security'.[34] In the space of a few years, the enemy of the state had changed position from being part of a 'total revolutionary onslaught', to being an acceptable partner in the search for peace at the negotiating table. More recent announcements, amounting to a 'one nation thesis', confirm the extent of these changes in the construction of social division.[35] One of the central questions with regard to these changes concerns the conditions of possibility for these radical shifts in political frontiers.

Borders . . .

One way in which the production of, and shifts in, divisions may be traced is via an investigation of the formation of and changes in state strategies pertaining to the 'drawing of borders'.[36] One aspect of apartheid that has always made it more contentious than other forms of racism has been the fact that it dared allow itself to become sedimented in visible form. It declared itself to the world; it created internal boundaries and fostered the birth of new states, the so-called 'homelands'. Apartheid, in so far as it not only spoke its racism, but also physically manifested itself, called forth contestations around those very boundaries. The eighties, in this respect, witnessed one of the most successful resistance projects to the legitimacy of those boundaries in a variety of forms. With the benefit of hindsight it is possible to regard the 1980s as the decade in which an ever more extensive challenge to those boundaries occurred.

Indeed, it could well be argued that one of the most significant consequences of resistance struggles has been the effective putting into question of a fundamental form in which these boundaries have become sedimented: the division between the 'homelands' and 'white' South Africa. The beginnings of the 'ending' of apartheid, if regarded as a historically specific discourse, can be traced back to the 1970s. In 1979 the Rhikhoto case caused a stir in South Africa for it declared the permanent right of a Section 10 worker to reside in what was considered to be white urban space. The occupation of this space continued to be central to the whole terrain of contestation between the state and the resistance movements in the eighties.

Urban space . . .

After the events of 1976, the position of urban Africans became one of the main issues on the state's reform agenda.[37] Having begun to think of including the so-called coloureds and Indians within a tricameral parliament, the issue of African political participation remained to be addressed. Avoiding a direct confrontation with the problem, the state opted for a series of reforms following from the recommendations of the Wiehahn and Riekert Commissions of Inquiry.[38] With regard to the settled urban black population, Riekert proposed a distinction to be introduced between what became known as the privileged 'urban insiders' and the 'rural outsiders'. The rationale behind this distinction was to facilitate the incorporation of the urban insiders by offering them a number of previously unavailable concessions – including permanent leasehold and home-ownership schemes, and a relaxation of restrictions on occupational and geographical mobility – while simultaneously tightening the controls and mechanisms of exclusion governing the presence of temporary contract and surplus labour.[39] In this way, urban areas could be 'cleared of "idlers and undesirables", the "illegals", and those without accommodation and employment'.[40]

The split between urban insiders and rural outsiders was at the heart of a new urbanization strategy which replaced direct controls of labour movement and migration with a more insidious, indirect means of control. In place of the notorious pass laws, Riekert proposed to manage the urban black population by regulating access to housing and employment, thereby hoping to shift part of the responsibility for the control of urban migration on to employers who faced increasingly severe punitive sanctions in case they engaged in 'unlawful' employment practices. Employers thus became part of an indirect policing system. This strategy differed from traditional apartheid policy in so far as it recognized, for the first time, the rights of a limited group of Africans to reside permanently in the cities. However, as was clearly stated in the Report, the inquiry would, in addressing the problem of manpower utilization, remain 'within the framework of certain parameters which were taken as given'.[41] In short, this meant the retention of the basic principle that Africans should exercise their political rights outside 'white' South Africa in the so-called homelands. It was, moreover, assumed that Africans would continue to live in segregated areas. The tentative inclusion of segments of the African population thus clearly stayed within the boundaries of traditional apartheid structures, not putting into question the distinction between 'white South Africa' and 'the homelands' where Africans were supposed to exercise their political rights.

This attempt at economic co-optation of the urban insiders, whose position was improved at the expense of the outsiders, has to be seen in the light of broader changes in official discourse. One of the most important elements of these changes was the increasing emphasis on a depoliticized 'free-enterprise' system as a solution to many of South Africa's problems and conflicts. In the logic of this discourse, markets and the economy were presented as governed by their own 'laws'.[42] The Riekert strategy clearly fitted into this wider emphasis by removing any obstacles to the exploitation of so-called market forces, as well as by trying to depoliticize the remaining measures of control. While the emphasis on free enterprise involved, on the one hand, a much closer co-operation between the state and big business, it simultaneously necessitated the construction of a black 'middle class', 'with a stake in the system'.[43] In this way it facilitated the delimitation of a space in which an (emasculated) 'blackness' could exist legitimately within the boundaries of 'white' South Africa.

The success of the Riekert strategy depended on its ability to maintain a clear insider–outsider distinction, and in this respect its economic viability and political legitimacy were of the utmost importance. A series of factors, however, worked against the maintenance of this distinction, as well as against the logic underpinning it – against, that is to say, the division between the homelands and white South Africa. As a result of its acceptance of the homeland–white South Africa division, the Riekert Commission could not address changes in the reproductive economy which undermined the very possibility of making any clear-cut distinction between the urban and the rural African workforce. One of the most salient changes taking place at the time was the rapid growth of an urban population in the homelands which was dependent on metropolitan employment. The homelands thus no longer operated simply as 'dumping-grounds' for the 'surplus' population not needed in the central economy. The fast-developing sector of cross-border commuters, according to de Klerk, presented an anomaly for the traditional apartheid division assumed to be in existence by Riekert.[44] It also reflected a new regional stabilization of the African labour supply in which there was a de facto incorporation of parts of the homelands population into certain ('white') suburban peripheries (with the exception of Durban and Pretoria)[45] and deconcentration points.[46] Furthermore, the Riekert Commission did not take into account the ever-growing rural poverty in the homelands which contributed to the massive increase in movement from the countryside to the cities. Neither did it address the resultant mushrooming of peri-urban squatter areas.[47] Both of these sectors – the cross-border commuters and the squatter populations – carried the *potential* of undercutting the maintenance of an insider–outsider distinction. They represent what Bauman would call indeterminate elements,[48] not fitting into any of the official apartheid categories, and therefore producing endless problems in terms of its reproduction.

By early 1981 the state had introduced significant changes in its policy which reinforced the processes outlined above. Moving away from industrial decentralization – a policy aimed at the relocation of industries close to homeland borders, and thus based on the premiss of the homeland–white South Africa division – P. W. Botha introduced a new regional development plan at the Good Hope Conference. This plan, appropriately described as consisting of a 'soft borders approach', argued that development planning should take place within regions which were free of constraints imposed by 'political' borders.[49] As Cobbet and others have argued, this broke down apartheid's division of labour and replaced it with regional sub-economies, which were to form the basis of the construction of new local and regional authorities from the mid-1980s. The fact that the constitutional dispensation based on the homelands–white South Africa division was inadequate was also admitted. Simon Brandt of the Department of Finance stated that:

> the constitutional planning which revolved around the creation of separate national states, was accompanied by a refusal to accept the regional pattern of development brought on by spontaneous economic forces [sic], and by active measures aimed at creating a viable economic base for each of the intended national states.[50]

Brandt, however, only argued for a rethinking of the constitutional relationship between Black Local Authorities, the national states and 'the higher echelons of governments in the Republic of South Africa'.[51] It took almost a decade of struggle before the question of the existence and political viability of the so-called homelands and independent national states as such could be opened up to radical critique from a political perspective within the dominant bloc.[52]

Now, although these economic changes were important in so far as they produced increasingly larger groups of people simply not able to fit any longer into the logics upon which the apartheid discourse had been premissed, they could not, by themselves, effect a disarticulation of it. For this to happen, they had to be articulated to a broader resistance discourse. It is here that the political factors working against the implementation of the Riekert strategy assume their centrality. The three areas of black resistance discussed by Hindson are of particular importance in this regard. The first concerns struggles by the independent trade-union movement which played a decisive role in undercutting the insider–outsider strategy by refusing to admit the division of the working class and by deliberately setting out to organize migrants, commuters and settled workers alike into single organizations.[53] Moreover, it challenged wage differentials between migrant and settled labour and thus undercut employers' attempts to reserve unskilled lower-paid jobs for migrant labourers.[54] The second set of resistances developed around the growing squatter communities who offered strong resistance to removal and resettlement by the state. Hindson concludes, with reference to the struggles at Crossroads and Kayalitsha, that

> more than any other single factor it is their struggles that have finally forced the state to concede the *failure* of the insider/outsider strategy, the *impossibility* of total territorial apartheid, and the *inevitability* of African urbanisation outside the homelands.[55]

The third set of resistances was located in the African townships. The recommendations of the Riekert Commission came in the wake of an emerging local government crisis manifesting itself, inter alia, in a proliferation of community-based grassroots movements which were to become united, by 1983, under the banner of the United Democratic Front.[56] The articulation of local township grievances into a broader anti-apartheid discourse served further to undermine the very logic upon which the social division of apartheid was relying. It exposed the co-optation, most forcibly by focusing on the unaddressed problem of political representation for the African population at a national level, and rejected all attempts to get the African population to participate in their own oppression. As a result of the growing militant and unified opposition, it became increasingly difficult for the state to hold on to, and utilize, its discourse – which was still premissed on a dichotomization of political and social spaces.

As is clear from the foregoing discussion, this dichotomization could only be perpetuated by an increasingly complex construction of strategies of inclusion and exclusion. There are many examples of this growing, and increasingly tangled, web of practices endeavouring to balance the various inclusionary/co-optational and exclusionary/repressive measures. One of these was the use of *kitskonstabels* – 'instant' policemen trained for only six weeks – to support right-wing vigilante groups in squatter communities which resisted forced removal. Another consisted of the undermining of grassroots resistances in the townships by bolstering the political and financial positions of the town councils through their inclusion in the well-funded Joint Management Centres.[57] In this way, it was hoped that the creation of so-called model townships, by upgrading housing, infrastructures, services and facilities, would undercut resistances and 'win over the hearts and minds of the people'. The WHAM strategy, involving selective control and containment, complemented the shift in state strategies away from influx control, to controls *within* the urban areas.[58] Boraine summarizes it in the following way:

> Rather than trying to keep Africans out of white-designated urban areas, the state is currently attempting to maintain control through a combination of selective allocation of resources to bolster conservative elites and vigilante forces, and the repression of democratic community organisations.[59]

By the mid- to late 1980s, in the context of the State of Emergency, there was a proliferation of 'enemies' of the state; and it became almost impossible to maintain clear and consistent lines of inclusion and exclusion. In this context, it is interesting to look at what happened at this point with respect to the portrayal of violence on television. Posel argues that one of the main intentions in the depiction of violence had been to contest representations of township violence as a people's war, 'a mass-based struggle, with an articulate and democratic leadership and a clear programme and strategy'.[60] The state, in its interventions, fell back on the 'agitator' theory: 'external' elements, such as the ANC and the SACP, were said to have 'infiltrated' the otherwise calm townships, and sparked off mindless and destructive violence. The violence, nevertheless, was not portrayed in simple black–white terms. As Posel remarks, while the discourse on violence played on long-standing 'white' fears of the 'black mob', it simultaneously had to override any crude racial depictions, for the whole of the transformist strategy depended upon the state's ability to co-opt support from 'moderate blacks' – excluding 'radicals' and 'communists' – whilst simultaneously selling the idea of 'power-sharing' to the white population.[61]

To orderly urbanization . . .

In the face of this developing crisis, the state abandoned any attempt at implementing the Riekert influx controls. In April 1986, the pass system was scrapped in its entirety, and influx control was replaced with a policy of 'planned or orderly urbanization'. In short, this involved a shift away from direct prohibitions over movement, residence and employment, to the use of indirect ones (notably regionally differentiated financial penalties and positive incentives, such as tax reliefs and the waiving of health standards in places of employment to influence settlement patterns).[62] This method of control over urbanization was said to be 'positive', since it allowed for the 'use of market forces, subsidies and development' to encourage people 'to settle in certain suitable areas rather than forbidding them to move to urban areas'.[63] And yet, the racially 'neutral' and indirect character of the measures, however, did not mean that all direct controls were given up. Indeed, even more insidious controls were, and have been, utilized. An example of this is the controlling of housing on the basis of legislation dealing with health and trespass laws. Nevertheless, a certain opening up of the situation, and modification of the insider–outsider distinction has occurred with the acceptance of differentiated accommodation. A far greater urban population was now legally resident in what was formerly 'white' South Africa. However, they were to be more differentiated in terms of housing, services and living conditions.

The orderly urbanization strategy no longer relied on the homeland–white South Africa distinction. Instead it was now linked to a new regional industrial dispersal strategy that aimed at a relocation of industrial activities away from metropolitan areas to 'deconcentration' points. South Africa as a whole was divided into nine development regions which cut across homeland borders in some cases, and which formed the basis of the framework for a variety of state institutions (such as the Development Bank, the Regional Development Advisory Committees and so on).[64] In its turn, from 1985 onward, each development region incorporated certain metropolitan regions which were governed by Regional Services Councils (RSCs). In this sense, the orderly urbanization strategy formed part of a larger series of incentives by the state to contain the deepening crisis by trying to depoliticize the provision of services, and to introduce a measure of political legitimacy at the local state level. The Black Local Authorities, which had all but collapsed, were given representation on the RSCs together with 'white' municipalities, the latter of which were funded by taxation on business turnovers, wages and salaries. (This, it was hoped, would act as a disincentive for the employment of more Africans in the metropolitan areas, directing it to the deconcentration areas where the standards of acceptable housing were lowered, and the requirements in terms of health and safety provisions waived.) Thus, the RSCs did on a political level what the Development Regions did on an economic one: they cut across the 'white' South Africa–homeland borders.

These strategies, forming part of the second wave of state reforms, followed in the wake of the rejection of other methods of control by the black community. They constituted a complete rejection of the notion that the homelands formed independent political and economical units.[65] The movement of state strategies over the past decade, from Riekert to orderly urbanization, thus involved an increasing dissolution of the very premises – those premises which were historically founded – of apartheid itself. This dissolution, I would argue, could be understood only by means of the crisis induced by resistances which continually questioned the various and increasingly complex insider–outsider distinctions upon which apartheid discourse relied.

Theoretically, it is important to consider some of the evaluations of these changes. Hindson has argued that while the changes signified an unshackling from apartheid, they also created a rejuvenation of capitalism. This needs very little comment. It is more than obvious that the state hoped to legitimize its transformist strategy by an increasing withdrawal from direct intervention, leaving the terrain open for 'neutral market forces' to do their work. However, this 'depoliticization' was not allowed to take place, and the 'free enterprise' discourse continues to be challenged.

On the other hand, the comment by Cobbet et al., namely that the 'new reforms go beyond the political and territorial premises of apartheid, though not necessarily [beyond] those of race or ethnicity' needs more elaborate discussion.[66] In the first place it is asserted that the reforms of the mid-1980s went well beyond what could be understood as the historically specific divisions instituted by apartheid. However, I would argue, as I did with respect to the failure of the Riekert strategy, that for these changes to become effective they had to be articulated to wider resistance discourses. The so-called 'structural' disarticulation of apartheid logics, while important in itself, is not sufficient to bring about the disarticulation of the political logics that have shaped the society. A dislocated structure merely opens the space for a multitude of possibilities of rearticulations which are, by definition, indeterminate. That is why the political factors working against state strategies are to be given a certain primacy, for it is only from there that we can address the construction of an alternative order. Finally, it could be argued that Cobbet's statement only makes sense if we read for 'race and ethnicity' what I have called the logic of apartheid. But even if we do this, we still face the possibility of going beyond the historical limits of apartheid discourse, while its wider logic, its modern character, is not put into question.

Identity and Modernity: Ambiguities

In order to develop this argument more fully, I shall draw on certain suggestions put forward by Bauman in a recent article in which he sets out a number of important notions that may be utilized in coming to a closer understanding of the nature of the crisis we are experiencing in South Africa today. The crux of Bauman's argument is that the modern project of cultural unity – of which apartheid could be said to be *the* example and to which is closely linked the ambitions of the national state – produces the conditions of its own unfulfilment.[67] This, we could argue, is the condition of modernity. Bauman proposes that we think of modernity, then, as a time when 'order . . . is a matter of thought, of concern . . . a practice aware of itself'.[68] Bauman, moreover, points out that the very notion of order can only become central in so far as the *problem* of order appears. Our world is thus shaped, he argues, by 'the suspicion of brittleness and fragility of the artificial man-made islands of order among the sea of chaos',[69] and our existence is modern in so far as it contains the alternatives of order and chaos.

Here the argument takes an interesting turn, for Bauman proposes that the struggle for order is not a struggle against chaos. Rather it is a struggle against ambiguity and the miasma of the indeterminate and the undecided; it is a struggle against indefinability and incoherence. It is in this sense that the statement that the modern state produces the conditions of its own unfulfilment must be understood. As Bauman points out, it is the modern practice of the state to exterminate ambivalence: 'to define precisely – and to eliminate everything that could not or would not be precisely defined'.[70] While the state needs chaos to go on creating order, the element of indeterminacy is that which has the possibility of radically undercutting the logic of the state.

Crisis Revisited

For Bauman, then, the indeterminate has a subversive potential precisely because it undermines the very logic of identity upon which the order–chaos polarity is found. Indeterminacy resists reduction to either of the categories, and thus subverts the very principle upon which oppositionality and, as others might argue, the whole of Western metaphysics is based. This brings me to possible ways in which one may begin to think through, both theoretically, as well as politically, the current crisis in South Africa. I have argued that the very logic of apartheid is based, not upon an either–or form, but on what could be called a 'both–and one'. This, I have tried to elaborate earlier, is precisely the reason why it has been so difficult to think the nature of apartheid: for while the 'both–and' logic on one level defies the logic of identity upon which apartheid rests so heavily, it reinforces it on another. Thus, the both–and logic, on the one hand, defies identitary thinking exactly because it refuses to be reducible to a single identity. And yet, on the other hand, the logic of identity is *not* radically put into question by its both–and nature. This is so because it still remains within the very logic of apartheid discourse itself. In fact, it is precisely why the discourse has been so powerful in its construction of social and political identities. To take up Bauman's point in this respect, what would undermine the logic of identity in a radical fashion is an element which cannot be categorized in terms of the complex series of inclusionary and exclusionary strategies fostered by apartheid discourse: an indeterminate element.

This argument could be extended to deepen our understanding of the crisis. Rather than reducing the complexity of the crisis to a single underlying factor, such as positing it as the result of a crisis of capital accumulation, one would have to investigate the conditions of possibility for the crisis. And these conditions I have located in terms of a discourse or discourses which could undermine the *logic* of apartheid. A crisis, on this view, can be described as a situation in which the *horror of indetermination* has manifested itself.[71] That is, a situation in which the dominant discourse is unable to determine the lines of inclusion and exclusion according to which the identity of the social is constituted. Apartheid discourse, then, is in a crisis precisely in so far as the indeterminacy and ungovernability of the social have become the dominant form of sociability.

On Bauman's reading, this undecidability or ambiguity originates in the failure of the naming or classifying function of language. He stresses, informatively, that classification 'consists in the acts of inclusion and exclusion' and that this operation invariably 'is an act of violence perpetrated upon the world, and requires the support of a certain amount of coercion'.[72] This logic, drawn primarily from a reading of the works of Derrida, could be further radicalized, for undecidability refers not only to the 'ambiguity' of elements that cannot be classified according to a certain logic, but to the originary terrain constituting the very condition of possibility for the act of classification. The question then becomes one of how to *account for* the fact of a particular classification. And here it is necessary to return to the *political* logics constitutive of social division. In this way, political struggle, contestation and resistance are put at the heart of any discussion of the crisis. As a result, it could be argued that any positing of a necessary link between the event of crisis and the discursive responses to it would be untenable. The gap between a dislocated structure or logic of a discourse and the principles of reading provided for it can only be filled provisionally by a contingent articulating principle.

A number of clarificatory remarks are necessary at this point. First, the mere fact that the structure is dislocated does not mean that 'everything becomes possible'. Dislocation always takes place in a *determinate* situation: 'that is, one in which there is always relative structuration', and the continuing existence of a symbolic universe of representations.[73] Second, a dislocated structure opens up the space for a multitude of possibilities of re-articulations which are by definition indeterminate. A dislocated structure is thus an open structure in which the crisis can be resolved in a variety of directions. From this it is clear that any attempt at re-articulation will be an eminently political project. There can be, as a consequence, no possibility of thinking a necessary or teleological link between dislocated structures and the discursive attempts to re-articulate them. The very logic of the notion of dislocation rules out such a possibility. The articulations provided by a variety of resistance organizations cannot, therefore, be argued to be a necessary result of 'objective' conditions, but are always the results of particular political logics, and reflect in that sense the logic dominant in the resistance discourses.

The space opened up by a dislocation is thus the space from which we can think the possibility of hegemonic re-articulation. It is from this space that the possibility of post-apartheid society will have to be articulated, and it is only to the extent that this articulation will take a form different from that logic characteristic of apartheid that we will be able to speak of a *post*-apartheid settlement. That is, it is only to the extent that we succeed in weakening the totalizing logics of modernity that we will be in a terrain different from the one where the logic of apartheid has reigned supreme.

Notes

1. Quoted in Derek Sayer, *Capitalism and Modernity. An excursus on Marx and Weber* (London: Routledge, 1991) p. ix.
2. Ibid., p. viii.
3. For some of the more influential interpretations of the crisis, see: C. Charney, 'The National Party, 1982–1985: A Class Alliance in Crisis', in W.G. James (ed), *The State of Apartheid* (Boulder, Colorado: Lynne Riener, 1987), pp. 5–36; Stanley B. Greenberg, *Legitimating the Illegitimate. State Markets and Resistance in South Africa* (Berkeley: University of California Press, 1987); M. Morris and V. Padayachee, 'Hegemonic Projects, Accumulation Strategies and State Reform Policy in South Africa', *Labour, Capital and Society*, 22(1), 1989 pp. 65–109; M. Murray, *South Africa: Time of Agony, Time of Destiny* (London: Verso, 1987); and John Saul and Stephen Gelb, *The Crisis in South Africa* (USA: Zed Books, 1986).
4. My remarks here refer to the decades-long controversy in the literature on South Africa as to the appropriate mode of analysis. For a general overview of the debate, see Harold Wolpe, *Race, Class, and the Apartheid State* (London: James Currey, 1988), and D. Posel, 'Rethinking the "Race–Class Debate" in South African Historiography', *Social Dynamics*, 9(1), 1983, pp. 50–66.
5. The notion of 'undecidability' used here draws on the work of Jacques Derrida, particularly as it is developed in his *Edmund Husserl's 'Origin of Geometry: An Introduction'*, trans. with preface and afterword by John P. Leavey (Nebraska: University of Nebraska Press, 1978); and as well, his *Dissemination*, trans. Barbara Johnson (Chicago: Chicago University Press, 1972). As well, I am using 'undecidability' as it has been developed in Rodolphe Gasché's seminal analysis of the notion of infrastructural undecidability, *The Tain of the Mirror, Derrida and the Philosophy of Reflection* (London: Harvard University Press, 1986). The argument has been developed in a more political context by Laclau, in his *New Reflections on the Revolution of Our Time* (London: Verso, 1990) pp. 172ff.
6. Roger Simon, *Gramsci's Political Thought* (London: Lawrence & Wishart, 1982) pp. 37–8.
7. It is necessary to retain an analytical distinction between the *event* of the crisis, and the *discursive articulation* of that event as a crisis. Theoretically, this involves a logic of articulation premissed on the notion that there is no necessary logic creating a correspondence between the 'experience' of a radical rupture and the interpretation of that rupture as a crisis. Thus, it is held (i) that a rupture may be articulated such that it does not appear as a crisis, and (ii) an interpretation or construction of a crisis may take more than one form, depending on the

particular discursive horizon dislocated by the rupture. A fuller discussion of the conditions of possibility for theorizing this may be found in Laclau, *New Reflections*, pp. 40–41.

8. Murray, *South Africa*, p. 432.

9. Jacques Derrida, 'Racism's Last Word', *Critical Inquiry*, 1985, p. 292, n.12.

10. Z. Bauman, *Modernity and Ambivalence* (Oxford: Polity Press) p. 1.

11. Sayer, *Capitalism and Modernity*, p. ix.

12. Ibid., p. xi.

13. Chris Fynsk, 'Apartheid, Word and History', *Boundary 2*, XVI (2), 1989, pp. 1–12.

14. Ibid., pp. 1–2.

15. Derrida argues in 'Racism's Last Word' that apartheid may be regarded as 'the first "delivery of arms", the first product of European exportation' (p. 295). Throughout this text, references are made concerning a possible relation between apartheid and the 'West'.

16. Fynsk, 'Apartheid', p. 7.

17. Derrida's critique of Western metaphysics, as developed over the last three decades, may be read as involving a theoretical 'critique' of the attempts in philosophy to present itself as grounded in 'totalizing' meta-narratives. See Jacques Derrida, *Of Grammatology* (Baltimore: Johns Hopkins University Press, 1974).

18. The notion of the *co-constitutivity* of a discourse is taken from Foucault's work on the simultaneity of the development of certain epistemes and the construction of their objects of analysis. See Michel Foucault, *Madness and Civilization* (London: Tavistock Publications, 1967).

19. Derrida, 'Racism's Last Word', p. 291.

20. Ibid., p. 292.

21. See for example Harold Wolpe, *Race, Class and the Apartheid State*, and Posel, *Rethinking the 'Race–Class' Debate*.

22. The notion of an *empty signifier* is drawn from the critique of structuralism in which a split between the signifier and the signified was thought. This split facilitated the possibility of theorization of the logic of articulation, based on the non-fixation of any signifier to a signified. In extreme cases, such as in the situation of an organic crisis, the ambiguity of signifiers may have proceeded to such an extent that no general agreement exists on their interpretation. The argument here is that this is the case with the notion of apartheid.

23. For a full discussion of the initial theorization of *political frontiers*, see in particular Ernesto Laclau and Chantal Mouffe, *Hegemony and Socialist Strategy* (London: Verso, 1985) pp. 104–45. As it is used here, it has been enriched by drawing on the notion of the *constitutive outside* developed by Staten's commentary on Derrida and Wittgenstein in his *Wittgenstein and Derrida* (Oxford: Basil Blackwell, 1985) pp. 1–27.

24. This argument may further be elaborated with reference to the later Wittgenstein's remarks on the identity of games, especially the exchange with Frege on the drawing of boundaries around concepts. See in particular Ludwig Wittgenstein, *Philosophical Investigations*, trans. G.E.M. Anscombe (Oxford: Basil Blackwell, 1953) pp. 65–88.

25. Recently, a number of commentators have chronicled the constitution of the identity of the 'West' with reference to the production of a variety of 'others'. The following writers have also remarked on the *constitutive* nature in the process of identity construction: N. Cohn, *Europe's Inner Demons* (London: Heinemann, 1975); Edward W. Said, *Orientalism* (London: Penguin Books, 1985); and R. Webster, *A Brief History of Blasphemy. Liberalism, Censorship and 'The Satanic Verses'* (Southwold: The Orwell Press, 1990).

26. Paul Smith, *Discerning the Subject* (Minneapolis: University of Minnesota Press, 1989) p. xxx.

27. Michel Foucault, 'Nietzsche, Genealogy, History', in D.F. Bouchard, ed., *Michel Foucault: Language, Countermemory, Practice* (New York: Cornell University Press, 1977) p. 162.

28. As quoted in V. Descombes, *Modern French Philosophy* (Cambridge: Cambridge University Press, 1980) pp. 138–9.

29. Liberal historians have been castigated by 'neo-Marxists' in debates on South African historiography for silencing the black population by denying them a voice in history. See S. Marks, 'Towards a People's History of South Africa? Recent Developments in the Historiography of South Africa', in R. Samuel, ed., *People's History and Socialist Theory* (London: Routledge 1981) pp. 297–308. The attempt here is, rather, to show how the production of political frontiers has created the conditions under which it became possible to exclude the 'other'.

30. See in particular, A. Gramsci, *Selections from the Prison Notebooks* (London: Lawrence & Wishart, 1971) pp. 58–9.

31. A. Mapheto, 'The Violence. A View from the Ground', *Work in Progress*, 69, 1990, p. 6.

32. Ibid.

33. F.W. de Klerk, 'Walk Through the Door and Let Us Talk', *The Independent* (UK), 2 February 1990.

34. Ibid.

35. F.W. de Klerk, 'Politicians Can Work Out New South Africa but They Can't Make It Work', *The Sunday Times* (SA), 3 February 1991.

36. The notion of strategy utilized here follows that by Glazer, in so far as it is based on the primacy of the political and does not presume a coherent and single strategy developed in a conscious fashion by the state. Rather, it is argued that emerging strategies result from a series of intra-state struggles – struggles between state and civil society – and, as well, from antagonisms developed between the state and the radical forces of resistance. See Daryl Glaser, 'A Periodisation of South Africa's Industrial Dispersal Policies', in R. Tomlinson and M. Addleson, eds, *Regional Restructuring under Apartheid: Urban and Regional Policies in Contemporary South Africa* (Johannesburg: Ravan Press, 1987) pp. 28–54, esp. pp. 48ff.

37. The following discussion of what has been termed the first and second 'waves' of reform draws heavily on the various aspects of regional reform strategies as elaborated in the seminal work of Cobbet et al., Glaser, and Hindson. While I am in full agreement with the emphasis on the primacy of the political found in most of these articles, I would argue that the moment of the political and its relation to the crisis remain under-theorized in these works. See W. Cobbet, D. Glasser, D. Hindson and M. Swilling, 'A Critical Analysis of the South African State's Reform Strategies in the 1980s', in P. Frankel, M. Pines, and M. Swilling, eds, *State, Resistance and Change in South Africa* (London: Croom Helm, 1988) pp. 19–51; Glaser, 'A Periodisation', and D. Hindson, 'Orderly Urbanisation and Influx Control: from Territorial Apartheid to Regional Spatial Ordering in South Africa', in Tomlinson and Addleson, *Regional Restructuring*.

38. See Wiehahn (chairperson), *Report of the Commission of Enquiry into Labour Legislation*, Republic of South Africa (Pretoria: Government Printer, [R.P. 47/1979]); and Riekert (chairperson), *Report of the Commission at the Inquiry into Legislation Affecting the Utilisation of Manpower (Excluding Legislation Administered by the Departments of Labour and Mines)*, Republic of South Africa (Pretoria: Government Printer, [R.P. 32/1979]).

39. As cited in Murray, *South Africa*, p. 65.

40. Ibid., p. 150.

41. See A. Ashforth, 'On the "Native Question": A Reading of the Grand Tradition of Commissions of Inquiry into the "Native Question" in Twentieth-Century South Africa', Ph.D. thesis, Trinity College, Oxford, 1987, p. 305.

42. Ibid., p. 315.

43. For a detailed summary of the various important moments in the changes between the state and organizations operating in civil society, see Michael Mann, 'The Giant Stirs: South African Business in the Age of Reform', in Frankel et al., *State, Resistance and Change*, pp. 52–86.

44. F. de Klerk, 'Some Recent Trends in Bophutatswana: Commuters and Restructuring in Education', South African Research Service, ed., *South African Review II* (Johannesburg: Ravan Press, 1984) p. 271.

45. See Cobbet et al., *A Critical Analysis of SA State's Reforms*, p. 22.

46. Hindson, *Orderly Urbanisation*, p. 104. Glaser summarizes the distinction between decentralization and deconcentration in the following manner: 'Decentralisation is the term used to describe traditional dispersal policy, the aim of which was to foster bantustan economies. It entailed the attempt to induce industry to locate in remote border areas. Deconcentration refers to the policy of encouraging industrial dispersal mainly on the outer peripheries of the metropolitan centres' (Glaser, *Periodisation*, p. 53).

47. Hindson, *Orderly Urbanisation*, p. 104.

48. Bauman, 'Modernity and Ambivalence', *Theory, Culture and Society*, 7 (2–3), 1990, p. 148.

49. Cobbet et al., *A Critical Analysis of SA State's Reforms*, p. 27.

50. S. Brandt, 'Die Wisselwerking Tussen Ekonomiese en Konstitusionele Hervormings in

Suid Afrika', paper delivered to the Conference of the Political Science Association of South Africa, Rand Afrikaans University, 1981, p. 6.

51. Brandt, 'Wisselwerking', p. 16.

52. The possibility of publicly questioning the political viability of the homelands became a rather moot point after the release of Nelson Mandela, though it has occurred in a context in which the role played by 'traditional leaders' in the restructuring of South Africa was placed squarely on the agenda of the 'progressive' movements.

53. Hindson, *Orderly Urbanisation*, p. 86.

54. Ibid.

55. Ibid, p. 87.

56. For a detailed discussion of the crisis of local government, see J. Grest, 'The Crisis of Local Government in South Africa', in Frankel et al., *State, Resistance and Change*, pp. 87–116.

57. For a discussion of the National Security Management System, of which the Joint Management Centres form a part, see D. Geldenhuys and H. Kotze, 'Aspects of Political Decision-Making in South Africa', *Politikon*, 10 (1), 1983, pp. 33–45; and J. Selfe, 'South Africa's National Management System', in Jacklyn Cock and Laurie Nathan, eds, *War and Society. The Militarisation of South Africa* (Cape Town: David Phillip, 1989) pp. 149–58.

58. The WHAM strategy is discussed in some detail in M. Swilling, 'Whamming the Radicals', *Weekly Mail* (SA), 20–26 May, 1988, p. 15.

59. A. Boraine, 'The Militarisation of Urban Controls: The Security Management System in Mamelodi, 1986–1988', in Cock and Nathan, eds, *War and Society*, p. 173.

60. D. Posel, 'A "Battlefield of Perceptions": State Discourses on Political Violence, 1985–1988', in Cock and Nathan, eds, *War and Society*, pp. 262–74.

61. Ibid., p. 273.

62. Hindson, *Orderly Urbanisation*, p. 89.

63. President's Council Report as quoted in Hindson, *Orderly Urbanisation*, p. 89.

64. Hindson, *Orderly Urbanisation*, p. 93.

65. Ibid., p. 88.

66. Cobbet et al., *A Critical Analysis of SA State's Reforms*, p. 20.

67. Bauman, 'Modernity and Ambivalence', p. 163.

68. Ibid.

69. Ibid., p. 164.

70. Ibid., p. 165.

71. Ibid.

72. Ibid., p. 2.

73. See in particular Laclau's remarks on this point, *New Reflections*, p. 43.

6

'A Country of Words': Conceiving the Palestinian Nation from the Position of Exile

Glenn Bowman

Mahmoud Darwish's poem 'We Travel Like Other People' opens with 'We travel like other people, but we return to nowhere.' It closes:

> We have a country of words. Speak speak so I
> can put my road
> > on the stone of a stone.
> We have a country of words. Speak speak so we
> may know
> > the end of this travel.[1]

Darwish's words, like so many of those of the 4,920,000 Palestinians living either in exile or under Israeli occupation as of 1986,[2] attempt to articulate the trauma Palestinians face in identifying themselves as Palestinian in a world in which there is no longer a country called Palestine. In this chapter I will essay a mapping of the 'country of words' that has come to stand in the place of Palestine in Palestinians' thoughts and activities. Here, then, is a survey, a Palestinian 'topography', that investigates how this recent diasporic people constructs and maintains a sense of a national identity when the territorial base to which that identity refers is occupied by another national movement – itself constituted through the denial of the legitimacy of any Palestinian national aspiration. Central to this inquiry is the way Palestinians, in the numerous places to which they have been scattered by the loss of their homeland, discursively construct images of themselves, their homeland, and the antagonists that have prevented them from achieving the national fulfilment which grounds their identities. What Edward Said has called the 'various and scattered . . . fate'[3] of the Palestinians after the originary 1948 loss of their homeland has resulted, I will argue, in the construction of a number of different 'Palestines' corresponding to the different experiences of Palestinians in the places of their exile. The nation-building process which

Darwish refers to in the final lines of his poem is, I contend, made difficult by the different senses of what it means to be Palestinian engendered by more than forty years of dislocation and dispersion. Issues of tactics as well as of identity are foregrounded by this diversity. Questions must be asked not only about whether the 'roads' laid by various Palestinian communities will be recognized by other communities as routes to a place they too would recognize as Palestine, but also about whether the members of these various communities will recognize each other as allies or as antagonists if, and when, a Palestinian state is re-established.

The war of 1948 gave birth to the State of Israel, scattering indigenous Palestinians throughout most of the world's countries.[4] The 1949 armistice, which fixed the borders of the territories taken by Israel in the war, left 73 per cent of what had been Mandate Palestine within the borders of the new Israeli state, and 711,000 (82.6 per cent) of the 861,000 Palestinian Arabs who had lived on that expropriated territory in exile outside its borders.[5] The war of June 1967 resulted in the rest of what had been Mandate Palestine falling under the control of Israel, with another 200,000 Palestinians (20 per cent of the total population of Gaza and the West Bank – many refugeed for the second time in less than twenty years) being forced to flee the territory. Most of the 2,880,000 Palestinians living outside of Israeli control as of 1986 trace their banishment back to those moments at which they, their parents or their grandparents were forced to flee their houses and lands.[6]

Additionally, there are approximately 2,040,000 Palestinians living within the territories occupied by Israel, and these, too, have witnessed the loss of their homeland even though they still reside on the territory that was once Palestine. The situation of Palestinians living in Israel (within the borders set in 1949) and in the Occupied Territories (the West Bank, Gaza and the Golan Heights, all taken in 1967) is effectively also one of exile. The intensive dislocations and disruptions which have taken place with the setting up and 'defending' of the Israeli socio-political order (386 villages were destroyed in 1948 alone, and subsequent developments have led to the mass relocation of populations, effective destruction of agricultural communities by forcing wage labour on peasants, and ever-escalating expropriations of lands for military and settlement building) have led Palestinians 'inside', like those 'outside', to perceive the territory which is the locus of their identity as mutilated and stolen. The fact that these people, technically, still live on the land that was Palestine in no way refutes their assertions that they are exiled from their homeland. For 'homeland' is itself a term already constituted within nationalist discourse; it is the place where the nationalist imagines his or her identity becoming fully realized. A domain wherein Palestinian identity is denied cannot be considered the Palestinians' homeland, even if it were the very same ground on which they imagine the future Palestinian nation will be built.

It is a central contention of this volume that all ideas of community are 'imaginary' constructions in so far as community always exists through the imaging of the group of which one conceives oneself a member. Darwish's phrase, 'a country of words', has pertinence not only to Palestinians and others who have suffered from nation theft and can only locate their countries in reminiscences, stories, songs and histories, but also to those who, living within existent communities, take the presence of those entities as given. All communities are 'countries of words' in so far as the rituals of inscribing borders, picturing territories and populations, and thematizing issues salient to those terrains and the communities believed to occupy them occur within discourse. In both oral and literate societies, the community is not a 'thing' in itself but a way of speaking, and thinking, about others who are 'like us'. People create communities rhetorically through thinking that some people are 'like' themselves while others are 'unlike' them. In this respect, demographic contiguity is only one element among many that can be drawn upon in stressing similitude and difference.[7]

Processes of conceiving likeness and unlikeness change, however, with changes in the media of communication which bring knowledge of others to mind. Benedict Anderson has argued that the particular systems of communication characterizing societies with popular literacy allow the imagined population of the imagined community to be extended far beyond the bounds of the knowable or face-to-face community of societies characterized by oral communications.[8] He demonstrates such extension in his description of the 'mass ceremony' of reading the daily newspaper through which the reader, 'in silent privacy, in the lair of the skull', concerns himself with a field of national events and conceives himself, through that concern, as like the 'thousands (or millions) of others [fellow readers] of whose existence he is confident, yet of whose identity he has not the slightest notion'.[9]

Although Anderson's own theorization of the phenomena of identification through text tends finally to be materially deterministic (asserting that it is the presence of the text as commodity which 'precipitates' the construction of the category of nation), implicit in his description is the recognition that the newspaper, like the novel, provides a ground on which readers can constitute their own subjectivities through identification with scenarios set out in the text. The reader of the newspaper, novel, or other narrative-bearing medium may (or may not) recognize himself or herself in a subject position produced within the narrative. By projecting that constituted subjectivity on to others who he or she believes engage that text, the reader can imagine a collectivity of persons positioned like (or unlike) himself or herself in relation to the concerns that the texts set out. This elaboration of the process of imagining community challenges Anderson's deterministic assumptions in so far as it foregrounds the problematic – seemingly not at all recognized by Anderson – as to why a person should (or should not) invest himself or herself in scenarios set out in texts. For the act of reading a newspaper or a novel does not automatically interpellate the reader within the subject positions they proffer; the text, and its positions, are objects to be interpreted, and, as Bourdieu has variously demonstrated,[10] the positions one takes in relation to various social texts are influenced by a wide range of factors. It seems likely that, in situations like those discussed by Anderson, there is already in play in the reader an identity which enables him or her to recognize the appropriateness to personal experience of subject positions within a text.[11]

The reader does not, in other words, 'find' a national identity through imagining a simultaneity of thousands (or millions) of others who are reading the same text at the same time. Instead, a national identity is constituted by discovering a set of concerns he or she 'recognizes' as his or her own within a text or texts. Through identification with the position set out in such discourse, the reader is carried out of the isolation of individual experience into a collective phenomenon which the discourse articulates in national terms. This re-evaluation of Anderson's theorization of the process of imagining community not only shifts attention from commodity form (that of the novel or newspaper) to the narrative content enveloped within those forms, but also emphasizes the relationship between text and audience through which the text plays a role in fixing the identity of its reader. The reader, in assenting to that identification, comes to see the text (form and content) as signifying a community of which the reader can imagine his or her self a part. This reassessment also enables one to move beyond texts per se into the wider analysis of discourse in which all cultural artefacts become, in effect, social texts providing fields for identification.

The recognition that national identity is a discursive production impels the analyst of nationhood and nationalism to examine the process of articulation through which elements of everyday experience come to connote the presence of a thing which is never actually evidenced in full, that is, the national entity. Whether this national entity is made up of those persons one imagines are one's fellow nationals (as with Anderson's imagined community) or is actually something even more nebulous – the 'Nation' itself – its most distinguishing characteristic is that it appears to be signified by its parts and is never perceivable as a whole. This, Anderson points out with reference to the imaginary aspect of community: 'the members of even the smallest nation', he writes, 'will never know most of their fellow-members, meet them, or even hear of them, yet in the minds of each lives the image of their communion'.[12] Žižek, elaborating on the fantasy of 'the Nation', writes that the nation thus

> appears as what gives plenitude and vivacity to our life, and yet the only way we can determine it is by resorting to different versions of an empty tautology: all we can say about it is, ultimately, that the Thing is 'itself', 'the real Thing', 'what it is really all about', and so on . . . the only consistent answer is that the Thing is present in that

elusive entity called 'our way of life'. All we can do is enumerate disconnected fragments of the way our community organizes its feasts, its rituals of mating, its initiation ceremonies – in short, all the details by which is made visible the unique way a community *organizes its enjoyment*.[13]

Both the national community and the nation itself will be imagined, consequently, by an abstraction of images of a 'way of life' from one's experiences of the persons and practices one has come to know or has come to imagine one knows (whether through personal acquaintance or through the imagination of familiarity that comes through the various media). These images are then projected on to the generalizing screen of the 'national imaginary' as fetishes of the nation which *stand in* for the thing itself.

The national entity is, then, signified synecdochically (the whole being designated by one or more of its parts). In an instance where the character of the whole is not known, this is problematic in a way it is not when, for instance, the knowledge of the nature of a boat makes the designation 'sail' clear. People coming to imagine the entirety of a national community through their familiarity with a small sector of its members or conceiving the character of the nation through an extension of their knowledge of localized customs will find themselves severely at odds with others who construct their images of the national community and nation on the grounds of their experiences of entirely different groups with entirely different customs. Clearly, of course, the members of these different communities have knowledge of each other through the various media which extend the borders of the imagined community beyond the knowable community, but, as I have noted above, the positions they take up regarding the narratives presented in those media will depend on their experiences of their own milieu and of persons, or powers, which are seen to impinge on those milieu from a place they interpret as an 'outside'.

This problem of imagining the nation is foregrounded in instances like that of the Palestinians in which the national community is scattered through a multitude of very different milieus. Thus, as I will demonstrate below in the cases of Edward Said, Fawaz Turki and Raja Shehadeh, the imaginings of Palestine by Palestinians located within the various sites of the diaspora (respectively New York, Beirut and Ramallah in the Israeli-occupied West Bank) will differ substantially, and may lead Palestinians from one domain to see those from another as foreigners, or even as enemies. However, such dissonance is also likely to occur within established communities and nations. A nation or social order that is fixed or 'real' is as much a discursive construct as one that is dislocated, disassembled or fantastic. In the former instance, however, the nation is taken as a given and voices that could deny its realization are muted or marked as criminal, alien or insane. Such hegemoniz-ation effects a general common sense acceptance of the nation in the interiority of individual consciousnesses, promulgated not only by texts such as newspapers and novels, but also by the proliferation in the external world of signs (institutions, monuments, rituals and other 'sediments') alluding to the nation and rendering its presence irrefutable.[14]

It can be said that the 'national field' of discursivity operates with the nation as its parameter, and, though conflict and dissension are perceived as occurring against the backdrop of the nation (indeed, the political is generally seen to be either intra-national or inter-national), they are not perceived as putting into question the actuality of that entity (indeed, a threat to the nation, either from inside or outside, actually offers substantive support to its reality). Debate may occur as to who is part of the nation and who is its enemy, but such debate, within which major conflicts between differing modes of interpretation and identification are played out, rarely throws into question the existence of the nation. This is in large part because in a heterogeneous social field, with multiple foci of conflict and consensus, a situation of what Laclau and Mouffe refer to as a 'total equivalence', where the discursive space of society 'strictly divide[s] into two camps', rarely occurs.[15] (Civil wars and revolutions, in which diverse antagonisms are mobilized around a single set of oppositions, are exceptions, but even here the defence of the real nation is the slogan under which both sides of the conflict fight.) The hegemonic discourse of the nation, like any mythology, makes the cultural – that is, the arbitrary and fashioned – appear natural and fixed in the order of things.

Where the nation is taken as a given, national identity serves as a backdrop to the various identities adopted within the context of the national community. Antagonism is perceived (if it is perceived at all) as threatening subsidiary identities rather than the national identity which engulfs them. Thus, in the example given by Laclau and Mouffe of a peasant prevented from being a peasant because a landowner is expelling him from his land, antagonism is perceived with reference to the identity 'peasant'.[16] A rhetoric of national rights may well come into play in the articulation of the conflict between peasant and landlord, but the conflict remains one between peasant and landlord, and not between non-national and national. (Although, as in Anderson's previous example where colonial officials were trained by the imperial bureaucracy only to be denied the opportunity of acting as civil servants in the Empire, the blocking of one identity by antagonism can give rise to struggles to constitute new identities which may undermine acceptance of the hegemonic discourse.) In established nations, lands are also dispossessed, employment curtailed or cut off, educational opportunities denied and persons unjustly incarcerated, but such events are discursively articulated as the *consequences* of either the operations of capital, the greed of landowners or businesspersons, the injustices of demographic settlement or localized racist practices, the incorrect interpretation of law by inept or corrupt officials, and so forth. Such agencies may be seen to impede the full realization of the national ideality, but these are discrete faults within the national order rather than antagonisms which challenge that order. Only in rare instances when the hegemonic hold of the concept of national identity has lost its grip on portions of the population are such events seen as signs of a denial of the national identity to those who suffer them.

The 'nation' in the discourse of an established national entity is an imprecise and effectively nebulous mythological concept which is, because of that imprecision, open to appropriation by all of its readers. In other words, the concept of the nation retains its grip on the imaginary of its population precisely by remaining unfixed. In this way, a wide range of persons and collectivities can identify themselves as constituent parts of it without having their readings and their allegiances to it challenged or denied by particular and exclusionary definitions. This unfixity can only be maintained, however, as long as the persistence of the nation is taken for granted; as soon as the nation is discursively posited as endangered, battle lines are drawn and processes of selective exclusion/inclusion are set in play. Thus, when certain hegemonizing groups claim the nation is threatened with dissolution or decay (as has been done in Britain by Thatcherite Tories and in the United States by McCarthyites and the 'Moral Majority') and attempt to 'correct' or fix the character of the nation along moral or political lines, constituent parts of the national entity are marked off as enemies. If the discourses of those groups are sufficiently influential, processes of division or fragmentation are set in play giving rise to conditions where equivalences can be made between seemingly disparate groups. Such processes are, however, generally curtailed by the state which isolates and marginalizes the groups promoting them through the operations of ideological apparatuses or, when such groups prove sufficiently disruptive of national consensus, by criminalizing and suppressing them. Such processes of division and fragmentation do, after all, assert what Laclau and Mouffe refer to as 'the impossibility of society' and threaten to set in play the dissolution of the national imaginary and thus the disintegration of the nation itself.[17]

When a nation is lost or unrealized, as when it is perceived as threatened, the issue of defining what impedes its realization becomes salient.[18] Persons who conceive of themselves as nationals without a nation (like those who feel their national identity is endangered) will interpret all manifestations of antagonism effecting their 'subsidiary' identities as symptomatic of the denial to them of their nation. Within Israel and its Occupied Territories dispossession, unemployment, closure of schools and colleges, and imprisonment are interpreted by Palestinians as evidence of the Israeli state's systematic programme to eradicate a Palestinian presence. The same can be said of those occurrences that, to an outsider, seem unmotivated such as a drop in the number of tourists purchasing goods from Palestinian merchants in the markets of Jerusalem's Old City.[19] Here, in effect, all acts of threatening or disallowing particular identities (those of landholder, worker, student, and so on) are read as particular instances of a global denial of national identity. This equation renders equivalent all agents of antagonism as well as, by deduction, making 'the same' all those who suffer the effects of those antagonisms.[20] Such collectivities are, in other words, discursively constructed out of the recognition that all of their members (retroactively posited) suffer the 'same' oppression by the 'same' antagonist. Once such a construct is acknowledged, the process of totalizing equivalences can be realized, and a strict border can be drawn between those who deny identity and those who are denied it.

The identity that arises out of such a process, and the politics to which it gives rise, both depend on the various experiences each group (or each individual) mobilizes in its particular construction of identity, as well as on the way those elements are articulated in discourse. It is here that issues of the different experiences of communities in different locales of diaspora become central to the issue of nationalist politics. I suggested, in my revision of Anderson's theory of the way in which national identity is constituted, that the process of interpellating oneself within a nationalist discourse necessitates that one already have some sense of identity through which one can recognize the appropriateness (or inappropriateness) of the subject positions provided by that discourse. That initial identity provides the subject with the means of recognizing and evaluating antagonism; one can sense that one's identity is denied only if one has a sense of an identity to be threatened. The process of equivalence, therefore, requires that the specific identity undermined by antagonism can be extrapolated so as to be seen as constituting an element within a wider, collective identity. Thus the Palestinian street merchant whose business is eroded can come to see through the recognition of an antagonism he interprets as Israeli that he is not simply a street merchant but, like the members of the community of other persons he perceives as threatened by Israel, also a Palestinian. He is a street merchant who sees himself as a Palestinian because the economic deprivation which endangers his well-being is not simply economic but also a matter of a state policy which manifests itself in domains other than simply that of the market in tourist goods. As long as he perceives antagonism solely in economic terms the perceived source of the antagonism is as likely to reside in other merchants on the street or in the foreign tourists themselves as it is in the activity of Israeli policy.[21]

Clearly the elaboration of a Palestinian nationalist discourse plays a significant role in establishing this set of equivalences. In part, this happens by providing the merchant (and others) with a means of generalizing their particular situations so that they appear as specific manifestations of more generic troubles – troubles which in turn are seen as afflicting all members of the community to which they belong (or come to imagine themselves as belonging). In fact, the very existence of the term 'Palestinian',[22] which derives its contemporary significance from the antagonism towards 'Palestinians' manifested by agencies and allies of the Israeli state, provides any Arab who conceives of his or her origins in the territories now occupied by Israel with a subject position within a narrative of generalized Israeli hostility – a narrative that can make meaningful all sorts of experiences of antagonism aimed at this Palestinian.

However, in a situation like that of contemporary Palestinians, where the national community is spread all over the world in a number of relatively autonomous enclaves, the nebulousness of the term 'Palestinian', which enables it to serve as a label of identity for all Palestinians, simultaneously renders it incapable of providing any sense of the distinguishing characteristics which would allow Palestinians in milieus where they suffer from particular antagonisms to recognize their situation as 'like' that of other Palestinians in different situations. A street merchant witnessing the harassment by Israeli soldiers of a peasant who has come to the city is likely to feel a consanguinity with that other 'Palestinian' because he recognizes the source of the other's difficulties as being the same as his own. He is, however, unlikely, to feel any affinity with a Palestinian bourgeois he meets while visiting Jordan, even though the latter may be an exiled victim of the activities of the Israeli state. In such a situation the affliction the bourgeois Palestinian experiences in his or her life in exile will not appear to the former to be anything like that which threatens the merchant under occupation. Furthermore, the exiled Palestinian's response to the particular antagonism that afflicts him or her (a response that, in Jordan, involves attempting to build up economic influence and prestige so as to strengthen 'Palestinian' power in Jordanian society) will not be recognized by the visitor as an activity appropriate to a real 'Palestinian' even though the exile may deem it fully appropriate to the situation. Thus Raja Shehadeh, a West Bank solicitor whose *The Third Way* will be examined below, writes: 'I don't go to Amman . . . seeing in the Jordanian capital men who have grown rich and now pay only wildly patriotic lip-service to our struggle is more than my *sumud* in my poor and beloved land could stomach.'[23]

The problem is that, in the absence of any generalizing positivity defining the Palestinians as a whole, the experience of antagonism itself comes to provide the determinative marker of identity. In the diasporic situation, where each community experiences different forms of antagonism, the members of each particular community will imagine their co-nationals as those who suffer 'the same' antagonisms as they do. They are unlikely to recognize as 'like themselves' others who suffer from different forms of assault on their identities, in so far as those other assaults are not the same as those they see constituting a 'Palestinian' identity. Palestinians with whom I spoke during my fieldwork in the Occupied Territories (1983–85) regularly referred to Edward Said, a person widely recognized in the West as a spokesman for the Palestinian movement, as 'that American'.

As Laclau and Mouffe indicate, any representation of the nation is 'at the same time a fiction and a principle organizing actual social relations'.[24] The envisioning by the nationalist of who it is who makes up the imagined community of which that person conceives himself or herself a part determines the political means mobilized in the struggle to realize the national rights of that community. The relative isolation of the various worldwide Palestinian communities means that in a very real sense each fights for a particular portion of the Palestinian population by means that are seen as appropriate to countering the threat to that particular portion. Unlike in established nations, where the struggles of parts of the population are subsumed within a national framework by the operations of a hegemonic ideology, in unrealized nations like 'Palestine' there are few, if any, mechanisms that can effectively serve to translate all the particular struggles into manifestations of a single global battle for nationhood.[25] Consequently, until the time of the *intifada* and, as I will argue in my conclusion, up to the present day, each Palestinian community has seen its particular situation as 'Palestinian'. It has consequently disallowed or ignored the 'Palestinian' character of other groups' struggles. Often, instead of seeing other Palestinians as 'like' themselves, Palestinians in particular milieus have seen the efforts of other groups as undermining or threatening their own 'Palestinian' interests. Thus, ironically, as the internecine struggles between guerrilla organizations and the conflicts between Palestinians on the 'inside' and the 'outside' have shown, Palestinians can play the role of antagonists to other Palestinians.

In the following pages I will examine a triptych of Palestinian self-portraits which variously elaborate the meaning of Palestinian identity in the pre-*intifada* period so as to illustrate the way particular articulations of Palestinian identity can function to fragment the Palestinian nation rather than bring it together. These texts are Fawaz Turki's *The Disinherited: Journal of a Palestinian Exile*, Edward Said's *After the Last Sky: Palestinian Lives*, and Raja Shehadeh's *The Third Way: A Journal of Life in the West Bank*.[26] The Palestinian lives described in each differ widely, as the reader would expect in narratives which derive respectively from the experiences of a person raised in the Lebanese refugee camps, from the life of a Palestinian university lecturer in New York, and from the perceptions of a solicitor working in Ramallah on the Occupied West Bank. What the texts have in common, other than the intention of elaborating Palestinian identity, is that all three authors, in describing who they and their people are, do so in very large part by describing the antagonisms which beset them. In accordance with the theory of identity-formation elaborated above, I want to show how these different antagonisms give rise to different imaginings of community and, in so doing, create a plethora of distinct strategies for realizing the Palestinian nation rather than a unified nationalist movement.

The Disinherited

Fawaz Turki states in the first pages of *The Disinherited* that '[i]f I was not a Palestinian when I left Haifa as a child, I am one now' (*TD*, 8). Although born in Haifa, Turki left at an age that ensured his childhood memories would come from squalid Beirut refugee camps where he was raised rather than from the Palestinian city from which his family was driven. The 'Palestine' he did not remember was, however, ever-present in the murmurings of older Palestinians who gathered in tight knots to re-create, compulsively, every detail of the lives which had been so suddenly wrenched from them:

> The moths would gather around the kerosene lamps and the men would mumble between verses '*Ya leil, ya aein*' ('My night, my mind – they have fused'). It is a typical Palestinian night, Palestinian mind. And we would know we were together in a transplanted village that once was on the road to Jaffa, that once was in the north of Haifa, that once was close to Lydda. (*TD*, 45)

Such obsessive re-creation of the past is not unusual in persons who have been brutally separated from their previous ways of life. Peter Loizos' *The Heart Grown Bitter* (1981) charts similar reactions amongst Greek Cypriot villagers driven from their lands by the Turkish invasion, and Peter Marris, in *Loss and Change* (1974), likens displaced peoples' compulsive memorialization of the past to the neurotic reactions of family members who cannot accept the loss of a loved one.[27] For Palestinian peasants, who made up 'the overwhelming majority of those in the camps',[28] village life had provided the frame of reference for all experience, and the loss of that frame effectively led to the disintegration not only of their world but of their conceptions of self as well. Thus Rosemary Sayigh, who has done extensive work within the Lebanese camps, writes:

> The village – with its special arrangements of houses and orchards, its open meeting places, its burial ground, its collective identity – was built into the personality of each individual villager to a degree that made separation like an obliteration of the self. In describing their first years as refugees, camp Palestinians use metaphors like 'death', 'paralysis', 'burial', 'non-existence', etc. . . . Thirty years after the uprooting, the older generation still mourns.[29]

This kind of nostalgia does not, however, provide a foundation for national identity, since in large part the collectivities being imagined in the villagers' reminiscences are their own obliterated village communities (which were, whenever possible, demographically reconstituted in the new settings of the camps).

Fawaz Turki and his generation did not learn what it was to be Palestinian from these nostalgic fantasies. Instead, their identity was forged out of the painful intolerance and harassment inflicted upon them by their unwilling hosts – initially the Lebanese authorities – but later, as migrant labouring forced them to travel through the Middle East, from their treatment at the hands of business and state personnel throughout the Arab world. Turki's generation were taught that to be Palestinian was to be cursed at, harassed, exploited and imprisoned by those powers who despised them but who had nonetheless created them by the treatment meted out to them within the camps. Thus, for these younger, lumpen-proletariat, camp Palestinians the enemy eventually ceased to be those who had driven their people from Palestine and became, instead, first the 'Arab' in general and then everyone else who exploited them in their exile:

> To the Palestinian, the young Palestinian, living and growing up in Arab society, the Israeli was the enemy in the mathematical matrix; we never saw him, lived under his yoke, or, for many of us, remembered him. Living in a refugee camp and going hungry, we felt that [while] the causes of our problem were abstract, the causes of its perpetuation were real. (*TD*, 53).[30]

Just as the enemy is given the features of the particular tormentors of the camp Palestinians, so too the population of the imagined 'land' of Palestine becomes those who share the camp Palestinians' experiences of being 'Palestinian' rather than all those who are descended from persons who lived in Palestine. Since these experiences are based on poverty and exploitation rather than on national characteristics, this population, at first, is seen to be made up of all Arabs who suffer under the unjust leadership of reactionary Arab states – 'The revolution is Palestinian in its origin and Arab in its extension' (*TD*, 103). In time, however, as the drift of diasporic life introduces Turki to the worldwide extension of reaction and corruption, the Palestinian community comes to be further redefined as 'a commonwealth of peoples heavily laden, heavily oppressed' (*TD*, 54). The struggle for the homeland becomes the struggle to constitute a ground on which human beings can have integrity. The liberation of Palestine thus becomes the

> liberation of [all] men and women . . . Palestine is not a struggle that involves only Palestinians. It is Everyman. . . . [We are] confronting the whole mosaic or racist mythology in the West and in Israel that essentially claim[s] that certain races are inherently cowardly, inferior, backward, and incapable of responding to the fierce exigencies that press on the human spirit. (*TD*, 176)

The Palestinians created by camp life in the *ghurba* (exile or dispersion) grew up with no links to a past and with few non-oppressive connections to the present. The experience turned a number of them, like Turki, into revolutionaries working within internationalist, rather than nationalist, parameters:

> We grew up in a vacuum. We belonged to no nation. We embraced no culture. We were at the bottom. The only way for us to go was up. . . . We had nothing to lose. We lived on the edge of the desert. On the fringe of the world. We had little to risk. . . . We made common cause with the oppressed. The oppressors made common cause against us. (*TD*, 154)

After the Last Sky

The bourgeoisie, who for the most part managed to flee Palestine just before the 1948 catastrophe, were not, like the peasantry, hurled into a vacuum but were welcomed into an established and well-to-do expatriate community.[31] From the mid-nineteenth century onwards, the urban elite of Palestine had established settlements throughout the Middle East, Europe and the Americas. Here their children could have cosmopolitan educations and they themselves could escape the Ottoman draft, British taxation and the depredations caused by Zionist penetration.[32]

The bourgeoisie of the *ghurba* have always been socially and economically assimilationist,[33] yet its members, despite integration into the cultures surrounding them, have maintained a strong sense of Palestinian identity. This persistence of Palestinianism reflects to some degree the importance of family ties and loyalties based on place of origin to social and business relationships, but it also plays a significant role in maintaining a feeling of 'rootedness'. It helps to provide a fixity of identity for individuals scattered across a number of continents who become integrated into a multitude of culturally heterogeneous societies and are thus subject to numerous radically different economic, social, political and confessional influences.

The loss of the homeland exaggerated these émigrés' already-present awareness of displacement and severance by making it impossible for them, literally, to 'go home' – to perform, in the flesh, the pilgrimage constantly made in the imagination to remind themselves of who they were and where they came from. Cut off from that past, the bourgeois found himself or herself inescapably immersed in the anomie of the post-industrial world

> where no straight line leads from home to birthplace to school to maturity, all events are accidents, all progress is a digression, all residence is exile . . . The stability of geography and the continuity of land – these have completely disappeared from my life and from the life of all Palestinians. (*LS*, 20–21)

This world, unlike that of the camp Palestinians or that of the Palestinians of Israel and the Occupied Territories, is one in which individuals, alone or hived off in nuclear families, live in relative isolation from extended Palestinian communities. Here the connections between wider networks of Palestinian families and friends are not constantly rehearsed in daily life but instead run sporadically along telephone lines or scheduled air flights.

In such a context national identity is a fragile thing maintained not so much through contemporary patterns of action and affiliation as through fetishized links to a common past:

> Intimate mementoes of a past irrevocably lost circulate among us, like the genealogies and fables severed from their original locale, the rituals of speech and custom. Much reproduced, enlarged, thematized, embroidered and passed around, they are strands in the web of affiliations we Palestinians use to tie ourselves to our identity and to each other. (*LS*, 14)

This 'Palestine', embodied in objects, images and gestures, cannot constitute an imagined simultaneity of like persons dreaming of (and working towards) a future state. The diversity, and the isolation, of the members of the diaspora's bourgeoisie is too great to allow them to imagine Palestine as anything more than a past moment in which all the now-scattered people of their homeland were once together. Rituals of remembrance serve therefore to provide a touchstone, like a memento from childhood, offering sensed continuity to lives almost wholly defined by the practices and the rituals of the surrounding communities in which the Palestinian bourgeoisie is immersed. Only in 'domestic shrines' (such as those displayed in the photographs Jean Mohr provided to illustrate *After the Last Sky*) are these individuals momentarily able to make contact with an island of identity afloat in the sea of their difference.

Despite working from one of the several distinct locales of Palestinian diaspora, Edward Said has succeeded in producing a well-researched body of writings which appear to transcend precisely those impediments to the articulation to a global image of Palestine described above. Once, however, one considers the role played by the antagonist in the activity of defining identity, Said's work can be seen to be continuous with the context out of which it emerges. If, as is suggested, the core of identity for the displaced bourgeoisie is memory and its mementoes, then the chief enemy of their form of national identity is the corrosive impact of time and misinformation. Years and miles bring about a gradual blurring and smearing of the contours of a remembered land and this gradual destruction is aggravated by the systematic misrepresentations of Palestinian history engaged in by Zionist and pro-Israeli manipulators of the media. Said's works range from explicit attacks on the media's anti-Palestinian calumnies and obfuscation[34] to philosophical-literary disquisitions on the question of how to begin to tell a story when one is always already *in medias res*.[35] His projects approach from various directions the question of how forms of representation can be true to the objects they claim to represent. The structure of Said and Hitchens's *Blaming the Victims* exemplifies this: a series of ten essays, all describing the mechanisms by which Palestinian history and the Palestinian people have been and are being misrepresented, leads up to a long piece entitled 'A Profile of the Palestinian People' which 'sets the record straight' by describing in detail the subject distorted by the previously discussed discourses on Palestine and Palestinians.

After the Last Sky, with its profiles and its portraits, is a similar attempt to re-present a fragmented subject. However, the diasporic experience of the bourgeoisie determines the character of the entity Said reconstitutes in that the Palestinian nation Said senses is, like the Palestinian community of which he is a part, a group composed of individuals tenuously tied together by what is lost rather than by what is held in common:

> To be sure, no single Palestinian can be said to feel what most other Palestinians feel: ours has been too various and scattered a fate for that sort of correspondence. But there is no doubt that we do in fact form a community, if at heart a community built on suffering and exile. . . . We endure the difficulties of dispersion without being forced (or able) to struggle to change our circumstances. . . . Miscellaneous, the spaces here and there in our midst include but do not comprehend the past; they represent building without overall purpose, around an uncharted and only partially surveyed territory. Without a centre. Atonal. (*LS*, 5–6, 129)

There is little room in such a presentation for the revolutionary internationalist programme of a Turki or the stolid solidarity in suffering evident in the people described by Shehadeh. Said's 'Palestinian' is a composite of the Palestinians he knows, and these are persons who, caught in the web of exile amid the anomic milieus of the late capitalist world, find occasional but brief respites from alienation in the celebration of an identity set off against that world.

Finally, and like most persons caught up in our dynamic but decentred world, they are people whose identity is always elsewhere and whose knowledge, like ours, is made up of the central fact that wherever they are it is always away from home:

> Whatever the claim may be that we make on the world – and certainly on ourselves as people who have become restless in the fixed place to which we have been assigned – in fact our truest reality is expressed in the way we cross over from one place to another. We are migrants and perhaps hybrids in, but not of, any situation in which we find ourselves. This is the deepest continuity of our lives as a nation in exile and constantly on the move . . . (*LS*, 164).

Thus, although Said's 'Palestine' can occasionally be seen in the 'exhilaration and energy and pleasure . . . [the] cheerfully vulnerable triumph' which flashes in the eyes of a Palestinian child and reminds the watcher that 'movement need not always be either flight or exile', that glimpse is always momentary and epiphanic (*LS*, 165). This nationhood, sensed in a moment lost by the time it is recognized, is a ground for redemption, but it is a redemption promising integrity to the uprooted individual and not one promising, or enabling, the political re-establishment of a fragmented community.

The Third Way

Said's nostalgia and Turki's revolutionary internationalism seem not to share common ground on which an allied nationalist movement could be built; the strategies each reading of the situation suggests are at odds, and the populations to be brought together by those strategies would not, one suggests, be willing to abide with each other within shared boundaries. This divergence is in large part the consequence of the Palestinian dispersion, since both the international bourgeoisie and the camp Palestinians (groups differently constituted since well before 1948) have developed in isolation from each other and have consequently cultivated their respective images of the Palestinian past, present and future under very different sets of influences.

The situation within the borders of historic Palestine is different because there a heterogeneous Palestinian population has shared the burden of Israeli domination. This is not to say that all social groups within these borders have been influenced in the same ways by the Israeli occupation, but that, since the Palestinian populations of the Israel established in 1948 and those of the territories occupied in 1967 were brought into contact, there has been, throughout the occupied land, a continuous Palestinian population growing increasingly more aware that the antagonisms each encounters in his or her contacts with the Israeli state are aspects of a generic antagonism all Palestinians suffer under occupation.[36]

In light of these remarks, I would contend that a bounded territory does not in itself create a collective consciousness even if it contributes in important ways to the preconditions of the articulation of such awareness. Regardless of whether it exists within the bounds of a continuous territory or over a range of discrete sites, two preconditions are required for the establishment of a conception of national identity in the absence of a state apparatus fomenting such an identity: (i) that an antagonism exists that people can recognize as 'the same as' that which troubles others in their imagined (but no less real) community; and (ii) that people are able to recognize that others are, like themselves, suffering that antagonism. Continuous territory in the instance of Israel and the Occupied Territories provides a setting for the development of 'Palestinian' consciousness because, first, as the field of the nationalist project of the State of Israel, it is a circumscribed stage on which antagonism to the

Palestinians is acted out, and second, because Palestinians circulating within those territories can witness a particular antagonism not only operating on themselves but also on others who come to be seen as 'like them'. These two preconditions, that is, the recognition of antagonism and recognition of others who, in suffering under that antagonism, are like oneself, are, as the work of Said and Turki have demonstrated, possible in instances other than that of a continuous territory.

However, as I will illustrate below, the particular way in which contingency intrudes into the lives of Palestinians under occupation militates against the fixing of images of self and antagonist which can occur in diasporic situations. Palestinians in Israel and the Occupied Territories are less likely to adopt forms of identity and identification which commit them to the realization of specific and exclusive images of a future nation than are those 'outside'. Images of the nation articulated under Israeli rule remain, for the large part, closely linked to the struggle against antagonism per se and are thus open, as the character of antagonism shifts, to modification and to the modification of strategies of resistance which devolve from them.

The population of Israel and the Occupied Territories that has come to consider itself as 'Palestinian' is quite heterodox. Not only do Christians and Muslims coexist under the Palestinian rubric, but even those communities can be differentiated along sectarian lines. Among the minority population of Palestinian Christians there is a wide range of sects (predominant among them Greek Orthodox, Franciscan Catholic, Greek Catholic, Syrian Orthodox and Anglican) among which are religious groupings with distinct religio-national loyalties (largely Armenians and Copts). More substantial distinctions can, furthermore, be made between Palestinian groups in terms of categories such as residence (rural and urban) and occupation (peasantry, mercantile, professional).

In the past, the various rulers of this area (Ottoman, British, Egyptian, Jordanian and Israeli) have promoted those differences in order to break the indigenous population into mutually antagonistic groups incapable of collectively mobilizing against their powers.[37] However, the radical transformations effected by the Israeli occupation (massive expropriation of agricultural lands, militarization of vast areas, development of a migrant labour market to serve newly developed industrial and service sectors, and closure of Palestinian banks, businesses and industrial concerns coexisting alongside intensive inculcation of Western capitalist culture and full-scale political repression) have undermined the old patterns of life on which such distinctions were based. Those transformations affect all Palestinians in Israel and the Occupied Territories in a number of ways that threaten their particular identities (as peasants, as land owners, participants in religious groups, members of familial and other communal units in which prestige accrues from local economic activities, entrepreneurs, and so on). Their recognition of the duality of their identities, both in terms of those particular fields of activity as well as in terms of a generalized Palestinian identity, is assisted by the open antagonism of Israelis to 'Arabs' as such (irrespective of those specificities). In effect, the latter provides Palestinians with a category, articulated by Israeli antagonism, within which all those antagonized can see themselves as the 'other' to the Israelis. In their contacts with the other Arabs of the Israeli-occupied lands they move through, this recognition of a situation which they can see is effectively collective impels them to acknowledge the inadequacy of old confessional, factional and territorial divisions and to adopt an overarching Palestinian identity.

A traditional opposition, like that between Christian and Muslim Palestinians in the Old City of Jerusalem, will only be maintained as long as the context out of which it has grown remains pertinent. However, when life is sufficiently disrupted to undermine or disable the efficacy of traditional allegiances, people are able to subordinate old oppositions to the need for new alliances.[38] The presence of an antagonist who, in the main, does not differentiate between those it antagonizes provides its victims with a new category in which they can recognize as equivalent themselves and others who they, in the past, might have considered enemies.[39] In such situations, attempts by the state to mobilize old categories and divide the dominated population will tend to be recognized as such, thus further undermining the hegemony of the traditional categories and promoting an even stronger awareness of a collective identity.[40]

Raja Shehadeh's *The Third Way*, although very much centred on the experiences of a West Bank lawyer based in Ramallah, draws on a wide range of Palestinians in describing the state of the nation. One can imagine the 'nation' Shehadeh claims is drawing together in the face of a common enemy through his evocations of the strength of the women's groups, his descriptions of peasants becoming aware that land expropriations threaten the homes on which their traditional 'my home is my castle' attitudes have been built, his vignettes of professional and academic lives distorted and blocked by state and racialist interventions, his recounting of the degradations brought on by touristic development and so forth. Shehadeh's image of the population of 'Palestine' is neither as indeterminate as Turki's nor as definitive as Said's; the text, in part because of a narrative style which allows both Shehadeh and the people he meets to articulate their situations, gives the impression of a heterogeneity embraced by an overarching unity forged out of recognition of common antagonism.

Movement by foot, by car, by aeroplane provides a constant refrain in *The Third Way* as it does in Said's *After the Last Sky* and, to a lesser extent, Turki's *The Disinherited*.[41] Unlike Said's 'Palestinian restlessness', which always leads the author to an empty site from which Palestine has already been stolen away, Shehadeh's movements bring him into contact with a land in the process of being transformed by the activities of an antagonist and with a wide diversity of people who are both being hurt by those multiple transformations and recognizing the necessity of resisting them. In contrast to Turki's 'migrations', in which Turki always encounters oppression but, already knowing its 'real' nature, never grants the people suffering it the authority to articulate their experiences for themselves, Shehadeh's movements bring him into contact with individuals and groups whose increasing awareness of the nature of the antagonist they face enables them to articulate strategies of resistance which are both valid for their particular situations and commensurate with those of others whose identities they are coming to recognize as their own.

Shehadeh's historical awareness and his constant contact with the actual transformations of historic Palestine enable him to treat the development of the contemporary situation as a continuing process rather than as an abrupt shifting of images from the idyllic to the demonic. Unlike Said's text, which is redolent with a sense of irrecuperable loss, or Turki's, which stands just this side of an apocalyptic transformation that has not yet been set in play, Shehadeh's is very much located in a present moment which is as open to definition as it is penetrated by contingency and antagonism. Instead of sketching an opposition of perfect past to perfidious present, or perfidious present to utopic future, he maps out for critical examination those aspects of past Palestinian lives which have lent themselves to the production of the alienated present. This historical interest is far from nostalgic; Shehadeh condemns aspects of a past others render as bucolic in so far as he reads the present as a product, rather than a violation, of the past. Thus, for example, he analyses and critiques the structures of authority and of trust that were developed in pre-Zionist days and sees in them a major contribution to the loss of the land and the subsequent muting of political activism: 'No effort is needed to control a society so geared to paternalism that it barely matters who the authority is which does the ordering' (*TW*, 29).

This evaluation is complex in so far as it takes away the Edenic image of that stolen 'thing' nationalists invoke to fantasize their inherent perfection[42] by suggesting that Palestinian behaviour too has been (and without careful scrutiny will continue to be) a source of the dilemmas of the Palestinians. In this way it renders contingent and permeable the border between the community to which the self belongs and that of the antagonist which is so carefully delineated and defended by others like Said and Turki. As a result, he is inclined neither to imagine a pure past which existed before Zionism destroyed Palestine nor to evoke a perfect post-revolutionary world which will follow the collapse of the capitalist order of which Zionism is a part. Instead he represents the contemporary moment, with its antagonisms, as one in which a particular form of struggle has to be carried out, but implies that future struggles will follow. Israel and its agents are, at the present moment, the most telling threat to the survival of the people who have conceived themselves as a community in the face of that threat, but when the struggle against that antagonism has been concluded there will be other struggles in which allies in the contemporary struggle may turn against each other.

Thus, in his portrayal of Palestinian women, he suggests that a temporary concurrence of their identities as women and as Palestinians has made them superb street fighters, but implicit in that description is the idea that if they succeed in defeating the enemies who have made them recognize that they are *Palestinian* women, they are likely to then take on the antagonists who threaten their being as *women* per se:

> Sometimes I think that those few women who manage to survive this are the strongest of all *samidin* and it is they who will finally lead the revolt. They have the least to lose and no ego to be pampered, hurt, or played on by the Israeli rulers. You see them fearlessly head demonstrations and shout at soldiers at road blocks. They have been used to brutal oppression by men from the day they were born, and the Israeli soldiers are not a new breed of animal to them. (*TW*, 115).

In representing women as strong allies in the struggle against occupation, Shehadeh does not simply subsume their particular identities as women under the rubric 'Palestinian'. Instead he demonstrates that their resistance to Israeli soldiers is a particular extension of their antagonism to male oppression (particularly that of Palestinian males) and, in so doing, suggests that the strength they gain through struggling against the Israeli state can, after its defeat, be turned against other, sexist Palestinian, antagonists.[43]

This recognition of the unfixity of identity is inscribed throughout *The Third Way* in a manner not matched either in *The Disinherited* or *After the Last Sky*. Each of the latter two books posits pure and essential identities which Palestinians must realize if they are to be true to themselves; in Turki's text it is that of the revolutionary internationalist inalterably opposed to the machinery of capital while in Said's it is the (finally irrecuperable) ideality of the Palestinian who existed before Zionism deformed and scattered his or her identity and stole Palestine. Since, as I have argued above, these identities are forged in the fire of the contemporary situations of Turki and Said, they are not universals or vague generalizations but particular extensions of specific, context-bound experiences of antagonism. They are therefore not necessarily identities that other Palestinians, whose experiences differ, are able to recognize as their own and take on. Shehadeh's recognition that the identities that have been melded under the Israeli occupation are particular manifestations of that situation leaves the future, in effect, open to the formation of new identities which might not, at the moment at which he writes, be conceivable. His text does not 'fix' Palestine and the imagined community which might fill its as yet indeterminable borders, but designates a particular struggle which has to be engaged before one can even begin to imagine the boundaries and the population of a future national ground.

It is thus indicative that he comes to elaborate the mechanisms of mobilizing, and transcending, that struggle in the course of conversation with an American Jewish writer he claims to 'like a lot' (*TW*, 85). Robert Stone, his friend, talks with him about the 'pornographic' relationship to the land of Israel that the Jews in diaspora developed in their longing to return to it:

> When you are exiled from your land . . . you begin, like a pornographer, to think about it in symbols. You articulate your love for your land, in its absence, and in the process transform it into something else. . . . [W]hen Jews came to settle here this century, they saw the land through these symbols. Think of the almost mystical power that names of places here have for many Zionists. . . . As for what it really looked like, they tried to transform it into the kinds of landscape they left in Europe. . . . It is like falling in love with an image of a woman, and then, when meeting her, being excited not by what is there but by what her image has come to signify for you. You stare at her, gloating, without really seeing her, let alone loving her . . . (*TW*, 86–7)

Shehadeh, subsequently musing on this discussion, realizes that Palestinians, exiled from their land while still on it, are themselves being placed in such a 'pornographic' relation to that land by the experience of having what they know and love taken away piece by piece.[44] He becomes aware that he is transforming that with which he, himself, has had an intimate and unarticulated relationship into a symbol of what he must join with others to consciously struggle for:

> Sometimes, when I am walking in the hills . . . – unselfconsciously enjoying the touch of the hard land under my feet, the smell of thyme and the hills and trees around me – I find myself looking at an olive tree, and as I am looking at it, it transforms itself before my eyes into a symbol of the *samidin*, of our struggle, of our loss. And at that very moment, I am robbed of the tree; instead there is a hollow space into which anger and pain flow. I have often been baffled by this – the way the tree-turned-symbol is contrasted in my mind with the sight of red, newly turned soil, barbed wire, bulldozers tearing at the soft pastel hills – all the signs that a new Jewish settlement is in the making. . . . [I see] the image of an uprooted olive as a symbol of our oppression. (*TW*, 87 and 88)

Shehadeh realizes that this 'identification of the land with your people and through that with yourself' (*TW*, 87–8) is taking place in the hearts and minds of Palestinians throughout Israel and the Occupied Territories.[45] He recognizes that such identification lifts those people out of the isolation enforced by their earlier and immediate experiences of their private lands, making them citizens of a common land – even if that land is one that is forfeit and must be redeemed:

> Before the occupation there was no national symbolism and cohesion specifically connected with the West Bank. . . . [Now] even Abu-'Isa, who always thought of himself and his house as a separate kingdom, is beginning, through the threat of an Israeli incursion, to extend his horizons. Although I am glad that this is happening – we could not hope to fight off the Israelis without it – I cannot but allow myself a moment of anger and regret. I feel deep, deep resentment against this invasion of my innermost imagery and consciousness by the Israelis (*TW*, 88).

What, however, is salient in Shehadeh's description of this process of nationalistic pornographizing is his acknowledgement of the 'anger and regret' which rises in him when he watches the olive tree shudder and turn into a symbol of the nation. The thing which is transformed for the struggle is not, at the same time, lost to everything but the struggle; the particular experiences which are metamorphosed into symbols in the mobilization for nationalist struggle are not forgotten but, in Shehadeh's text, remain simultaneously as elements which can be rearticulated for different identities and different strategies;

> [W]e who have lived a silent love for this land are left with the grim satisfaction of seeing that the Israelis will never know our hills as we do. They are already making endless, ignorant mistakes. For all their grand rhetoric, they are strangers. We *samidin* may be turning into pornographers – but our love is not forgotten. The reason for our grief is also our strength . . . (*TW*, 89).

The process of turning elements of the experience of Palestinians into symbols of the national entity for which they must fight is essential to the mobilization of a unified community. As essential to Shehadeh, however, is the knowledge that those things which stand behind the symbols, like the particular lives of the people who become 'Palestinians', are always more than simply moments of the articulation of a national entity. In large part because he can meet, talk with and respect the particularities of the widely heterogeneous population of Palestinians living within Israel and the territories, Shehadeh recognizes and retains recognition of the fact that the imagined community of Palestinians is both a very diverse population suffering under all sorts of oppression (of which the particular Israeli antagonism is but the currently most telling) *and* a single collectivity now united in the contemporary struggle to hold on to the land and their lives in the face of Israeli incursions. There are many identities at play beneath the nationalistic identity of *samidin*, and the political strength of the Palestinians in the Israeli-occupied Territories will lie in – if it can be maintained – the recognition that the diversity which is the foundation of unity is also the grounds on which a democratic and pragmatic state can be built. In Shehadeh's book, unlike in the texts of Turki and of Said, there is no 'Palestinian'; there is only a plurality of Palestinians. For Shehadeh, as a result, both tactics and allies in this particular struggle are open to processes of re-evaluation. Such processes, which are vital to the formulation of strategies in a situation where the forms of oppression and opportunity are labile, would be rendered unworkable by more fixed conceptions of antagonism and identity.

The *Intifada* and Beyond

The Disinherited, After the Last Sky, and *The Third Way* were all written and published before the *intifada* broke out in December 1987. That popular struggle has taken on a mythical character in the self-imaginings of Palestinians throughout the world, and has given rise to activities – both inside and outside the Israeli-occupied Territories – which may lead to a political settlement providing some sort of autonomy for a Palestinian entity in the territories now occupied by Israel. In closing this paper I would like briefly to consider some of the implications of the way the *intifada* or, as it should be translated into English, the 'shaking off' has been received inside and outside the territories. Some of the conflicts now arising within the Palestinian nation-in-waiting (independence was formally declared on 15 November 1988) in response to the American-sponsored 'peace talks' are, I believe, consequences of the different processes of identity formation which took place throughout the Palestinian diaspora before 1987.

Shehadeh's text was written during a period in which Palestinians in Israel and the Occupied Territories were becoming more and more aware of their common interests as Palestinians in resisting Israeli policies pertaining particularly to military control, land expropriations and colonial forms of economic development. The stance of *sumud*, articulated in *The Third Way*, was in large part a policy of holding fast – of 'stay[ing] put, . . . cling[ing] to our homes and land by all means available' (*TW*, vii) – in a situation in which the increased militarization of the territories inaugurated by the Likud's 1977 electoral victory made more open forms of struggle unfeasible. In the ten years that followed the Likud's ascension to power land expropriation increased dramatically as settlements blossomed throughout the territories (by 1987 55 per cent of the land area of the West Bank and 30 per cent of that of Gaza were in Israeli hands). Political oppression escalated to unbearable levels, especially under the 'Iron Fist' programme Yitzhak Rabin inaugurated in August 1985. By 1987 illegal expulsions of Palestinians had become common, and popular Israeli support for right-wing policies of 'transporting' entire

Palestinian populations out of 'Greater Israel' and into surrounding Arab countries was growing.

On 8 December 1987 an Israeli tank transporter swerved to the wrong side of the road at an Israeli checkpoint in Gaza and flattened a car full of Gazan workers who were waiting to be cleared to cross into Israel so that they could go to work in Tel Aviv; four residents of the Jabaliya refugee camp were killed in the incident. By that time, such an 'accident' could only appear to Palestinians throughout the territories as a symbol of what seemed like a general Israeli state policy of exterminating the presence of Palestinians in the areas under state control. I would argue – and discussions I had with Palestinians in Jerusalem, Ramallah and Beit Sahour in August 1988 confirm this interpretation – that, at the moment news of the killed Gazan workers reached them, Muslim and Christian, villager and shopkeeper, revolutionary and housewife recognized that there was nothing evinced in Israeli activities towards Palestinians in general that would have prevented it from being any one of them who was flattened in that car. As news of the workers' deaths spread throughout the Occupied Territories and Israel, men and women from all walks of life, whose only common trait was their 'Palestinianness', recognized their own in the mangled bodies in the car.

I would contend that the *intifada* was conceived as Palestinian experiences of Israeli-state antagonism flooded in, filling that iconic moment and creating what Laclau and Mouffe describe as a situation of 'total equivalence' in which, in the Palestinian instance, the society of Israeli and Palestinian constituted under occupation 'strictly divide[d] into two camps'.[46] However, such a 'spontaneous' response demands more than the manifestation of what is taken to be genocidal policy; certainly betweem 1979 and 1982, when Shehadeh was writing, enough of a recognition of solidarity forged by oppression existed throughout the territories to provide the tinder for any of several events to spark into conflagration. Had Palestinian reception proved appropriate the assassination attempts on Palestinian mayors in June 1980 and the bombings by the extremist Israeli Kach movement which accompanied them could have provided such a spark. A collective recognition of a people's fate at the hands of a hostile force is not enough to spark active insurrection; there is as well a need for something to suggest that success resides in active resistance.

Interestingly, in late November 1987, a successful attack by an external Palestinian group (the Popular Front for the Liberation of Palestine – General Command) had been carried out across the northern border resulting in the deaths of six Israeli soldiers. This attack (virtually the first successful guerrilla action across the Lebanon–Israel border since the Israeli invasion of the Lebanon) served to prove, at a signal moment, that Israeli power was not invincible. Confidence that Israel was not omnipotent was, furthermore, augmented by the escape from prison in August of that year by a number of Islamic Jihad activists who, while successfully avoiding recapture, succeeded in assassinating a Captain of the Military Police in Gaza. These proofs that the enemy was vulnerable, occurring at the same time as other events showed that the policy of *sumud* was not sufficient to restrain the antagonism of the Israeli apparatus, pushed the Palestinians in the Occupied Territories and, soon after, in Israel itself into a new and different form of resistance.

Certainly, however, if the insurrection were to last (as it has now for nearly six years), it was vitally important for it to organize in a manner which would enable it to convince people that it *could* provide an alternative future to that promised by Israel. It had, in other words, to inscribe in the consciousness of the Palestinian community a set of alternative institutions which would make visible a Palestinian alternative to Israeli rule. A Palestinian infrastructure was rapidly coordinated out of the various institutions which had separately developed under the period of *sumud* described by Shehadeh: medical, educational, legal and advisory groups, which had previously operated autonomously, rapidly established links and attempted to take on the problems raised not only by the insurrection but also by the attempted disengagement of the Palestinian economy from that of Israel.[47] The United National Leadership of the Uprising (UNLU), which quickly organized without assistance from outside as the insurrection promised to continue, called on Palestinian landowners to cease collecting rent from people who were separated from their incomes by the insurrection (especially those who had, until the *intifada* called for disengagement, worked as labourers within Israel).[48]

Such assertions of the possibility of surviving without Israel also occurred at local levels. I was told, in 1990, that one family of stonemasons, who continued to work for Israeli contractors after the onset of the *intifada*, was shamed out of what was seen as collaboration by a delegation of villagers who carried a number of sacks of wheat to the house of the family and presented them to the head of the household, saying: 'We are sorry that you are so poor that you must work for the enemy, and we have collected from amongst ourselves this food so that you will no longer have to.' Such mutual support, given sincerely as well as ironically, asserted to Palestinians that they could survive as Palestinians without maintaining the economic ties with the Israelis that until then they believed they needed to perpetuate in order to endure. In so doing it also institutionalized the boundary between Israel and Palestine which had been taking form through the period leading up to the *intifada* and which had been deeply and irrefutably scored in Palestinian consciousness by the Gazan episode.

The external leadership of the Palestine Liberation Organization was taken by surprise by these activities of the Palestinian community under occupation, which 'presented the organisation with an unmistakable challenge . . . [by taking] its future into its own hands'.[49] The 'outside', which had until then dismissed Palestinians under occupation as incapable of thinking for themselves and had seen its role as that of instigating and directing internal resistance, suddenly found itself faced with a people which did not conform to its image: 'Almost before anyone knew it, a unique way of doing things had taken hold in the territories along with a new vision of the population as a self-propelled body that was both leading and waging the struggle against Israel on its own.'[50] Arafat and the PLO were quick to respond to this challenge, however, and within days were working

> to create the conditions to allow the *intifada* to continue; they had somehow to integrate in their own organizational framework the scores of new leaders that were emerging; they had to bring into play the political programme of the PLO in a way that would respond to both 'the crowd's sentiments' and the 'new target' the leaders outside knew had a chance of being achieved considering the changing balance of power the *intifada* was bringing about.[51]

Nonetheless, as Baumgarten points out, even the PLO had difficulty in conceiving the difference between the struggle that was taking place within the territories from that which it deemed appropriate to the 'Palestinian' situation. Until 7 March 1988, when Fateh's disastrous attack on Dimona proved that military attacks damaged, rather than contributed to the *intifada*, PLO communiqués and strategies presumed that the popular uprising conformed to the PLO's image of an appropriate response to Israeli hegemony, in being an armed struggle.[52] Other guerrilla groups, linked with – as well as opposed to – the PLO, continue, until the present day, to use the PLO leadership's subsequent support of the non-violent character of the uprising as a means of articulating their attempts to discredit the PLO and the internal leadership.[53]

Nonetheless, in the period following the advent of the *intifada*, that uprising was transformed from a particular response of a particular Palestinian community in a specific situation into an icon of Palestinian aspirations throughout the diaspora. By early March 1988 the various organizations which constituted the main body of the PLO (Fateh, the Popular Front for the Liberation of Palestine, the Democratic Front for the Liberation of Palestine, and the Palestine Communist Party) had settled their oft-times fratricidal differences and announced their solidarity in supporting and maintaining the *intifada*. On 15 November 1988, the Nineteenth Palestine National Council announced its full support of the Palestinian Declaration of Independence which had been drafted by the internal leadership, and subsequently gave its backing to the PLO–US dialogue which seemed to give credibility to the national 'road' on which the *intifada* appeared to have set all Palestinians. A year later there were celebrations throughout the Palestinian diaspora ('inside' and 'outside') of the first anniversary of the yet-to-be-established state of Palestine.

The movement from the moment at which one can conceive oneself as a part of a national community to that in which the nation is realized through the establishment of a state is, however, not only one of struggle against antagonism but also one of compromises, sacrifices and the fixing in place of those institutions that will become hegemonic in the future state. It is, in other words, a process of definition. Palestinians throughout their dispersion were able to see their freedom and fulfilment in the icon of Palestinian aspirations the *intifada* initially provided; but as the uprising began, against great odds, to make progress on its path towards Palestinian statehood within a portion of the territories occupied by Israel, many Palestinians – both those 'inside' and 'outside' – began to question whether the Palestine those persons backing the United National Leadership of the Uprising were beginning to gain sight of was actually the promised land to which they aspired. Within the territories, Hamas[54] contested the leadership of the *intifada* – often by violent means – because of UNLU's commitment to a democratic, secular state. On the 'outside', various guerrilla factions, with their allegiances to particular refugee populations outside of the borders of the Israeli state, came to fear that any settlement which created a state in the Occupied Territories per se would leave the Palestinians they claimed to represent – many of whom had originally resided in the territories annexed by Israel in 1948 – without any right to return to the homes from which they had been driven.[55] Some of these groups began to fight for the interest of Palestinians 'outside' against the gains being made by the Palestinians 'inside'. A telling example of this struggle, and its disruptive power, was the 1990 attack by the Palestine Liberation Front on a Tel Aviv beach which succeeded in breaking off negotiations between the US and the PLO.

As the peace talks proceed along their tortuous and impeded way and the negotiators (of whom Raja Shehadeh is one) succeed in eking small, but vital, concessions from the Israeli team, groups inside and outside the territories come to see that whatever might come out of the negotiations is not likely to fulfil their fantasies of what Palestinian nationhood should mean. The resulting dissension can only please the Israeli government, since it appears as proof of its assertions that the Palestinians are a people who do not deserve a nation; Palestinians are too 'fractious', too 'extremist', too 'fundamentalist', and too 'fanatic' to be allowed to control their own lives, homes and lands. This Orientalist rhetoric is, of course, an example of what Said and Hitchens term 'blaming the victims'. It suggests there is an essence of fractiousness which is inherent within 'Arabs' in general, and Palestinians in particular, whereas in fact the divided character of the Palestinian people in exile is a product of that involuntary exile. However, in so far as reality is discursively constructed, such a rhetoric can succeed in turning many non-Palestinians into advocates of a pax Israeli, despite the sympathy they have come to feel for Palestinians under occupation as a result of witnessing in newspaper stories and on television screens the brutality with which Israeli soldiers and settlers have attempted to crush the *intifada*.

The chief problem afflicting Palestinians in the current situation, aside from the antagonism of Israel, is what Laclau and Mouffe call the 'impossibility of society'. One's fantasy is always far more (and, in ways hinted at by Shehadeh, far less) than what can be realized, and the fantasies of 'Palestine' constructed in its absence prevent those people who see themselves as 'Palestinian' from recognizing places for themselves in the Palestine that is currently being put together. The long period of exile from Palestine, in which no hegemonic apparatus served to fix an image of the nation in the minds of its involuntary émigrés, has resulted in people imagining what the nation could be if the antagonisms which prevented it were to disappear, and these imaginings have generated a number of diverse, and idealist, images of the future state. As the power of the antagonist afflicting one particular Palestinian community begins to wane, a nation that may answer to some of the needs and aspirations of that population is beginning to take form. As Palestinians in the Occupied Territories inch closer to the realization of statehood, the ideal image of the 'Nation' is tarnished and diminished by the concessions and pragmatic sacrifices necessitated in building a state from the ground up. The Palestine that results from that process of state formation will not be one that gives back to all Palestinians all that they have lost, nor bequeaths to them all they imagine could be gained were the antagonisms that have made them what they are to evanesce. Many of them will not recognize, in the subject positions it provides for its citizens, a place in which they can locate the identities their experiences have constituted for them. That Palestine will not be their Palestine.

Although a future Palestinian state in the rump of what was Palestine may provide a means through which more widely satisfying solutions to the 'Palestinian problem' might eventually be found, this can only happen if those Palestinians who cannot recognize in the form it is beginning to take anything resembling their promised land do not, out of frustration and fear of an even more permanent dispossession, assist in preventing its establishment. It cannot be satisfying for people who have been waiting for their homeland for forty-five years to be told that they must wait, and work, longer. The phrase 'after the last sky', which provides the title for Said's book, is taken from another poem of Darwish, 'The Earth is Closing on Us', which queries:

> Where should we go after the last frontiers,
> where should the birds fly after the last sky?[56]

The slight satisfaction available to Palestinians exiled outside their land can only be found in knowing that there are no final frontiers, there is no last sky.

Notes

1. Mahmoud Darwish, 'We Travel Like Other People', *Victims of a Map* (bilingual text in Arabic and English) trans. Abdullah al-Udhari (London: Al-Saqi Books, 1984), p. 31.

2. David McDowall, *The Palestinians: Minority Rights Group Report no. 24* (London: Minority Rights Group, 1987), p. 31.

3. Edward Said, *After the Last Sky: Palestinian Lives* (London: Faber and Faber, 1986) p. 5.

4. See Laurie Brand, *Palestinians in the Arab World: Institution Building and the Search for State* (New York: Columbia University Press, 1988). Statistics cited by Brand show that in 1982, 40.5 per cent of Palestinians lived within Israel and other Israeli-occupied territories, while 25.1 per cent were resident in Jordan, 10.4 per cent in Lebanon, 6.4 per cent in Kuwait, 4.8 per cent in Syria, 7.3 per cent in other Arab countries, 2.1 per cent in the United States and 3.0 per cent in other non-Arab countries such as Australia, Germany and Chile (p. 9).

5. Benny Morris, *The Birth of the Palestinian Refugee Problem, 1947–1949* (Cambridge: Cambridge University Press, 1987) pp. 297–8.

6. McDowall, *The Palestinians*, p. 31.

7. A topographically unbroken landscape can be shattered by the representations of several groups which may mutually inhabit it and yet envisage themselves as discrete and discontinuous communities. A striking example of this is set out in Raymond Williams's *The Country and the City* where, in discussing Jane Austen's rural landscapes, Williams demonstrates that for the agrarian aristocracy the distances between one country house and the next were seen as unpopulated territories despite the dense inhabitation of those lands by the rural peasantry (R. Williams, *The Country and the City* [St Albans: Paladin, 1975] pp. 135–57). In this instance, as in that of the pre-state Zionist declaration that Palestine 'is a land without a people for a people without a land', it is clear that the recognized population is made up of groups and individuals with whom the definers see themselves sharing common interests and projects rather than simply a tract of land. Armenians and Jews in diaspora, furthermore, engage in frequent religious gatherings in which they liturgically celebrate themselves as parts of a national entity constituted in eternity and working towards historical reconstitution on the land on which their nations and their religions were formed. In the absence of literal land, 'Israel' and 'Armenia' are figured in a liturgical landscape in which 'standing on' sacred ground prefigures return to the lost territories. Such persons, engaged in ritualized reminiscences in spaces which symbolically participate in the territories of Israel or Armenia, are able to see themselves as parts of worldwide communities of others sharing both their exile and their projects of recuperation.

8. Benedict Anderson, *Imagined Communities: Reflections on the Origin and Spread of Nationalism* (Verso: London, 1991) pp. 22–36. See also Brian Stock, *The Implications of Literacy: Written Language and Models of Interpretation in the Eleventh and Twelfth Centuries* (Princeton: Princeton University Press, 1983) pp. 88–92.

9. Ibid., p. 35.

10. See Pierre Bourdieu, 'The Production of Belief: Contribution to an Economy of Symbolic Goods', *Media, Culture and Society*, II:3, 1980, pp. 261–93, and *Distinction: A Social Critique of the Judgement of Taste*, trans. Richard Nice (Cambridge, Mass.: Harvard University Press, 1984).

11. Anderson's later consideration of the role played in fomenting national identity by the colonial policy of neither allowing substantial advancement to indigenous officials within the colonial bureaucracy nor permitting them to serve as officials in areas outside those from whence they came, supports this assumption (*Imagined Communities*, pp. 56–7). The training of the apprentice bureaucrat in the ways of the colonial bureaucracy enables him to see himself as an official of the empire but this identity is subsequently denied by an act of symbolic violence which prevents him from operating as an imperial officer outside the boundaries of the colony of his birth. This subject thus is open to recognizing his own impeded situation in the stories of others who have experienced the same or similar constraints to advancement and is to join with those with whom this identification identifies him in processes of reimagining or rearticulating identity – processes which, as Anderson points out, give rise to the creation of new, in this case nationalist, identities.

12. Anderson, *Imagined Communities*, p. 6.

13. Slavoj Žižek, 'Eastern Europe's Republics of Gilead', *New Left Review* 183, September/October 1990, pp. 50–62.

14. Theoretical concern with the inscription of the ideological on the material can be traced from Durkheim and Mauss's *Primitive Classification* (1901–2), trans. Rodney Needham (London: Routledge, 1963) to Duncan's *The City as Text: The Politics of Landscape Interpretation in the Kandyan Kingdom* (Cambridge: Cambridge University Press, 1990). Trotsky, describing Lenin's 'desire to unfold the party's programme in the language of power' through, among other things, the constant issuance of revolutionary decrees, demonstrates how, in the early days of the revolution, putting markers of the new social order in place was a major project of the Soviet bureaucracy: 'It was impossible to tell in advance whether we were to stay in power or be overthrown. And so it was necessary, whatever happened, to make our revolutionary experience as clear as possible for all men. Others would come, and, with the help of what we had outlined and begun, would take another step forwards. That was the meaning of the legislative work during the first period. . . . He [Lenin] was anxious to have as many revolutionary monuments erected as possible, even if they were of the simplest sort, like busts or memorial tablets to be placed in all the towns, and, if it could be managed, in the villages as well, *so that what had happened might be fixed in the people's imagination, and leave the deepest possible furrow in memory*' (Leon Trotsky, *My Life: An Attempt at an Autobiography* [Harmondsworth: Penguin, 1975] pp. 356–7; my emphasis).

15. Ernesto Laclau and Chantal Mouffe, *Hegemony and Socialist Strategy: Towards a Radical Democratic Politics*, trans. Winston Moore and Paul Cammack (London: Verso, 1985) p. 129.

16. Ibid., p. 125.

17. See further ibid., p. 122; and Ernesto Laclau, *New Reflections on the Revolution of Our Time* (London: Verso, 1990) pp. 89–92.

18. Here one finds that the recognition of the 'other' is central to the constitution of any identity, as Derrida and Staten have indicated in their discussions of the 'constitutive outside' (see Derrida, *Of Grammatology*, trans. Gayatri Spivak [Baltimore: Johns Hopkins, 1976], pp. 39–44; and Henry Staten, *Wittgenstein and Derrida* [Oxford: Basil Blackwell, 1985] pp. 16–19). Moreover, as Laclau and Mouffe have stressed in their elaboration of the concept of antagonism, alterity in antagonism takes on a threatening role which demands a resistance if identity is to be maintained (see Laclau and Mouffe, *Hegemony and Socialist Strategy*, pp. 122–7). The 'nebulousness' of national identity in an established nation can be seen to be a result of a passive relation to the constitutive outside; one is British because one is not French, and to maintain this identity one need define it no further than to say it is not the same as that of the other. In a situation of antagonism, on the other hand, one is impelled by the assertion of the power of the antagonist to attempt to make positive – to define – the position that antagonism attempts to negate.

19. Glenn Bowman, 'Letter from Jerusalem', *Middle East International*, 299, 1 May 1987, p. 20.

20. Laclau and Mouffe, *Hegemony and Socialist Strategy*, pp. 128ff.

21. Bowman, 'Letter from Jerusalem', p. 20.

22. 'Palestine' was constituted as an imaginable entity at the moment of its loss; as such, there were few explicitly national traditions for its members to carry into exile. As Nels Johnson has shown in *Islam and the Politics of Meaning in Palestinian Nationalism* (London: Kegan Paul International, 1982) the inter-factional feuding of the political elite of pre-1948 Palestine, as well as the localized interests of the Palestinian peasantry, meant that identity was tied tightly to local, factional or class interests and not to some idea of national or nationalist solidarity. Resistance to Zionist encroachment was couched in terms either strictly regional (focusing on resistance to land loss) or broadly international (pan-Islamic or pan-Arabist) by the various groups concerned (see p. 57 and *passim*). Consequently there was no pre-existent vehicle that could be mobilized to create, in the exile, a sense of national simultaneity and a promise of territorial re-establishment – at least not in the way the Armenian Orthodox liturgy could for the Armenians, or the way 'that mixture of folklore, ethical exhortation and nationalist political propaganda that we call the Bible' could for the Jews. (See Eugene Kamenka, 'Political Nationalism – The Evolution of the Idea', in Kamenka, ed., *Nationalism: The Nature and Evolution of an Idea* [Canberra: Australian National University Press, 1973] p. 4.)

23. Raja Shehadeh, *The Third Way: A Journal of Life in the West Bank* (London: Quartet Books, 1982), p. 8. *Sumud* is an Arabic term referring to Palestinians under occupation whose identity derives from their dedication to holding on to their homes and lands by all means available. See also p. vi.

24. Laclau and Mouffe, *Hegemony and Socialist Strategy*, p. 119.

25. The Palestine Liberation Organization is organized around a structure allowing relative autonomy to each of the groups represented therein: 'The apparatuses and the country organisations each have their own budget and organisational structure, with their lines of control meeting only at the level of the Central Committee. This unique organisational structure was developed by the leadership primarily to ensure the survival of the movement in the face of repeated Arab efforts to infiltrate, split or otherwise undermine it; but it also enabled them to isolate any source of ideological ferment, thus keeping the ideological common denominator of the movement at the intentionally low and all-embracing level with which it was founded' (Helen Cobban, *The Palestinian Liberation Organisation: People, Power and Politics* [Cambridge: Cambridge University Press, 1984], p. 26). As a result, although the PLO, with the Palestine National Congress which is effectively its legislature, serves as a government in exile, it is able to do little more than stand as a symbol (the 'ideological common denominator') of Palestinian aspirations while each of its autonomous units works in the interest of the discrete communities of the diaspora they represent.

26. Fawaz Turki, *The Disinherited: Journal of a Palestinian Exile*, 2nd edn (London: Monthly Review Press, 1974) hereafter within text as *TD*; Edward Said, *After the Last Sky*, hereafter within text as *LS*; and Raja Shehadeh, *The Third Way*, hereafter as *TW*. All page references to these titles are listed in the text within parentheses.

27. Peter Loizos, *The Heart Grown Bitter: A Chronicle of Cypriot War Refugees* (Cambridge: Cambridge University Press, 1981); and Peter Marris, *Loss and Change* (London: Routledge and Kegan Paul, 1974).

28. Pamela Ann Smith, 'The Palestinian Diaspora, 1948–85', *Journal of Palestine Studies*, XV:3, Spring 1986, p. 93.

29. Rosemary Sayigh, *Palestinians: From Peasants to Revolutionaries* (London: Zed Press, 1979), p. 107.

30. The Israelis have, of course, come to play a more immediate role in the demonology of camp Palestinians since they began to take a more unmediated role in the persecution of Lebanese Palestinians. The increasingly active participation of Israelis in the inter-communal strife of the Lebanon through the 1970s culminated, in the early 1980s, in actual Israeli occupation of significant parts of the country. This, in part by proxy and in part directly, continues at the time of writing. Just as the 1967 Israeli Occupation of new territories of historic Palestine led eventually to a sense of solidarity between 'Israeli Arabs' and the Palestinians of the Occupied Territories, so it might be hoped that eventually the Palestinians of Lebanon will grow more empathetic towards the Palestinians of Palestine who share with them Israeli occupation.

31. With respect to this exodus, see Salim Tamari, 'Factionalism and Class Formation in Recent Palestinian History', in Roger Owen, ed., *Studies in the Economic and Social History of Palestine in the Nineteenth and Twentieth Centuries* (London: Macmillan, 1982) p. 180; and Ian Lustick, *Arabs in the Jewish State: Israel's Control of a National Minority* (Austin: University of Texas Press, 1980) p. 48.

32. See Smith, 'The Palestinian Diaspora', pp. 17–37.

33. Although recent restrictions on Palestinian economic influence in the Middle East in general and the Gulf States in particular – including widespread imprisonment, banishment and execution – may cause interesting redefinitions of position.

34. On this point see Edward Said's *Orientalism* (London: Routledge, 1978); his *The Question of Palestine* (London: Routledge, 1979); and his *Covering Islam: How the Media and the Experts Determine How We See the Rest of the World* (London: Routledge, 1981). Also see Edward Said and Christopher Hitchens, *Blaming the Victims: Spurious Scholarship and the Palestinian Question* (Verso: London, 1988).

35. Edward Said, *Beginnings: Intention and Method* (New York: Basic Books, 1975).

36. For the Israeli strategies of occupation within 1948–67 Israel, see Lustick, *Arabs in the Jewish State*. For the occupation of the West Bank and Gaza, see Jan Metzger, Martin Orth and Christian Sterzing, *This Land is Our Land* (London: Zed Press, 1986). On the experience of the West Bank peasantry, see Tamari, 'Building Other People's Homes: The Palestinian Peasant's Household and Work in Israel', *Journal of Palestine Studies*, XI:1, 1981, pp. 31–66.

37. See Steven Runciman, *The Historic Role of the Christian Arabs of Palestine* (London: Longman, 1969); and Lustick, *Arabs in the Jewish State*.

38. See my 'Unholy Struggle on Holy Ground: Conflict and Interpretation in Jerusalem', *Anthropology Today*, II:3, 1986, pp. 14–17; and also Loizos, *The Heart Grown Bitter*, p. 132.

39. See my 'Religion and Political Identity in Beit Sahour', *Middle East Report*, 164–5, May–August 1990, pp. 50–53, and 'Nationalizing the Sacred: Shrines and Shifting Identities in the Israeli-Occupied Territories', *Man: The Journal of the Royal Anthropological Institute*, XXVIII:3, September 1993, pp. 431–60.

40. For an analysis of Israel's unsuccessful attempt to strengthen the rural/urban divide and thus weaken Palestinian identity, see Salim Tamari, 'In League with Zion: Israel's Search for a Native Pillar', *Journal of Palestine Studies*, XIII, 1983, pp. 41–56.

41. In *The Third Way*; see in particular pp. 30–33, 96–8.

42. On this point, see Slavoj Žižek, *Looking Awry: An Introduction to Jacques Lacan through Popular Culture* (Cambridge, Mass.: MIT Press, 1991), pp. 213–14.

43. A similar statement of the recognition that the struggle against Israeli occupation will not end the problems of the Palestinians was made to me by a Palestinian leftist in Jerusalem in 1985: 'We have two battles to fight; the first is the war of national liberation, and after that is the revolution.'

44. Shehadeh's use of the term 'pornography' suggests that one loses the object of desire in pursuing an image of that object into which one has actually invested desire. I would stress here that the issue is not one of the real as opposed to the fantastic (which is Shehadeh's construction) but instead an issue of the way the 'pornographic' discourse of desire fetishizes the image and perversely 'fixes' it outside of the historical and political domain in which the object exists.

45. For the centrality of the issue of land, see Geoffrey Aronson, *Israel, Palestinians and the Intifada: Creating Facts on the West Bank* (London: Kegan Paul International, 1990). The foregrounding of the land as the field in which all activities characterizing and maintaining Palestinian lives take place results from the fact that one of the most salient aspects of Israeli domination is the state's theft of Palestinian lands. The land thus is transformed into an emblem of Palestinian existence and its theft becomes the sign of the Israeli will to efface the Palestinians. A Beit Jala woman, talking of her brother's death by heart attack when he heard his property had been confiscated by Israeli settlers, told me: 'When you see a big healthy man fall over dead in his prime it is because of land – land is all they have, it is their connection. Land is the issue on the West Bank.'

46. Laclau and Mouffe, *Hegemony and Socialist Strategy*, p. 129. In the following week, violent demonstrations, starting in the refugee camps and spreading quickly to the towns, broke out throughout the territories. This process of polarization and mobilization seems to follow quite closely that described by Fanon in *The Wretched of the Earth* (Harmondsworth: Penguin 1967); see especially the effects on the development of revolutionary consciousness of the 'hecatombs' of the slaughtered (p. 56). The particular policies of relatively non-violent resistance successfully promoted by the United National Leadership of the Uprising differ from the violent strategies engaged in the opening phases of the Algerian revolt, and this may be a consequence of the way that in the territories communication (not only that effected by media and telephones but also that brought about by travel – both voluntary and that forced by taking on employment away from one's residence) rendered the gap between urban and rural consciousness less abysmal than that which existed in Algeria.

47. Joe Stork, 'The Significance of Stones: Notes from the Seventh Month', in Zachary Lockman and Joel Beinin, eds, *Intifada: The Palestinian Uprising against Israeli Occupation* (Boston: South End Press, 1989) pp. 67–79.

48. On this point, see further: Ze'ev Schiff and Ehud Ya'ari, *Intifada: The Palestinian Uprising – Israel's Third Front* (New York: Simon and Schuster, 1990) pp. 188–92; and also Aronson, *Israel, Palestinians and the Intifada*, pp. 328–32.

49. Aronson, *Israel, Palestinians and the Intifada*, p. 328.

50. Schiff and Ya'ari, *Intifada*, p. 188.

51. Helga Baumgarten, ' "Discontented People" and "Outside Agitators": The PLO in the Palestinian Uprising', in Jamal R. Nassar and Roger Heacock, eds, *Intifada: Palestine at the Crossroads* (New York: Praeger, 1990) p. 218.

52. Ibid., p. 210.

53. Ibid., pp. 219–22.

54. Hamas is the 'Islamic Resistance Movement', an offspring of the fundamentalist 'Society of the Moslem Brethren' that conceives of Palestine not in national terms but as sacred territory dedicated as a *waqf* (religious bequest) to God.

55. The 1948 war led to the expulsion of 83 per cent of the Palestinian population of what then became Israel; any settlement which recovers only the West Bank and Gaza will not, in even a territorial sense, recover the homes of these people and their very numerous descendants.

56. Darwish, 'The Earth is Closing on Us', *Victims of a Map*, p. 13.

7

Rastafari as Resistance and the Ambiguities of Essentialism in the 'New Social Movements'

Anna Marie Smith

The rewriting of leftist orthodoxies through the confrontation with post-structuralist, post-modernist and contemporary psychoanalytical categories has been enormously productive and strategically critical. The 'new social movements' – the highly decentralized, informal, autonomous, local and yet simultaneously transnational struggles – could not be accurately described as long as they were reduced to an epiphenomenon of class struggle. There is much evidence to suggest, however, that the decentring of the class struggle is only an initial step in the development of a more useful political analysis of these movements. What actually has become uncommon in discussions of the 'new times'[1] is the lack of references to the women's movement, the peace movement, the environmentalist movement, the lesbian and gay movement, and ethnic and racial minorities movements. Positioned as additional elements, the discursive function of these references is ambiguous. Will these 'additions' be included without modifying the central principle (*plus ça change . . .*), or will their subversive potential be recognized?

The problem with an uncritical reproduction of this list is that it tends to simplify, and indeed collapse, the field of oppositions out of which they have emerged. And yet, these oppositions do not have a simple binary structure. In the struggles against racism, for example, there is no singular 'enemy' figure and no singular 'liberating' figure. Indeed, in post-war Britain, the racist exclusion of blackness has been articulated with various discursive elements, such as nationalism, anti-criminality, anti-intellectualism, anti-local government and so on. In the case of the 'Salman Rushdie Affair', racist arguments were advanced in the name of the supposedly European democratic tradition. It was argued by various British right-wing politicians and intellectuals that the Muslim 'extremists' had to be opposed because their foreign religious fervour constituted a threat to the Western principle of the right to free speech. Through this articulation, the censorious and racist extremism of the Thatcherite discourse were momentarily concealed.

Resistances against racism are equally complex. Homi Bhabha and Edward Said, for example, responded to the 'Salman Rushdie Affair' by expressing support for Rushdie's right to challenge orthodox Islam. However, they also distanced themselves from the racist defence of Rushdie by insisting that the orthodox Muslim responses to *The Satanic Verses* should be considered in terms of the specific context of Islamic histories, and warned against the redeployment of an Orientalist caricature of the Muslim positions in the guise of a defence of democratic freedoms.[2]

On the other hand, and in an attempt to describe the complexity of contemporary social movements, many writers have attempted to make a distinction between two different moments in these discourses.[3] Broadly speaking, the first moment could be identified as one in which social demands are organized around an essence, that is, a fixed, ahistorical 'woman-ness', 'blackness', 'lesbian-ness', or 'gayness'. The demands in this moment centre on a liberation and restoration of these essences, all of which have been suppressed and colonized by the diverse forces of domination. The strategies emerging from this moment are conceptualized in terms of redressing discriminatory exclusions: demands are made for full and equal inclusion in the social (such as the extension of democratic rights and freedoms); a replacement of stereotypical imagery with 'positive images'; proportional representation in public and official discourses; and affirmative action in employment practices. Demands are also made for the construction of exclusive spaces, within which the work of recovering these essences can progress.

The second moment – which is, at the same time, both complementary and contradictory with the first – is one wherein essences such as 'woman-ness', 'blackness', or 'gayness' are reconsidered. The singularity of each essence is shown to mask an actual plurality of positions. Strategies of this type show, for example, that instead of a homogenic notion of a black subject, there is instead a plurality of blacknesses sharing only a 'family resem-blance' to each other, rather than an essential core. Through this weakening of the essentiality of these elements, the entire purpose of each social move-ment is called into question. Lesbian and gay activists, for example, some-times strategically invoke the myth that lesbians and gays constitute a fixed subject which occupies 10 per cent of the population; some of them also (more or less) believe in this myth. At the same time, lesbians and gays often argue that no one should regard their sexuality as naturally predetermined, that everyone should have the freedom to choose their sexuality in a mean-ingful way, and that sexualities can be reconstructed and promoted. Simi-larly, various feminist discourses have questioned the conception of a natural 'woman' and theories that argue that female sexuality is determined by this essence.

Given these complexities, though, how can this juxtaposition of contradictory moments in the discourses of social movements be analysed? It may be useful here to refer to a similar problematic in philosophy and deconstruction. 'Essentialism', or, in Derridean terms, the 'metaphysics of presence', has a complex relation with 'anti-essentialism', or deconstruction. Deconstruction is positioned vis-à-vis presence as a supplement,[4] not as an exterior entity or as an opponent. Deconstruction only appears to come after presence, and only appears to be imposed on the text from the outside at the whim of an author. Deconstruction actually 'takes place', wherever there is something.[5] There is no self-conscious author of the critique of presence; in a sense, one always finds oneself already thrown into position, already engaged in deconstruction.

There is never, then, a 'pure' deconstructive practice that escapes the metaphysics of presence; one finds oneself, inevitably, doing something and, to an extent, doing its discursive opposite – precisely at the same time.[6] Supplementation in the form of deconstruction is possible only because deconstruction is always already at work in the original foundations of the text itself. Without the possibility of deconstruction, there would be no text whatsoever. Or, to put it slightly differently, the deconstructive 'act' – an apparently intentional initiative – is both a profoundly heroic interruption and, because it is always already 'done', a movement without an author, place or time. The deconstruction of essences is always there and not there, always already present in the origin and never complete in the end. In a perverse dialectic, the movement of *différance* simultaneously shows the failure of, and makes possible, the very essentiality with which it is endlessly intertwined.

Deconstruction shows the impossibility of pure and complete essences, but never replaces essences; it instead shows that what appear to function as essences are actually located on the terrain of contingency, rather than the terrain of necessity. In an infinite invasion/preservation of otherness, deconstruction and the metaphysics of presence are simultaneously positioned as each entailing the very conditions of impossibility, and yet also the very conditions of possibility, of each other. In the case of the essentialist and anti-essentialist moments in the discourses of social movements, these two moments should be seen not as separate phases, not as 'incorrect/correct' alternatives, but as supplements, in a manner analogous to the relation between the metaphysics of presence and that of deconstruction.

One way to describe these identity games is to speak in terms of essence-claims. From the original moment in which an essence-claim is made, the essence-claim is already being undone; there never was/never will be a pure 'blackness', 'woman-ness', and so on. These strategic claims to essences nevertheless do have important political effects, allowing for self-naming and other-naming in the mapping out of antagonisms. Claims to essences should always be placed in terms of their particular context of particular strategies, such as the struggles against domination, rather than be considered in abstraction. The effect of an essence-claim which is deployed as part of a resistance strategy cannot be predicted in advance. It may function as a condition of possibility for further subversion of domination, or as a limitation, depending on its particular context.[7]

'Essence' and Essentialism

To illustrate the implications of this approach to social movements, I propose to examine one influential black resistance discourse – Rastafari – as an essentialist resistance strategy against domination. However, because the terms 'essentialism' and 'essence' are used in many different ways, I shall first attempt to provide some working definitions by returning, in part, to their philosophical origin, namely to Aristotle's *Metaphysics*. For Aristotle, we obtain knowledge of things only in so far as they contain something universal, some singular and constantly identical characteristic.[8] That universal characteristic, *eidos* or form, is also its 'cause'; that is, it is also the characteristic most primary, immanent, and indivisible in the thing. The *eidos* or form is that which alone gives Being, definiteness, concreteness and boundaries to the thing.[9] With this conception of Being, Aristotle constructs the opposition between form and matter, essence and accidents.

Aristotle offers an analysis of the male citizen Socrates: his human-ness, his quality of being a rational animal, is his essence. Other terms – that is, accidents – are predicated to this person, but there is no necessity in these predications. For example, his human-ness is said to be wholly unaffected by his facial features and their purely exterior elements; hence, these elements have no essential meaning. Lacking necessity, there can be no scientific knowledge of the accidental; and, in fact, the accidental in Aristotle is closely akin to the nonexistent.[10] The gender, race and socio-political status of this subject is, not surprisingly, 'necessary' (and thus not accidental). Indeed, Aristotle holds that only male citizens are endowed with full rationality, as opposed to the females and slaves of the polis; to define Socrates's human essence as a rational capacity is thus to define him as a free male, and to exclude, strictly speaking, females and slaves from humanity.[11]

From the Aristotelian viewpoint, then, a sensible thing is properly understood as a compound, consisting of that which truly causes its Being and knowability, that is, its form, and of that which, in the thing, cannot be known and has no being per se, that is, its matter.[12] Form is that which remains the same, identical throughout accidental physical change. Matter is secondary to form, serving merely as a medium for form. Although it is indispensable to the concrete thing, it has no reality of its own. In short, form is essential to the thing, while matter is accidental; form and matter are analytically divisible. Indeed, without the possibility of conceiving the form of the thing apart from matter, there would be no possibility of knowing the essence of the thing; the thing would remain unknowable and without Being.[13] Form is eternal actuality, while matter exists only potentially, with the non-necessary possibility of coming to Be.[14]

In the *Metaphysics*, Aristotle does not consider form–matter compounds alone, but also asserts that there is a prime mover – the only pure actuality, a pure Being; a form which is prior to all other forms as the efficient and final cause of all things; a form which is not combined with matter; an essence unadorned by accidents. The prime mover causes all motion, but is separate from that which it moves and is itself unmoved.[15] A thing, then, is known to the extent that its essence, rather than its accidents, is 'grasped'. A thing *is*, in the true rather than apparent sense, to the extent that it is form rather than matter. The accidental must be purely external and secondary to the essential, since, for Aristotle, without a separate and constant element, Being and knowability collapse into flux. Pure *eidos*, then, is precisely that which is most knowable, even if such knowledge is in practice the most difficult to obtain.[16]

Since the utterly self-sufficient prime mover is pure Being, Aristotle argues that the highest pursuit of which 'man' is capable is a pursuit that has itself for its own end; hence, the exertion of the best part of 'man' is reason, in the contemplation of the noble and divine, the realm of pure forms and the prime mover. This most virtuous practice is a turning away from the world of appearances towards that which truly *is*, working against the temptations of the false goods and lesser pleasures of the material and the bodily, towards, instead, the cultivation of pure wisdom. Although the contemplative life is not for the many, since only a few are endowed with higher natures, it is through this activity that 'man' can attain the highest degree of perfection possible for a mortal being.[17]

Now, borrowing the category of 'essence' from this philosophical trajectory opens many different possibilities, particularly in terms of discourse analysis. Discourses which tend to be organized around similar themes as the Aristotelian attempt to distinguish between form and matter can be grouped together under the name 'essentialism'. Social practices within these discourses tend to be shaped by a shared conception of a social identity, and this identity tends to be considered as fixed, unique, undivided and ahistorical. This identity also tends to be conceived as that which 'lies beneath' the surface of multiplicities; the former tends to be recognized as the truth, while the latter tends to be regarded as mere appearance. 'Essentialist' arguments, in terms of identity, tend to claim that the 'essence' or true character of an identity has been concealed through the work of forces which are external to that 'essence': that is, the forces of oppression and domination. A turning away from surfaces and appearances towards the recovery of the underlying 'essence' tends to be considered not only as a possibility, but as a strategy of crucial importance. Such a 'liberation' of a true identity, both individually and collectively, becomes the highest possible achievement. Decision-making is increasingly brought within this structure, with the presupposition that there ought to be a direct correspondence between what one essentially is and what one does. This entails, of course, a thorough criticism of predominant value systems and the construction of an alternative value system that is specific to the particular identity in question. This 'return' to a true identity is only accomplished through a total criticism of values and practices – a fundamental transition from the realm of appearances to that of truth, goodness and happiness.

The Essentialism of Rastafari

Considered in these terms, Rastafari discourse can be described as 'essentialist'. The informal process of turning towards Rastafari values – the 'journey to Jah' – is a turning away from white Western influences, Christianity, competitive individualism, and, in the British case, a rejection of traditional British values and racist conceptions of blackness. This process entails an identification with 'I and I' – the true self. This return to the true self is achieved collectively through 'reasoning', discussion, and reflection on spiritual questions. In 'I and I', the splitting of the original and natural collective unity through individuation, and the division between the divine and the self, is overcome. 'I and I' expresses the presence of the God of Africa in the self, and the fundamental continuities binding individuals together underneath individual differences. It signifies an essentially unified spiritual brotherhood. In Rastafari discourse, the 'I and I' identity creates a sense of a *gemeinschaft* community whose spiritual links span historical periods, national borders and individualist tendencies, recasting those tendencies, borders and periods as examples of many false and oppressive divisions.

This return to essence, however, must be placed in the context of strategies of resistance. Rastafari beliefs provide an all-embracing framework for the understanding of, and resistance to, virtually all experiences of oppression. Condensing these diverse opposed elements into the symbol of Babylon, Rastafari draws a single frontier between the white racist system and the suffering black people. It is in reference to this single frontier that the meaning of everyday experience is constructed. The 'Babylonian conspiracy' nevertheless functions as an extremely flexible device: it accommodates virtually any particular experience and novelty. For the Rastafari, the history of their people and the apparent triumph of the white oppressors constitutes an essentially continuous tradition. Experiences of oppression confirm the identity of the brotherhood as the chosen ones, those who by their moral nature are superior to the oppressors. Organized in this manner, the heterogeneous experiences of oppression are strategically reinterpreted as a singular phenomenon, and as that which paradoxically signifies a higher status.

This articulation of blackness with suffering, however, is combined with the representation of the effects of racist oppression as external to true blackness. The Babylonian system is represented as ultimately failing to penetrate and subvert blackness, such that the 'journey to Jah' always remains open as a possible strategy. The supreme value of this return becomes clarified in the Rastafari interpretation of the diverse experiences of exclusion from white society through displacement and condensation of all oppositional elements on to Babylon.

Jamaican Traditions of Black Resistances

The Rastafari form of black resistance, the total turning away from the white Western world towards a higher spiritual realm, is located in, and made possible by, a tradition of similar resistances based in Jamaican history. In that tradition, the strategy of turning to a spiritual 'beyond' has been deployed and redeployed for generations. This strategy made resistance thinkable in the face of almost overwhelming domination. As early as the seventeenth-century slave revolts, African peoples in Jamaica escaped white subordination by withdrawing to enclaves in the hill regions.[18] The equations of resistance with spiritual beliefs, oppressors with evil, liberation with a complete refusal of white society and the establishment of a radically separate world, and freedom with other-worldly salvation, were maintained in several subsequent resistance discourses: Jamaica's first millenarian movement, the revolt of the Mial people in the 1840s, and the movement of Alexander Bedward, a black Baptist leader and faith healer.[19]

Garveyism is also an important precursor to Rastafari, especially in terms of its radical reinterpretation of the identity of the Negro/African people. Through his influential Universal Improvement of the Negro Association, Garvey encouraged Afro-Americans and Afro-Caribbeans to organize themselves in terms of their racial identity first and foremost to achieve their freedom through unity and self-reliance and to strengthen the African 'nation': to liberate the actual colonies and to unify Africans throughout the world. The Garveyite principle of self-reliance and definition of race as a natural category set this discourse apart from other contemporary organizations, such as the National Association for the Advancement of Coloured People. Garvey saw pluralism and integrationism as a negation and/or dilution of the essence of the African people.

Another important aspect of Garveyism in terms of Rastafari is its pan-Africanism, and its promotion of the representation of Ethiopia as the mythical origin of this nation. Diverse peoples became, through this myth, unified as a single people sharing the collective dream of a spiritual return to Africa.[20] Garveyism shared the single frontier structure and the emphasis on spiritualism of its predecessors, and added pan-Africanism and the myth of Ethiopia to the tradition. In the Rastafari 'journey to Jah', the principles of these resistances, from the slave revolts to Garveyism, were taken up and redeployed in a further resistance strategy in Jamaica.

Why was this Jamaican spiritual belief system rearticulated as a resistance discourse by many young British blacks in the late 1960s and 1970s? It is possible that Rastafari discourse would have remained relatively obscure, rural- and Jamaican-oriented, and would have never been adopted by young British blacks, without the articulation of this discourse to alternative black music, namely reggae. Reggae was originally a fusion of African, traditional Jamaican, and American rhythm-and-blues music traditions. In the early 1960s, the electrified disc-jockey sound system displaced acoustic perform-ance, but brought traditional Jamaican music closer to the music favoured by young blacks in British and American cities. 'Toasting' DJs mixed records with their own African-inspired verses, adding commentary on contemporary ghetto experiences to the music. 'Rock steady' and reggae bands soon followed, reflecting in their music, both in the lyrics and the sound, the crises in contemporary Jamaica: high unemployment, inflation, food shortages, widespread poverty, political corruption, strikes, fights, shoot-outs, and battles with the police. In the massive migrations from the depressed rural areas to the urban centres, black teenagers made up a majority of the migrant population. Many of these young blacks lived in makeshift shacks and were unable to find work. Reggae music described their experience, and expressed their resistance, like other musical forms in a Jamaican tradition which dates back to the slave revolts.[21] Linton Kwesi Johnson comments:

> [The sounds of reggae] are the sounds of screeching tyres, bottles breaking, wailing sirens, gunfire, people screaming and shouting, children crying. They are the sounds of the apocalyptic thunder and earthquake; of chaos and curfews. The sounds of reggae are the sounds of a society in the process of transformation, a society undergoing profound political and historical change.[22]

Reggae artists became the most visible Rastafari, giving the belief system a contemporary form of expression that, in the music of Bob Marley, Peter Tosh, Burning Spear, Junior Murvin, Leroy Sibbles and others, secured for Rastafari an international audience.[23]

Alternative black music, then, became the principal mode of transmission of Rastafari discourse. The emergence of reggae in Britain followed the establishment of a separate black entertainment tradition in the 1950s. The black dance halls soon gave way to sound systems modelled after their

Jamaican counterparts. As a mass (white) youth entertainment industry rapidly expanded in the 1960s, the value of 'alternative' (black) music increased. The sound systems and blues party DJs prided themselves on playing exclusively independent and imported records from Jamaica, which were stocked by speciality record stores. Many British blacks were introduced to reggae music from Jamaica through the activities of these entrepreneurs well before Bob Marley and the Wailers first toured the UK in the mid-1970s.[24] Marley later became a successful recording 'star' in the mainstream charts as well, bringing a slightly less 'dread' message to a large black and white audience.

The Rastafari 'Total Experience'

With this mode of transmission, Rastafari was taken up by black British youths in the form of a highly informal, leaderless and flexible belief system. From a brief review of the practices of British Rastafari, it can be shown that this discourse constituted an essentialist 'total experience' in which virtually all of the social practices of the believers tended to be organized with reference to the 'I and I' identity.[25] Rastafari developed exclusive forms of expression, in terms of musical and oral discourses. And reggae music remained an important form for the promotion of Rastafari beliefs in the Caribbean, Europe, North America and Africa. Black music shops, black community centres, reggae clubs, festivals and, later, 'pirate' radio stations became important sites for the continued construction and promotion of Rastafari. The everyday, 'non-productive' practice – the enjoyment of music – was resignified by Rastafari as an important form of communication, especially in its exclusive, alternative-to-(white)-mainstream content.

The emphasis on the oral tradition in Rastafari discourse also had effects in terms of language. Taking up a previously devalued Afro-Caribbean language system, British Rastafari created a unique language out of a mix of various Afro-Caribbean linguistic elements with Cockney elements. The informal use of this unique linguistic system by both Rastafari and other blacks and some whites precluded the development of a strict division between 'members' and 'non-members'.[26]

Rastafari discourse also represents the body of the black man and the black woman in a different manner than popular British discourses. This representation is particularly opposed to the representation of the black body in racist discourses. The Rastafari practice of wearing dreadlocks, the long coils of hair by black men and black women, is exemplary in this respect. This practice was derived from early believers in Jamaica, who sought to imitate Ethiopian warriors and to follow the biblical teachings from the Old Testament. Only Negroid hair, if coiled, will continue to grow in genuine dreadlock coils;

Rastafari invested this banal biological fact with a meaning connoting the privileged status of blackness. Where the black body had been the site of disciplining and neutralization of difference, it was now redefined as a highly visible signifier of black pride.

The revaluation of the black body as goodness was coupled with a revaluation of sensual pleasures. Some of the British Rastafari adopted a special diet designed to contribute to the strength of the body and to protect it from harm. As the black spirit had to be cleansed of the destructive effects of the Babylonian system, so too did the black body need to be cleansed of Babylonian pollutants. For virtually all believers, the smoking of 'ganja' was viewed as a spiritual and collective ritual. Illegal drug use among British youths in general was fairly common in this period, and Jamaican marijuana was not consumed by the Rastafari alone. Ganja smoking signified deviance, criminality and perversity,[27] like any other illegal drug use. For the Rastafari, however, this ritual was also perceived as an element in the 'journey to Jah', a loosening of the insidious grip of the Babylonian system on 'I and I'. The privileging of drug use in Rastafari discourse constitutes a rejection of the traditional subordination of the bodily to the spiritual which is usually found in both religious and political resistance discourses alike.[28]

Another example of this revaluation of the black body can be found in Rastafari representations of sexuality. The heterosexual practices of Rastafari are highly privileged; the assertion of the goodness of blackness is articulated to the assertion of the virility of the black male and the representation of the black woman's fundamental role as a child-bearer. Sexual practices, as long as they do not contradict these principles, are revalued as good in themselves. Homosexuality, contraception and abortion, however, are usually represented as taboo.

The Rastafari, then, tended to conceive virtually all of their experiences in terms which reinforced their particular sense of blackness. They tended not to experience Rastafari-blackness as one blackness among many, but as the only true blackness. If a black person expressed anti-Rastafari beliefs, he or she would be represented as speaking under the influence of Babylon and as being temporarily misled as to their true identity. Blackness in this context came to have meaning not with reference to a multiplicity of heterogeneous positions and discourses, but through the all-embracing single frontier structure of Rastafari. The productivity of contiguous and overlapping discourses which contribute to differentiation of blackness, discourses organized around gender or sexuality, for example, tended to be muted. This singular Rastafari-blackness was articulated to goodness, and to virtually all good-nesses. A chain of equivalence of unlimited dimensions was established, embracing the equivalences Rastafari-blackness = essential blackness = goodness = the oppressed people = noble suffering = return to spiritual origin = Ethiopia = the divinity of Haile Selassie 'I' = a collective identity over individualism = black musical and oral expression = cleansed and strengthened bodies = harmony with nature = sensuality = virility = fertility = a divine other-worldly destiny = everyday resistances against policing, the white education system, state institutions, and so on.

The dimensions of the Babylonian conspiracy, the opposed camp in terms of the singular frontier, were also unlimited, such that it captured virtually all facets of oppression. For Rastafari, the constitution of identity was not a matter of a complex play of heterogeneous subject positions, of which Rastafari-blackness was one among many, but of an increasingly totalizing identity which did not admit contradictory identities (such as homosexual blackness or anti-Rastafari blackness). The return to essence entailed a total clarification of multiplicity and contradiction in experiences and identities, such that the social became represented as a simple two-camp system.

However, the informality of Rastafari discourse constitutes, in a sense, a logic which contradicts these totalizing and essentialist moments. The conception of a Rastafar*ian* membership, and indeed the very term, Rastafarian*ism*, are representations which are perhaps more central to academic observations rather than to non-academic cultural practices. The discursive effects of Rastafari cannot be limited to a neatly defined empirical group of people. Hebdige notes the importance of the cross-over between (white) alternative-to-(white) mainstream music and Rastafari-influenced reggae. For the white British punks, the 'conviction [and] political bile' of reggae offered an effective and credible form for their criticism of the vacuous nature of the white rock scene. Like the mod and skinhead appropriations of the styles of the West Indian rude boys, white punks borrowed from Rastafari and reggae to express their distance from the British mainstream.[29]

Gilroy explicitly criticizes the sociological attempts by writers such as Cashmore[30] to define Rastafari in terms of false and true members according to a strict definition of core beliefs. He draws attention instead to the 'lines dividing different levels of commitment' and to the 'broad and diverse use to which the language and symbols of Rastafari have been put'.[31] The 'interpretive community' which has been constructed through Rastafari discourse 'extends beyond Afro-Caribbean people who smoke herb, to old people, soul boys and girls, some whites and Asians'.[32] Gilroy also describes the complexities of the tensions and cross-overs between different types of reggae and between Rastafari reggae and soul music.[33] The late 1980s saw the emergence of the funky dreads like Jazzy B and Soul II Soul, who produced the most successful juxtaposition of the reggae, soul and dance music traditions. Other cross-overs are less popular and yet just as subversive in terms of their interruption of fixed boundaries between identities, such as performers like 'MC Kinky', a white British woman who often performs her reggae-ragga-sweet chatting-styled music in white dance clubs in London.

The Politics of Evaluating Rastafari Politics

Many writers have offered evaluations of Rastafari discourse; the most common assessment is that it is 'escapist'. This discourse, however, only appears to be escapist in the terms of a Western rationality which cannot represent spirituality as a resistance strategy. Cashmore, in his generally sympathetic study, argues that Rastafari is among the most important forms of black resistance in contemporary Britain. However, he categorizes the first-generation black immigrants as apolitical and quiescent, such that it is in contrast with their submissiveness that Rastafari appears to be radical. The unintended effects of this type of analysis can be problematic. As Gloria Yamato states,

> Now the newest form of racism that I'm hip to is unaware/self-righteous racism. The 'good white' racist attempts to shame Blacks into being blacker, scorns Japanese-Americans who don't speak Japanese, and knows more about the Chicano/a community than the folks who make up the community. They assign themselves as the 'good whites' as opposed to the 'bad whites' and are often so busy telling people of colour what the issues in the Black, Asian, Indian, Latino/a communities should be that they don't have time to deal with their errant sisters and brothers in the white community. Which means that people of colour are still left to deal with what the 'good whites' don't want to . . . racism.[34]

In a similar comment, Ezekiel Mzika also writes:

> I too am sick and tired of being told by white people what my responsibilities as a black man are, of being told that because I am black, I must always and only speak and write and think about blackness. White people own the world, while I am confined to being black.[35]

This is not to say that white writers have nothing to say about black culture, but that every evaluation of cultural practices should be informed by a conception that takes as given the inextricability of power and resistance. In other words – and this is where this Foucauldian notion of power is most crucial – instead of dismissing the practices of the 'first-generation' black immigrants in Britain as capitulations to oppressive cultures, Cashmore should have shown the operation of resistances beneath the surface of these practices, and should have noted their common-sense aspects.

Hebdige discusses Rastafari in his study of British youth subcultures.[36] He argues that, along with other subcultures, Rastafari constitutes a 'symbolic violation of the social order'.[37] Subcultures express a 'Refusal' of the social order through the informal revaluation of mundane objects as 'signifiers of difference'.[38] Hebdige's insights, however, are limited by the base/superstructure model of politics. Working with the 'subculture theory' framework,[39] Hebdige assigns subcultures an epiphenomenal status. Only the class struggle is considered as a 'real' political site. Subcultures are defined in terms of the class struggle, but because of their location outside the 'concrete' level, they fail to constitute true resistances. The solutions of subcultures can only be 'magical' since they are located at the 'profoundly superficial level of appearances; that is, at the level of signs'.[40]

It is nevertheless possible to analyse Rastafari discourse as a resistance strategy without using these problematic approaches; namely, through contextualization. What were the patterns of domination in which Rastafari emerged as a response? What was the subversive potential of Rastafari with reference to racist discourses? To sketch out the significance of British Rastafari, I shall briefly refer to the various constructions of blackness in both the colonized Caribbean and post-war Britain.

Disciplining Blackness: Not-whites, Immigrants, Criminals and 'Good Blacks'

Although we often now take the meaning of the term 'black' for granted, it should be emphasized that this term is a relatively recent construction which has achieved 'common sense' status only through extensive discursive interventions. One of the principal strategies of the colonization discourse was precisely the negation of presence to blackness. This negation was one of the non-coercive strategies for the containment of the threatening 'native'. On the one hand, the colonizer attempted to suppress any rituals and practices which linked the colonized with their African past, in an attempt to relegate 'native'-ness to a non-space. In itself, 'native'-ness appears in the colonization discourse as a nothing; it takes meaning only with reference to the colonizer. 'Native'-ness only signifies not-white, not-Western, not-civilized, not-Christian, and so on. On the other hand, the colonization discourse attempted to present its discursive space as the only possible space. In these terms, some version of 'native'-ness had to be included such that the colonized space could appear to be global and all-embracing. As a discourse claiming to be universal, it had to appear to account for virtually everything; all social elements, in some form or another, had to be given a place within the colonization discourse. That which the colonization discourse could not represent, namely the forms of blackness which threatened colonization with subversion, had to be concealed, and this concealment was constructed precisely through the representation of an included and disciplined blackness. Colonization therefore also entailed 'enlightenment' strategies, the Westernization of different strata of the 'natives', such as the household servants (as opposed to plantation slaves) and the Europeanized intellectual elite. The effect of these strategies was to mask the deep division of the social between the colonizer and the colonized. Colonization appeared not as the brutal war between two organized camps, but as a natural and humane cultivation of the colonized in terms of their own true interests: the transformation of a people who lacked history, culture, religion, and so on. With this concealment of the threat of subversion, colonization appeared to be a viable project; and with this disciplinary inclusion of blackness, colonization appeared as legitimate for a large proportion of the colonizers' population. This organization of consent would have been impossible if the hegemonic representation of colonization were structured in terms of a total war.

These disciplinary-representational strategies of the colonization discourse were only partially successful. As mentioned above, there were several slave revolts in Jamaica, and resistances were consistently deployed on an everyday level. Many plantation slaves, for example, thought themselves to be, in their position at the margins of the 'enlightenment' strategies, superior to their Europeanized counterparts at the centre of these same strategies.[41]

The effects of these strategies, especially in terms of the negation of presence to 'native-ness', were nonetheless extensive. Evidence suggests that as late as the 1960s, a subtle but highly influential system of 'pigment racism' operated in Jamaica. Hierarchical status valuations of different peoples were made according to different grades of skin 'shadings', with 'pure' whiteness being widely valued in hegemonic cultural discourses as superior to all, with declining values for lesser degrees of whiteness, and the lowest value for blackness. A pyramid distribution of the population according to socio-economic status could be mapped directly on to an equivalent shadings pyramid, again with whiteness corresponding to the highest status. The value of blackness was denied in many informal ways: there were no black fashion models, black history celebrations, or black cultural education in the schools. The black elite tended to value Western education, dress and cultural events as superior to any indigenous or African counterpart.[42] Any revaluation of blackness as positive, as having meaning not simply with reference to the whiteness which it was not, but in terms outside this negation, was positioned at the margins of the Jamaican social, outside the space of legitimate discourse. It was not until later in the 1960s that this hegemonic representation of blackness was fundamentally challenged. The shift towards a popularization of the representation of blackness as a positive element was marked by the success of Michael Manley's populism.

The strategies that have been deployed to negate the positivity of 'native'-ness or blackness in the colonization discourse can therefore be described as a complex of exclusionary and inclusionary strategies. The colonized was at the same time excluded from the terrain of the colonizer, and, in a highly regulated and neutralizing process of 'Westernization', included within that terrain. These different strategies are contradictory only in appearance, for their effects in terms of the negation of 'native'-ness and blackness were consistent.

A similar complex of strategies also negating blackness has been deployed in post-war Britain. Exclusionary strategies have included the widespread experiences of racism on an everyday level, in housing, employment, public services, violent attacks, and so on. What is even more revealing, however, is the extent to which the very categories used to refer to the African and Caribbean peoples in post-war Britain are the condensed signifiers them-selves of exclusionary strategies. Throughout the academic literature, these peoples are referred to as 'newcomers', 'strangers' and 'immigrants', as if these labels were natural, rather than strategically constructed.

First, to name these diverse peoples as 'newcomers' is to conceal the history of their already-established discursive presence in Britain. Various peoples of African origin have lived in Britain from the sixteenth century as slaves.[43] These peoples numbered eighteen thousand in London in 1770, about 3 per cent of the city's total population.[44] Following the first waves of anti-black reaction,[45] and voluntary and involuntary repatriation, these peoples all but disappeared from Britain in the late nineteenth century.[46] The two World Wars saw their return, especially Afro-Caribbeans, to Britain. There were, for example, ten thousand Jamaican servicemen in the armed forces during World War II.[47]

These peoples were also not 'strangers' to the established British; they were already 'known' through imperial discourse as the 'colonized'. Many analysts argue that imperialism was unimportant to the 'average' British citizen.[48] This argument, however, is part of the post-colonial attempt to 'forget' the influence and collapse of the Empire, rather than dispute the fact. While many British people may have remained ignorant of the intricacies of the imperial structure, the imperial discourse made a tremendous impact throughout civil society. Between the 1890s and the 1940s, imperial themes were common-place in popular advertising, theatre, cinema, radio, youth organizations, juvenile literature, overtly imperialist organizations, militaristic and mon-archical ceremonials, the discourses of elementary schools, Churches, prisons and reformatories.[49]

Indeed, references to the colonized as a homogeneous category, in spite of the plurality of these peoples, pervaded the imperial discourse. This colonial 'other' was used discursively in the construction of a new British nationalism, the unification of the British around a common national project. The most subordinate (white) British citizen could take pride in his or her superiority over even the most noble (black) colonial.[50] Mackenzie comments that of all the discourses that had the effect of 'disciplining class divisions', the imperial discourse was most effective in this period, achieving more in this regard than workplace and religious discourses.[51]

Blackness was therefore always 'within' Britishness, and was always 'known' by the British as the singular and inferior 'other'. Because the colonial discourse was central to the construction of a new hegemonic conception of

Britishness between the 1890s and the 1940s, decolonization brought about nothing less than a national identity crisis. With the migration of some of the former colonials to the metropole, especially the former 'natives' of Asia, Africa and the Caribbean, as opposed to the 'Europeans' of Canada, Australia and New Zealand, there was the possibility that these migrants would be defined in the same terms of the colonial discourse, as the anti-British 'other'. For the anti-black immigration lobby of the 1960s, they did become the 'most visible symptom of the destruction of the "British way of life" '.[52]

Finally, the naming of these diverse migrants as 'immigrants' is also highly problematic. The question of the stage at which this label ought to be removed is immediately posed; some writers insist on using increasingly absurd terms, such as 'second-' and 'third-generation immigrants'. The term 'immigrant' makes sense only with reference to a fixed frontier which is crossed by a particular element, moving from an outside to an inside. Although the frontier in this case may appear to be naturally fixed, its fixity cannot be taken for granted. If the colonized played the role of the supplement during the imperial era – as the addition which was needed to complete the inside, that against which the inside achieved its insidedness – then this apparently outside element was always in the inside as its condition of possibility. If, for example, the labour of slaves or colonized workers of African origin originally provided the capital for the development of various British socio-economic sectors, and then the direct descendants of these peoples migrate to the metropole, this movement can fairly be described as movement within a system, rather than the entry of an outside element into an inside.

The status of these peoples as immigrants, outsiders coming into an inside, was in fact constituted retroactively in a strategic deployment of frontiers. The sense that they were already elements within a system, migrating within that system, was explicitly recognized in the immigration laws of the 1950s. Migrants from the colonies had only to prove that they were subjects of the British Empire and, as holders of British passports, had no special visa or entry requirements. There were no distinctions between returning administrators of English descent and migrants of Asian and African descent. Laws had to be passed to legitimate the practice of keeping entry statistics concerning the movement of the Asian and African peoples.

In the context of decolonization, waves of violent racism in British inner cities, and the development of immigration lobbies in parliament, these peoples became British subjects with a difference.[53] The 1962 Common-wealth Immigrant Act normalized the racist perception that these peoples should not have the same rights as other migrants. Based on the wholly unsubstantiated argument that 'coloured' Commonwealth immigration levels were excessive, entry of these specific peoples was restricted according to employment categories.[54] In 1965 the Labour government reversed its previous stand and renewed the 1962 Act, arguing that fewer numbers of 'coloured' immigrants improved race relations.[55] This explanation revealed the rationale which had been previously masked by economic arguments, namely that the immigration question was a race issue, rather than a labour and employment issue.

Other immigration legislation specifically designed to regulate the movement of what had become a special racial category was passed in 1968 and 1971. The most significant piece of legislation in this respect was the Kenyan Asian Act of 1968. This Act retroactively invented a national border to exclude elements which had already been recognized *de jure* as already inside a broader system, and as having equal status in that system. The British government had agreed with the first independent Kenyan government in 1963 that all British passport holders would be given the opportunity to retain their British citizenship. In this agreement there was no reference to race, and no reference to the fact that some of the subjects in question were of English origin and that others were of Asian origin.

In 1967 there was a small acceleration of movement from Kenya to Britain, due to domestic Kenyan policies. The numbers of migrants of Asian origin who attempted to exercise their rights under the 1963 agreement were negligible in aggregate terms.[56] The significance of their entry, however, was dramatically redefined through the interventions of anti-black immigration lobbyists such as Powell[57] and Sandys. Following their campaign and extensive coverage in the popular media, the terms of the 1963 international agreement were changed. On 22 February 1968, the Labour government introduced immigration controls explicitly designed to discriminate against any British passport holder who did not have a parent or grandparent born in the United Kingdom. Because the migration of black peoples to the United Kingdom has only been significant since the 1950s, this qualification singled out an almost exclusively white group of passport holders. It ensured that the descendants of the colonial administrators and white migrants from the United Kingdom to Commonwealth countries would be granted a virtually free entry. These technical euphemisms effectively marked the not-white racial category within the broad category of passport holders for exclusion, without explicitly referring to race.[58]

With this legislation, the redefinition of the British frontier such that a specific group identified in racial terms became outsiders crossing into the inside, or outsiders barred from entry into the inside, was complete.[59] Blackness is represented as a 'newcomer', a 'stranger' and an 'immigrant' even though it has been within Britishness all along. This strategic 'forgetting' of the Empire is a crucial strategy within the post-colonial discourse on race and nation,[60] for it conceals the dependency of various Britishnesses on the exclusion and disciplinary inclusion of racial othernesses. The immigration legislation of the 1960s therefore constitutes one of the most important sites of the reorganization of a racially defined Britishness in the post-colonial era.

In anti-black immigration discourse, blackness was redefined. Blackness no longer signified not-white and inferior, but that which is located in Britain and is inherently anti-British. Britishness was also redefined such that the exclusion of blackness became a natural and legitimate defensive strategy. Through interventions such as Powell's anti-black immigration campaign in the late 1960s, a particularly exclusionary Britishness which stands opposed to the not-white 'enemies within', became hegemonic. The development of different senses of Britishness is of course possible. However, the organization and popularization of this particular Britishness did much to compensate for the trauma of decolonization. As the otherness of the colonized unified the nation in the imperial discourse, this new conception of blackness played a similar role in the organization of the Powellite and Thatcherite nationalism of the 1970s and 1980s.

However, these exclusionary strategies could not stand on their own. Britishness could not just signify anti-blackness; some elements of some type of blackness had to be simultaneously included. Only with this juxtaposition of exclusions and inclusions could officials effectively claim that their policies were 'fair' and 'even-handed'. There can be many ways of including an element, from the one extreme, wherein an element is brought into a space with its subversive supplementarity intact fundamentally disrupting that space, redefining all other elements without sacrificing its own 'otherness' in the process; to another extreme where that element is neutralized as it enters the space, and merely gives that space an appearance of completion, as a compensation for a lack. In the latter case, the element is wholly transformed in the process; its alterity and subversive potential is disciplined and neutralized. If the former case is one of radical interruption, the supplement in the latter case is included through assimilation, and becomes a harmless addition.

In 'official' discourses on race in Britain in the 1960s to 1980s, there is a tendency towards the combination of inclusions with exclusions, and these inclusions tend towards the assimilatory type. As mentioned above, the Labour government's 1965 Commonwealth Immigration Act was defended on the basis that it would improve 'race relations'. It was implied that blackness had to be considered in terms of quantity and quality: the nature of blackness is such that its qualitative effect depends on its quantity. The presence of 'too many' elements of blackness meant that they would revert to their original anti-Britishness and could not, consequently, be absorbed. Different signs of disruption in the social were understood to be the signs of 'too many': from the anti-black riots by whites and other 'race relations' problems, to labour shortages, social service shortages and even a general decline in morality.

The Labour government's rationalization therefore normalized the condensation and displacement of disruptions in the social on to the blackness signifier, and legitimized this kind of quality/quantity thinking on race. Powellism was organized in terms of a similar logic, but differed in that it had an almost total intolerance for multiplicity and disruption within the conception of the British social space. For Powell, almost any blackness was 'too many'. For both the Labour officials and Powell, the assimilable 'good black' was possible, but this assimilable goodness could be developed only if the quantitative presence of blackness was strictly regulated.[61]

The same Labour government that renewed the Immigration Act in 1965 also passed a Race Relations Act which imposed conciliation in cases of discrimination in places of public resort.[62] In 1968, Labour officials again insisted that the February immigration controls, which were specifically designed to exclude blacks, must be combined with new race-relations measures. Taken together, the new bills were supposed to be a 'fair and balanced policy on . . . race relations'.[63] The problem with this dual logic was that immigration legislation legitimated the sense that blackness was a subversive element at the same time that race-relations legislation was supposed to promote the dissolution of racial distinctions. The impossibility of this contradictory approach only increased the appeal of Powell's anti-black immigration campaign. Another problem with the 'race-relations' approach was the sense that, in resolving the problem of racial difference, blackness and not Britishness had to be transformed through assimilation. The Race Relations Act, for example, was used to discipline black activism in the case of the prosecution of Michael X. This activist was tried for allegedly uttering 'anti-white' statements.[64]

The combination of exclusions and inclusions, and the promotion of an assimilatory inclusion, can also be found in policing discourse. In the 1970s, a new articulation of blackness – especially young male blackness – with criminality suddenly acquired widespread credence. A dramatic escalation of the policing of this community, the increased use of coercive force, and popular media coverage of so-called 'waves' of specifically black crimes occurred.[65] In the coercive moment of this policing, the frontier that protected Britishness from subversion and that discursively organized blackness as part of disciplinary strategies was transported from its colonial location on actual battlefields, and from its national location in the invention of a national border to exclude black 'immigrants', to the inner cities within Britain itself.[66] This relocation allowed for a more local and more precise differentiation and discipline.

As the policing of the black community became more highly organized, however, extensive efforts were made to represent the policing frontier not simply as the line between whiteness and blackness, but as the line between different blacknesses: the law-abiding good blacks who conducted themselves in a sufficiently British manner, and the law-breaking subversive blacks who, through the signifier of their criminality, proved themselves to be recalcitrantly anti-British. On the other hand, the Asian community, although still considered 'black' in post-colonial Britain, is policed differently than the Afro-Caribbean community.[67] Different generations and socio-economic groups within black communities are also policed differently.

Police officials have even argued that Rastafari must be differentiated in terms of policing. They have distinguished between the 'true believers', a non-violent and largely passive group, and the 'imitators' who mask their criminality with the disguise of Rastafari beliefs.[68] It is through this differentiated application of coercion and legitimation that policing wins consent and is able to penetrate a space more deeply and to become productive. Policing does not simply say 'no' to blackness, but differentiates blacknesses, and incites the development of an assimilated blackness which would displace a subversive blackness. The use of policing in the 1970s and 1980s to differentiate blacknesses represents an entirely logical progression from the 1960s. Where the differentiation of blackness was originally pursued through the invention of a national border, this same strategy was relocated to a more productive discourse, on to a far more specific site in which far more flexible and effective mechanisms were available.

The Thatcher government also deployed a similar combination of exclusions and assimilatory inclusions. On the one hand, it renewed and strengthened the 1968 exclusions of those immigrants who could not prove 'patriality', that is, British-born grandparents, in the 1981 Nationality Act. On the other hand, the Conservative Party under Thatcher has actively sought electoral support among black voters. In an election poster analysed by Gilroy it is claimed that the Conservatives view the British people not as 'special' groups differentiated according to race, but as equal citizens. It says: 'With the Conservatives, there are no "blacks", no "whites", just people.' Referring to the poster's photograph of a young black man, it says: Labour says he's black. Tories say he's British.[69]

The text represents the Tories as the truly inclusionary party, as opposed to Labour's divisive approach. As Gilroy points out, however, this 'included blackness' is not just any blackness, but a business-suited single male, wholly Anglicized, and almost entirely assimilable in his entrepreneurial and isolated form.[70]

Another example of this exclusion/inclusion complex can be found in the New Right's discourse on education and race.[71] Ray Honeyford, a frequent contributor to New Right publications, declared that the schools play a critical role in 'socializing "Afro-Asian settler children" into the mores which the racially harmonious life in contemporary Britain required of them', while simultaneously arguing that 'the presence of these children in British schools was an impediment to the education of white children'.[72] Black children are supposed to constitute an alien anti-Britishness, which may be transformed into an assimilable blackness through intensive British education, but, in the transitional stages, their alterity could become a dangerous interruption.

A similar representation of race was deployed in the protest of the white parents who withdrew their children from a school in Dewsbury because of its 85 per cent 'Asian-British' population. They claimed that they did not object to the presence of these other children, but argued that the quantitative 'imbalance' had a qualitative effect on their children's well-being. One parent commented: 'If it was 50:50, fair enough, I'd be happy. But 85 per cent, that just isn't on.'[73]

The parents said that they were not racist, and they did not claim blacks were inferior, but they nonetheless expressed concern about the 'proper' Christian and British education of their children. The implicit argument is that black children ought to be included in the British education system, but in a carefully regulated manner, and that 'too many' of these children could subvert the education of the white children.

There is a continuity between these parents' protest and the reaction against 'multicultural' curricula in the schools.[74] In both cases, blackness is represented as dangerously subversive, and the identity of the white British children is regarded as vulnerable to this subversion. 'Tolerance' of cultural otherness is therefore seen as an abandonment of British traditions. Race-relations legislation does not provide a framework for the resolution of these conflicts. Deliberate policies of racial integration in the schools are actually prohibited by these laws. Local councils which do not want to produce racially-segregated schools must pursue integration policies covertly in the name of an efficient use of resources, without the support of legislation.[75]

Where the colonization regime constituted, with respect to native-blackness, a complex of exclusions and inclusions in which the inclusions tended towards the assimilatory type, an analogous complex of exclusions and assimilatory inclusions of an assimilatory type construct and discipline blacknesses in contemporary Britain. Blacknesses are defined in terms of the binary opposition, 'subversive blackness' – an inherently anti-Britishness element – versus 'good blackness' – an assimilated, British-ized blackness. Within racist discourse, there is a constant shifting between representations in which this distinction is collapsed, and those in which this distinction is accentuated. The differentiation of blacknesses and the undecidability between the two types of representations of blackness worked to undermine the construction of a unified and positive black identity.

Blackness: From Absence to Presence

It is in the context of these multiple racist strategies that diverse black resistances emerged. The significance of Rastafari, and that of its essentialist blackness, can be evaluated only with reference to these exclusions and assimilatory inclusions. In Jamaica, the Rastafari constituted an effective refusal of the colonial exclusion/inclusion game. Following the resistance-through-withdrawal pattern of their predecessors, Rastafari were able to constitute a separate space at the margins of the social in which blackness ceased to be disciplined 'native'-blackness and became revalued as the transhistorical and transnational spirit of Ethiopia. Members formed communes in the mountains and, later, in the urban shanty-towns. They rejected the intrusions of all Babylonians, including social workers, unions and the police. The fact that this separatism posed a substantial threat to the social order is confirmed by the intense harassment by the police and government officials that these communities endured until the mid-1960s.[76]

In spite of the separatism of the Rastafari, the harassment by state officials, and the lack of what would traditionally be understood as 'political resources', Rastafari discourse nonetheless constituted a highly effective interruption of colonialism. This interruption was later relocated from the margins to the 'legitimate' sphere of the social, but emerged first and foremost in the spiritual practices of this small movement from the slums, a movement based on Old Testament beliefs, traditional music, drug use and an other-worldly orientation towards oppression. Rastafari discourse showed that which could not be represented in colonial discourse, a positive blackness defined in terms of Africa rather than Europe. It also showed that the displacement of disciplined blackness with this positive identity could be accomplished only through a complete rejection of the existing social order. One Jamaican commented in 1968,

> It is significant that the Rastafari founded perhaps the only real piece of Jamaican culture Jamaica has experienced, and it fed on a hope that did not lie inside the island society. The Jamaicans who reacted against European aesthetics and grew their hair to resemble the jungles of their lost heritage rather than the straightened smooth gloss of England's green fields, instinctively sought for a symbol of black pride which they could not find then or now in Jamaica. When they coated themselves with honest earth, it was a symbolic . . . rejection of the pusillanimous middleman way of life existing parasitically upon the creations of others.[77]

It was only through the strategy of turning to a radically other (from the European point of view) discursive universe that the moral and spiritual bankruptcy of the colonial discourse could be exposed and rejected. Where the colonial discourse may have previously appeared to accommodate different blacknesses, the positing of this positive blackness, with its own tradition, showed the limits and rigidity of the colonial system. Where the radical division between native blackness and the colonizer had been concealed by the exclusion/inclusion matrix, resistances such as Rastafari discourse reinscribed that frontier and, furthermore, organized a collective crossing of 'the line'. In Fanon's terms, the resistance strategy of Rastafari is analogous to the general strategy of turning to the 'ways of the nigger' of other colonized peoples.

> When the colonialists . . . realise that these men whom they considered as saved souls are beginning to fall back into the ways of niggers, the whole system totters. Every native won over, every native who had taken the pledge not only marks a failure for the colonial structure when he decides to lose himself and to go back to his own side, but also stands as a symbol for the uselessness and the shallowness of all the work that has been accomplished. Each native who goes back over the line is a condemnation of the methods and of the regime.[78]

The collective crossing of the line between native blackness and the colonizer is profoundly threatening to the containment strategies of colonization. From the basis of this new discursive foundation, further resistances became possible which would have otherwise been unthinkable.

This turning to another discursive universe is necessarily a turning to a new 'nodal point', a term which, in its centrifugal effects, tends to organize the meanings of all other terms distributed around itself.[79] In the case of the Rastafari intervention, the conception of blackness as the transhistorical Ethiopian essence became this new nodal point. Rooted in a tradition of resistances against what was interpreted as a singular pattern of domination, the Rastafari identity emerged as the product of strategic repetitions. Blackness was no longer the not-colonized, but the spirit which united an entire people across diverse experiences of suffering at the hands of Babylon. The totalizing and essentialist dimensions of Jamaican Rastafari discourse make sense in the context of the complex strategies of colonialism. Given the all-embracing exclusion/assimilatory inclusion matrix of colonial discourse, blackness could only be redefined in terms of a resistance strategy which radically turned away from the discursive universe of the colonizer. It is in these terms, as a strategy of interruption of a totalizing discourse of domination, that the spiritualism, separatism and essentialism of Jamaican Rastafari discourse should be considered.

As the construction of a positive black identity in Jamaica emerged only through resistance strategies, the construction of a similar identity in the British context was also the product of resistances. There is substantial evidence that the migrants from the colonized Caribbean to Britain in the 1950s thought of themselves first and foremost not in terms of broad collective categories, but in terms of Caribbean village and sub-national regional identities. Even the category 'West Indian' appears to have been more important to white British researchers than to the peoples themselves. National identities were opposed to one another, such as the self-identified division between Jamaicans and Trinidadians.[80]

These migrants also did not think of themselves as a united people returning to a common 'motherland'. Contemporary population movements from the Caribbean are located in a long tradition of similar migrations, to Cuba, the Aruba oilfields, Panama, the United States and finally Great Britain.[81] Prohibitory immigration legislation in the United States, rather than a collective feeling of British subjecthood, was the catalyst for this latter phase of migration. In a survey of the migrants from the Caribbean, 78 per cent of the respondents said that they had chosen to come to Britain only because they could not emigrate to the first country of their choice. Only 10 per cent of the respondents said that Britain's status as the 'mother country' was an important factor.[82]

How has the 'black' identity come to be in Britain an almost natural category which spans these differences? On the one hand, there was a tendency in terms of the racist discourse, which reinscribed colonial categories, to group all former colonials from the 'New Commonwealth' (Asia, Africa and the Caribbean) together as 'blacks'. In this context, blackness signified not-British and not-white. The residual signification effects of the colonial discourse accounts for the inclusion of Asians in the 'black' category in Britain, where they would not be included in the American or Canadian context.

On the other hand, there was the emergence of resistance strategies against racist discourse which strategically reoccupied this all-embracing conception of blackness, but on different terms. In the wake of the 1958 white anti-black riots, for example, activists invoked a specifically West Indian identity to mobilize resistance. It was at this time that the *West Indian Gazette* and the West Indian carnival were established. Before this period, the various resistances to racial exclusions, informal self-help groups for savings and housing, social clubs, workers' and students' associations, and so on, tended to be organized around different Caribbean village, sub-national and national identities.[83] The West Indian category was broadened and politicized further with the founding of the Association for the Advancement of Coloured People, the Coloured People's Progressive Association and the Standing Conference of West Indian Organizations.[84] West Indian and Asian groups also joined together to form the Co-ordinating Committee Against Racial Discrimination and the Campaign Against Racial Discrimination.[85]

This wave of organizations was followed in the 1960s by various forms of militant black liberation discourse. This discourse posited a radically new sense of blackness centred on the Garveyite themes of consciousness, pride, self-help and self-rule. The resistance strategies shifted from local informal strategies based on everyday needs, and organizational strategies to oppose discrimination, to a revolutionary approach. Black liberation aimed not just at a reform of the existing social order, but at the politicization of every aspect of the social, the constitution of a new and separate black nation and the overthrow of the entire racist system.[86]

Combined with the polarizing effects of Powellism and the popular panic regarding black immigration, the impact of the militant movements was enormous. Not only did many more people see themselves as 'black', and see blackness as a positive identity. They also increasingly accepted the conception that the diverse experiences of oppression for blacks were the results of a single transhistorical oppression – racism – and that white-Britishness was inherently and essentially based on the domination of blackness; that the social was therefore divided between two fundamental camps, blackness versus white-Britishness; and that the liberation of blackness could only be won with the total defeat of the white-British order.

Previously disparate individuals experienced a collective identification process not dissimilar to the 'coming out' process of gay identification. One Wolverhampton nurse commented,

> Each day I'm getting more aware of the fact that I'm black because of the situations that one comes up against . . . therefore you try to find out your background, and the customs of your ancestors.[87]

Another nurse from Slough said,

> We had heard about slavery in Jamaica but didn't put it together and put ourselves within. We didn't think it happened to people we descended from . . . But, coming to this country, you get to realise that we're part of slavery.[88]

British Rastafari should be situated as genealogically following not only the resistances of Rastafari in Jamaica, but also these resistances in Britain. In the British context, the 'becoming black' process dating back to the 1950s also stands as a condition of possibility for the 'journey to Jah'. The terrain for the assertion of blackness as Ethiopian goodness, and the rejection of Babylon, had already been prepared in the development of a radical division of the social into two camps, blackness versus white racism. At the same time, Rastafari distinguished itself from the militant discourse in its directly Caribbean, rather than American, orientation; its emphasis on 'youth culture', music and drug use; its spirituality and apparently un-political form. These differences, however, only ensured the further promotion of virtually the same conception of blackness to different spheres in the social; they are not constitutive of an 'escapism' or an anti-political betrayal of black liberation. Both the militant discourse and Rastafari discourse entailed a thorough critique of the existing social order, the deployment of frontiers and the construction of new identities, such that previously unthinkable resistances became possible. The Rastafari movement, however, facilitated the repetition and reformation of the radical black identity politics of the 1960s in a particularly 'youth-oriented' form, and at a time when the militant leadership and organizations were under attack and in decline.[89]

Identification, 'Other' Images and the Rastafari Resistance Against Racism

In Britain, Rastafari was a continuation of the 'becoming black' process by different means. Through this identification, blacks named themselves the excluded but chosen people, and turned away from the system which told them that they were nothing, to take on a positive identity. Through the Rastafari intervention and the other radical black discourses, the racist strategies of exclusion and assimilatory inclusion were effectively countered. The radical solidarity of this positive black identity frustrated attempts to create divisions such as the differentiation between the assimilated 'good black' and the unassimilable 'subversive black'.

In the Rastafari framework, assimilation was equated with a surrender of true blackness to Babylon. British Rastafari not only saw themselves as different from whiteness-Britishness-Babylon, but also as privileged. For Rastafari, blacks occupied the position of the chosen ones. Experiences of domination only served to confirm Rastafari beliefs and superior identity. Whereas in the anti-black discourses, blackness was defined as that which lacked Britishness, Rastafari named Britishness as that which was lacking. The illegitimate newcomers for Rastafari were the Babylonians who had no culture of their own, but had only acquired a pseudo-culture through the violent plunder of the Ethiopians. Britishness was redefined to signify moral and spiritual bankruptcy. Its institutions and laws deserved only suspicion and contempt, and its traditions and customs were rejected as being inextricably linked with the domination of blacks. Britishness on its own, without this domination, was nothing. British patriotism became a cruel, dangerous and pathetic joke.

The meaning of Rastafari, however, is not exhausted in its anti-Britishness; it is fundamentally a turning to a 'beyond Britishness' in a recovery of the Ethiopian identity. This intervention in the conception of Britishness is nevertheless crucial. Where the exclusion of blackness was combined with assimilatory inclusion, radical black discourse, such as Rastafari, named assimilation as a lie that, for all its inclusionary appearances, was equally exclusionary in its effects. Where the exclusionary Britishness was represented in racist discourse as if it could naturally include blackness at no risk to itself, as if only some blackness was excluded not on the basis of race but on the basis of a non-racial rejection of subversion, this legitimation of a fundamentally exclusionary system was undermined. The radicalized, oppositional and essential blackness of Rastafari would not be appeased with 'fair and balanced policies', 'race relations', or 'equal opportunity in the market-place' systems. Rastafari, as well as other radical black discourses, instead rejected assimilatory compromise and named both exclusion and inclusion through assimilation as racism.

In other words, it is by placing the identification strategies which are deployed by Rastafari in the context of the fragmenting effects of racist discourse that the essentialism of these strategies can be evaluated. In Lacanian terms, identification is a transformational process, in which an image reflected at a distance, on some other surface, is accepted as a representation of the ego. The ego is not already an 'inside' space relating to this 'outside' image, for the acceptance and internalization of the image is constitutive of the ego as such. The strategic character of identification cannot be overestimated. The Lacanian text, 'The Mirror Stage' (a text central to contemporary psychoanalytic discussions on identification),[90] is permeated with strategic terminology.

The image reflected from the other surface is accepted as a reflection of the ego not just because of its content, but more importantly, because of its form (*Écrits*, 2). Identification provides a sense of a bounded identity which functions as an 'armour' (*Écrits*, 4) in terms of the rigidity and fixity that it offers. Without identification, the construction of the 'defences of the ego' (*Écrits*, 5) would not be possible. Lacan also states that the formation of the 'I' through identification is symbolized in dreams of a 'fortress' in which the subject searches in vain for a 'lofty, remote inner castle' (*Écrits*, 5).

Now, although Lacan emphasizes the alienating effects of identification – effects that result from the fact that the image of the ego remains irreducibly other such that identification is at the same time mis-identification – he also insists on the fundamental character of this process. Without the conception of the ego's identity as bounded and fixed, there would be no foundational reference for the 'I' which the subject has not yet spoken.[91] The construction of identity involves an impossible idealization which always fails to obtain the substantiality and permanence that is promised by the image; it is, neverthe-less, the only effective response to the fragmentary effects of oppression. To paraphrase Lacan, the motivation for such an identification derives from a sense of a lack of identity in the current juncture, and an anticipation of a fully formed identity in the future (*Écrits*, 4).

For young British blacks in the late 1960s and 1970s, the juxtaposition of the fragmentary effects of racism with the promise of a return to a positive black identity in black militant discourse heightened this fundamental sense of an identity crisis, the distance between the sense of one's identity in the present as lacking unity, and the promise of completion in an anticipated identity. Politicized by black militant discourse, and already aware of the representational bankruptcy of popular British discourses vis-à-vis blackness, the imaginary that could posit a 'solution' – albeit a temporary and imperfect one – to their identity crisis had to be radically other-than-European: the tradition of Caribbean and African resistances.

The blocking of the exclusion and assimilatory inclusion matrix of anti-black discourses, and the construction of a positive blackness, are the central achievements of radical black discourses. Rastafari is one form of radical black discourse that, with its emphasis on a flexible belief system, music, drug use and youth 'counter-culture', brought these radical conceptions to young blacks and to some young whites.

What, then, are the various resistances that this movement has in turn made possible, resistances that would otherwise have been unthinkable? And what is the significance of the fact that Rastafari and the other radical black discourses reject Britishness and yet remain located in Britain? If Britishness remains incompatible with blackness, what space is there for mobile strategies?

A non-neutralized, non-assimilated blackness is only incompatible with an exclusionary type of Britishness. For all its appearances of being natural and ahistorical, the Britishness of Powellism and Thatcherism is only one Britishness/Englishness among many actual and possible Britishnesses.[92] A radical democratic articulation of blackness and Britishness is possible in spite of the predominance of the assimilatory articulation of these two elements. If we are to speak of radical democratic hegemony, as opposed to authoritarian hegemony, then we must distinguish between these types of articulation. A radical democratic articulation, proper to the first type of hegemony, would be one in which articulation is not achieved through the neutralization of difference. The autonomy and the subversiveness of black-ness would be preserved and even deepened to the maximum extent possible in the case of a radical democratic articulation. Clearly, a pure instance of this articulation would be an impossibility, a contradiction in terms, but an articulation can nonetheless be said to have a radical democratic character in terms of degree.

Rastafari and other essentialist radical black discourses show that a tremendous amount of discursive work needed, and still needs, to be carried out on both the terms 'blackness' and 'Britishness' before an articulation between them with any degree of radical democratic character is possible. Against the negations of domination, blackness had to be redefined posi-tively, within its own tradition. Radical black discourse, however, remains located in Britain, within the terrain of the struggles around the definition of 'being British'.[93] A radical democratic articulation of Britishness and black-ness also requires the opening up of Britishness to difference, a transform-ation which only appears to be impossible in the shadow of the hegemonic authoritarian Britishness. To say that this construction of a new Britishness is impossible is not only to succumb to the naturalizing effects of the hegem-onic Britishness, but also to excuse the 'British Left' from an urgent project.

Rastafari contributed to the foundations for further black resistances. These new resistances reveal the multiplicity and heterogeneity of blacknesses that were always there, especially as they intersect with other discourses organized around classes, genders and sexualities. Unlike the essentialist discourses, the new resistances engage with, rather than suppress, these differences.[94] In the context of this emphasis on differences, the total strategy of 'liberating' a 'true self', or returning to essence, is represented as a failed myth. There is an important difference between the racist fragmentation of blacknesses and the creative development of differentiated blacknesses which still stand opposed to racism.

This opening up of strategies around blacknesses would be impossible as long as there were no effective resistances against the neutralizing, marginalizing and fragmenting effects of racist discourse. In other words, the essentialist moment is the moment of the object becoming subject which makes possible the placing of that subject 'under erasure'.[95] The once singular blackness is opened to differentiation, but these new differences retain the trace of resistance against racist discourse. The social is no longer represented in terms of a two-camp system, the chosen suffering people versus oppression, and the 'innocence' of blackness is suspended.[96] It becomes acceptable to recognize that the strategies of the essentialist moment may have oppressive as well as anti-oppressive effects. Questions such as 'To what extent are differences of gender and sexuality suppressed through the promotion of this particular blackness as the universal blackness?' and 'To what extent can a non-authoritarian Britishness be re-constructed?' become accepted as legitimate challenges. In an intervention about black film, Hall discusses the opening up of singular blackness to difference, and the inevitability of the involvement of contemporary black resistances in the struggle to define the meaning of Britishness.

> There can, therefore, be no simple 'return' or 'recovery' of the ancestral past which is not re-experienced through the categories of the present: no base for creative enunciation in a simple reproduction of traditional forms which are not transformed by the technologies and identities of the present. This is something that was signalled as early as a film like *Blacks Britannica* and as recently as Paul Gilroy's important book, *There Ain't No Black in the Union Jack*. Fifteen years ago we didn't care, or at least I didn't care, whether there was any black in the Union Jack. Now not only do we care, we must.[97]

Again, this is not a 'two-stage theory of revolution'; the different oppositional moments do not merely replace one another.[98] The complexities of systems of domination demand in turn complexes of resistances. The essentialist moment and the moment in which the essentialist subject is shown to be impossible stand as each other's supplements, paradoxically constituting both each other's limit, and each other's condition of possibility. The latter moment does not erase the work of the essentialist moment but opens up the possibilities for more local and more complex strategies. Finally, neither moment appears in a pure form but, inevitably, as always intertwined with each other in various degrees.

As is the case with all social movements, the evaluation of the Rastafari movement should not proceed according to predetermined conceptions of politics. Its separatist and spiritual characteristics should not be used to legitimate its categorization as a form of escapism. Rastafari can be instead evaluated as a resistance strategy, and can be located within a tradition of similar resistances which became effective at a certain juncture in the British context. The effects of essentialist discourses cannot be predicted in abstraction. Given the complexities of domination, the strategic construction of identities through essence-claims has both a central role – and a highly ambiguous legacy – in the organization of resistances.

Notes

1. The term 'new times' is taken from a series of articles published in *Marxism Today* and collected in Stuart Hall and Martin Jacques, eds, *New Times: The Changing Face of Politics in the 1990s* (London: Verso, 1990).

2. Their statements are published in L. Appignanesi and S. Maitland, eds, *The Rushdie File* (London: Fourth Estate, 1989), pp. 137–41 and 175–7.

3. I have taken the conception of 'two moments' in the logics of the new social movements' discourses from Stuart Hall's comments on the diversity of black resistances. 'New Ethnicities', *Black Film/British Cinema, ICA Documents 7* (London: Institute of the Contemporary Arts, 1988) pp. 27–31. Hall differentiates between struggles around the relations of representation and struggles around the politics of representation. A similar distinction between essentialist and anti-essentialist moments in the discourse of the lesbian and gay movement can be found in J. Weeks, *Sex, Politics and Society* (London: Longman, 1981) pp. 282–8, and his *Sexuality* (London: Ellis Horwood, 1986) pp. 69–88. Judith Butler offers a slightly different distinction in terms of the women's movement and representation: in the first moment, universal categories such as 'women' and 'the patriarchy' are used uncritically, and demands are made for equal representation in the hegemonic representational system as if the latter had no effect on the constitution of the represented subject. In the second moment, the exclusionary effects of these universal categories – the ways that their deployment depends on the exclusion of non-white, non-European women – are shown, and representation is no longer regarded as a neutral process. See her *Gender Trouble* (London: Routledge, 1990) pp. 1–6.

4. On the (non-)concept of supplementarity as one of the 'infrastructures' of deconstruction, see J. Derrida, *Speech and Phenomena* (Evanston: Northwestern University Press, 1973) pp. 88–104, and *Of Grammatology* (Baltimore: Johns Hopkins, 1976) pp. 141–64; R. Gasché, *The Tain of the Mirror* (London: Harvard University Press, 1986) pp. 205–12; and H. Staten, *Wittgenstein and Derrida* (Oxford: Basil Blackwell, 1985) pp. 111–60.

5. J. Derrida, 'A Letter to a Japanese Friend', in D. Wood and R. Bernasconi, eds, *Derrida and Différance* (Evanston: Northwestern University Press, 1988) p. 4.

6. G. Spivak, 'Translator's Preface', in Derrida, *Of Grammatology*, p. lxxviii.

7. This approach is opposed to that of Diana Fuss, who argues that the political value of an essentialist strategy depends on the subject position from which the strategy is deployed. She argues that the essentialist strategies of a hegemonic group can further domination, while those

deployed by a subordinate group can have subversive effects. *Essentially Speaking: Feminism, Nature and Difference* (London: Routledge, 1990) p. 32.

8. Aristotle, *Metaphysics* (London: Heinemann Loeb Classical Library, 1938) III, vi, 1; and III, vi, 9.

9. Ibid., V, viii, 1–3.

10. Ibid., V, xxx, 1; VI, ii, 1–2; VI, ii, 5; XI, vii, 5.

11. Aristotle, *The Politics*, 1260a. For Aristotle, this hierarchy in the 'natural' distribution of rational capacity is itself necessary rather than accidental. The adult male rules over the not yet fully rational male children and the imperfectly rational females and slaves in the household, and this rule is supposed to be a necessary part of his development of the virtues required in his role as a citizen. In this sense, the failure of rationality in females and slaves is necessary to the rationality of the polis as a whole.

12. Ibid., VII, viii, 4–5.

13. Ibid., VII, xi, 1–6; XII, v, 2–3.

14. Ibid., IX, viii, 16; XII, v, 2–3.

15. Ibid., XII.

16. J. Owens, *The Doctrine of Being in Aristotelian Metaphysics* (Toronto: Pontifical Institute of Medieval Studies, 1978) p. 45; P. Aubenque, *Le probleme de l'être chez Aristotle* (Paris: Presses universitaires, 1966) p. 58.

17. Aristotle, *Nichomachean Ethics* (London: Oxford University Press, 1925) X, pp. 6–8.

18. E. Cashmore, *Rastaman* (London: Unwin, 1983) pp. 13–14.

19. Ibid., pp. 17–19. And see also L. Barrett, *The Rastafarians* (London: Heinemann, 1977) p. 27.

20. T. Vincent, *Black Power and the Garvey Movement* (San Francisco: Ramparts, 1976) pp. 17–19; T. Martin, 'Garvey and Scattered Africa', in J. Harris, ed., *Global Dimensions of the African Diaspora* (Washington: Harvard University, 1982) p. 245.

21. Jah Bones, 'Reggae DJing and Jamaica Afro-Lingua', in D. Sutcliffe and A. Wong, eds, *The Language of Black Experience* (London: Basil Blackwell, 1985) pp. 52–68.

22. L. Johnson, 'The Reggae Rebellion', *New Society*, 10 June 1976, p. 589.

23. S. Davis and P. Simon, *Reggae International* (London: Thames and Hudson, 1983).

24. P. Gilroy, *There Ain't No Black in the Union Jack* (London: Hutchinson, 1987) pp. 164–6.

25. These practices have been well documented elsewhere. For more detail, see J. Plummer, *Movement of Jah People* (Birmingham: Press Gang, 1978); D. Hebdige, *Subculture: The Meaning of Style* (London: Methuen and Co., 1979); L. Garrison, *Black Youth, Rastafarianism and the Identity Crisis in Britain* (London: ACER, 1979); H. Campbell, *Rasta and Resistance* (London: Hansib, 1985); Greater London Council, *Rastafarianism in Greater London* (London: GLC, 1984); Cashmore, *Rastaman*.

26. Jah Bones, 'Language and Rastafari', in Sutcliffe and Wong, *The Language of Black Experience*, pp. 32–7. The conception of a defined Rastafarian membership is problematic; I shall return to this theme below.

27. Drug use as perverse in Barthes's sense of the term; i.e., the taking pleasure in a practice not considered 'profitable'. R. Barthes, 'Vocabulary', *Polysexuality: Semiotexte*, vol. VI, no. 1, 1981, p. 206.

28. The refusal of the body-to-mind subordination is therefore a refusal of the tradition in which Aristotle's philosophical discourse is located. The Afrocentric stance of Rastafari discourse is also a refusal of European ethnocentrism, in which Aristotle's elitist conception of reason constitutes a founding text. Both of these refusals indicate the extent to which the 'theoretical framework' and the 'case study' in this essay remain incommensurable.

29. Hebdige, *Subculture*, p. 63.

30. Cashmore, *Rastaman*.

31. Gilroy, *There Ain't No Black in the Union Jack*, p. 187.

32. Ibid.

33. Ibid., pp. 187–92.

34. G. Yamato, 'Something About the Subject Makes It Hard to Name', in G. Anzaldua, ed., *Making Face, Making Soul/Hacienda Caras: Creative and Critical Perspectives By Women of Colour* (San Francisco, Aunt Lute Foundation Books, 1990) p. 21.

35. E. Mzika, *Outlook*, no. 13, summer 1991, pp. 50–55.

36. See his *Subculture*.

37. Ibid., p. 19.

38. Ibid., p. 3.

39. On 'subculture theory', see J. Clarke et al., 'Subcultures, Cultures and Class', in S. Hall and T. Jefferson, eds, *Resistance Through Rituals* (London: Hutchinson, 1976) pp. 9–74; and P. Cohen, 'Sub-cultural Conflict and Working Class Community', *Working Papers in Cultural Studies 2*, University of Birmingham, 1972.

40. *Subculture*, p. 17.

41. E. Lawrence, 'Sociology and Black Pathology', *The Empire Strikes Back*, Centre for Contemporary Cultural Studies (London: Hutchinson, 1982), pp. 100–111.

42. G. Lewis, 'Race Relations in Britain', *Race Today*, vol. I, no. 3, July 1969, p. 80; K. Pryce, *Endless Pressure* (Bristol: Bristol Classical Press, 1985), pp. 5,7; D. Hiro, *Black British, White British* (London: Eyre and Spottiswoode, 1971) p. 107; K. Norris, *Jamaica: The Search for Identity* (London: Oxford University Press, 1962) pp. 58–9, 97–8; L. Barrett, *The Rastafarians*, p. 174.

43. F. Shyllon, 'Blacks in Britain', in J. Harris, ed., *Global Dimensions*, pp. 170–94; R. Kapo, *A Savage Culture* (London: Quartet, 1981).

44. Hiro, *Black British, White British*, p. 4; N. File, *Black Settlers in Britain, 1555–1958* (London: Heinemann, 1981).

45. P. Fryer, *Staying Power: The History of Black People in Britain* (London: Pluto, 1984).

46. Hiro, *Black British, White British*, p. 5.

47. Pryce, *Endless Pressure*, p. 20.

48. B. Porter, *The Lion's Share: A Short History of British Imperialism* (London: Longman, 1984) p. 339.

49. J. Mackenzie, *Propaganda and Empire* (Manchester: Manchester University Press, 1984) p. 253; B. Schwarz, 'Conservatism, Nationalism and Imperialism', in J. Donald and S. Hall, eds, *Politics and Ideology* (Milton Keynes: Open University Press, 1986), p. 166.

50. Hiro, *Black British, White British*, p. 301; and Mackenzie, *Propaganda and Empire*, p. 255.

51. Mackenzie, ibid., p. 258.

52. E. Lawrence, 'Just Plain Common Sense: The "Roots" of Racism', in *The Empire Strikes Back*, p. 47.

53. C. Mullard, *Black Britain* (London: Allan and Unwin, 1973) p. 46; S. Hall, 'Racism and Reaction', in J. Rex et al., *Five Views of Multiracial Britain* (London: Commission for Racial Equality, 1978) p. 27; Hiro, *Black Britain, White Britain*, p. 11.

54. R. Davison, *Black British: Immigrants to England* (London: Oxford University, 1966) p. 1; I. Katznelson, *Black Men, White Cities* (London: Oxford University, 1973); A. Sivanandan, *A Different Hunger* (London: Pluto, 1982) pp. 10, 18.

55. Sivanandan, *A Different Hunger*, p. 17.

56. About 7,000 Kenyan Asians emigrated to Britain each year between 1964 and 1966, and there was a slight increase in 1967, as 8,443 entered between January and September. Net figures for 1967, however, show a net emigration from Britain of 84,000, even with this increase. Hiro, *Black British, White British*, pp. 224–5.

57. I have discussed Powell's discourse in more detail in 'The Speeches of Enoch Powell', *Essex Papers in Government*, no. 66, November 1989.

58. Sivanandan, *A Different Hunger*, p. 23.

59. The idea that someone could actually become an immigrant – without changing residence – precisely because of race, is used in the film *For Queen and Country* (Martin Stellman, dir., UK, 1989). The protagonist, a black British soldier raised in south London, returns home from tours of duty in the Falklands and Northern Ireland and finds that he cannot obtain a British passport under the new Thatcherite citizenship legislation.

60. Hall, 'Racism and Reaction', pp. 25–6.

61. An example of this emphasis on assimilation can be found in the case of the deportation appeal by the Asian-British Pereira family in 1984. The appeal was successful, but only after a campaign was mounted in the popular media and by local neighbours in which it was argued that this family had shown a commitment to Britain and the English way of life, in terms of their Christianity and their participation in the village life with their (white) British neighbours. (Gilroy, *There Ain't No Black in the Union Jack*, pp. 63–4.) This decision implies that cases in

which the immigrants retain their non-white-English identities would not be judged in the same manner.

62. Sivanandan, *A Different Hunger*, pp. 17–18.

63. As quoted in Hiro, *Black British, White British*, p. 229.

64. S. Hall et al., *Policing the Crisis* (London: Macmillan, 1978) p. 49; Sivanandan, *A Different Hunger*, pp. 17–18.

65. Gilroy, *There Ain't No Black in the Union Jack*, pp. 72–111; Hall, 'Racism and Reaction', p. 29; Hall et al., *Policing the Crisis*; Sivanandan, *A Different Hunger*, pp. 23, 27, 32, 33.

66. Gilroy, *There Ain't No Black in the Union Jack*, p. 110.

67. J. Lambert et al., 'Police/Immigrant Relations: A Critique of the Select Committee Report', *New Community*, vol. III, no. 3, Summer 1974, pp. 172–92.

68. The West Midlands Police Force commissioned a study on the deteriorating relations between the police and the black community by John Brown (*Shades of Grey*, Cranfield: Cranfield Institute of Technology, 1977). Brown alleges that the 'most serious police problems' were caused by a 'particular group – some 200 youths of West Indian origin or descent who have taken on the appearance of the followers of the Rastafarian faith by plaiting their hair in locks and wearing green, gold and red woollen hats' (p. 3). Brown nevertheless asserts that a distinction ought to be made between this 'criminalised Dreadlock subculture' and the relatively harmless 'true Rastafarians' (p. 7). Cashmore reports that a police Superintendent told him that 'the first thing you've got to do when you're talking about Rastafarians is distinguish between the real followers and these kids who stick a few posters on the wall, grow plaits and call themselves "Rastas". Most of them don't know what they're on about and they're the ones who cause all the trouble for us' (p. 173).

69. As quoted in Gilroy, *There Ain't No Black in the Union Jack*, p. 58.

70. Ibid., p. 59.

71. For a detailed discussion of the New Right and race and racism, see G. Seidel, 'The Concept of Culture, "Race" and Nation in the British and French New Right', in R. Levitas, *The Ideology of the New Right* (London: Polity Press, 1985) pp. 107–35, and 'The White Discursive Order: The British New Right's Discourse on Cultural Racism', in I. Zavala et al., eds, *Poetics and Psychiatry* (Amsterdam: Benjamins, 1987) pp. 39–66.

72. Gilroy, *There Ain't No Black in the Union Jack*, p. 60.

73. *The Guardian*, 13 July 1988, p. 20.

74. For more detail on the New Right attack on 'multiculturalism', see Seidel, 'The White Discursive Order', *Approaches to Discourse*, pp. 53–5.

75. *The Sunday Times*, 17 July 1988, B1.

76. M. Smith et al., 'The Ras Tafari Movement in Kingston', *Social and Economic Studies*, vol. IX, no. 3, 1960, supplement.

77. As quoted in Barrett, *The Rastafarians*, p. 175.

78. F. Fanon, *The Wretched of the Earth* (New York: Grove Press, 1968) p. 221.

79. E. Laclau and C. Mouffe, *Hegemony and Socialist Strategy* (London: Verso, 1985) p. 112.

80. D. Midgett, 'West Indian Ethnicity in Great Britain', in H. Safa and B. du Toit, eds, *Migration and Development* (The Hague: Mouton, 1975) pp. 664–5, 76–7; P. Pollard, 'Jamaicans and Trinidadians in North London', *New Community*, vol. I, no. 5, Autumn 1972, pp. 370–77.

81. Lewis, 'Race Relations in Britain', p. 79.

82. D. Lawrence, *Black Migrants, White Natives* (London: Cambridge University Press, 1974) p. 20.

83. Davison, *Black British: Immigrants to England*, p. 103; Sivanandan, *A Different Hunger*, pp. 5–8.

84. Hiro, *Black British, White British*, pp. 43, 45; Sivanandan, *A Different Hunger*, pp. 1–16.

85. Hiro, *Black British, White British*, p. 55.

86. See for example S. Carmichael and C. Hamilton, *Black Power* (New York: Random House, 1967); O. Egbuna, *Destroy This Temple: The Voice of Black Power in Britain* (London: MacGibbon and Kee, 1970); Hiro, *Black British, White British*, pp. 56, 64; Hall et al., *Policing the Crisis*, p. 248; Sivanandan, *A Different Hunger*, pp. 20–23, 25.

87. As quoted in Hiro, *Black British, White British*, p. 103.

88. Ibid., pp. 103, 104.

89. 'After Dread and Anger', six-part radio documentary, written and narrated by Ferdinand Dennis, produced by Louise Purlow and Kathy Watson, Radio Four, UK, April 1989.

90. J. Lacan, 'The Mirror Stage as Formative of the Function of the I as Revealed in Psychoanalytic Experience', in *Écrits: A Selection*, trans. Alan Sheridan (London: Tavistock, 1977) pp. 1–7 (henceforth abbreviated in the text as *Écrits*, followed by the page reference). The definition of identification given above is taken from this paper (*Écrits*, 2).

91. J.P. Muller and W.J. Richardson, *Lacan and Language* (New York: International Universities Press, 1982) p. 38.

92. Schwarz, 'Conservatism, Nationalism and Imperialism', *Politics and Ideology*.

93. Hall, 'New Ethnicities', p. 30.

94. Ibid., p. 27.

95. Derrida, *Of Grammatology*, pp. 44–64.

96. Hall, 'New Ethnicities', p. 28.

97. Ibid., p. 30.

98. Ibid., p. 27.

8

The Crisis of Identity and the Struggle for New Hegemony in the Former Yugoslavia

Renata Salecl

The Yugoslavia constructed by Tito after World War II was a particularly cohesive creation, at least in so far as the ideology of self-management, fraternity and unity, along with the non-alignment symbolized by President Tito himself, acted as the 'cement' of the social fabric. Self-management was held to be the highest level of democracy, far ahead of workers' participation in capitalism; non-alignment was seen as the best chance of overcoming the division of the world into blocs; and Tito was the cohesive authority which guaranteed the equality of all the nations within Yugoslavia, as well as guaranteeing prospects for society's prosperity (high living standards, openness to the world, and so on). But with Tito's death came disillusionment. People soon learned that the miracle of the Yugoslav economy had been based on large foreign debts which the state had used to cover the investment failures of industry. Economic collapse was paralleled by significant international conflict: at first between Serbs and Albanians in the Serbian Autonomous Province of Kosovo, then amongst other Yugoslav nations, finally culminating in the country's disintegration and all-out civil war.

The paradox of Yugoslavia is that although its entire recent political reputation has been based on the break with Stalin in 1948 (and, later, the introduction of self-management in contrast to the real-socialist systems of Eastern Europe), these same states have overtaken Yugoslavia in the struggle for democracy. Yugoslavia's pause in the demolition of socialism has, thus, two causes: the first is the logic (and working) of self-management ideology itself; the second is that of nationalism.

It could be said that disintegration of the ideology of self-management – indeed, Yugoslav's utter economic and political chaos – confirms Althusser's thesis on ideological state apparatuses: that ideology is materialized in the entire organization of society.[1] So even though we can say, for example, that the self-management thesis about 'the disposal of surplus value to direct producers' might have been utopian, this utopia was nevertheless materialized in the organization of socialist firms – just as the utopia about 'self-management direct democracy' was also materialized in a complex delegate system; or the idea that 'public self-defence' was materialized in an intricate web of secret regulations and agencies which already penetrated every cell of society. Consequently, when the ideology of self-management was presented as a complete contrast to real-socialist ideology, it simultaneously seized its basic element (the Party as the guarantor of the system, the struggle for actual rather than formal freedom, dealing with enemies of the system, and so forth), and created the possibility of a considerably more effective way to silence the critics of the system than that postulated by real-socialism. Now, given that the self-management system was immanently revolutionary and self-critical, it thus, constantly, changed the system, 'revolutionizing' it with ever new legal norms – constantly changing the constitution, or continually making good those deficiencies in the system which had hitherto hindered direct management by the workers, and so on. But throughout all this activity, the sources of power (the Party, state organization, secret police) ended up maintaining the same roles as they would have had in a classical real-socialist system. Precisely because of this 'revolutionary' nature, the ideology of self-management was also able to neutralize oppositional critics of the system by stressing how the ideologists of self-management themselves were combating the same problems. So, for example, the ideology of self-management could counter the demand for 'anti-bureaucratization' by saying that it too was trying to get rid of the alienated bureaucratic structure and was fighting for direct workers' rule. The only really dangerous critics of the self-management system became, then, those who openly attacked the idea of self-management itself; and they were singled out as the worst of the enemy within.

The economic crises in the eighties provoked workers' revolts, but the workers' demands were deeply conservative: they demanded more pay and better working conditions, but seldom political pluralism or independent unions. Strikes and meetings were characterized by the lack of any positive programme of political change: people demanded changes not in the system itself, but only in the leadership which sought to betray the ideological foundations of the system (socialism, working-class interests, and so on). With the typical old Stalinist understanding that 'the cadres decide all', Yugoslav workers also wanted 'the right people in the right places'. This perspective has best been explained by the Yugoslav sociologist, Josip Županov, who argues that the basis of the Yugoslav system was the pact between the governing politocracy and the narrower, manually skilled section of the working class.[2] This working class was the real pillar of the establishment. The political bureaucracy was given total authority in exchange for maintaining the most minimal subsistence level, with social security and the 'right not to work'; that is, the right to a (low) standard of living, a secure position, and the right not to have to work terribly hard. The economic crisis meant that the ruling political bureaucracy was no longer able to meet its obligations under this pact, and therefore workers' protests could be seen as a desperate appeal to the polito-cracy to keep its part of the deal. The paradoxical features of workers' protest – the total absence of demands for democracy and independent unions – are probably best explained from this perspective. Workers called directly upon their rightful partner, embodied, from their perspective, in the Party, to pro-vide 'a life worthy of man'. Or, to put it slightly differently: they were looking for a Master whom they could empower, in return for their being looked after. Indeed, one of the elements in the rise of Serbian nationalism under Mil-ošević's leadership has been Milošević's capacity to build on this fact and his ability to recognize himself as the addressee of the workers' demands. And he has promised that, to the extent that he is given power, he will fulfil his part of the social pact, in contrast to the corrupt status-quo bureaucracies of the republics.

The ideology of self-management in Yugoslavia disintegrated in three stages. The first stage of self-management took place in the sixties and seven-ties when theoreticians centred around the journal *Praxis* attacked official ideology in the name of 'proper' (read: critical, creative) Marxism. According to the *Praxis* philosophers, the predominant 'statist bureaucratic' conditions in Yugoslavian society prevented the emergence of 'proper self-management socialism'. Consequently, they called for a programme to abolish the gulf between the ideal and the real, with the intention of making the concept of self-management more realizable and effective. In other words, the oppo-sition criticized the establishment in the name of a purified version of the establishment's own ideology. The second phase in the disintegration of self-management ideology started at the beginning of the eighties in the form of 'new social movements'. This period was characterized by a process of equal disintegration of both official and oppositional ideology. The disarticulation of official discourse showed that the establishment was no longer legitimized by any homogeneous ideological construction, but had come to use a whole series of heterogeneous, disassociated elements in its ideological discourse. For ex-ample, self-management and social ownership attempted to make contact with market economics; but as to the demand for independent journalism, the establishment answered in a real-socialist style, that is, that 'the freedom of the press does not exist anywhere'. Interestingly, a similar disarticulation oc-curred in the opposition: this expressed itself as a pluralist scenario of oppo-sitional subjects (for example, the feminist movement, peace movement, ecology, and so on) which not only questioned the basic socialist system itself but, rather, questioned the role of the state – all in the name of the struggle for a civil society. Characterized by ideological heterogeneity and apoliticism, this opposition was not organized into parties but took the form of a series of informal movements which exerted pressure on the establishment through public protest.

The third and final phase in the disintegration of self-management ideology emerged at the end of the eighties when opposition groups created formal political parties and declared the power struggle open. This meant that the establishment, at least in its public statements, also had to abandon its sacred position and acknowledge the Communist Party as just one of many political subjects – one that could lose power at any time. Official ideological discourse in this period began to abandon self-management and Marxism in favour of socialism with a capitalist face. Because of ever stronger opposition, official discourse was forced to fold elements of the opposition's discourse into itself: thus it began to stress the struggle for human rights, freedom of thought, and a state based on the rule of law and the market, and so on. But even then its strength was still preserved because, in spite of the changing discourse, the state apparatus, the army, and the secret police simply maintained their old positions, thus allowing the establishment to continue working in the same way as it always had done up to that point.

This background allows us to pinpoint the exact moment when the disintegration of the ideology of self-management began. The main ideologue of self-management, Edvard Kardelj,[3] put forward a thesis in the 1970s about the importance of the 'plurality of self-management interests' as a crucial element of a self-management society. This thesis, which at first glance seemed to be just another empty phrase from the self-management vocabulary (constantly emphasizing that the worker is the only owner of the means of production, the only one who can decide about production and surplus; and that real self-management resolves all alienation and so on), suddenly proceeded to generate a multitude of interpretations and thus to mark a site of radical contingency. Why? Because the 'pluralism of self-management interests' could be interpreted as undermining the Party monolith – since, up to now, Party ideology had never used the concept of pluralism of opinions, ideas or interests; rather, it had clung to the notion of unity at any price. But as soon as a pluralism of interests is introduced, this unity is challenged; for in reality, a pluralism of interests equals political pluralism. So an apparently surplus syntagm became the point at which the system began to fracture, that is to say, the point where elements, which had until then formed an ideological structure, now achieved independence and began to function as 'floating signifiers' awaiting new articulation. Thus the struggle for hegemony began, that is, a struggle for what this concept would include in its series of equivalences.[4] Official Party ideology tried in vain to retain the 'pluralism of self-management interests' within its confines; yet even though Kardelj himself later abandoned the term, already this 'pluralism' had taken on a life of its own, becoming a trademark of the alternative, opposition movement. Along with the crumbling of the ideological structure, the struggle over which discourses would 're-sew' the free-floating disparate elements was now firmly under way.

Although the federal authorities and the army (JNA) desperately tried to preserve Tito's Yugoslavia, the rhetoric of 'fraternity and unity' and the slogans of both the revolution and the national liberation war no longer served as the points of identification that had held the Yugoslav symbolic universe together for forty years. At the end of the eighties, a new series of, primarily national, points of identification emerged which totally redefined the terms of the struggle for ideological hegemony. As a result, we can isolate three blocs around which various conceptions of the form of a future Yugoslav society crystallized at the end of the eighties. The most disreputable was the right-wing populist Serbian bloc with its concept of a unitary state, a strong party, and a centralized government under Serbian domination. This bloc, in addition to the Republic of Serbia with its autonomous province of Vojvodina, included Serbian inhabitants in the province of Kosovo, Montenegro, members of the Orthodox Church, part of the federal administration and senior staff of the army, and Serbian inhabitants in other parts of Yugoslavia, along with Serbian emigrants abroad. Since the Serbian population is numerically the strongest and Belgrade is simultaneously the capital of the Republic of Serbia and of Yugoslavia, this bloc had considerable influence in federal agencies. It is also important to bear in mind that a large proportion of employees of the federal administration and the military leadership were of Serbian nationality. This bloc was characterized by economic underdevelopment, high unemployment and an ongoing dispute between Serbs and Albanians in Kosovo. Opposed to this bloc was the Slovene bloc, which was working towards greater independence of the republics and a pluralist, multi-party organization of society. Along with both leadership and opposition in the Republic of Slovenia, this bloc included part of the opposition and a smaller part of the leadership of Croatia, as well as certain opposition groups in Bosnia and Herzegovina and in the province of Kosovo. Characteristic of this bloc was relative economic success, low levels of unemployment, and political liberalism in Slovenia. However, this bloc's weakness stemmed from its small influence on the activities of federal agencies and the army.

In any case, the strongest and the most 'official' was the 'status quo' bloc, consisting of the army, parts of the federal administration, the secret service, military industry and the bulk of the leadership of Bosnia and Herzegovina and Macedonia. This bloc had maintained its position by repression and wanted to withstand the crisis through cosmetic adjustments, according to the strategy of 'changing things so that nothing changes'. In its desire to maintain its position, this bloc stood against both of the other blocs. In principle, it favoured market economics, although its economy was hopelessly ineffective – as evidenced by the ossified organization of the army, unwise industrial projects in the republics, and widespread corruption.

Nationalism

The national threat became the strongest point of identification on which the opposition as well as the establishment relied. So, on the one hand, local establishment figures strengthened their position by stressing their role in defending the nation against other nations while, on the other hand, part of the opposition also presented national sovereignty as the main aim of the political struggle.

Given this scenario, two views of nationalism were, and have remained, predominant in official Yugoslav politics since the outbreak of national conflict. The first tried to distinguish 'progressive' nationalism (non-aggressive, defensive, civil) from 'regressive' nationalism (aggressive, promoting hatred, directed at the re-establishment of homogeneous national communities). The second view stressed that national frictions were simply the means by which the governing politico-bureaucracy maintained division amongst the nations, and so prevented people from uniting against the real enemy, namely the governing bureaucracy. Is it not true that every nation is offered a myth of how others exploit it in order to disguise how the people themselves exploit others? Such a myth was only an updated variation of the good old Stalinist myth of honest, innocent working people who are never anti-socialist. Thus in Yugoslavia we had the myth of the innocent, honest, democratic public which would never be nationalist – it would only have been manipulated into nationalist attacks by a *corrupt* politico-bureaucracy. Just as the 'honest working people' actually exist only as a mythical reference point for the Party (thereby legitimizing its power), so too the myth of an innocent, non-nationalist public only exists to legitimize the power of the current establishment.

Paradoxically, then, the first step toward real democratic maturity would be, of necessity, the unconditional recognition of the 'depravity' of the people. For example, it might be said that 'it's not true the Albanian people are basically honest and that irredentism is only an idea by which they are poisoned by manipulators', or that 'it's not true the Serbian people are basically honest and that Greater Serbian nationalism is only an idea by which manipulators poison the people', and so forth. With this kind of strategic sentiment, it's not hard to see the transparent delight with which the masses surrender to the manipulation; nor is it hard to see how they maintain their most intimate identity through the 'myth of nationalism'. Likewise, Greater Serbian nationalism, constructed through the myth of a Serbia that wins in war and loses in peace, is the ideological means by which individuals experience their innermost, everyday, concrete burdens; it is their way of finding a scapegoat, which in this case is the Croats. What must be acknowledged here is that the people cannot be deceived unless they are already structured in such a way that they want to be deceived. Or, to put it another way, people themselves articulate a desire for their own deception.

Psychoanalysis enables us to avoid both the simple condemnation of nationalism as well as the false solution of dividing it into 'good' (progressive, anti-imperialist, and so on) versus 'bad' (chauvinist, colonizing, and so on) elements; it enables us to conceive of the nation as what 'always returns' as the traumatic element around which fantasies weave. Thus it enables us to articulate the fantasy structure that serves as a support for ethnic hatred. For both national movements – right-wing opposition and authoritarian populism – have built their power by creating specific fantasies about a threat to the nation, and have, as a result, put themselves forward as the protectors of 'what is in us more than ourselves', that is, that which makes us part of a nation.

It is necessary to emphasize that, as with all nationalism, national identification with the nation ('our kind') is based on the fantasy of the enemy: an alien which has insinuated itself into our society and constantly threatens us with habits, rituals – indeed, discourses – that are not of 'our kind'. No matter what this Other 'does', it threatens us with its existence. The fantasy of how the Other lives on our account, is lazy, and exploits us, and so on, is repeatedly re-created in accordance with our desire. For example, there exists a common notion that immigrants are lazy, lack good working habits, and so on, which is accompanied by the simultaneous accusation that they industriously steal our jobs. The Other who works enthusiastically is especially dangerous – for that is precisely their way of deceiving us and becoming incorporated into 'our' community. The same can be said with immigrants who assimilate: they are usually accused of retaining their strange habits, of being uncivilized, and so on. But if they adopt our customs, we then assume that they want to steal from us 'our thing': the nation.

We are disturbed precisely by the fact that the Other is Other and that he or she has his or her own customs, by which we feel threatened. As Jacques-Alain Miller says, hatred of the Other is hatred of the Other's enjoyment, of the particular way the Other enjoys. For example, when Croats are irritated by the Albanian 'mafia-type' of business, or when the Slovenes find unbearable the way 'Southerners' (Bosnians, Serbs, Montenegrins, and so on) enjoy themselves, what they are identifying is the threat of the way the Other finds enjoyment in a different way than we do. As Miller says:

> Something of that kind could consist, for example, in the fact that we ascribe to the Other an enjoyment in money exceeding every limit. I am willing to see my neighbour in the Other but only on condition that he is not my neighbour. I am prepared to love him as myself only if he is far away, if he is removed . . . When the Other comes too near, when it mingles with you, as Lacan says, new fantasies emerge which concern above all the surplus of enjoyment with the Other . . .
>
> The question of tolerance or intolerance is not at all concerned with the subject of science and its human rights. It is located on the level of tolerance or intolerance toward the enjoyment of the Other, the Other as he who essentially steals my own enjoyment.

> ... When we are considering whether the Other will have to abandon his
> language, his convictions, his way of dressing and talking, we would actually like to
> know the extent to which he is willing to abandon or not abandon his Other
> enjoyment.[5]

This Other who steals our enjoyment is always the Other in our own interior.
Our hatred of the Other is really the hatred of the part (the surplus) of our own
enjoyment which we find unbearable and cannot acknowledge, and which we
transpose ('project') into the Other via a fantasy of the 'Other's enjoyment'.
The hatred of the Other, in the final analysis, is hatred of one's own
enjoyment. Intolerance of the Others' enjoyment produces fantasies by which
members of particular nations organize their own enjoyment.

Serbian authoritarian populism has produced an entire mythology about
the struggle against internal and external enemies. The primary enemies are
Albanians, who are perceived as threatening to cut off the Serbian autonomous province of Kosovo and thereby to steal Serbian land and culture. The
second enemy is an alienated bureaucracy which threatens the power of the
people: alienated from the nation, it is said to be devouring the Serbian
national identity from within. The third enemy has become the Croats who,
with their politics of 'genocide', are outlawing the Serbian population from
'historically' Serbian territories in Croatia.

All images of the enemy are based on specific fantasies. In Serbian
mythology, the Albanians are understood as pure Evil, the unimaginable: that
which cannot be subjectivized – beings who cannot be made into people
because they are so radically Other. The Serbs describe their conflict with the
Albanians as a struggle of 'people with non-people'. The second enemy – the
bureaucrat – is presented as a non-Serb, a traitor to his own nation and, as
such, also effeminate. The Croats are portrayed as the heirs of Goebbels, that
is, as brutal Ustashi butchers who torment the suffering Serbian nation – a
nation whose fate is compared to that of Kurds in Iraq. And the Muslims are
named Islamic fundamentalists, extremists who would like to expand their
religion all over the world.

However, along with Albanians, Slovenes have also emerged as the enemies
of Serbian nationalism: they share with the Albanian separatists the wish to
constrict the political hegemony of Serbia. What do we get when we combine
these two enemies? Remember that Albanians are presented as dirty,
fornicating, rapacious, violent, primitive, and so forth, while the Slovenes are
presented as unpatriotic, anti-Yugoslav intellectuals, and as non-productive
merchants who exploit the hard work of the Serbs. If we simply put the two
pictures together, if we add an Albanian to a Slovene, what happens? You get
the Jew, the typical anti-Semitic portrait of the Jew: dirty, fornicating, but at
the same time an intellectual, non-productive, profiteering merchant.[6]
Moreover, in Serbian mythology, the enemy is revealed to be both rapacious

and impotent. Just as English conservatives describe the threat to Britain from immigrants (especially blacks) as 'the rape of the English race',[7] so the Serbs portray Albanians as rapists of the Serbian nation, who steal the Serbian national identity in order to instal their own culture. Reinforcing this figure of rape are allegations about actual attempts by Albanians to rape Serbian girls. But what is important here is that the rape is always only an attempted – that is to say, failed – rape. A picture of the enemy thus takes shape as an Albanian who tries to rape Serbian girls but is actually unable to do so. This portrayal is based on the fantasy of the enemy's impotence – the enemy tries to attack, to rape, but is confounded, is impotent, in absolute contrast to the macho Serb.

The mythology of the new Serbian populism constantly stresses the difference between real men – workers, men of the people – and bureaucrats. In this mythology, the bureaucrat is portrayed as both a middle-class feudal master and a kid-gloved capitalist, with top hat and tie, 'clean outside and dirty within'; in absolute contrast to the worker, the man of the nation, 'dirty on the outside but pure within'.[8] The essence of the argument is that the bureaucrat is not a 'real' man: he is effeminate, slug-like, fat; he drinks whisky and eats pineapples – as opposed to the macho worker, who eats traditional national food and dresses in workers' dungarees or national costume. Bureaucrats are not men because of their alienation from tradition and their betrayal of the heroic Serbian people.

To demonstrate its ties to the nation, then, Serbian populism invokes the heroic dead – not just their names, but their actual bodies. In the new Serbian populist mythology, current fighters for Serbian sovereignty are constantly compared to the Serbian heroes who fought the Turks six hundred years ago. Bones play a special role in this dramatic identification with the heroic past. Serbian populism has rediscovered the old Orthodox custom by which the mortal remains of a ruler are carried through all the monasteries of the country before burial; so the restoration of the real Serbian identity was confirmed in 1989 by the transfer to Kosovo, after more than six hundred years, of the bones of the famous Serbian hero, King Lazar, who died in battle with the Turks. When the old Orthodox ritual of carrying the bones around the monasteries was reinstituted for Lazar's remains, it designated the new birth of the Serbian symbolic community. The bones can be seen here in Lacanian terms as the Real, that 'something more' which designates the symbolic community of the Serbian nation. Indeed, the national 'Thing' comes out precisely in the bones. Thus Lazar's bones function as the Real which has returned – as it always does – to its (rightful) place. Lazar's return to Kosovo constitutes symbolic confirmation of the 'fact' that Kosovo has always been the cradle to 'that which is Serbian'.

As Lacan says, race becomes established according to how a particular discourse preserves the symbolic order. The same can be said of the concept of a national community: in the case of Serbia, the ridiculous ritual of transferring bones functions both to reinstate and preserve the symbolic order. On the factual level, what we have here amounts to no more than a pile of trivial bones, which may or may not be the king's, which may have some archaeological or anthropological value; yet within the Serbian ideological discourse, these bones also represent that which 'the enemy has always wanted to deprive us of, that which we must guard with special care'. The national conflict between the Serbs and the Albanians, as well as the struggle between Serbs and Macedonians, has always exploited the symbolism of bones stolen from Serbian graves. For example, one myth has grown up around the claim that Albanians have supposedly dug up the graves of Serbian children; another myth claims that Macedonians supposedly used the bones of Serbian soldiers who fell in World War I for anatomic studies in their medical faculties. Moreover during the war in Croatia, the bones of the Serbs, killed by the Ustashi in World War II, acquired a special meaning and once again the rituals of transferring bones and ceremonial reburials with ideological speeches started to appear.

Nationalism and the Struggle for a New Hegemony

In the past ten years nationalism has played a crucial role in the struggle for a new hegemony in Serbia. This struggle began when a group of Serbian politicians around Slobodan Milošević first took up the problem of Serbs emigrating from the autonomous province of Kosovo. This group later openly demanded the formation of a Greater Serbia by way of an annexation of territories that were part of other republics. This populist movement in Serbia successfully united two apparently disassociated elements: a neo-Stalinist party politics and the concept of civil society (though in a nationalist guise).

What first happened was that certain neo-Stalinist goals were achieved by putting the party above the state. Surprisingly, this move garnered popular support. Milošević's success here turned on combining a host of heterogeneous elements into a populist nationalist project, a kind of rag-bag assortment containing the most extraordinary mixture of elements:

(i) *traditional Stalinism*, with its appeals to both unity and 'differentiation' through purges and reactivation of an ideology that more or less ran along the lines of a self-declared anti-self-management chain – Tito-the party-the army-fraternity-unity;

(ii) *proto-fascist right-wing populism*, with its state-of-emergency hysteria and its 'street pressure' brought to bear through mass rallies directed at particular enemies, replayed at a national level;

(iii) *étatism*, with its emphasis on a strong, unified state that rigorously upholds the law;

(iv) *the mythologization of nationalism*, with its more or less directly expressed thesis of Serbia as the pillar of Yugoslavia, the essence of Yugoslavness; and of the Serbs as the only 'real' Yugoslavs, via resuscitation of old Serbian myths aimed at countering the thesis of a 'weak Serbia as a condition of a strong Yugoslavia';

(v) *bourgeois liberalism*, with its emphasis on economic liberalism and the human rights of Serbs in Kosovo, in addition to Milošević's timid flirtation with bourgeois democracy.

What could possibly hold all these disparate elements together? The figure of a strong leader, a need for decisiveness ('now is the time for history, not for discussion'), and a clear image of the Enemy.[9] Significantly, this heterogeneity has been Milošević's strength, not his weakness. Indeed, Milošević fully succeeded in re-establishing an effective 'series of equivalences', to use the terminology borrowed from Laclau and Mouffe.[10] Specifically, he honed the Stalinist rhetoric of the iron fist, archaic nationalism, and a civil rhetoric of human rights, and so on, into a unified discourse set against the status quo of the federal bureaucracy.

Milošević's populism has also been based on his effectiveness at interpellating individual segments of society (workers, the intelligentsia, technocrats, the party bureaucracy and so on) in such a way as to neutralize their potential antagonism. As Ernesto Laclau has noted:

> the basic method of this neutralisation lies in a transformation of all antagonism into simple difference. The articulation of popular-democratic ideologies within the dominant discourse consists in an absorption of everything in it which is a simple differential particularity and a repression of those elements which tend to transform the particularity into a symbol of antagonism.[11]

The Serbian populist movement confirms the thesis that no element belongs naturally to a fixed ideology. Accordingly, it would be incorrect to say, for example, that the fanatic devotion of the masses to a leader is a part of fascist ideology by nature; or that the totalitarian project of a strong party above the state is always Stalinist per se. Indeed, Milošević has shown that elements which might have been considered part of a defined ideology can be re-articulated as entailing a totally new meaning. But having said that, another characteristic of Milošević's populism has been that it is impossible to say which element is pre-eminent. Essentialists have constantly harped on this problem, maintaining that communist ideology has served Serbian nationalism as a means of finding its own expression; others have advocated an opposing thesis according to which the Stalinist-communist project has served nationalism in order to survive. Both lines of reasoning are fundamentally flawed: they fail to take into account that the position of the various elements is only created by articulation.

How has the struggle for a new hegemony progressed? Crucial to this struggle has been the resurrection of old myths, folk songs and stories portraying the historical struggle of the Serbian and Montenegrin nations against the Turks. Symbolic identification with the popular heroes of Serbian mythology has given the new leadership a special status: not only have they acquired an aura of sanctity as folk heroes, but this new, sanctified status has also enabled the leadership to repair the historical damage incurred by the loss of the battle of Kosovo in which the Serbs were defeated by the Turks in 1389.[12]

Through the rearticulation of old myths into official political discourse, Milošević constructed new myths that were easy to identify with, at least in so far as they replaced the socialist jargon of the bureaucracy. Self-management had introduced a specific jargon that transformed businesses into 'organizations of associated labour'; workers into 'direct producers'; and directors into 'individual business organs'. With the aid of a kind of 'demystification' of the language, self-management could be portrayed as a really direct form of democracy. The success of the 'anti-bureaucratic revolution' lay in the recognition that this rhetoric of self-management represented a total obfuscation of the effective social relations. But, moreover, this 'anti-bureaucratic revolution' was also successful because it replaced self-management rhetoric with a return to the old national myths – so long ignored in the supranational socialist ideology. For the old epics and heroic songs are models of effective rhetoric, with their short clear sentences and visionary stresses; they contrast dramatically with boring political speeches.

As a struggle for hegemony, the struggle for a new rhetoric of the 'anti-bureaucratic revolution' has thus been characterized by the need to structure the discourse around a newly created reference point. For the Titoist ideology, the main reference point was the National Liberation Struggle (NOB), which was simultaneously presented not only as a victory against the occupier but also as the victory for the socialist revolution. The sort of 'founding word'[13] of this discourse was Tito's slogan: 'It is necessary to maintain fraternity and unity like the pupils of the eyes.' In the case of the anti-bureaucratic revolution, the point to which the discourse continually refers is the moment when, in the Montenegrin town of Zuta Greda, police truncheon striking miners. Milošević's phrase, 'Nobody has the right to beat the people!' gained the status of the 'founding word'. Not only did this motto become a reference point for all other attempts to stop protest marches by members of the Serbian and Montenegrin nations, it became above all the point which restored meaning to the heterogeneous elements of the anti-bureaucratic discourse in its articulation phase. 'Nobody has the right to beat the people' literally means the empty phrase 'the people are the only authority', but its actual significance is that it gives complete legitimacy to all forms manifest in the 'anti-bureaucratic revolution'. As in all communist projects, the people again become the imaginary bearers of the revolution in whose name the party abrogates power;[14] only this time the struggle is between one communist power and another, or, as an anti-bureaucrat would say: 'real workers' power against alienated power'.

The key to the success of Milošević's discourse turned on the delicate balance between what he said and what he left unspoken. He knew that the effect of signification of an ideological discourse is always supported by some fantasy-frame, by some unspoken fantasy-staging which organizes its economy of enjoyment. To explain this idea we should turn to the theory of French linguist Oswald Ducrot, especially the distinction that he draws between presupposition and surmise.[15] Presupposition is an integral part of the speech act; responsibility for it rests upon the speaker, that is, it is the speaker who, by pronouncing a certain proposition, guarantees its presuppositions. For example, if I say 'I promise you: I will avenge your father's death', I assume hereby a whole network of symbolic, intersubjective relations and my place within it. I accept as a fact that the father's death was the result of an injustice; I assume that I am in a position to compensate for it, and so on. On the other hand, the surmise is the place of inscription of the addressee in the enunciation; that is, it is the addressee who assumes responsibility for it, who has to derive the surmised content from what was said. The surmise emerges as an answer to the question that the addressee necessarily poses to him- or herself: 'Why did the speaker speak that way? Why did the speaker say that?' The surmise thus concerns the way the addressee must decipher the signification of what was being said; and hence, that is why the surmise necessarily touches upon fantasy. In Lacan's graph of desire, fantasy is specified as an answer to the famous '*Che vuoi?*'; that is, to the question 'What did he mean by saying that?'

To clarify the surmise with respect to Milošević, let us take as an example one of his statements: 'My foot shall not touch the Kosovo ground as long as Kosovo is not free.' This apparently neutral statement of one's intention not to go to Kosovo until the Serbians there are freed from Albanian domination carries a clear political message: a call to liberate Kosovo from the Albanians. This surmise is easily recognized by each Serbian addressee, although it is not directly implied by the utterance, nor is it a presupposition of the utterance nor part of its illocutionary force.

We could offer a generalization about this split between presupposition and surmise: it entails a necessary distance between the field of meaning of an ideological discourse and the level of fantasy functioning as its surmise. Let us again take the case of Milošević's authoritarian populism: as has already been shown, at the level of ideological meaning, his achievement has been considerable; in the main, because he succeeded in reuniting in the same discourse elements that were hitherto regarded as incompatible (such as old Stalinist Communist Party rhetoric, proto-fascist elements, and economic liberalism). However, the key to the success of his discourse is the delicate balance between what he has said and what is left unspoken. On the level of ideological meaning – when Milošević speaks for the strong, unified Yugoslavia where all nations will live in equality and brotherhood – he presents his movement as a new, 'counter-bureaucratic revolution', a broad, democratic populist movement rebelling against the corrupted state-and-party bureaucracy, and an attempt to reinstal Tito's legacy, and so on.

However, behind this programme lies another programme, another message, which is easily deciphered by his supporters as the answer to the question 'Why is he telling us this?': Milošević's true aim is to crush the Albanians by turning them into second-rate citizens. He wants to unify Yugoslavia under Serbian domination by abolishing the autonomy of other republics. He presents the Serbs as the only really sovereign nation in Yugoslavia, as the only nation capable of assuring state sovereignty, and he promises to the Serbian masses revenge for the supposed exploitation of Serbia by the more developed republics of Croatia and Slovenia, and so on. Thus we find as the surmise of his discourse a bricolage of familiar, heterogeneous elements, each of which inflames the desire of the Serbians. Such elements include the revival of old Serbian nationalist myths, the glorification of the Orthodox Church as opposed to the intriguing, anti-Serbian Catholic Church, not to mention the continuation of sexual myths about 'dirty Albanians' fornicating all the time and raping innocent Serbian girls – in short, the whole domain of fantasies on which racist enjoyment feeds.

The same can be said of all other successful neo-conservative populist ideologies: their very success rests upon the distance between ideological meaning (the return to the old moral values of the family, of the self-made man, and so on) and the level of racist sexual fantasies which, although unmentioned, function as surmise and thereby determine the way the addressee deciphers the signification of ideological statements. But far from being something deplorable, this very distance is perhaps exactly what marks the difference between neo-conservative populist ideologies, still attached to democratic space, and so-called totalitarianism. 'Totalitarianism' – at least in its radical version – can be understood as an ideology which operates by stating directly and openly what other ideologies only imply as a surmise (an example being Hitler's direct appeal to racist, sexual, and anti-Semitic fantasies). One of the usual self-designations of extreme-right politicians (Le Pen in France, for example) is precisely that they say openly what others (their fellows of the moderate right) only allude to between the lines. Milošević's populism has been a hodge-podge of heterogeneous elements; when, at a given moment, these elements begin to attain independence, this hodge-podge starts to disarticulate itself. At first it seemed as though Milošević himself would have triggered this process. But once other political parties in Serbia began to utter openly the nationalist fantasy which Milošević measured only by mood, the result was a new, more radical nationalist ideology. Real political pluralism became the worst enemy of the anti-bureaucratic revolution.

The anti-bureaucratic revolution is in exactly the same relation to 'normal' self-management socialism as fascism is to 'normal' capitalism. We can appreciate this parallel by considering good old Marxist dogma and by asking ourselves: what is fascism? Fascism is the attempt – by means of a radical revolutionary discourse and with the support of a violent mass movement – to restore national unity and thus to preserve the existing relations of (capitalist) production. The key to such fascism is the introduction of a permanent state of emergency, legitimized by the need to fight some external Enemy – the Jew, the Communist. Of course, all the anti-capitalist thunderings against the 'Jewish plutocrat' do not deceive anybody: fascism fights only against the 'excesses' of capitalism; its real enemy is the communist.

Here is where the anti-bureaucratic revolution is precisely homologous to fascism. No 'anti-bureaucratic' rhetoric can deceive us, since the real enemies are not the bureaucrats (that is, the former politocrats – because those who have shown a timely submission to the new masters survived without difficulty). The real enemies are the forces of democratic pluralism. In order to take away their popular appeal, these forces must be portrayed as the national enemy (Albanians, Slovenes, and those Croatians reputed to be genocidal), just as in fascism the enemy was deceitfully presented in the form of the Jew. It is a desperate attempt to maintain the existing balance of social power by mobilizing an atmosphere of national menace, a threat to the nation. This is an old fascist trick; Hitler, too, came to power through deft manipulation of German national humiliation following World War I. In fact Milošević's favourite metaphor, wherein Serbia and Montenegro are 'two eyes in the same head', derives from Hitler's speech on the '*Anschluss*' of Austria in 1938.

Milošević has also, successfully, included in his discourse the demands made by the opposition for parliamentary democracy and a multi-party pluralistic political system. Radically nationalist as well as liberal democratic parties opposed both communism and Milošević's populism. They hoped that it would be precisely their anti-communist stance that would bring them electoral victory. But again it was nationalism that won the day for Milošević; and, indeed, liberals who failed to incorporate nationalism into their discourse were the biggest losers in the elections. However, the radical nationalists who openly stated their nationalist-racist fears also lost because Milošević spawned the fear that the victory of the opposition would plunge the country into economic and political chaos. Thus Milošević succeeded in promoting himself as the only guarantor of the unity and prosperity of the Serbian nation. He succeeded in creating what may have appeared to be a multi-party system but was instead a system operating under the absolute control of the Socialist Party. At the same time he articulated the growing discontent of the working classes by forging a new enemy: the Croats.

In March 1991, when students dramatically protested against Milošević and demanded democratic changes (above all, freedom of the press), it seemed as though Milošević's regime was finished. This seemed to be the case because Milošević used force to crush the demonstration; the sending in of tanks only catalysed a greater revolt of the opposition. But once again Milošević stayed in power by shifting attention away from the internal antagonisms of Serbia to the threat of an external enemy: the Croats. The Serbian ideological machine started to present the new, democratically elected Croatian government as a mortal threat to Serbs living in Croatia; that is, as a neo-fascist regime planning the 'genocide' of the Serbs.

Resurrected once again was the familiar method of creating national tensions (a method already used by the Serbs in their conflict with the Albanians). This time, however, what was emphasized were the old traumas of the Serbo–Croat quarrel (in the main having to do with the collaboration of the Croatian government with the fascists during World War II and the subsequent slaying of the Serbian population). Milošević demanded that, in the case of the secession of Croatia from Yugoslavia, the 'Serbian' parts of Croatia should stay attached to Serbia. At the same time, Serbian politicians also provoked conflicts in ethnically mixed Bosnia and Herzegovina, again demanding the attachment of territories populated by Serbians.

In the last instance the only way Milošević's regime could survive was to begin an imperialistic war, which Milošević declared with the famous statement, 'It is the legitimate right and the interest of the Serbian people to live in one state – this is the beginning and the end.' For it was only with war that Milošević could silence the demands made by the opposition for democracy, while at the same time preventing the revolt of the working classes who – due to the fall in the standard of living – were on the brink of demanding a change in the leadership of the country.

The Yugoslav People's Army

Let me preface my remarks on the Yugoslav army (JNA), by saying this: if anyone has had their world destroyed by the disintegration of Titoist ideology, it has been, first and foremost, the Yugoslav army. The army has viewed everything, from the stirrings of nationalism to the beginnings of political pluralism, with great distrust and it has, as a result, compulsively clung to old ideological forms. Above all, the army has constantly stressed its purity and has rejected any attempt at 'secularization' by resisting such things as public disclosure of its activities, the introduction of civil military service, and the nomination of a non-military minister of defence. It has sought to separate itself from the social crisis at all costs, disapproving of the crisis from a safe distance and constantly denying that it has played any role in generating the crisis.

Through its 'spontaneous ideology' the JNA experienced itself as Yugoslavia's pillar, the purest embodiment and guarantor of brotherhood and unity, 'as a crystal tear', excluded from the struggle of particular interests characteristic of 'profane Yugoslavia'. If the JNA did not appeal directly to God, it was nonetheless clear that the place the army occupied and spontaneously experienced was seen as consecrated space; it was a 'sacred space', with kinship to the status of the divine right of kings. Any criticism of its activities or questioning of its role was labelled as a grave attack, not only on the JNA, but also (precisely because of its sanctity and its sacred place) as an 'attack on Yugoslavia'.

The claim that attacks on the JNA were attacks on the Yugoslavian nation as a whole can be read in terms of the slogan: the JNA is 'Yugoslavia in miniature'. Furthermore, it can be interpreted through Lacan's distinction between the big Other and the *objet petit a*, that is, where the JNA is the *objet petit a* of Yugoslavia as the great Other self-managing socialist republic: the symbolic network and a foreign body at its very heart. It is that core which is 'in Yugoslavia more than Yugoslavia'; a sacred, untouchable place in Yugoslavia's heart. In this context, the JNA presents two, apparently incompatible, claims about itself: (i) the JNA is the personified, purest expression of Yugoslav society – it is society in miniature, a school for self-management, brotherhood and unity; and (ii) because of its nature, the JNA is not – and cannot be – organized on a self-management basis; rather, it must be organized on the basis of command lines and on an unconditional performance of commands. Thus the JNA reveals itself as both internal and external to the fundamental Yugoslavia – and so, too, the point of the nation's 'extimacy' (Lacan). This is precisely how the JNA apparatus has perceived itself in its spontaneous ideology: as a non-self-management guarantor of self-management, as the point of exception from the system of self-management, but nonetheless as the point that holds together this very same system.

Obsessed with portraying itself as 'blameless' in a deviant society, the JNA has always presented itself as an island of brotherhood and unity, purified of nationalism, liberalism, technocratism and similar abominations feared by 'those outside'. As such a reservoir of purity, it stresses that every segment of Yugoslavia has been tainted with nationalism – except the JNA. Despite open conflicts among various factions and disagreements over development in Yugoslavia, the JNA still perceives itself as exempt from social antagonism, occupying a superior position as the unsullied final guarantor of social unity.

Given this perception, we can now formulate why this unblemished view of themselves is – if we invoke Hegel – a view of the highest Evil. Real Evil, the real impediment to the stability of Yugoslavia, has not been perpetuated by particular interests, but by the structuring of the social field itself which has prevented divergent socio-political interests and projects from being articulated and thus from taking part in the democratic struggle. Such divergent interests have instead been understood as disintegrative, that is, as threatening to the cohesion of Yugoslav society. When the JNA took to weapons and force, first in Slovenia and then in Croatia, its discourse of claiming a need for war came from the hypothesis that only the JNA could (and does) defend the integral wholeness of Yugoslavia, preventing national conflicts and so forth. But behind this level of ideological meaning, the JNA's hypothesis made it quite clear that the JNA was in fact fighting for socialism. The JNA never did come to terms with the collapse of socialism in Slovenia and Croatia, but when it could no longer openly declare these two republics as the enemies of socialism it declared them secessionist and through that act made the military intervention legitimate.

How can we interpret the fact that after the war in Slovenia, the JNA openly went to the side of Serbia in its war over parts of Croatian territory? After the collapse of socialism and the anticipated disintegration of Yugoslavia, the JNA found itself in a kind of transitional period; it was desperately looking for a new role, a way to survive. It was precisely at this point that the move over to the Serbian side offered the JNA a way to give a new meaning to its struggle for Yugoslavia. Because the connection between the JNA and Serbia does not originate from some 'deep' ideological unity and because it does not reflect an admission by either side of mutual need or co-operation, it is therefore thoroughly contingent. Nevertheless, this connection results from a pragmatic realization made by both the JNA and Serbia that each can survive only if united with the other.

In the past the JNA was always suspicious of Milošević. It criticized his nationalism because the JNA perceived itself as the supranational guarantee of peace in Yugoslavia. But in the wake of the collapse of Yugoslavia, it was Serbia and its desire to create a Greater Serbia (or a smaller Yugoslavia) that offered the only island where the JNA could survive. The JNA sent messages to the Serbs which (between the lines) read: 'The only way by which you can realize your desire for a Greater Serbia is to say that you are fighting for Yugoslavia and then we can fight together.' For Serbia the acquisition of the JNA had a very important meaning in its imperialistic war. Serbia presented the alliance with the JNA as something natural, taking into consideration the historical Serbian partiality for the army, their warrior pride and the simple fact that the majority of the officer cadre of the JNA was Serbian. During the 'purification' of the JNA of officers of other nationalities, this majority cadre also considerably helped the JNA to move to the side of Serbia.

The Articulation of the Political Scene after the Fall of Communism

The Slovene political scene in the eighties has been marked by an extraordinary swing to the 'alternative' movement created out of a variety of heterogeneous groups, including groups usually not on speaking terms with each other. This movement encompasses national-democratic-oriented people working in the arts, subcultures such as 'punk', the post-Marxist 'new left' and the 'new social movements' (ecology, peace, feminism, gay) right up to the spontaneous dissatisfaction of individual strata and professions which suddenly took on an organizational form. These new forms sprang from the oppositional activities of individual groups such as philosophers and sociologists, from the founding of the independent farmers' union, and from other unionizing initiatives. Also included must be the Socialist Youth Organization (ZSMS) which had always been a kind of bridge between 'official' and 'alternative' politics and thus provided an umbrella for the new social movements.

Although all this fomentation was not clearly structured, there nevertheless hung in the air an unspoken consensus that the 'alternatives' themselves had grouped into two divisions: the 'left' (new social movements, subcultures) and 'nationalist democracy' (mainly arts workers). The 'power struggle' was a syntagm by which the alternative movement opened the space for democratic political struggle. In socialist ideology, anyone who fought for power had been characterized as an enemy, as one who undermines the power of the working class. The open claim to a fight for power, first expressed in Slovenia by the Socialist Youth, was initially greeted as a dangerous, hostile act, although its clear expression immediately restructured the field of political struggle. Thus even the Party itself started saying that it would not only give up power and organize free elections, it would also acknowledge the collapse of the self-management system.

Before the general elections, then, the political scene in Slovenia was spontaneously constructed from three blocs: the communists and the two oppositions, consisting of the new social movements with the ZSMS, and the national-cultural opposition united in Demos (Democratic Opposition of Slovenia). Demos favoured parliamentary democracy and the complete independence of Slovenia, including the possibility of secession. It linked the importance of the national question to the problem of the low Slovene birthrate, in the name of which the parties grouped in Demos more or less openly stressed the need for a 'population policy' that would restrict the right to abortion. The paradox of Demos was the heterogeneous nature of the parties grouped within it. Before Demos was formed, it was uncertain whether the Greens, who were an ecological wing of the new social movement, would join the conservative Christian Democrats in a group bloc and support part of its ideology. Accordingly after joining Demos, the Greens have given ambiguous statements on the question of abortion: 'not for, not against'; instead, they have accepted the ideology of a 'national threat' and generally have lost the character of an alternative movement.

Precisely this heterogeneous nature of Demos has reconfirmed the contingent nature of alliances in the political struggle. In the formation of the opposition blocs in Slovenia, a struggle for a claim on the 'Green problem' has taken place between Demos and ZSMS-Liberals. The Greens have had the status of a new social movement formerly associated with ZSMS; the ecological issue has had the character of a citizens' initiative above party politics; it has been more a call for a new life style than a political platform. But when they joined Demos, the Greens lost their autonomy and became one of the elements included in the global-national-defence-political project. In a similar fashion, the ecological project thus changed its 'colour' from being just Green: once it was chained to the discourse of national democracy, the ecology movement was reduced to a marginal element in it. The discourse of national democracy rearticulated the ecological demand into the demand for the 'preservation of the culture and the natural heritage of the Slovene nation'. Ecology was thus inscribed in the ideology of the national threat or the general war against 'pollution' which threatens the national substance and which includes everything from polluted nature to 'spiritual pollution', from pornography to soulless contemporary man.

Alternative movements (ecologist, feminist, peace, gay, and so on) and ZSMS had radically transformed the political arena with their demands. They had stressed the primacy of political over national demands, and their chief focus had been the struggle for political franchise. This meant the dismemberment of the socialist state apparatus and its reconstruction along the lines of Western democracy. The key contribution of the alternative movements had been their ability to interpret in a new, fresh way the relationship between the social and the political. Whereas, as we have seen, the whole logic of self-management socialism had been based on the negation of the political. Laclau's observation that in Marxism the political is merely the supplement of the social,[16] is all the more precise with respect to the ideology of self-management. With its idea of immediate democracy and the complete power of the workers over production and collective leadership, self-management completely realized the project of subordinating the political to the social.

Interestingly, the first oppositional organizations in the new social movements also persisted in affirming the primacy of the social over the political. They promoted the idea of separating civil society from the state because such a separation would enable the creation of an independent sphere for civil society outside the official discourse of self-management. They saw their struggle against power above all in the form of public pressure directed at the organs of power from a space external to the system of power. But it was precisely with the proclamation of the syntagm 'a bid for power' that the demands of the new social movements could, and indeed had to, articulate themselves into a political discourse: thus they became the subject of parliamentary discussions; and slowly they too were taken up by the discourse in power.

The whole political scene changed after the elections. In every Yugoslav republic one could witness the emergence of three blocs: the former communists (who changed their name to 'socialists' or 'reformers'), the national right, and the liberals. In every poll, the winning bloc was the one that had included nationalism in its struggle for hegemony. As we have already seen, in Serbia (and in Montenegro) this bloc was the communist one; in Slovenia, Croatia, Macedonia, and Bosnia and Herzegovina the nationalist parties also won the elections. However, these parties defined themselves in opposition to communism, and the majority of them were right-wing in political orientation. In both cases those who lost out were the liberals. The reason for their failure can be located precisely in the fact that they were unable to articulate nationalism. Even though the liberals had the best political programme – one that was open to minorities, and was able to articulate the problems of women and ecology, and above all tried to resolve the economic difficulties facing a society on its way out of socialism – the voters did not identify with liberal politics because they defined themselves as non-national. The liberals did not realize that what mattered is not so much the economic problems as the way these problems are symbolized through ideology. For example, unemployment and poverty are of course hard facts, but what matters in a political battle is how they are perceived, how they are symbolically mediated and structured. An essential feature of the ideological efficiency of the nationalist parties was their ability to subordinate all real (economic) problems to the problem of national identity: they succeeded in convincing the voters that a solution to the national question would solve all other questions as well.

The 'trick' of a successful political discourse is not to offer us direct images with which to identify, not to flatter us with an idealized image or an ideal ego, and not to paint us the way we would like to appear to ourselves; instead, the 'trick' is to construct a symbolic space, a point of view from which we can appear likeable to ourselves – in other words, to construct the discourse in such a way that it leaves the space open to be filled out by images of our ideal ego. In the political discourse of Yugoslavia, it was precisely the national problem which designated the place of identification. Both kinds of nationalist parties – the communists and the right – succeeded in making the question of national sovereignty the element which shaped the symbolic space in which people could recognize themselves. This space was filled not only with images of hatred of other nations but also with images of the 'happy' future which was to arrive with national liberation. Liberals who perceived nationalism as an element of authoritarian-populist proto-fascism lost elections because they were not able to replace this negative image of nationalism with a positive one. They could neither incorporate the struggle for national identity into their political programme, nor find a way to include this identity into a series of plural and democratic equivalences.

The Socialist Moral Majority

National identity serves as the basis upon which the specific ideology of the moral majority depends. This is the moral majority we encounter both in Slovenia and Croatia, as well as in other East European countries. However, it does not have the same significance as the moral majority in the West. In view of its structural role, the moral majority in socialism is democratic and anti-totalitarian: its voice is an oppositional one. Moral revolt against a real socialist regime predominates in its criticism of the authorities. It thus articulates the distinction between civil society (in the name of which it speaks) and the totalitarian state as a distinction between morality and corruption. A return to Christian values, the family, the 'right to life', and so forth, is presented as a rebellion against immoral real socialist authority which, in the name of the concept of communism, permits all sorts of state intervention into the privacy of the citizen.

Paradoxically, the moral majority in the East, in spite of its oppositional role, is comparatively more socialist than conservative in relation to its Western counterpart. Where the latter is characterized by an anti-socialist market ideology in which people answer first for themselves and the state is not the guardian of their well-being, the new post-socialist moral majority, in the name of an organic national ideology, reforges a link with the socialist heritage. When it calls for the reinforcement of national affiliation and Christian values, this moral majority simultaneously stresses that we must not surrender to soulless capitalism; that we must create a state-supported national programme, and so on.

The difference between Western and post-socialist moral majorities can also be seen in their different perspectives on the issue of abortion. First we must point out that in Yugoslavia, as in the majority of other Eastern European countries, abortion is legalized and within easy reach of every woman: indeed, it has often been the only available form of contraception. It was the Catholic-nationalist opposition that first raised the possibility of restricting abortion, but it did so in terms unfamiliar to Western anti-abortion movements. For the traditional 'moral majority', as it is known in Western countries, does not oppose abortion on the grounds of the threat it poses to the nation, but in the name of the Christian values of sanctity of life, the sacred significance of conception, and so forth, from which it derives the claim that abortion is murder. But objections to abortion by the moral majority in Slovenia and in Croatia are connected to their claim that abortion poses a threat to the nation. Linking images of abortion as a crime against humanity to images of abortion as a threat to the nation produces an ideology through which support for the Slovenes or the Croats becomes synonymous with opposition to abortion. When the former Croatian opposition writes that 'a foetus is also Croat', it clearly demonstrates that an opinion about abortion is also going to be an opinion about the future of the nation.

The production of these kind of fantasies of a national threat must of course be seen in terms of the political struggle they engender. The strategy is to transform the internal political threat of totalitarianism into an external national menace which can only be averted by an increase in the birthrate; in other words, by limiting the right to abortion. Thus emerges the hypothesis that to be a good Slovene or a good Croat means primarily to be a good Christian, since the national menace can only be averted by adhering to Christian morals.

In the ideology of national threat, women are pronounced both culprit and victim. The strongest former opposition party in Croatia, the Croatian Democratic Community (which then went on to win the elections), has gone so far in this that it has publicly blamed the tragedy of the Croatian nation on women, pornography and abortion. 'This trinity murders, or rather hinders, the birth of little Croats, that "sacred thing which God has given society and the homeland".' The Croatian moral majority regard women who have not given birth to at least four children as 'female exhibitionists' since they have not fulfilled 'their unique sacred duty'. Women who, for whatever reason, decide on abortion have been proclaimed murderers and mortal enemies of the nation, while gynaecologists who have assisted them in this 'murderous act' are pronounced butchers and traitors.[17]

Women, then, are pronounced guilty; yet at the same time, they are depicted as the victims of overly liberal abortion laws. Ideologists of the post-socialist moral majority take as their starting point the notion that a free decision about how many children a person will have is an inalienable human right, and that society is obliged to maintain population policies that enable people to have the desired number of children. These ideologists believe, therefore, that a state that prioritizes the right to abortion is refusing its citizens access to this second right – that of having a desired number of children. Here the real victims are women.[18] This fantasy of the woman-as-victim is based on the hypothesis that the woman and the nation share the same desire: to give birth. If a woman is defined by maternity, then abortion is an attack on the woman's very essence; but it is also an attack on the essence of the nation, since the national community, according to this ideology, is defined by the national maternal wish for an increased population.

The ideologists of the national threat invoke the same logic as that used by

Ceauşescu's: when a journalist asked him whether the ban on Romanians travelling abroad was not a violation of human rights, Ceauşescu's answer was that since the most important human right is to be able to live in one's own country, the ban on travelling abroad simply guarantees this right. So, too, the ideologists of national threat represent their desire to limit the right to free abortion as simply reinforcing the human right to have the desired number of children. Interestingly, then, this ideology – the ideology of the national threat – has also produced in Croatia a specific form of anti-Semitism, linked, in this case, to the national conflict between Croats and Serbs. To better understand this, it is first necessary to stress that Serbs see themselves in their mythology as Jews – at least in as much as they see themselves as the chosen nation of Yugoslavia. According to the Serbian philosopher, Jovan Rasković, the Serbian nation has always been a nation of tragic destiny, some sort of God's nation; a nation which lost, in Kosovo, its 'sacred country'. So the Serbs understand the Kosovo problem in terms of a struggle for their holy land, that is, the cradle of the Serbian community. The Albanian population is thus constantly presented as immigrant, although this immigration took place in the middle ages and the Albanians are arguably the descendants of much earlier Illyrian inhabitants of the region.

It is precisely this Serbian self-depiction as the 'Jews of Yugoslavia' that reinforces Croat anti-Semitism. For in its mythology, the Jews and Serbs have together implemented a conspiracy against the Croat nation. Here we find, then, the traditional anti-Semitic fantasy of the Jew as Shylock – the sly cheat who lives on the labour of others – united now in the image of the Serb as the national enemy who threatens Croatian sovereignty. That this anti-Semitism is used entirely arbitrarily in the national struggle is confirmed by the Serbs themselves: on the one hand, they proclaim themselves the Jews of Yugoslavia and thus reinforce Croat anti-Semitism, while on the other hand, it is actually the Serbs themselves who construct anti-Semitic enemies (as has been already shown: adding together the images of their own two Enemies, Albanians and Slovenes, in order to get the Jew).[19]

War and the Fantasy of the Homeland

If the Serbian leadership easily succeeded in presenting to the West their imperialist war in Croatia as an ethnic conflict because of their conflicts in the past, during the war in Bosnia and Herzegovina they had more difficulty in doing so. The Muslims, in contrast to the Croats, at the beginning of the war, did not perceive their territory (Bosnia and Herzegovina) as a homeland in a national way. They did not form a narrative about their country which could be called a fantasy structure of the homeland. Before delving into this a bit more, let us recall how this fantasy structure usually works. As noted earlier, in

Lacanian psychoanalysis fantasy is linked to the way people organize their enjoyment: the way they structure their desire around some traumatic element which cannot be symbolized. Fantasy gives consistency to what we call 'reality'. Social reality is always traversed by some fundamental impossibility (by an antagonism, in the language of Laclau and Mouffe), which prevents it from being fully symbolized. It is precisely fantasy which fills out this empty place of the social. Fantasy thus functions as a scenario for concealing the ultimate inconsistency of society.

In the fantasy structure of the homeland, the nation (in the sense of national identification) is the element that cannot be symbolized, for the nation is an element in us that is 'more than ourselves', something that defines us – but is, at the same time, undefinable. We cannot specify what it means, nor can we erase it. We may even say that the nation is linked to the place of the Real in the symbolic network. In Lacanian psychoanalysis, the Real is an element which is always missing, but which at the same time always emerges; it is the element society tries to incorporate in the symbolic order and thus neutralize, but which always exceeds its grasp. Even though the social symbolic order is oriented toward a homeostatic equilibrium, it can never attain this state because of this alien, traumatic element at its core. It is precisely the homeland, then, that fills out the empty place of the nation in the symbolic structure of society. The homeland is the fantasy structure, the scenario through which society perceives itself as a homogeneous entity.

The aim of war is to dismantle this fantasy structure of the enemy country. The aggressor tries to destroy the very way the enemy perceives itself, the way it makes national myths about certain territory, the way it takes this territory (or political system) as something sacred, as a symbol of its existence. This is why the aggressor does not intend merely to impose its beliefs on the enemy's beliefs. The aggressor's aim is, in the first place, to destroy the enemy's belief and to take from them their identity.[20] Thus when the Serbs occupied a part of Croatia, their aim was not primarily to capture Croatian territory but to destroy the fantasy structure the Croats had about that territory. The Serbs forced the Croats to redefine their national identity, to reinvent national myths, and to start perceiving themselves in a new way, without linking their identity to the same territories as they did before.

In the case of Bosnia and Herzegovina we do not encounter this kind of fantasy relation towards the nation. The Muslims, at the beginning of the war, still organized their fantasy scenario of the homeland around the idea of Yugoslavia: the Muslims were the only ones who took literally the trans-nationality of the Yugoslav federation and believed in the notion of 'brotherhood and unity'. The whole existence of Bosnia and Herzegovina was, in a way, a realization of the socialist aim to erase the element of the nation from social organization. The Muslims persisted in this transnational attitude even after their towns had been bombed; they did not want to call the attacker by name; they did not want to give the attacker a national connotation. Thus at the beginning of the war, the aggressors were referred to as 'criminals, hooligans', and only much later did they get the name of chetniks or Serbian nationalists.

The inhuman persecutions of the Muslims by the Serbs reveal, among other things, the fact that the aggressor is disturbed by the very lack of the fantasy structure of the homeland with respect to the Muslims. It is as if it were unbearable for the Serbs that the Muslims do not organize their fantasies of the homeland on national ground. This is why the Serbs are desperately trying to create the impression of the enemy's national-religious extremism and are naming the Muslims 'fighters of Jihad', 'green berets' or 'Islamic fundamentalists'. By torturing the Muslims, the Serbs are actually trying to provoke Muslim fundamentalism. Thus the primary aim of the Serbs is to belittle the Muslims' religious identity by ruining their mosques or by raping young Muslim women. Rape is for Muslim women an especially horrible crime because their religion strictly forbids any sexual contact before marriage; rape, for a young Muslim woman, thus has the meaning of a symbolic death. If the aim of the war is to destroy the fantasy structure of the whole population, then the aim of rape – as the aim of any other form of torture – is to shatter the fantasy structure of the individual. The very manner in which Muslim women are being raped, the very fact that rape is seen by the aggressor's soldiers as a kind of 'duty' they have to perform on the captured woman, reveals the aim of the aggressor to destroy precisely the fantasy structure of the individual woman in a way that will touch her religious and sexual identity. These attacks aim at dismantling the very frame through which a Muslim woman perceives the outer world and herself as consistent; the way she organizes her identity and the identity of her world. Rape as a form of punishment always aims at humiliating the victim, at ruining her world, so that she will never be the same again and will never perceive herself in the same way as she did before. For this purpose, the aggressors are inventing the most horrible forms of torture, where women are raped in front of their mothers or fathers, where incest is demanded, and so on.

If, in the case of the war in Croatia, the aim of the aggressor was to destroy the fantasy structure of the enemy, the objective situation in Bosnia and Herzegovina is just the opposite: here it is the aggressor who, in a violent way, is forcing the Muslim to forge a fantasy structure of national-religious identification. The war actually constructs Bosnia and Herzegovina as a homeland; it creates the fantasy dimension necessary so that Muslim soldiers are willing to die for their own country. This uneasiness with the very lack of national identification on the side of the Muslims is apparent also in the way the Western media report the war in Bosnia and Herzegovina. The first thing that strikes one is the contrast with reporting about the 1991 Gulf War, where we had the standard ideological personification: instead of providing information on social, political and religious trends, antagonisms, and so on in Iraq, the media ultimately reduced the conflict to a quarrel with Saddam Hussein, Evil personified, the outlaw who excluded himself from the civilized international community. Interestingly, even more than military destruction, the true aim of the Gulf War was presented as psychological – as the humiliation of Saddam who had to 'lose face'.[21] In the case of the Bosnian war, however, and notwithstanding isolated cases of the demonization of the Serbian president Milošević, the predominant attitude has been that of the quasi-anthropological observer: the media outdo one another in giving us lessons on the ethnic and religious background of the conflict. Traumas hundreds of years old are being replayed and acted out, so that, in order to understand the roots of the conflict, one has to know not only the history of Yugoslavia, but the entire history of the Balkans from medieval times. In this conflict, it is therefore not possible simply to take sides, one can only patiently try to grasp the background of this savage spectacle, alien to our civilized system of values . . .

Yet this procedure involves an ideological mystification even more cunning than the demonization of Saddam Hussein: for the assumption of the comfortable attitude of a distant observer and the evocation of the allegedly intricate context of religious and ethnic struggles in the Balkans here enables the West to shed its responsibility towards the Balkans, that is, to avoid the bitter truth that, far from simply being an exocentric conflict, the Bosnian war is a direct result of the failure of the West to grasp the political dynamic of the disintegration of Yugoslavia.

Notes

1. See Louis Althusser, 'Ideology and Ideological State Apparatuses', in *Lenin and Philosophy and Other Essays* (London: New Left Books, 1971).
2. Josip Županov, 'Delavski razred in dru "bena stabilnost"', *Teorija in praksa*, 11, 1986, p. 1153.
3. See Edvard Kardelj, *Democracy and Socialism*, trans. Margot and Bosko Milošavljević (London: The Summerfield Press, 1978) pp. 115–40.
4. See on this point Ernesto Laclau and Chantal Mouffe, *Hegemony and Socialist Strategy* (London: Verso, 1985).
5. Jacques-Alain Miller, 'Extimité', unpublished seminar, 1985–86.
6. Mladen Dolar, 'Kdo je danes Žid?', *Mladina*, Ljubljana, 11 March 1988.
7. Bhikhu Parekh, 'The "New Right" and the Politics of Nationhood', in *The New Right* (London: The Runnymede Trust, 1986).
8. Ivo Zanić, 'Bukvar "antibirokratske revolucije"', *Start*, 30 September 1989.
9. On the image of enemy in totalitarianism, see Claude Lefort, *The Political Forms of Modern Society* (Cambridge: Polity Press, 1986).
10. Laclau and Mouffe, *Hegemony and Socialist Strategy*.
11. Ernesto Laclau, *Politics and Ideology in Marxist Theory* (London: Verso, 1977) p. 173.
12. Zanić, 'Bukvar "antibirokratske revolucije"'. The process of exchanging the old leader for the new, i.e., Tito with Milošević, was also an exceedingly important element of the new rhetoric.

First of all it should be stressed that Milošević never directly referred to Tito, although he sometimes used Tito's formulations. At the same time, it is symptomatic of his strategy that he never directly attacked or criticized Tito, in spite of how the whole anti-bureaucratic project was aimed at the Titoist ideology and its scheme of federation. It is of interest to note that the anti-bureaucratic rhetoric exchanged Tito with Milošević in two contradictory ways. On the one hand, it was stressed that Milošević was the only real successor to Tito, a new son of a great leader, to which the lyrics from a newly composed popular song bear witness: 'Slobodan, proud name, Tito taught you well.' On the other hand, there is the much stronger thesis whereby Milošević's accession is the only solution to Tito's errors, as the lyrics continue: 'Slobodan, proud name, you are better for us than Tito.' The apparently contradictory relations are accounted for by the mythical place Tito still maintains in the eyes of the nation; Milošević's project has to be understood as an apparent continuation, and at the same time an extension, of Titoism.

13. On the notion of 'founding word', see Jacques Lacan, *Le Séminaire, livre III: les psychoses* (Paris: Seuil, 1981) p. 315.

14. Lefort, *The Political Forms of Modern Society*.

15. Oswald Ducrot, *Le dire et le dit* (Paris: Minuit, 1986).

16. Ernesto Laclau, *New Reflections on the Revolution of Our Time* (London: Verso, 1990) pp. 56ff.

17. *Dnevnik*, Ljubljana, 26 February 1990.

18. Ante Vukašović, 'Zavaravanje "ena"', *Danas*, Zagreb, 3 March 1990.

19. The thesis about the Judaic nature of the Serbian nation also attempts to substantiate the image of Albanians as terrorists. Since peaceful demonstrations of Albanians crying 'We want democracy' are difficult to characterize as classical terrorism, the Serbian media have had to produce the fantasy of a secret terrorist organization that uses the struggle for democracy only as a veil. Notably, the Serbs have been calling the Albanians terrorists only since the disintegration of real-socialism in Eastern Europe; prior to this they had been using the term 'counter-revolutionary'. Encapsulating them as terrorists is also much more effective: it tries to create, at a more worldwide level, the impression that the Serbian struggle against the Albanians means, for example, the same as the Western struggle against Gaddafi's terrorism or the Jewish struggle against Arab terrorism, and so on.

20. Elaine Scarry, *The Body in Pain: The Making and the Unmaking of the World* (Oxford: Oxford University Press, 1985).

21. For an analysis of the media's report on the Gulf War, see Samuel Weber, 'The Media and the War', *Alphabet City* (Toronto) Summer 1991.

9

The Green Threshold*
Zoltán Szankay

The people has the right to progress as well as to begin.

BENJAMIN F. HALLET
(Boston, 1848)

The planet has become an object of environmental planning. Was there ever a stronger reason to streamline the world than saving the planet?

WOLFGANG SACHS
(Berlin, 1992)

We definitely do not give enough thought to the nature of action.

MARTIN HEIDEGGER
(Freiburg, 1947)

The symbol of unity gives a greater play to human experience than the unity itself.

DONALD W. WINNICOTT
(London, 1986)

Perceiving a Threshold of Our Time

Threshold and border should be most sharply distinguished from each other. Threshold is a *zone*.[1]

WALTER BENJAMIN

Let us consider the (not very numerous) moments of positive political invention since the end of World War II, in an area that could be called, in a

---

* It will be clear from what follows that this chapter, and in particular the remarks concerning context-retrieval, could not have seen the light of day without the theoretical and practical space of the *Grüner Aufbruch*; nor, therefore, without the political contact of friends such as Antje Vollmer, Ralf Füchs and Bernd Ulrich. Hans Scheulen of Bremen University made an important contribution to its first version. Finally, I would like to thank Sue Golding for her thorough conceptual editing and reordering, which served to clarify many of the essential ideas in this text.

broad sense, the West. And let us consider them in light of the question: which of these moments have created a new space, so to speak, in the syntax of a 'political nation' – a syntax that resonates with consequences far beyond its own 'space'?[2] This would be tantamount to asking which of these moments has introduced a degree of field-changing into the operation of the political syntax of our late modernity, a paradigm shift perhaps barely discernible, and yet one that has still crept into a political-historical elucidation of the problems and oppositional patterns. Or, to ask the question slightly differently: At which moment have we been able to discern, perhaps with some surprise, a creative voice for which our political categories (practically all embedded in our patterns of opposition going back to the nineteenth century) may *not* have been suitable?

If we turn our political and historical attention to these questions, we come up against two such moments that, at first glance, may seem odd having been put together – even though they made their appearance at almost the same instance. On the face of it, they involve quite *disparate* renewals, carrying all the weight of a scarcely retouched actuality. These two renewals have been the Solidarnosc phenomenon in Poland, and, in the Federal Republic of Germany, the more modest phenomenon of the Greens. Interestingly, and as we shall explore in this paper, it has been the latter that has entailed greater diversity in its effects, expressing and rebuilding a kind of 'threshold' of the political horizon itself. For what we shall call the 'Green threshold' refers to that unforeseen locus that, in the late seventies, inserted itself – with a kind of friction at first hard to identify – into the pattern of conflict and party politics of the German as well as (albeit indirectly), the West European political landscape. At that time, and even though it emerged as a *party space* making itself felt at the level of parliament, it did not simply emerge out of a conglomeration of 'the ideological development + awareness of the ecological problem', which is how it was – and still is – largely presented. Rather, it took shape out of concrete and often painful *political decisions* – decisions that were bitterly contested to the very end, since they had often been negotiated from opposite sides in the schema dominating political syntax. Suddenly, political and cultural-political threads were knitted together in a way that would not have been possible before. We could now advance a step further conceptually, too, focusing on the term 'political decision'. That term is used, generally, in contexts of deliberate strategic-political actions, where well-known alternatives are clearly in sight. Within this context, the conscious or historically latent 'we-identities' of those who decide are not at all involved. Now, the context of the Green threshold (as well as of the space of Solidarnosc) was quite different: it clearly involved these identities. For the kind of political-historical space that it began to demarcate was a space that opened the site for something like a new category of party (able to affect the traditional conflict pattern of the existing political parties and therewith, in lesser and greater degrees, able to change those traditional schemata). That is to say, its context was one where a space of politics appears which is both 'conscious' *and* 'unconscious' at exactly the same time.

What could conceivably be meant, both practically and analytically, by this reference to the simultaneity of the 'political unconscious'? Or rather (and more to the point) how could it be that a political unconscious might bear out a newer, different, concept than what had gone before; and, in so bearing, what might be the importance (if there was one) of the link to Green politics or to that of Solidarnosc? For as we know, this expression, 'political unconscious', has been a well-oiled but rather vague term. Indeed, when the term has arisen in the political or social-psychological literature, it is conceived practically everywhere as a pure 'mode of deficiency'; that is, exactly in the way it is *not* conceived in the Freudian enlargement of the thinkable. For all its questionable features, Lacan's approach, insisting on the now infamous statement 'the unconscious is structured as a language', seems to bring us closer to the heart of the matter. Why? Because what becomes clearer in re-posing that statement (and others, as we shall note later) is that there is a peculiar terrain or space, a peculiar 'something', brought to bear when examining the unity of both a presence and an absence (where neither represent empty signifiers). Let us look more closely at this matter. When we talk of a reactive way of being able to think of a unity, as for example with the 'I-self' and the 'We-self', we have in mind quite a definite vicious circle. There is the focal point (let's say, in this example, the 'I-self'), outside of which remains all the rest (that is, the 'We-self'). For a long time this 'worked' – at least in the sense of a mutually reinforcing impoverishment of the analytic ways in which the objectified individual-psychological ego and the sociologi- cally objectified We-Group, with their socio-psychologically 'grounding' association, were conceived.

Thus, only the rationalistic, certainty-securing modes of determination, forcibly limiting our experiential dimension, that is, our familiar/uncanny (*heimisch/unheimliche*) language-embedded responsiveness, worked together – and still do work – in a modern world where the 'we-selves' are thought outside of the 'I-self', and vice versa. (And here it could be said, not without a touch of irony, that the 'organic' ways of conceiving the collective and the – ultimately fully rationalist, that is to say, immanent and non-political – 'community' were not tied to concrete signifiers but were, instead, abstractly *counter-social* and, by that measure, doubly reactive.) This rationalist, reactive way of conceiving the political and the social has also, not surprisingly, another dimension, in this case focusing around the twin problems of avoidance and assurance. For, without the (in a liberal, and at first sight, clear and univocal) connection between totalitarianism and the assertion of 'collective identities', it would have taken until several decades after the Second World War for the protective and dominant methodological individualism of rational choice

theories to develop (where it could be said that they developed methodologi-
cally reliable ways of grounding 'collective action' in a way in which the
'supra-individual' could be, and had to be, excluded *ab initio*).

Isn't that so? As if we could have today – or in specific moments of this today
– a 'freer' access to the interplay of the I-selves and we-selves? A kind of move
'daring' to interrupt their assured dichotomization? One that becomes a
threshold-zone, which, in spite of being constantly overstepped by modern,
fully secularized historicity, is *not* to be converted into something definitely
surpassed, being a complement to any horizon? One could say, in fact, that it is
only *today* that this kind of terrain is even thinkable as a kind of social; that is, a
kind of *political* social, where the two ultimate and ruthless exclusions made
invisible in modern rational sociality (the one linked with the sovereign reason
of state and the one linked with the ecological – the visible 'social' exclusions
being, presumably, an overlapping effect of both) could and should have the
chance to become politically confrontable? Confrontable from spaces where
the time – and the right – to progress does not exclude the time – and the right
– to begin?

Presumably, nothing is theoretically more important here than to be able,
really, to stumble upon our language-embedded political nature, rather than
to leap, continually, over it. For it is only as political, language-embedded
beings, that the I-self and the we-selves can be thought together non-
reductively. Only thus can we, following both Freud and Heidegger, perceive
how the I-self is capable of speech only through the *presence of an absence* – just
as it is the historical-political presences of absence which make the 'us' (as a
language-embedded 'we' and not as an 'us-group'; that is, not as the pure
'among us' of a 'we the here presents') capable of both being addressed and
addressing. And yet, today in Germany as elsewhere, the overwhelming
response of academics and social scientists to something introduced in this
way is not unlike the kind of table-thumping that Clifford Geertz speaks about
at the end of his latest book: someone shouts indignantly, 'Where are the
facts?'; the others shout back, 'No, where is the question of power?'[3] In our
recent history there is a sobering, noteworthy event wherein part of the answer
to this twin table-thumping lies. . .

During a particular constellation in the summer/autumn of 1989, as we
know, a 'people' (a 'we-selves') got the chance to speak in the former GDR,
thereby forcing the 'surrender' of a totalitarian regime that had been as
convinced of its rationality, progressiveness and humanism as it was of its
so-called 'ethic of responsibility'. No other form of this 'collective' ability to
speak so clearly marked the breakthrough from protest to a 'revolutionary'
new claim to sovereignty as did the Leipzig demonstrations, where the
world-famous 'We are the people!' suddenly burst forth. Let us now ask our
table-thumping colleagues: Who was it that spoke as 'we' in the streets of
Leipzig and, yes, meddled in 'power'? What was it, exactly, that spoke there,

and from where? Can this so-called fact of 'the people' be understood as a collective action with an underlying, pre-given – that is to say, apolitical or supposedly neutral – collective identity? Or did it come about through the 'rational choice' of individual demonstrators calculating their interests, who remained on the lookout for 'free-riders'? Or, better yet, was it the textbook example of 'expressive behaviour' at the margin of the irrational, if not to mention consensus-oriented 'communicative action', keeping itself at a distance from power? If one is not to be too disrespectful of the supposed facts, not to mention power, all these alternative analyses of social theory, with their concomitant conceptualization of the 'we-selves', and therewith of 'collective' action, are irritating at best; but, at worst, when the whole problem is considered, they really do not make much sense at all.

So let us begin again: how is this 'us' to be conceived? Let us say, along with Lacan, that the 'us' is a political language-embedded being. Well, if this is the case, *how* does this political language-embeddedness impact on the conceptualizing of the 'us' – for shouldn't it matter (and if not, why not?) to remember that for decades the central sovereignty-message of the GDR regime was: 'The people are us!'?[4] That is to say, shouldn't it matter that there is a *history* to this language-embedded being? For it has also to be said that on the streets of Leipzig a (non-self-identical) subject, a political 'we' linked to the sovereignty of the subject – not as a we-group but as a 'language-embedded being' – emerged, though it was one that emerged in the *reversal* of that historical sovereignty-message. Indeed, has it not become plain 'to whom' this (inverted) message was directed?

Let us return to the Green threshold. From the aforesaid, it should be clear that the term does *not* refer to the 'party organization of the Greens' (though also being constructed at roughly this time and 'place', albeit through a different kind of action from that involved in the creation of the *Green space*). Nor does it refer to what is called a programmatically and ideologically defined 'political position', even though the organization of a political force (or party) can be 'built', like that of any 'voluntary association'.[5] We shall advance another small step only if we realize, instead, that the modes of political action that created a place such as the Green threshold or Solidarnosc (or an 'intermediate zone' in Benjamin's sense), cannot be grasped within our conventional categories of political science or 'the sociology of parties'. They cannot be grasped with that kind of sociology in part because one of the specific and constitutive features of such places and of their particular 'temporality' is that from them odd sorts of things, like for example a 'political nation', are being addressed (by, among others, J. G. A. Pocock, M. Walzer, and a multitude of republican discourses of Western history) with a different, but continuity-guarding accent – so that, in the end, it may yield answers in an overt way. All the political places of the classical parties of the West 'began' in such a way. Even the forms of political action under discussion cannot be grasped by our usual political philosophies and social-scientific categories. The reason is because, here too, the individual connections that emerge and can only be established through such forms of partial objectification of the social – and that can, also, have their partial legitimacy – are not just partial kinds of reality. They also swing around and block the very conceivability of the political and, with it, political action (that is, action that is not completely objectifiable). If one relies on so-called objectified individual connections, then, the social-political effects and identity-forms whose temporality is not reducible to a (quasi-physical) co-presence or a universal linear (that is, spatialized) temporal succession are not only de facto excluded, they are also denied 'in general', in their very 'type' of reality. And this is true even if political thought and action *itself* constitutes experience again and again, as for example in the modes of fear and guilt – of referring to remote surroundings and deferred or belated realities, or of referring to the *penetrating* of the spatialized time-complex by decision and/or by play. Among other things, this means that the perceptibility of the Green threshold and of the disjunctive specificity of the Solidarnosc-space depends upon the dissolution or relaxation of this 'rebound blocking'. (In this sense, the writing/setting of this text might also be that of an exercise in conceptual 'unblocking'.) This unblocking in relation to the type of temporality dominant within sociological and 'politico-logical' conceptions of rational systematic effectiveness (that is, suffused with the notion of presence which, in being hegemonic, is as reality-shaping in historical discourse as is the manner in which political actors themselves explain their action) immediately makes something else appear: namely, a *(re-)opening* of the *question of the nature of political things*, as Leo Strauss has put it – that is, the question that must count as *the most closed question* of all in any hegemonic regime.

This leads me to remark on what I would call the misunderstanding about new social movements: it is not easy to see the full extent of this 'closure' in a way that is not foreshortened in either a functionalist or in a historical sense. For, with the historically overwhelming consequences of the political victory of what J. G. A. Pocock analyses as a liberal-oligarchic 'court space' (a point I will return to below), the progressivist schema for the relation between a society dissolving other political community associations and a new kind of state sovereignty assuring legal security, growth, and progress, acquires a largely syntax-forming and partly politics-erasing self-evidence. (Without the victory of the early-modern 'other space' in Jefferson's post-revolutionary United States – which Pocock and others call 'country-space' – we would perhaps no longer perceive the political-historical *specificity* of the triumph of the centralist 'court'.)

The restricted character of the question 'what is the nature of political things?' in our social-political theory shows again how resistant it is when the 'blueprint' of the above relation, at first certainly historical, is again beginning to assume *political* contours. We can see this from a recent historical example. Between the mid-sixties and the end of the seventies, starting from a reopened source of conflict within the political syntax of the historical space of the United States, a unique dislocation developed within the history of late modernity. (Its often pacified consequences, but also that to which it gave life, are still discernible in the early nineties despite the ways in which they are ideologically concealed.) The most important elements of the 'addressing/acting we-forms' it implied could not be arranged under any of the subjectivities; neither as 'class subject' nor as 'subject with particular interests'; neither as 'reactive subject' nor as 'subject with authoritarian identifications', and so forth – that is, arrangements through which *social* subjectivity was conceived in the political-sociological thought of recent modernity as always entailing a temporality of presence or one spatialized in the tunnel of the 'stream of progress'.

These addressing 'we-forms' – which, despite their perceptible resistance to the hegemonic political syntax, were quite rapidly assigned in the sixties to the 'left', or so-called autonomous camps – could certainly not be derived from structures or functions. Nevertheless, this historic dislocation (*Verwerfung*), which at the beginning was also a rejection (*Verwerfung*) in the prevailing objectification and patterns of opposition of modernity, was not at first able to stimulate social theory. Even the critical and politicized domains of the social sciences which focused on this historic refusal were not in a position to experience it as a disruptive challenge to their fundamental schema of objectification. Since the question of the nature of political things remained closed, the crucial bearers of action within this dislocation were categorized – despite the many discontents connected with it – as a 'sub-class' belonging to an essentially *pre-political* socio-historical form of reality, supposedly discovered in the first half of the nineteenth century; that is, as ('*new*') *social movements*. Thus, on the one hand, use of the term social movement has objectified, for more than a hundred years, an impulse layer of social action inscribed in the 'history of progress', downstream from institutional politics and spontaneous by nature – a spontaneity which is always represented pre-politically because it is conceived in terms of a pre-given 'nature of need'. If, with A. O. Hirschmann, we see in the hegemonic new order of references – between (threatening) passions and (rational, society-constituting) interests – one of the main founding achievements of the political hegemony where state and society (as they are 'naturally' for us) come into being together, then it should also be clear that, in the end, social movements (qua merely 'social') always have assigned to them an already *subaltern* space.[6] And though it is a 'movement' space, though indeed it may be 'moving', it can neither appeal to the political nation nor have an effect upon political syntax itself. Reactive fascist movements only appear to be an exception, for in essence – and as institutionalized – they accept remaining fixed in their rule over an irrational space (of puberty, as Winnicott puts it[7]) which is hegemonically assigned to them. (Which, of course, does not affect their destructiveness.)

On the other hand, in the so-called discovery of 'new' social movement (with its implied actual will to establish pure movement or activity), there is a moment of the fateful modern exacerbation of the active/passive dichotomy. This dichotomy, as Heidegger first showed, was latent ever since the beginnings of Western metaphysics. In a way which could be thought simple only by formalization, that is, only by the constructivist opposition between determining form and passive empirical material, it is associated with what psychoanalytic and feminist thought calls the 'gendered logic' of autonomy.[8] Finally, 'social movement' is often pictured as subjectivity conceived naturally in a quasi-physical temporality of presence and space. Through its political reference, it is not possible to conceive either the latencies reaching through time (*Zeitdurchgreifenden*) or the political nature of the secular relations of hegemony which affect the Green threshold and the space of Solidarnosc, and are affected by them. Thus, also, a determination to grasp the 'historic refusal' of the sixties through the concept of the (new) social movements partly post-Hegelian and partly 'naturalistic' in their way of conceiving latency, conceals the politically *decisive* factors that, in their *contingency*, have brought forth the Green threshold and the space of Solidarnosc.

It could be said, then, that the impossibility of opening up the question 'what is the nature of political things?' was as important in its absence as was the emergence, the presence, of the Greens. Notwithstanding the obvious fact that this formation conformed to none of the existing party categories, this occasion could also not be used to question the 'self-evidence' of that strange modern beast, the political party, within the syntax of a political nation, with its divisions no longer based on objective interests nor able to be reduced to a code of difference – something still perfectly possible in the political thought of a Burke or a Karl Rosenkranz.[9] Instead the Greens, who initially (like Solidarnosc) proclaimed themselves a movement, were forced into one of the already-existing party boxes or turned into a kind of a hybrid class of parties, invented by freelance politology of the new class of 'West European left-libertarian' parties that, at least for the author of *The Logics of Party Formation*, had included the 'renovated' Communist Party of Sweden.[10]

This latter categorization is a particularly striking example of how, in the hegemonic capping of the question 'what is the nature of political things?', as well as the resulting divorce of late-modern political science from political thought (where a dispute over the *res publica* is at issue), a high professionalism of the political scientist could perfectly well go hand in hand with political illiteracy – in the exact sense of a manifest inability to read the political and its *not wholly* rationalizable 'nature'. Returning to the blocking of the question of political things and to its unblocking, then, it can be said that a peculiar form of assistance is offered for the latter by the very perception of the Green threshold itself. On the one hand, we can sense – with the help of this perception – the so often blurred difference between scientific or ideological discourse on the 'ecological' (without any possible effect on the concrete political syntax through which the 'problems' are elaborated); and, on the other, we can sense a political discourse which, speaking the language of political democracy, addresses a political nation with the 'ecological' in a way that affects the political syntax itself. (We can presume, hereby, that the very setting of the classical Western European political syntaxes, tied exclusively to the 'time to progress' and its left–right patterns, are exactly the ones *least* able to sense, not to mention to face, the 'real' exclusion marked by the ecological.) The same is valid for the perception of the space of Solidarnosc. Here, also, as we shall see in the following, the (albeit quite different) underlying East European political syntax had to be opened by 'free' identity-affecting political decisions, so as to make possible, *as well*, the breaking of the spell of a 'reason of state' appearing with the dignity of an ethic of responsibility.

In this way, Solidarnosc itself was thereby able to *reopen* the question at issue.[11] Where *this* question is reopened, so too is that of the 'good' ability to think together the 'I-self' (Winnicott speaks of the 'true self' as 'the *place from which* to live')[12] with that 'we-self' from which we always speak and act when we do it truly *politically*; that is, also in the significant, transmitted sense of this word.

Green Threshold/Solidarnosc Space

Let us now return again to our 'Green threshold'. If we consider it in the context described, it first appears to those steeped in the fundamental modes of modernity (that is, those who conceive the political as socially 'grounded' and as 'derived') as something like a *stumbling-block threshold*.[13] For, closely regarded, the even course of a political continuity-thinking oblivious to syntax (for example, those fixed on strategic-instrumental and/or moral solutions – a course which has become natural), here falls out of step.[14] At this point, it is secondary whether we locate such continuity-thinking within the hegemonic political sociology of the 'academic community', or amongst the 'self-evident truths' of hegemonic political discourse itself. It is therefore not really surprising that the treatment of the threshold in question, and of its effects beyond its original space – whether within progressive or neo-conservative political sociology, or in the discourse of more conservative or progressive bearers of political syntax from the classical parties – at first always amounts to a *levelling* of this threshold. Levelling, in this context, means to render the syntactic break *imperceptible*, by *reducing* the reality of that political renewal of 1979 to an addition of general 'ecological' and 'pacifist' *contents* and/or to equally general political *forms* of so-called grassroots democracy (or plebiscitary democracy). Through such levelling, these contents and forms appear to become 'syntactically detached' and 'freely available'. It is then possible – and it is this impression that must be solidified – that they will be 'taken over' by some historical or ideological 'party space' of the inherited political syntax (whether conservative, liberal, 'social-democratic' or 'left-libertarian'). In this sense, then, the *rendering of the threshold as unrecognizable* thus coincides with the *superfluous rendering* of the (party-) political space to which the 'break' refers.

Interestingly, it must be said that remarkably similar to the stumbling-block threshold has been the fate of the political space through which, and from which, the 'appeal' of Solidarnosc became possible. Here, too, we can observe how what constitutes, *in* this space, a certain 'stumbling-block threshold' for political thought and political experience is embedded in the hegemonic party-political and ideological discourses, as well as in the ways of treating it in social or political science. The specific historical-political productivity and efficacy of the 'Solidarnosc space' – what makes it questionable or memorable, or even worthy of being questioned and remembered (*frag-würdig* and *denk-würdig*) – thereby disappears from sight. It is equated, at the level of general ideological-political content and schemata of difference, with that which was, subsequently, objectified as the Central and East European dissident and civic movement – the last phase of the Soviet Empire and the attempts by a 'real-socialist reformism' not yet free of the totalitarian element to save itself. In this way, it has been incorporated as a particular moment into this (concealing) generality, since it is a question of levelling that passes into the category of empirical reality, and hence cannot be redressed through purely historical-historicist individualization.

And yet, the 'interruption' that the *space of Solidarnosc* made in a specific political syntax of modernity (without guarantees or justification around some historical level of development, as is also the case with the Green threshold) is still *less perceptible* than that of the Green threshold. For in its case, the levelling we have spoken about proceeds still more easily and as a matter of course, while in the political space of the Greens – despite the hegemonic levelling practices – there always was (and still remains) a public perception (even if unclearly defined) that the political space in question brought with it a certain disturbance to the traditional syntax and categories of West European politics. In the space of Solidarnosc (especially outside Poland) there is hardly any perception of this kind. What distinguishes the 'addressing space' of Solidarnosc from that of all other opposition or reform forces of that period in Central and Eastern Europe – a period expressing the almost impossible combination of a Polish-Catholic Christianity, articulated by 'anti-totalitarianism', and laden with an originally libertarian-secular and combative intellectual current of modern Polish history (not to mention the overstepping of this very combination itself) – is perceived, before anything else, as the product of a conjunctural *negative alliance*. It is this self-explaining image of a *tactical* alliance that covers up the decisive difference between Solidarnosc and the widely isolated dissident 'civic movements' on the one hand, and the compromised and one-track nature of reform communism, on the other. The effects of the newly created political space, in this case widely and really interrupting the underlying political syntax of Middle and East European spaces, cannot become visible in this way. This political syntax, in its (more than one hundred years old) modern form, is marked by a kind of dividing line of political identities that can never have the pure spatial clarity of a left/right dichotomization.

Adam Michnik, for whom the left/right divide makes no sense in the post-communist countries, describes in the chapters of his *La Deuxième Révolution* (1990) this same split in several ways: first, as one between populists and urbanites; second, as a split between Slavophiles and Westerners (in predominantly Slav-Orthodox countries); third, as one between ruralist and urbanites in Hungary (or as one between 'culture and civilization'); and finally, as a split marking the conflict of two cultures.[15] It is crucial to note here that Michnik – who has continued to speak and act from the 'political space' of Solidarnosc despite his clashes with its charismatic leader-figure – nowhere succumbs to the temptation to portray the destructive, highly imaginary 'overturning' of this antagonism (with which the history of the entire region was marked again and again) as a necessary consequence of the appearance of *one* of its antagonistic moments. Interestingly, this is the case despite his well-known proximity to the so-called urbanite, as well as to the so-called Westernizing and civilizing, side of the divide. Understanding this (re-)mark is crucial: for only then do we draw closer to the realization that the political space of Solidarnosc, far from *fitting into* this specific political syntax (much more perceptible now, after 1989, in the hard conflicts between Western-liberal and populist-type political forces and parties), 'interrupts' it in a manner that displays astonishing parallels with the kind of break (complete with its weaknesses and provisionalities) that the Green threshold achieved in the political-syntactic version of modernity dominating the German/West European space. Moreover, we also suddenly notice what the perception of this specific parallelism (and, in some respects, 'sameness' though not 'equality') has put into question and continues to make difficult. It is not only that the 'interruption' of the Solidarnosc-space can hardly take shape if we cannot connect it to the historical specificity of that 'totalitarianism' to which it was an answer (and not a reaction).[16] But it can only become more clearly visible if we perceive the historical qualities of the basic political conflict-pattern that *operates* in the 'historical region' of Solidarnosc.

And yet, is it not precisely this latter perception that is obscured both by 'our' (that is, Western European) political syntax, as well as by the ways its hegemonic pattern of political conflict 'entered' social theory, where it acquired an even 'clearer' (because socially and rationally founded) natu- ralness. For, even where the fact of another kind of polarity is formally recognized, that polarity is read in terms of a clear-cut register of political opposition 'produced' in the West European political-historical space. The 'other' polarity, then, is supposedly one that has, despite its diversity, the same nature (though more imaginary-abstract than symbolic) as that which came to prevail out of the West European political space. The character of this polarity tends to be expressed publicly/politically in the Western European 'natu- ralized' definition of a left/right divide of a (closed) political space. (Even more obvious than the progressive/conservative divide connected to it.) It is this distinctive, desymbolized detachment (*Abgelöstheit/Absolutheit*) of its imagin- ary surface – detached from any concrete name or significance which marked in pre-modern times the rallying points of opposite political camps – that has made possible the easy comprehensibility and ubiquitousness of this register in the modern world. In principle, then, the objective topological site of each and every relevant political-ideological position can be inscribed and represented within it. Starting from what appears to be a merely political- parliamentary original semantics (in the context of the French Revolution), it has subsequently been able to gain access, almost universalistically, to the political syntax of almost all political-historical spaces (albeit as an overlapping of other kinds of opposition patterns). Furthermore, it is present in ideological classifications of the most diverse institutions and in their internal differenti- ations – in the churches as well as educational establishments, in the media and even the administration of justice. The entering of this abstract polarity in political sociology produced the generalized concept of 'cleavage' used to mark the (purely internal) division of *any* socio-political unit, according to pre-political social or cultural differences/oppositions *expressing* themselves ideologically or politically. Now, the kind of conflict-pattern interrupted in a peculiar way by Solidarnosc is not only different from the left/right- dominated syntax of Western Europe; it is of a different nature.

Rethinking Opposition

Let us now take a further step in thought and observation. If we come to say now, with a certain emphasis, that when political sociology, in a broad sense, *thinks* that it is working with a concept ('cleavage') universally applicable to *all* divisions of the social, in *reality* it is referring to a special nature of polarity; that is, to the one 'evident' only in strictly immanent positively closed social space. So this must appear, in the first instance, to most of present-day political thought as an irrelevant assertion with a displaced emphasis. For why should we *not* refer – living as we do in societies where the transcendence-relatedness of pre-modern societies has definitely disappeared – to society as a positive immanent unit?

And yet, the point here in question could begin to yield a different set of interests, if we could show – with the help of political sociology – how the decisive dimension of that difference between West and East European political syntaxes found in the first instance, in an empirical, descriptive way, could be discerned. Let us begin again with the assertion: the political divisions marked by our West European, left–right and progress-fixed political syntax (which, obviously, do not coincide with the syntax working in the political space of the US) have, as their condition of possibility, a self-referential social inner space, in which all constitutive references to an 'outside' (or, to put this in a different register, to the Other) are erased. It is this erasure that converts the present-fixed working of this political syntax to something – at the one and same time – autonomous and representable in space. On the contrary, all opposed moments described by Michnik display dividing lines which *cannot exist as such*; the East European *political* space could not be imagined (as can the West European) as existing on its own. This means: the dividing 'lines' opposing these moments are clearly not 'cleavages' of an internal space. All of them have spatially non-representable constitutive references to an Outside, to what can be viewed, at first glance, as 'full' Western Modernity.

Now, at first sight, the external dimension of these Central and East European contrasts (which is implicit in the so-called 'Slavophile-Orthodox' versus the 'Westernizing', as well as in other variants) involves only *positive differences*: that is, in their distinctive positivity and definable oppositions to the 'Western' in the various dimensions of the latter (that is, market-connectedness, universalist affirmation, and so on). However, if one thinks through the problem, one notices that through this external reference 'both sides' also have to deal with a different problem. We notice this when we realize how, through the danger of full identifications of both sides in this conflict-pattern with exclusive, but strictly secularized figures of the 'true West', the 'other side' becomes the impossible fullness of a liberal-progressive or of a national-popular identity of the political nation. (And, in so becoming, also becomes an element whose elimination is imperative for a we-identity.) This is precisely the kind of imaginary polarization that Ernesto Laclau and Chantal Mouffe refer to as antagonism which, in the end, makes 'impossible' the objectively, and purely intentional, social. It impinges, at the same time, on what we can call here the 'answering-possibility' of the transferential threshold.[17] It is crucial here to add that, contrary to (often false) appearances, this kind of 'opposition' cannot be grasped as a *formalized* relation (that is, as one freed of the political signifiers and their syntax), in this case, between 'urban-liberal' *openness* and 'popular-national' *closure*. To think otherwise, however, is not just a matter of distorted appearance: it arises from the fact that the political syntax of Central and Eastern Europe is also *overlaid* by the West European inner-space contrast often declined in terms of 'left' and 'right'.[18]

Deceptive too, then, is the common-sense notion that it is possible, fundamentally, to attach a specific external reference (comparable to the one we have located in the distinctiveness of the Central and East European political syntax) to the left/right opposition within society (which mainly 'does' as though there were no state) and to the poles of that opposition. This applies to the 'war and peace' question: for the social-political left may, for example, be just as prone to violence at a world level in the struggle against despotism as it is radical-pacifist within the hegemony of the liberal, evacuating denial of antagonism. (And the reactive right also has its free-floating forms.) What does this mean for a sharper awareness of the Central and East European schema of opposition? Only if 'we' (that is, we 'in' spontaneous Western political thought, with its conceptualization of the political) are able to resist our inclination, by now become natural, to read the Central and East European schema of opposition of the respective political nations, with their more open antagonism potential and with their conflict lines charged with multi-dimensional temporality, in terms purely of schema of intra-*societal* (and/or 'ideological') patterns of difference – only then will the meaning of the external reference (or dual character) of this 'other' opposition become accessible for our whole approach to the question, touching also on the question of the nature of political things. This dual character applies in *all* variants of this other opposition: in some of them (for example, the variant of 'Slavophile-Orthodox' versus 'Westernizing'), it is directly legible from 'outside', without closer knowledge of the history; in others, it is apparent 'only' for the Central and East European political-historical consciousness (and for 'Westerners' with a good knowledge of history – for example, with regard to the different versions of the 'populist versus urban' opposition, and the presence of the dual character within it).

Historical Excursus

Let us now consider these remarks in the form of an excursus. The Hungarian historical example shows that the contrast in question is completely false if 'Western' (or 'civilizing') is given a one-dimensional and univocal significance. For example, in the *népies* ('folkish') tradition in Hungary – which, unlike the *narodnik* tradition in Russia, was associated not only with 'ideological' but also with political sovereignty-signifiers of a republican type – there is an effective nexus whose historic bearers of meaning and conflict have had affinities with Hungarian Calvinism, along with its remote milieu of the Netherlands (and also with the Calvinist political-religious world in Walzer's

'oppositional' sense). This nexus must be understood *as against* the hegemonic articulation of sovereignty in the Enlightenment-Absolutist, rationalist-
centralist 'West'. The extraordinary research of J. G. A. Pocock helps us to
understand more clearly than before two things: the transferential capacity of
political language and how far the hegemonic sedimenting of our political-
ethical thought (right up to the way in which we deploy the particularist/
universalist opposition) bears the stamp of the (almost) total victory of what
Pocock calls the Whig-Liberal 'court space' of modernity.[19] This nexus might
then be located, within an exaggerated Pocockian terminology of counterposition, in the 'country-space' as against that of the 'court'. Indeed, Pocock
(and the historians close to him) researches into the 'latency dimension' of
historical-political effects and lifts those effects out of the mechanistic-
naturalistic imagery of spheres of action (within the pure co-presence of
motives and objective structures). One could argue, following Pocock, that
only in this way could (and can) the specific 'fusion' which produces the
hegemonic political background syntax take place – a fusion whereby the split
Christian-Western signifier of sovereignty becomes unified by virtue of the
fact that, as 'court space' in oligarchic-liberal hands, it is the universalist-
centralist *guarantor* of modernity's promise of security, freedom and welfare.
This fusion, effected in the power dimension of the signifier, combines with
the spaces of difference and law of civil society to make possible the concrete
realization of what Walter Benjamin called 'capitalism as religion'.[20]

On the other hand, even the 'capitalism-opening' Bank of England – which
provides a sovereign guarantee to the specific time-referent of the economy of
modernity – can be understood as an 'economic fact' only in retrospect.
Concretely it arises on the welded ground of sovereignty resulting from the
(ultimately contingent) political victory of the court, and not as some necessary
outcome of purely positive economic and social developments untouched by
the constitutive outside. Within the 'sphere of the West', only the historical
space opened up by decisions taken in the struggles following the North
American Revolution have conserved and deployed a political syntax which
has been formed by a 'different character of opposition' and a different
'victory'. The Jeffersonian victory in the post-revolutionary arrangement of
1800 gave to a country-space occupied by republicans an effectiveness which
shaped the relationship in the United States between liberal society and state,
and republican 'community'. The hegemony weakened by this arrangement –
the one created by Hamiltonian federalists and by later party Republicans –
wagered on an American reproduction of the English social paradigm of state
and economy, defined by the court-space, which already had the compelling
appearance of political rationality and modernity. The unique US victory of
the country-pole (which, as political signifier, is definable with a distinctive
temporality, not just 'ideologically') is what, until today, has made possible the
stubborn resistance, so irritating for West Europeans, of an American political

schema of opposition to a more 'rational' political syntax, linked clearly to the progressive-conservative and the left/right division. (As Pocock and others have shown, in England itself after the post-revolutionary arrangements of the early eighteenth century, the country-pole could only be a Tory-occupied, conservative/anti-oligarchic oppositional space: the same may apply to most of Western Europe.)

There are few better examples of hegemonic absorption and inscription than the (for us) evident rationality of the West European schema of political opposition, which are further reinforced, of course, by the fact that the French-Jacobin Revolution, with consequences for the West European socialist imaginary, has occupied the court-space, just as though it were a matter of course. Thus, it was always necessary in Europe to seek (rather peculiar) 'negative reasons' to explain why what happened politically in the United States would *not* count as 'modern normality', why the Left/Right opposition would *not* (or, more precisely, would not on the whole) determine the political division of space, not to mention also why 'there', in the US, the working class (conceived, on political grounds, as having a pure social existence) has found no party 'expression'.

This excursus is not meant to suggest an equivalence between the 'awkward' US political syntax and the Central and East European political syntax pervaded by the different schemata of opposition. Instead it should clarify some of our initial questions concerning actual turning points of the Green threshold and the space of Solidarnosc (albeit within their respective political syntaxes). It also allows us to formulate the following questions. First, once Pocock and others have made visible the latent 'schism' in the (Anglo Saxon-impelled) liberal-progressive tradition, how far does something like an initial 'threshold zone' of political modernity come to light? Second, in surfacing 'as such', why is it that it can be transgressed or 'crossed' but not transformed *into something that has definitively been transgressed*? Third, might it be the case that not only the Federal German 'Green threshold' and the 'space of Solidarnosc', but the very perceptibility of this initial threshold of political modernity, be bound up with a reintensification of its latent schism – and, as a consequence, with a weakening of the 'naturalness' of that (mainly) West European political syntax of progress which 'does as if' purely internal, transferential thresholds-free, antagonism-free, differences were alone at work *within* it. Fourth and last, is there not a great deal to suggest that the American process that emerged as a certain 'horizon of progress' took shape, beginning in the so-called Progressive Era of the early twentieth century and continuing through the 'New Deal' and the 'Great Society' *might now be coming to an end*? That is, that the former *rendering imperceptible* of the decisive (not fully secularized) dividing line of US political syntax is now losing its hegemonic foundedness? If so, then the communitarian critique of liberalism, which some have conceived as an ultimately free-wheeling and self-repeating production,[21] would, in the end, be something *more* than mere repetition. (And that is quite apart from the fact that, as Laclau shows in *New Reflections on the Revolution of Our Times*, repetition without displacement does not exist politically, nor for that matter in any other way.)

In attempting to respond to these questions, I should like to address my remarks to a scarcely considered, and rather remote, milieu: one that also casts some light on the fact that all through the 1980s students in US universities showed a livelier and more widespread interest in the West German Greens than did their counterparts in any other country of the 'West' – a highly curious fact, which, in a few quarters, still remains mysterious and almost offensive for some 'progressive' German political scientists. In the opening speech of Clinton's electoral campaign for the US presidency, reference was repeatedly made to the third of the three terms: 'Opportunity – Responsibility – Community', though the speaker explicitly distanced himself from 'liberals', from 'conservatives' *and* from long-term state regulation of what might fall into the sphere of the 'community'. In this way, a space of political address was marked out again and redefined. If we further consider that a prominent figure committed to an assuredly not 'naturalizable' ecology was chosen as candidate for the vice-presidency, it is clear that these characteristics mark also a space *closer* than any other significant political space in the 'West' to the space (or 'zone') of the Green threshold. The old-new name of what is referred to as the 'Clinton space' is certainly not without interest: it is not called 'New Deal' but 'New Covenant' – which highlights the Protestant/Old Testament parallel to the Catholic element in the space of Solidarnosc, and hence also the developing significance of the intimate connection between the strict, rationalistically forced, immanent closure of society and its 'capitalist religion' of self-evident, infinite progress. (This 'proximity' in question is one that is simultaneously separated by a hard-to-define and even more difficult to implement 'limit to political promises'. But it also sheds light on something that the most conscious 'Green sounding' remarks accomplish least of all.)

But within the hegemonic, 'univocalized' West European liberal relation between 'that which is social' and 'that which is the state', the original, 'political' self-definition of the Greens in 1979 (in terms of 'grassroots democracy') was clearly a stopgap that was 'somehow' supposed to express a distance from the hegemonic political statism. Nevertheless, from the beginning, but rather subliminally, the discourse of the Greens was able to speak, breaking through the conservative-progressive order of differences to the whole of the nation, touching not only on central themes, but also on the same political-historical conscience. In the later ideologically univocalized and polarizing attempt to clarify matters on the wrong side, there was on one hand (the 'fundamentalists') a classical left-subaltern and autonomous opposition to the state, with an *implicit* acceptance of the hegemonic liberal definition of the sphere of the state; and on the other (the merely pragmatic

Realos) a full liberal-rationalist acceptance of a Pocockian 'court state', with the implicit acceptance of a purely immanent sphere of society founded upon interests and presence in which ecology could never be more than the 'environmental question'. These political self-definitions of the Greens, taunted by ideological reoccupations, might have a thing or two to learn from the *political* controversy between liberals and communitarians in the United States (though not from the academic version with its by now tiresome moral 'founding discourse'). But this we can do only if we do not try to solve too rapidly what we may call the 'American paradox of the politics of modernity'. Or, to put it slightly differently, only if we are able to perceive this paradox at all, and in all its distinctiveness outside of (or completely different from) our own usual linear-historical and socio-politically univocal categories – so that the 'play of difference' can be heard within it – can we learn 'a thing or two'.[22]

The 'American Paradox' of the Politics of Modernity

We shall here leave to one side the question of how far this paradox 'speaks' to us, only if we are capable of *using* the (further expanded) operating space which the 'political signifier' of the Green threshold (or of the space of Solidarnosc) has opened up in the European political syntaxes.[23] Briefly stated, this paradox consists in the fact that the operating space of US politics has long since been the *most limited* and yet also the *most open* of all those discernible within the 'political nations' of the West. It has become the *narrowest operating* space because nowhere else in the recent Western world have there been such tight limits to the political decisions and alternative horizons directly relating to hegemony. And nowhere else, for a long time, did the decisions of political parties appear so *secondary* beside the imperatives of the religion of progress, the power of technology to deliver, and the supremacy of money in the sphere of politics.[24] As stated before, however, it is also *the most enigmatically open* operating space. Indeed, the American setting of political conflict, for all the intellectual-rationalist and Europeanist striving, could not be transformed into a 'truer' conflict pattern able to mirror social or 'class' realities. By making political decisions, it remained able – often only in catastrophically weakened forms – to transmit the concrete, political signifiers and their generative medium that had taken shape through the Jeffersonian historic arrangement. Through this setting, then, a 'time-crossing' tension remained *politically* alive, transmitted from the conflictive beginnings of modern political rationality (in shifting and paradoxical ways, to be sure) connected with the exclusions, the specific closedness and power-centredness of its order demanded and enforced. It was this tension which could enter the American political language; and the multi-vocal temporality of its We The People, meanwhile, became imperceptible in the political conflict-language of

Western-Europe – which acquired their democratic spaces, also after 1789, on the levelled-in terrain of court-hegemony and its closed, indebted temporality.

In this way, what becomes perfectly obvious is that the political language that carries through its opposition patterns and through its half-hidden reference to an Outside, the aforesaid tension, has nothing to do with something imagined, as a classical-republican ideology passed on psychologically. Today we can also see that the tensions so politically transmitted are connected (in a conflict-ridden way) to modern-hegemonic demands that have turned out to be potentially totalitarian or destructive for any democratic-political community. This means, then, also that the specific conflicting spaces between the two political formations of the US, conserving their own potentials for question-thematization and for making more 'hearable' the excluded, may once more become larger, after long decades of narrowing. It can be said that in our contemporary times, the real space of tension between the two American parties is larger than that between the classical West European parties in contest.

Now, if we consider this 'difference-retaining' and exclusion-sensing tension in American political language, we first think of it as operating like the Western European political syntax, related only to the internal space of a political arena. And yet, once we take a step back and mark out and listen to the differences at work, we find that this transmitted tension points very well to a kind of constitutive outside – or carries with it something that is fundamentally addressing the European-Western forms of modernity. Thus one could also say that the tension of the paradox in the political language of the US, in its latent or even suddenly emergent forms, referred to and still refers (in the well-known sense of *correction* and *new beginning*, always with their religious, ethical or moral uses) to that which is underneath in the 'old-world' order, with its entanglement of power and of war, and its ignorance of the temporally interwoven symbolic natural references. It is in this context, then, that this theoretical and historical *reconnoitre* circles around the question of how far the break and the emergence of what has been called the Green threshold and the space of Solidarnosc make politically possible something like a 'European translation' of the syntactically preserved American 'communitarian' concept. Here, ostensibly, the loosening of the hegemonic and objectifying fixation of the political takes place only in the repeated passage of a 'virtuous circle'.

This means, first, that our setting must be 'good enough' for our question (concerning the nature of political things) to be reopened within it – for only then will the interruptive character of the Green threshold and the space of Solidarnosc become *visible*. At the same time, however, it is these interruptions – as conscious/unconscious addressing-acts with characteristic responsibility and temporality references that cannot be understood in terms of either 'strategic action' or 'communicative' or 'value-escorted' action. Hence, they *take away* from modern-European (political) syntaxes that self-evidence through which they (largely) present themselves as 'natural political languages' of 'the' social interests and 'the' cultural-normative differences. They are thus also a *condition* for (epochal) revival of the question of the nature of political things. This also means, then, that it is in these 'passages' where we notice the forcedly subaltern and reactive character of the (mainly ideological) places from where – inside of the non-interrupted-hegemony of modern political temporality – the attempts were made to reintroduce critically the problematic of 'nature' and of 'reason of state' into the political.[25] Here it is not only important to perceive the de facto 'marginal' political character of conservative protection of the environment on the one side, and of left-emancipatory anarchism with its libertarian variants on the other side. More crucial is the fact that 'inside' these critical spaces the hegemonic preliminary decision on what 'nature' and 'state' *are* (on what their temporality *is*) is fully accepted. The proof of this acceptance is that what emerges in these 'critical' positions is an antagonism 'contrary' to what appears hegemonically as 'nature' (that is, the measurable, quantitative nature of natural science) and as 'state' (that is, the original dimension of contractual and institutional constraint, set up in a 'natural', need-satisfying sociability). It is in this way that we see emerging two critical positions, pretending to occupy – ideologically – the 'green' and 'libertarian' area. On the one side, a 'critical' ideological discourse of 'deep ecology', with an 'ecological' fixed to a kind of holistic, vitalistic nature, involving 'human nature' in the same literal and objective constraints as the nature of natural science. And, on the other, the simple and direct state- and constraint-negations of radical 'liberation' and emancipation, fixed in the discourses of direct and grassroots democracy. (Working with the same kind of sociability of the social, and where, exactly as in the 'classical modern' co-position of state and society, there is no political language, and so, also, no possible reference to what *law* can mean in 'polis', in 'res-puplica' or in 'covenant'.)

But the hegemonic effect of modern-European (political) syntax can finally also be seen in another remarkable fact: namely, that the two above-mentioned ideological spaces for these (subaltern) attempts to reintroduce critically 'nature' and 'state' in ideological-political discourse are located – as fragments of a successful, radical dissociation – at the two opposite 'ends' of the left/right continuum inscribed in the hegemonic syntax. Within a fully operational 'dissociation' of this kind, it would be absurd to imagine that the two spaces (which are mostly fixed to 'positions') could have anything at all to do with each other. The 'noticing' of this hegemonic-dissociating effect becomes theoretically significant if it is a question of perceiving what is specific in the difficult breaks and *identity-affecting* decisions through which, around 1980, the addressing-space of the West German Greens made its first appearance. (We say 'first', because there is much to suggest that today, in the early 1990s, a comparable threshold, also affecting the political syntax, is appearing on the horizon in France.) But the emergence will be concealed if, as in all variants of strictly rationalizing-immanentist political sociologies, the so-called 'critical' impulses and 'value-positions' of Green politics are identified *independently* of their political-syntactic interruptive and addressing effects.[26]

What is important here is the connection between, on the one hand, the two already mentioned ideological intents to (re)introduce 'ecological critique' and contestation-linked state-critique in politics (both in a 'local' and 'internationalist' vein, over-springing the political nation and its temporality) and, on the other hand, the Janus-faced *double reality* of political organizations in the 'Green-Alternative-Area' – something we find practically everywhere in contemporary politics beginning from the early 1980s. For where the emergence of these forms have not simultaneously been connected with an interruption in the 'naturalness' of the classical-modern West European political paradigm, they appear to encompass in *a dual form*, first, as 'ecologically centred' conservationist 'Greens'; and, then, as 'left-alternative' (or 'left-libertarian') 'Greens'. The hegemonically pre-given nature of political things remains so *untouched* by the modes of address of these two forms, however ideologically 'radical' discourses and their actions may be. These 'double-headed' forces appearing as Greens do not emerge as marginal only in political terms; they have also geared themselves to the margins of the respective ideological-political 'camps' as subaltern. Thus they inevitably remain *dependent* in their very existence upon conjunctural situations. As 'for instance' spectacular worsenings and neglectings of environmental conditions and issues, overwhelming other political themes or salient technocratic or state-bureaucratic levelling and abuses. The history of the Greens of the German Federal Republic (now transformed into 'BÜNDNIS 90 – DIE GRÜNEN' after the merger in the spring of 1993 with Bündnis 90 [alliance '90] of the ex-GDR, carrying therein the spaces and discourses which made possible the Democratic Revolution of 1989) shows also, to be sure, that any political space emerging initially as a rupture of the dominance of the two ideological poles governing elsewhere the fates of organizations and parties of the 'green area' is not (and cannot) be free of ideological or moralistic reoccupations; that is to say, the ones parting from the two aforesaid poles, or from regionally centred green politics, abandoning the place from where the political nation could be addressed. These reoccupations continue to receive their force from the hegemonic 'nature' of political things. In such cases what is lost is the possibility, within the perspective of the Green threshold, of also making hearable (that is, together with the 'pragmatic' moments of Green discourse) that moment which Laclau's theory of the political expects from us (with a still inadequately grasped radicalness): that is, the non-closeability not just of the last 'future horizon' of human development (which, after the historic events of the last few years, can be abandoned without any political cost and as part of the prevailing trend), but above all of the naturalist-rationalist 'grounding horizon' of the history of our sociality made free of displacement and events, whose operational space is thus the (sovereign) space of promise and its 'problem solution'. Indeed, it becomes a space where, finally, it appears possible to plan even the 'salvation of the planet'. Because such a moment – a moment touching the nature of political things – should so acquire, in spite of it all, a moment of playing, it was not the worst of interpellations when, surprisingly, a Green poster addressed the people, in 1990, by saying: 'If you vote for us, you will become rich, happy and famous. You have our word. The Greens.' (In fact, in recent Federal German history this 'you have our word' has received the same significance as has Bush's 'read my lips' in the United States.) It is curious to note the precise effect signatures have on messages, particularly in this example. In the German political space at least, it is only *this* signature which makes the political message *not* preposterous and *not* aggressive or cynical. What constitutes the imposing force of the 'last reason' of modern/rational political action, the fully secularized space of the absolutist court's *raison d'état*, has by no means disappeared as a result of the emptying of its 'centre'. It has become a surrounded power-place. The closed circle of those who surround it (however wide or narrow it may be) may thus imagine that it, as a body representing The People, is sovereign, in the absolutist sense: that it can decide according to its present Will. The presence-fixed closedness of this 'amongst-ourselves' (of this *entre nous* as the French say)[27] is what we may call the fatal misunderstanding of the 'democratic revolution', running through the new states of the world as 'democracy'. The centrality of the 'court', the *raison d'état* dimension of that space, has by no means disappeared as a result of its 'emptying', for it is also a *reordered* space. The closed circle of its 're-orderers' may thus imagine that, as a sovereign circle, it is 'by itself'.[28]

A Provisional Conclusion

This text began as an attempt to trace the emergence of the 'interrupting' space of the Green threshold, and also (but to a lesser extent) that of Solidarnosc. Later, as it was being 'updated', several forebodings, present at the time when I was actually taking part in creating an 'intervening' place (and discourse) of *Grüner Aufbruch* within the Federal German Green Party (1987–90), were confirmed by the subsequent events. This time period – probably one of the more decisive moments in the short history of *Die Grünen Aufbruch* – came into existence as a bearer of an identity-related discourse: for it tried to identify and to contest the double-sided 'ideological reoccupation' of the Green space by a 'fundamentalist' (that is, 'red–green' and 'deep green') party executive. It was, in other words, one that came to represent a politically more sensitive but, hence also, a more reactive part of the party, fighting the fundamentalists from a purely pragmatic political place that blurred completely the contours of the Green threshold itself. (Indeed, this conflict was about to split *Die Grünen* – and *Aufbruch* was one of the main moments that blocked this split. It was after this blocking that the 'fundamentalist' party executive could be deposed in December of 1988.) My reading of the situation included the perception that, within the space for action, key moves were persistently eluding us at a historical-political turning-point (or 'threshold context') at a time when we had to speak and decide politically – eluding us because, among other reasons, of the effects of what we have here called the 'hegemonic political syntax'. In spite of this (or perhaps, because of it) the tracing of this project thus changed into – a never quite successful – one of *trying to catch up with* a context that was *already* action-effective.

Only after this project was fully under way did I realize the full significance of the space of Solidarnosc and the space of 'communitarian' discourse as linked with – and separated from, in strange ways – the Green threshold. As was the case with the emergence of the Green threshold in 1979 – ultimately through a (by no means 'compelling' and thus power-related) majority decision at a founding congress, and *against* the discourse prevailing in all intellectual and party milieus of the left at that time – so too were *identity-related* questions concerning processes of perception, thought and decision at the forefront in the emergence of Solidarnosc. In fact, at the moment of the decision which founded the Green threshold, there were two main forces trying to *maintain* a continuity of existing ideological/political identities: one trying to give to the *Grünen* the character of a more or less loose alliance of different social and political forces (so as to allow the emergence of, and to retain the sense of, strict and radical left-wing identities), and one proclaiming that the *Grünen* must bear the identity already pre-existing (that is, closed and ideologically settled) in the different deep-green currents. Both were *counterposed* to a break in identity which raised the stakes on creating and forming together a political place from which the great majorities of the German society could be addressed and confronted with the 'ecological cause'.[29] By focusing in this way on the process of identity formation, something often lacking in even the best 'sociological' analyses of Solidarnosc is able to become more visible: namely, the extent to which its very constitution involved painful, identity-affecting perceptions and decisions. Moreover, this focus allowed us to achieve 'more' than what an instrumental accounting or classical progressive alliance of Catholic and secular-enlightened intellectual currents would have done. This 'more' depended upon the break-up of the historical and political space fixated on immanence and therefore *raison d'état*.

In this respect, too, what became obvious from the beginning was the importance of a political theory that could most effectively articulate the question of antagonism/confrontation and bring with it concepts of political identity (from the seemingly remote location of post-structuralism and Lacan, and the late Wittgenstein and Heidegger's move beyond phenomenology) into the neighbourhood of politics and political purpose itself. In attempting here to keep abreast of today's, actually effective, context of political action – a project which has referred us back to similar theoretical traditions and breakthroughs by a variety of theorists (perhaps with the decisive exception of Winnicott's work and its strange connection with the 'late' Heidegger) – one can say that even when their own formulations have been debatable, the gateways opened by Laclau and Mouffe have been crucial for this task.

Two Kinds of Threshold: An Opening and Closing Note

It can be said, then, that the way in which Walter Benjamin marked here the metaphor of 'threshold' helps us to avoid the kind of fixity we find used almost everywhere in socio-political and socio-historical literature – a fixity that only employs the metaphor in its univocal sense. This imposes itself, as Sloterdijk has pointed out often enough,[30] automatically and for as long as these scientific discourses fully accept a 'place' located purely 'inside' a linear and processional history wherein the closing dimension of modernity condemns itself as the last era, only capable of conceiving an infinite deferment of an end, but never a *novum*. This univocal sense of the threshold metaphor is that of a disempowering critical border, separating two historical spaces of the same continuum (or levels) of an evolution (or 'phase-logic'). *This* threshold is then only understood as a threshold of transition (*transitio*) for a 'moving' but self-identical social unit for 'collective subjects' progressing in the closed time-tunnel of all historicist settings. This threshold is also a critical one: not to cross it, that is, to lack the capacity or will to cross it, implies also that it is a menace. In fact, in this sense of the metaphor, we 'meet' the threshold as a challenge to our collective self-preservation, as our 'old' collective coherence has weakened; as our 'system of differences' cannot cope any more with new dislocations. In this way it implies, in other words, a *demand*, an *Anspruch*.

Having said this, it is of secondary importance, therefore, if we represent our so-called objectivated collective subjects as the processual or projectual subject of modernity on the way to his or her rational self-foundation; that is, as the anthropological subject of a 'human species' or as a 'cultural' unit or nation. They all have exactly the same univocal temporality, the same setting inside a literal processual historicism, guaranteeing the hegemony of the fully secularized, death-estranged and language-expunged dimensions of modern collective identities. (That is, expunging with the reduction of language to 'communication' or to a 'cultural code' its uncanny element, the 'self-destructive, eschatological element within the language itself', to use the exact poetical formulation of Joseph Brodsky.)[31]

Alain Touraine formulates *this* socio-historical sense of the threshold metaphor in an exemplary way. 'We are already half-way out of the industrial society, and only on the *threshold* towards a post-industrial society, dominated by the cultural industries.'[32] In Touraine's notable effort to reconstruct an actor-oriented sociology, the threshold metaphor comes to mean two things: (i) threshold as a disempowering, dangerous border of an 'already-not' and a 'not-yet', where there can be no strong, socially grounded collective actor; and (ii) threshold as a crossing, whence we arrive at the new (but of course repetitive) terrain of modernity. This will allow a new grounding, a new rationality of socio-political cleavages, and also of action, exactly in the same way as the 'industrial society' and its central 'industrial conflict' provided the grounded social actions called 'social movements'. The crossing of this threshold will produce, then – and at one blow – the possibility of progressive socio-political action, not to mention sociology itself. The forced literality of the transitional threshold and its fixed time-relatedness is exclusive towards all those resettings of the political and of the theory of its praxis after World War II, in which a specific holding and opening dimension of Western political tradition is working in the medium of its republican and Christian-liberal languages. This dimension cannot be separated from what Hannah Arendt called the 'wonder' of an action, the wonder of a *prattein* that 'begins'. Neither can it be separated, as shown by Bruce Ackermann, from that pluri-dimensional American 'We The People', obscured and sociologized after the Progressive Era for almost a century.

But, it is also no less the case, as we have seen, that with historical sociology, classically linked with the purely transitional threshold, we can observe another characteristic of that particular kind of 'the political' which is linked to the temporality of the same: there is an insistence on taking as a given its fixed reactive essence. Even in such lucid work as that of Zygmunt Baumann (*Legislators and Interpreters*), his 'threshold of the Modern Era' still has to appear with this kind of reactive fixity. The intentions and practices which constitute the same can be thought purely and exclusively as present-fixed *reactions*, not as possible *answers*, applying pluri-dimensional language to the structural dislocations threatening the 'efficiency of social reproduction' in the times preceding the modern era. Let us, rather, concentrate on the other sense of the threshold metaphor; that is, the one less linked with demand, will and advance. It is, as Benjamin emphasizes, a threshold of *transmissio* and transference. For us, this sense of the metaphor points to that potential space *which is precisely political*, and which, even when turned into absence in the temporality of an unfolding history, is not turned into a void or vacuous non-being.

If we are able to speak today, in the context of action and of the political, about a threshold in this transference-sense (which of course can never be separated completely from its other sense), it is undoubtedly due to the increased theoretical audibility of the specific effects of the working of transference and temporal retroactivity (*Nachträglichkeit*) in the setting of *Freudian* psychoanalysis. This audio-ability is, for its own part, due to the fact that the scientistic misunderstandings, enclosing this setting in the pure inside of psychology, are, as a result of multiple events, much less hegemonic than some decades before. One of these events was the second great interrupting-setting of our century (with respect to temporality and language, to death-relatedness, to the addressing and addressee identities of all that is said or implied with the 'I' and the 'we'): the (late) Heideggerian setting of thought and its loosening, de-grounding workings (which, obviously have nothing to do with grounding nor of one-gendered ontology). The space of the *Freudian* setting can appear as such – along with the essential help of the admirable sensitivity of Winnicottian thought and practice – that is, as it appeared from the beginning: as the event of a unique potential space of co-acting, the holding and the transference of which can loosen the closed – and so, forward fleeing – temporality of modern identities, inventing and discovering a space of free play, a *Spielraum*, one that is found neither by will-efforts nor by self-reflection. Is it not possible, then, in reaffirming this, to also perceive how the thought of Hannah Arendt points exactly to this space, when she links the potentiality of Beginning with the interruption of Forgiving? And is it not also possible now to hear how the early Heideggerian thought knocks at the same door, translating – audaciously, as Gadamer reports – the Aristotelian *phronesis* as *Gewissen* (the voice of conscience); that is, with a term that points here to something doubly paradoxical – to a *common and contested* voice of the *political* conscience?

Notes

1. Walter Benjamin, Collected Works, V, p. 617.
2. We prefer the term *political syntax* as opposed to that of *political grammar*, as used by H. Laski, E. Laclau and C. Geertz. Its association with sentence and *praedicatio* makes both more perceptible and more time-bound the retroactive effect of its type of order upon the identity of the articulating (and thus also that of the politically self-articulating) 'We'. Together with Derrida, we are thinking here of the 'syntactic/semantic' difference as *opposed to* the 'form/content' difference. It also highlights a parallel play with its Greek translation, where syntax means also 'order of argument', and indeed 'order of battle'.
3. Clifford Geertz, 'Works and Lives', *The Anthropologist as Author* (Stanford: Stanford University Press, 1988) p. 138.
4. Does it help to remember that Jacques Lacan, in the *Actes de Bonnevales*, said that 'the word's behaviour appears less as communication than as the founding of the subject in an essential statement'? And that: 'The behaviour of the word, in so far as the subject wants to ground himself on it, is of such a kind that if the transmitter is to communicate his message, he must have

received it from the receiver, and he completes this by sending out his message in the inverted form'?

5. This position strikes us as something whose *ultimate basis* generally lies in a 'one-way' political will (of an individual or a group). There is no room for the two-way, rhetorical element of addressing-site (*Ansprechplatz*) within a historical-political space – a site, the hearing dimension of which is also directed towards a possible common (but not unanimous) decision taking form in a political controversy.

To put this point differently, it is to say, then, that there is a subterranean nexus linking (i) Kant's absolute, univocal difference of the ethical realm, radically separate from the political, and opposed to the realm of the naturally determined – a difference which he desperately saves by means of the moral 'pure *will*' (by definition divorced from experience) – to the hegemony of a particular, historically and politically distinct West European (and, as we shall see, not simply 'Western') mould; (ii) a kind of sovereignty, only approximately definable as 'centralist', which accelerates development and has become effective on a planetary scale; and (iii) denial of the listening (and thus also the historical and power-related) dimension of any 'we-site' involving any 'space of address' – a site, therefore, that cannot be defined purely as strategic-rational because it is *not* synonymous with a collective ego whose identity can be established in advance and independently of language.

The same nexus is at work in the moral-political version of the grounding of the political. It appears as an alternative to the scientific, objectivist 'will to ground', or as a complement to it. It is, like the objectivist grounding which is historically oriented on 'real' interests, woven into the background syntax of political modernity. In certain situations, this Kantian type of normative univocal replacement of the political (also as univocal replacement of the emancipatory in that which can be 'scientifically demonstrated' to be 'objectively progressive') assumes a certain importance. Where this happens – for example, in the 'left complement' of the hegemonic rationality of progress – the 'hearing' dimension of the 'addressing place' from where we speak in our political language of democracy becomes even less perceptible than in the open, semi-pragmatist modes of perception of the liberal rationality of interests: less perceptible, that is, to the extent that the 'deafening' exclusiveness and duality – 'norm-oriented politics' versus 'populist, power-oriented politics' – retains a more determining weight, a greater exclusiveness. Through late-Heideggerian thought, then, the strange but close affinity of Kant's 'moral medium' with Nietzsche's 'will to power', apparently so remote from morality, becomes clearer in quite a different horizon. Nothing is more unsupportable for the 'discourse ethics' of Apel and Habermas – a way of thinking which, located in the Kantian tradition but also driven by the shock of the first German post-war generation that had to face the consequences of Nazism, insists on producing a univocal, morally guaranteeing standard for social action.

6. Albert O. Hirschmann, *The Passions and the Interests: Political Arguments for Capitalism Before Its Triumph* (Princeton, Guilford: Princeton University Press, 1977).

7. See D. W. Winnicott, 'A Discussion on the Aims of War', in his *Home is Where We Start From*, essays by D. W. Winnicott, compiled and edited by Clare Winnicott, Ray Sheperd, Madeleine Davis and D. W. Winnicott (New York: Norton, 1986).

8. See Jessica Benjamin, *The Bonds of Love: Psychoanalysis, Feminism, and the Problem of Domination* (New York: Pantheon Books, 1988).

9. See Burke's definition of a political party, where he writes: 'Party is a body of men united, for promoting by their joint endeavours the national interest, upon some particular principle in which they are all agreed' (Burke, 'Thoughts on the Causes of the Present Discontent', in *Works* [London: Bohn, 1864], as quoted in B. Parekh and Thomas Pantham, eds, *Political Discourse* [London: Sage Publications, 1987]). It is interesting to note also that as early as 1843, Karl Rosenkranz, articulating the Hegelian *Philosophy of Right* for liberal politics, spoke of the modern 'amalgamation of the science of principle with that of interest'. In his understanding, this 'de facto' amalgamating was rationally upheld through Hegelian philosophy. (See further, *Die Hegelsche Rechte*, edited by Hermann Lübbe, 1962.)

10. Herbert Kitschelt, *The Logics of Party Formation: Ecological Politics in Belgium and West Germany* (Ithaca, New York: Cornell University Press, 1989).

11. The compulsiveness of Max Weber's dichotomy (ethics of conviction/ethics of responsibility) as a split ethical-moral *foundation of will* in the political realm, is precisely the mark of that 'elimination of the specifically political nature of the victorious practices' of which Laclau speaks.

Interestingly, one also finds that Leo Strauss explicitly connects a 'limit' of the moral-political (or rather, the visibility of a limit) with his above-mentioned question, 'What is the nature of political things?' He writes, 'Insight into the *limits* of the *moral-political sphere* as a whole can be expanded fully only by answering the question of the nature of political things.' Leo Strauss, *What is Political Philosophy* (New York: The Free Press, 1959, reprint 1973), p. 94 (emphasis added). To see a direct proximity to Nietzsche in this kind of Straussian 'reference to limits', as is often done, obscures more than it illuminates. In Strauss's commemorative speech on Kurt Riezler there is a reference to Heidegger in which these 'limits' do not appear as merely 'objective' (that is, in Nietzsche's terminology, 'psychological'). And in this reference one can detect that Strauss conceives Heidegger's distance from the ethical *as* 'will-founding', not simply as an observation of 'limit'. He also ascribes to it a special kind of perceptual dimension, saying: 'Heidegger . . . denies the possibility of ethics because he feels that there is *a revolting disproportion* between the idea of ethics and those phenomena which ethics pretended to articulate.' (*Strauss*, p. 246 [emphases added].) Here one may ask: is it not out of place in this context to insist on the limits of the moral-political sphere and on its connection with the nature of political things, if the space of Solidarnosc – as one would gather from most of its discourses – appears to emerge precisely from a revaluation of the moral-political sphere? (And is this revaluation not also the theme of many discourses about the Greens?) How little this is out of place, however, will become clear only if we also realize that 'ethics of responsibility' and 'ethics of conviction' belong to the same regime of hegemony (which as the 'political' makes itself invisible). Nothing is easier, then, than to demonstrate the limits of the one from the terrain of the other. Strauss's reasoning speaks precisely against this 'easy' kind of 'demonstration of limits', which in one way or another stems from knowledge.

This, then, affects the bearer of responsibility/security-guaranteeing itself. Indeed, how little the effects of the space of Solidarnosc depend on simple revaluation of the moral-political sphere can be seen in its difference from the 'dissident groups' of Central and Eastern Europe. For all their merit, these groups could not achieve the *interrupting* political space, and thus remained confined to opposing the 'ethics of responsibility' and legitimation discourse of the *post*-Stalinist reform regimes on the 'same kind' of ground; that is, on that of a pure 'ethics of conviction'.

12. D. W. Winnicott, *Human Nature* (London: Free Association Books, 1988), p. 162.

13. Of course, it is not a question here of 'allocating blame'. In reality, parts of the discourse of the Greens themselves unavoidably participated, and still participate, in this 'imperceptibility' of the specific historical 'space', to the benefit of (the well-known fixation on) the addition of general programmatic points and on 'intrinsically' superior 'moral positions'. But the positive (that is, non-reactive and democratic) disturbance of our political syntax was, and is, a partly selective and partly subliminal disturbance of hegemony. On the other hand, the levelling 'stumbling-block threshold' is that of a working political space of dialogue, which *disturbs* and partly interrupts in two chief respects. It disturbs the perception of the political schema of opposition, and thus also in part, disturbs that of the political syntax as a quasi-natural or social *a priori*.

Having said that, then, and despite the pragmatic dimension of the Greens' discourse, it does not become entirely (*restlos*) possible to treat the political handling of the 'ecology question' *purely* in terms of this environmental 'question'. This too is syntax-affecting, also through the way in which this subliminal broadening of address reaches beyond the objectively thematic, and an expansion of democratic-political response (or possibility of response) comes into play. It should not be lost on the reader just how little of this can be grasped in the framework of 'communication theory'.

14. 'Oblivious of syntax' here principally refers to the (also theoretical) fixation on direct contents – qua strategic-instrumental or moral political solutions – in which the historical specificity of the bearers of the political articulations and decisions, as well as the schemata of conflict in which they are embedded, completely 'disappear' behind these immediate meanings (that is, behind 'the semantic').

15. Despite his having taken very clear and distinctive positions on the matter, the extent to which Michnik is able to shake off a 'campist' view becomes clear when he speaks of the 'rebirth of two great traditions of Hungarian history' in relation to the conflict between the League of Free Democrats and the Hungarian Democratic Forum (the one more 'city-centred' and liberal-libertarian, the other more popular-Christian with a greater stress on cultural history). The same applies when he looks at the Russian 'followers of Solzhenitsyn' and the 'followers of Sakharov'

(and, therefore, also at the opposition between the camps, even beyond Russia). For Michnik, the future chances of democracy for the whole region are bound up with the 'ability of sensible people in both camps to compromise'. See Adam Michnik, *La Deuxième Révolution* (1990). For a general introduction to his work in English, see Adam Michnik, *Letters from Prison and Other Essays*, trans. Maya Latynski (Berkeley: University of California Press, 1985).

16. Only on certain points can we invoke this 'totalitarianism' – that is, East European Leninism-Stalinism – as the constitutive 'negative reference' of this political syntax of the historical region. In its violent way, this 'totalitarianism' was the first interruption in the 'regional syntax' wherein the two opposite moments were 'integrated'.

17. Laclau's thought unfolds precisely by taking seriously the 'stumbling-block threshold' of left-wing and Marxist political-theoretical thought, as evidenced in the fact that the antagonisms of a Peronist populism, introduced into the Argentinean political nation cannot be 'translated' purely into differences within society. Rather, it is an 'introduction' that also took place as a kind of 'updating' of the 'Argentinean' conflict configuration between, on the one hand, *unitarios* as both Jacobin and liberal-oligarchic party supporters of the relationship produced by the court-victory between the social and state instances under the imperative of 'progress' and 'up-to-date Europeanization'; and, on the other hand, *federales* as party supporters of an 'American wilfulness' qua revival of the so-called 'better' tradition of Western Christianity or Western liberty, with either ultra-montanist *or* anti-Absolutist signifiers. (And which, in a certain way, is the 'same' conflict configuration as the American one, between [the later] Democrats and Republicans, but on a terrain much more marked by court-victory and country-weakness, and so much more exposed to 'corruption', as can be noted in our contemporary times.) The (completely spatial) metaphor of 'closure and opening', used to characterize the opposition between 'popular-nationals' and 'liberals', is thus, as Laclau shows, one of the impossible spatial translations of the political itself – since antagonism, as one of the possibilities of directed identity, cannot be grasped with any code of difference (that presupposes a spatially closed 'equi-presence').

18. For this reason, the discourse which criticizes state and power 'in principle' – both arising from the subalternity of the pure sphere of civil society in the eighteenth century, and the present-day version that speaks of society assuming the functions of the state – does not know about the things of which it speaks. Society – as the neutralizing mode of the social in modern times, accented by freedom and (in Hirschmann's sense) 'exit' – is essentially related to the state. It emerges as a system of difference 'cleansed of antagonism' (which is why, as Laclau shows, it can never really exist according to its own standard of positivity), by virtue precisely of the state-expanding evacuation of that aspect of social-historical identities which is determined by addressing antagonistic dimensions. Thus, growing efforts to establish pure 'society' (which tends to 'evacuate' everything incapable of reciprocity) means – and demands (*heißt*) – growing statehood (of the hegemonic type). More succinctly put: the more society, the more state. But of course, formalizations of this kind 'topple' into an objectifying 'setting'. They 'do as if': as if one were talking of an already overstepped limit of relations (or lack of relations) between the self in Winnicott's sense and the 'addressing We' through which we are able to speak and be spoken to.

19. See, above all, J. G. A. Pocock, *The Machiavellian Moment: Florentine Thought and the Atlantic Republican Tradition* (New York: University Press, 1975); *Virtue, Commerce, and History* (Cambridge: Cambridge University Press, 1985); and *Politics, Language and Time* (London: Macmillan, 1960). Especially in this early book, we come up against yet another feat of Pocockian Workings. As far as we know, he is the only 'recognized' historian seriously given to the task of making thinkable, in political history, the Kuhnian difference between 'normal science' and 'paradigm-creation'. Among other things that means he incorporates the notion of a *discontinuous* history; i.e., the utterly impossible inside of the history of hegemonic historicism and their 'movements' (whether of '*longue durée*' or not). This discontinuity points in two directions: towards the difference of 'higher politics' and 'normal politics' as articulated by Bruce Ackermann (in *We the People – Foundations* [Cambridge, Massachusetts: Harvard University Press, 1991]) and towards the Heideggerian 'essential discontinuous destiny of being' exactly seized by Robert Bernasconi in his 'The Fate of Distinction between Praxis and Poiesis', *Heidegger Studies*, Vol. 2, 1986.

20. Walter Benjamin, *The Collected Works*, Vol. VI (Frankfurt A.M., 1991) p. 100. I owe the reference (together with a thoughtful illumination of the 'ecological') to Michael Jaeger (Berlin).

21. See Michael Walzer, 'The Communitarian Critique of Liberalism', *Political Theory*, vol. 1, 1990, pp. 6–23.

22. The political-historical scene in the USA in the last decade was the most vivid display of egalitarian 'rights-discourse' (previously called 'New Social Movements'), which inserted itself in an alternative-subaltern manner into the hegemonic discourse of the Reagan era. As a round-table of the journal *Telos* showed in 1988, the self-reference of this 'radical-libertarian' discourse went hand in hand with an 'actionist' loss of political speech, where purely 'quantitative' media attention of those 'taking measures' was at the centre of concern. At another level (a level that only appears to be quite different), much of the violent events of autumn 1992–summer of 1993 in Germany can be explained by the fact that the hegemonic discourses of the new Federal Republic (in their 'left' as well as their 'right' variants) were simply not able to address the 'most shaken' youth identities in the ex-GDR: literally not a single word was to be heard about the horizons and holding symbolic union of a renewed German 'political nation'. Not surprising, then, that those who are not spoken to do not themselves usually speak; they 'act'.

23. This means: only if we can use the historical-political opportunity whereby two causes can now be addressed and confronted which previously, within the rigid hegemonies of the classical-modern, West and Central/East European syntaxes, could ever be addressed and confronted in the terms of political democracy. These two are the *ecological cause* – the 'natural residue' which suddenly concerns us and stares us in the face (*ça nous regarde*, as is said in French), and which is not 'dissolving' within the rationality of our economic-scientific action because it cannot be converted into pure 'nature as raw material'; and the *cause* of the *totalitarian danger* facing the democracy (and the solidarity-bearing political nation and social sphere) – which can only 'meet up' with us if the modern, self-referring *raison d'état* having to pass judgement on the rationality or irrationality of political action, is suddenly no longer 'good enough', revealing its potential totalitarian complicity.

There can scarcely be any doubt that in Poland in 1980 it was General Jaruzelski (or the 'reform communist' Rakowski enjoying broad 'West European' sympathy) who acted in a 'modern, statesman-like manner', or even 'in the Polish national interest', and *not* Lech Walesa or Adam Michnik. For, the crucial point in the 'space of Solidarnosc' – what turned it into a threshold space no longer fully 'within' the hegemony by which the distribution of 'modern-rational' and 'emotional-irrational' spaces of political action can be assured – was that a different kind of 'common responsibility' emerged within it, whose 'mode of address' no longer allowed it to be represented with any effect as reactive-'fundamentalist' behaviour. This space of common responsibility does not coincide with the *Realpolitik* space of a classical ethic of responsibility, nor with its moralistic opposite. But neither did it emerge without a difficult and painful 'syntactic break', precisely with respect to the politically *not* secularized strands of Polish Catholicism, which, in playing a constitutive role together with lay strands of former Marxists and critical rationalists, 'moved' in their political identities.

Precisely for this reason, it was action/praxis 'able to begin' in the sense of H. Arendt, which led to the creation/discovery (in a Winnicottian sense) of the space of Solidarnosc – political action which, in so far as it could not be made to disappear by the otherwise effective dual strategy of everyday repression and an opening to privatization, 'interrupted' the *Realpolitik* rationality of the so-called reform-communist continuation of a 'slackened' Soviet empire. This interruption, which was later facilely normalized as dissidence so as to adapt it to the hegemonically produced 'nature of political things', opened a whole decade of abnormality in Poland, and therewith, also, in Central/Eastern Europe and the Soviet Union. Timothy Garton-Ash could still write in 1988: 'The impossible is still happening in Poland.' And this *impossible*, which, as a scope – as a *Spielraum* was living evidence to counter the notions about the 'objective limits' of the operational spaces of politics in Eastern/Central Europe, developed together with the not-unrelated changes in Moscow in 1988–89. It even took effect where the specific 'syntax-interrupting' action that led to Solidarnosc had not come about, or had done so only in the discourse of individuals such as Vaclav Havel (i.e., where the pre-war constellations of political opposition – as well as the 'kept-alive' patterns of thought and power of 'reformed totalitarianism', with their eerie proximity to democratic *raisons d'état* – were almost universally determinant). Thus, what we have called above the 'use of operational space' does not only stand against a complete reactivation of the classical-modern schema of political opposition and its levelling of thresholds. It also stands for that opening in which the 'ecological cause', as well as the 'cause' of a reductive 'national interest', can come to *meet* us – a meeting which, throughout the sphere of the full hegemony of classical-modern European opposition-patterns, is constitutively *impossible*.

24. John M. Murray writes: 'the political defeat of Federalism did not destroy the old Court forces in American society at large. . . . They discovered that they did not have to dominate politics . . . to manipulate America's vast resources. . . . Thus . . . they shifted their activities . . . to the state and local levels of the Northeast and later of the Northwest, where their enterprise, boosterism, ability and greed ran amok across the land . . . while Jeffersonian and Jacksonian opponents stood impotent guard over the inactive virtue of the central government' (in 'The Great Invasion, or Court versus Country', in J. G. A. Pocock, *Three British Revolutions, 1641, 1688, 1776* [Princeton, Guilford: Princeton University Press, 1980] p. 427). Murray's analysis also touches the weakest point for the Jeffersonian pole: the lodging of slavery, despite Jefferson's attempts to avow the contrary, within the Country-field. The above 'breakdown of control' had the result that Murray, like nearly all progressive intellectuals of his generation in the United States, could in the end only see the setting of the US schema of conflict as an anachronism, in comparison with the (vaguely 'social-democratic') adaptation of the political to society. There is much to suggest that this imaginary/social-democratic reference of a 'social-natural' political setting is today disappearing in the United States.

25. In answer to Sue Golding's query as to what, precisely, constitutes 'mainly, *purely*, ideological spaces', the following could be said by way of clarification: they are the ones localized inside 'the project of ideology'. They are the ones that express themselves 'most importantly', as Zygmunt Baumann puts it, in his *Legislators and Interpreters*, 'in the shifting of responsibility for the production and reproduction of the "good society" from the holders of the secular political power of the state to the professional spokesmen of Reason, showing their own science, ideology and expertise as the legitimation for their unique position' (p. 102, *passim*). It is in this sense, then, that for its bearers – speaking from a guaranteed, 'rational' identity place which can never be at stake – the question of political identity is radically incomprehensible.

26. This concealment happens in comparative studies too, when the 'national' specificity of the party-political model of opposition enters the picture. On closer inspection, these studies can focus only on the different 'national' *chances* for the 'green' or libertarian 'value position' (posited as fully positive and self-identical references) to become politically important, against other, predominant ones. That is to say: all 'Green forces' are treated as purely ideological groups, within a fictitious detachment of addressing- (or rhetorical-) dimensions, 'opening' identities and affecting political syntaxes (and not fictitious 'values').

27. No pre-modern body of people has ever been able to understand itself in this literal manner. The gods, The Law, The Ancestors (and so, the descendants) were also 'here', through the implicit acknowledgement of the language-embeddedness of the 'We'-s and the 'I'-s.

28. Precisely the pure continuity of what Laclau and Mouffe (in relation to the turning-point of '1789') call the 'democratic revolution' and its 'egalitarian logic' is *constitutively* more closed in on itself than any other 'symbolic system'. That is to say, vis-à-vis the 'interruption', vis-à-vis *answering* the experience of the 'constitutive outside' (i.e., to the identity-concerning incompleteness of what sovereignty and the rationalist 'handling of nature' make 'complete' in their different ways). Behind that stands the pure dimension of claim and justification (*quid iuris*) of 'egalitarian logic' and its struggles. Because these are admitted into the nature of the modern political will, they have as their 'natural' horizon sovereign measures which are directly justice-creating and problem-solving: that which makes demands does not then speak as addressee and addressor, but speaks sovereignly from its own grounded place and as directed to that which brings forth the measures. In the passage through the contra-rotating moments of the 'democratic revolution', one also notices what is *concealed* in Claude Lefort's talk of the 'empty i.e. emptied by the actions of the French Revolution space of the sovereign', a concept which has rightly become important in Laclau's most recent writings.

29. See further, Adam Michnik's *La Deuxième Révolution*.

30. See in particular, Peter Sloterdijk 'Nach der Geschichte', in Wolgand Welsch, ed., *Wege aus der moderne* (Weinheim: 1988) pp. 272ff.

31. Joseph Brodsky, 'Less than One', *Selected Essays* (New York/Toronto, 1986) p. 287.

32. Alain Touraine, *Plädoyer für die Rettung des Sozialen (Pleading to Save the Social)* (Berlin: World Media/Tageszeitung [TAZ], 1990); my emphasis.

Sign O' Times: Kaffirs and Infidels
Fighting the Ninth Crusade[*]

Bobby Sayyid

> If confusion is the sign of the times, I see at the root of this confusion a rupture between things and words, and the ideas that are their representation.
>
> ARTAUD

According to Rorty, all people have a set of words and phrases that they use to justify the things they do and believe. He describes such a set of words as a person's final vocabulary.[1] It is the vocabulary that one resorts to in order to tell a story about one's self. It is final in the sense that beyond these words there is only tautology, silence or force. A final vocabulary consists of a set of 'thin words' such as 'truth', 'good', 'justice', 'evil', and more specific 'thicker words' like 'Revolution', 'Reason', 'Democracy', 'Socialism'.[2] I call the cluster of 'thin words' ethical, and the cluster of 'thick words' political. It is through this political cluster that more general, flexible words are given shape. The big vague concepts such as 'good' are explained by reference to more particular thicker words such as 'Liberalism' or 'Fascism'. To put it slightly differently, the content of the thin words is provided by the thicker words. It is these thick words which are more commonly the subject of political conflict. We tend to agree on the need for 'justice' and 'goodness'; the problem arises when we try to define these words, and suggest ways of achieving them.

In recent years, an increasing number of Muslim communities have experienced changes in their final vocabularies. Many Muslims have started to

---

* I would like to thank: Kishver Nasreen, Lilian Zac, Chay Senave, Dhanwant K. Rai, Louise Miller, Ernesto Laclau, Barnor Hesse, Nur Betul Celik and Warren A. Chin. They have all contributed in various ways to the preparation of this chapter. Needless to say, whereas the above mentioned are responsible for much of what may be good about this paper, they are equally accountable for its shortcomings. I would also like to thank Kim Travers, the Alternative Working Girl, for her help with the typing of this manuscript.

use metaphors like 'Islamic Revolution' or 'Islamic State' to (re-)describe the meaning of words like 'justice', 'truth', and 'good'. This shift towards vocabularies centred around Islamic metaphors has come to be described by alarmed political analysts, and journalists alike, as 'Islamic Resurgence' or 'the rise of militant Islam', and, with increasing popularity, 'Islamic Fundamentalism'.

One of the major difficulties raised by the emergence of 'Islamic Fundamentalism' is the way it seems to be rejecting modernity. We in the West are used to seeing political struggles being conducted in a vocabulary that refers to 'Islam had long vanished from the stage of history at large.'[3] things such as 'liberty, fraternity and equality', 'bread and land', 'socialism or death'. We can understand these slogans and the projects they articulate because they are a part of a political tradition that has been dominant for the last two hundred years, and which we claim as our own. This political tradition is grounded in modernity.

Muslims, by using a final vocabulary that is centred on Islamic metaphors, highlight the limits of our traditional political discourses, and put into question our pretensions to universalism, by drawing attention to the particular nature of modernity. In other words, Muslims who use Islamic metaphors draw our attention to the fact that there is another way of doing politics which does not seem to rest upon the dominant language games of the last two hundred years. One of the main reasons why 'Islamic Fundamentalism' causes so much disquiet is because it seems to suggest that we may have confused the globalization of a political tradition with its universalization. By rejecting the dominant political discourses, 'Islamic Fundamentalists' make it difficult for us to describe them, since so many of our theoretical tools are bound up with this dominant political tradition.[4]

Most accounts of 'Islamic Fundamentalism'[5] begin with one of three main events: the Six Day War, the First Oil Shock, or the Iranian Revolution. 'Islamic Fundamentalism' is often understood as a response to the humiliation of military defeat or to the power of petro-dollar propaganda or to the fanaticism of revolution, or some combination of the three. These events are seen to be symptomatic of a deeper set of crises such as urbanization, expansion of the state, integration into the world economy, and so forth.

1. Islam and Crisis

The logic of these accounts can be expressed in Leninist algebra as: crisis + Islam = 'Islamic Fundamentalism'. With this kind of formulaic algebra, one can see that there is nothing in the various crises that makes the articulation of Islam necessary. Processes such as industrialization, urbanization, expansion of bureaucratic structures, and population growth are simply 'common' to the South.

For the moment, let us take that as a given, however problematic that 'given' clearly must be. Still, the question remains, even within that framework: how do upheavals associated with modernization translate into specifically *Islamist* projects? Why is it that these crises taking place in Muslim communities trigger 'Islamic Fundamentalism'? Because, as the tautology of definitional logic would conclude, they take place in Muslim communities. In other words, Islam is treated as a residual category. Islam exists as a backdrop, 'a reserve army of symbols', that one can call upon to inscribe global phenomena into 'Islamic Fundamentalism'. The effects of modernization are refracted through the prism of an Islamic culture to produce 'Militant Islam'.

'The life that had come to Islam had not come from within. It had come from outside events and circumstances.'[6]

But what I want to do here is to question the possibility of any identification of a unified culture outside a scheme of reading that would produce that identification. Culture (or any form of unity) cannot be a unified object of analysis independent of its articulations and readings. In other words, cultures have no intrinsic or essential identity or unity – outside history or politics – that can be reached by a 'transparent' reading. Rather, cultures are created and interpreted by human practices.[7] Islamic cultural practices, like all other practices, are a product of articulation, rather than a manifestation or uncovering of an Islamic essence. For example, if Islam were intrinsic to Iranian society how would we explain the different places Islam has occupied at different moments? When Reza Shah himself physically attacked Ayatollah Modaress (one of the most senior Ayatollahs of his day), it did not unleash social unrest. However, in 1964, when Reza Shah's son sent his troops to attack theology students at Qom, rioting ensued throughout Iran. Or did Iran only have an Islamic culture in 1978–79, when the Pahlavi regime was toppled by massive popular mobilization around Islamic metaphors?[8]

In fact the narratives which rely on the effects of urbanization, industrialization, and so on, to trigger 'Islamic Fundamentalism' rest, implicitly or explicitly, upon the explanatory power of another factor: the dislocation of cultural authenticity and tradition. It is the dislocation of Islamic order and unity which leads to 'Islamic fundamentalism'.[9] The various processes of modernization produce a certain disjunction between the demands of modernity and the rigidity of traditional culture. Ultimately, what is being dislocated is a structure understood as an Islamic culture. Now, not only do these accounts avoid the problem of understanding how Islam enters the picture; they also assume that it is possible to know what form a new inscription will take by 'knowing' the order that has been dislocated. Or, to put it in its usual form: because it is an *Islamic* culture that has been dislocated, the attempts to reinscribe it will be carried out by 'Islamic Fundamentalists'.

For these accounts, then, the use of Islamic metaphors can be explained by pointing to the identity of the culture prior to its dislocation. This, however, as Laclau points out, is not possible: the relationship between a dislocation and an inscription is contingent.[10] In the case of 'Islamic Fundamentalism' the very identity of Islam and Islamic practices will be transformed – and re-signified by any new attempt to reinscribe a culture – as being Islamic. The current struggles between 'Islamic Fundamentalists' and their enemies revolve around these attempts to name cultures, histories and societies.

By using metaphors from Islamic texts, 'Muslim Fundamentalists' are considered to be using the power of ethical words to do political work. Or to put this in terms favoured by most commentators, they are 'manipulating' religion for their own political ends. 'Muslim Fundamentalists' reply that Islam is not merely a religion but a total way of life, one that includes the political. The 'Muslims' fundamentalist' demand for an 'Islamic State' is different from a celebration of 'liberal bourgeois democracy'; not because the metaphors are different, but because there is difference in the 'thickness' of metaphors. In other words, 'Islamic state' refers to a thinner signifier than 'liberal bourgeois democracy', because it refuses to acknowledge that it is simply a political signifier. As many critics of 'Islamic Fundamentalism' point out, 'Islamic Fundamentalists' tend to be rather coy about articulating the concrete form of an 'Islamic State'. Part of this vagueness is no doubt due to reasons of political calculation, but part of it is due to the fact that the 'Islamic state' is not a metaphor for a particular institutional arrangement; rather it is a description of a moral universe. It is a description of a moral universe because Islam continues to be articulated as both an ethical and political signifier. Not only is Islam used in such a way to give content to notions such as 'justice' and 'goodness' but it is also a thin word requiring a content.

The impossibility of deciding whether Islam operates as a political ('Islam') or an ethical ('Islam') signifier makes it difficult to know where and how to place it within the accounts of 'Islamic Fundamentalism'. On the other hand, without its inclusion there can be no 'Islamic Fundamentalism'. In other words, 'Islamic Fundamentalists' use Islam to forge their projects, but their use of Islam also involves the construction of the identity of Islam itself. This relationship between Islam and 'Islamic Fundamentalism' cannot be discovered by reference to an Islamic essence. We still have to put Islam in the picture. But before we do that we have to clear up a little matter: so far I have been using the label 'Islamic Fundamentalism', but I am unhappy with this description.[11] I think it makes an understanding of these movements difficult by making them look simple.

Fundamentalism as a label first emerged during the 1920s to describe various Protestant sects in the United States who took the Bible to be the literal word of God.

'I have decided to retain the label modern Islamic fundamentalism. This is because in the West, both in the mass media and the academic journals and books, this movement is described as Islamic fundamentalist.'[12]

It was reactivated during the mid-1970s to describe the growth in the USA of the so-called Moral Majority, the phenomenon of Born Again Christianity. It was then expanded to include the various movements which use Islamic metaphors to (re)describe their political projects. But Muslims resist the label of 'Islamic Fundamentalism' on several grounds.

First, if by fundamentalism is meant a literal interpretation of canonical texts, this does not apply to 'Islamic Fundamentalists' since their interpretations are imaginative redescriptions of the canon. This explains why in general the Sunni ulema has tended to oppose 'Islamic Fundamentalism' because they regard the 'Fundamentalist' interpretations as too metaphorical. (The position of the Shia ulema is slightly different, though it has to be noted that the senior ulema in Iran have, on the whole, remained aloof from the Islamic Republic.) Second, Muslims would argue that fundamentalism is more a signifier of US foreign policy – a policy that calls its clients 'moderates' and its opponents 'Islamic Fundamentalists'. For example, in Afghanistan it is the fundamentalists who on the whole have wanted elections and the erosion of tribal identities in order to construct a more populist position. It is the moderates who have opposed elections, and sought the restoration of the monarchy. Or take the Saudi monarchy's Wahabbism, which had more to do with a conventional understanding of fundamentalism than the Islamic ideology advocated by Iran. Third, if by fundamentalism is meant a rejection of modernity, even here the position is more complicated as we shall later explore. 'Islamic Fundamentalists' tend to reject traditional folk Islam. Sociologically, 'Islamic Fundamentalists' come from the ranks of those with modern education rather than traditional religious seminaries.[13]

People who use Islamic metaphors to convey their hopes, to think their political utopias, and to narrate a story of their destiny, call themselves Islamists.[14] (To try and ward off any accusations of Orientalism in my move, let me make the disclaimer that this is not to suggest that all Islamists are identical in their beliefs; no more than it is to suggest that all bourgeois liberals are part of a monolith.) In the next part of this chapter I will turn to look at the various attempts to de-Islamize Muslim communities – a delegitimation that has provided the context for the Islamist projects of (re-)Islamization.

2. The End of the Caliphate: Putting Islam in the Picture

In 1924, Mustapha Kemal abolished the Caliphate and signalled the emergence of a new hegemonic order in the Muslim world. The abolition was the sign of the ultimate fragmentation of Islam; the Caliph could no longer act as a quilting point that represented the unity of Islam, helping it to maintain its political identity. Henceforth, Islamic presence in Muslim communities was confined to the private sphere, as a system of religious practices and laws governing personal status.[15] All other major Muslim communities were either directly governed by European powers or were under indirect European control. In this way, Islam was exorcized from the political sphere.

Those Muslims who rejected the use of Islam as a political signifier and who sought to bring, however mediated, a reconstruction of society in which the role of Islam would be analogous to the role of Christianity in post-reformation Western Europe; all those Muslims who rejected the use of Muslim metaphors, who felt that Islam should not interfere with the state – all those people I will call Kemalists.

'As for the Caliphate it could only have been a laughing stock in the eyes of the civilized world enjoying the blessings of science.'[16]

Kemalists took seriously the Weberian answer to the riddle of the 'European miracle'; that is, that the reasons behind Western advancement could be located precisely in Western cultural practices.[17] Kemalism understood modernization not just as a question of acquiring technology, but as something that could not be absorbed without a dense network of cultural practices which made instrumental thought possible. For the Kemalists, these cultural practices had a specific identity; they were the cultural practices of the West. The discourse of modernity was centred in the figure of the West: the West as Progress, as Reason, as the destiny of Man. The Kemalists thought that modernization would only be possible by maintaining the link between Western rationality and technology. Mustapha Kemal made a self-conscious effort to reproduce 'Western civilization' in Turkey. The Grand National Assembly followed its abolition of the Caliphate by passing a series of laws that attempted to construct Turkish society as Western society: the New Turk was to be firmly rooted in 'Western civilization', without Arabic script, without the Sharia, without Fez.

The response to the abolition ranged from various attempts to re-establish the Caliphate (for example, Fuad of Egypt, or the Khalifat movement of South Asia), to schemes to reform it (for example, Rashid Rida), to questioning its relevance (Abd al Raziq), to accepting the necessity of its abolition (Mohammed Iqbal).[18] By abolishing the Caliphate and instituting a programme of radical modernization in what had been the most powerful Muslim state, Kemalism transformed the horizon of what had been considered politically possible. Kemal's project of constructing Turkey as a modern national state, self-consciously modelled on the West, found resonance in many other Muslim societies.

The discourse of Kemalism included the Pahlavis; it included Bourguiba who declared that his aim was to make Tunisia a modern nation on the principles of the French Revolution; it also included Nasserism, Baathism, Bhutto's 'Islamic Socialism'. Indeed, all of these projects can be seen as variants of Kemalism. They were all constructed on a horizon opened by Kemal Atatürk.

Kemalists sought to represent the unity of their communities not by reference to Islam, but by articulating nationalism. It was the 'Nation' that was used to undermine Muslim identity, and weaken the claims of Islam as foundation of the various Muslim societies. Linked to this articulation of the nation as prime source of loyalty and solidarity was the formation of a historical narrative that became the foundation of the new order. In Turkey the (re)invention of 'The Turk' was used to replace 'The Muslim' as a historical subject. It was the 'Turks' who were considered a 5,000-year-old people, the descendants of the Hittites, and so forth. For the Pahlavis, it was the narratives of Aryans and '2,000 years of continuous monarchy of Persia' that had articulated their final vocabulary. For Saddam Hussein, Baathist Iraq was precisely heir to Nebuchadnezzar's Babylon.[19]

In order to constitute themselves as Western, the Kemalists had to deny and repress any traces of the Orient.[20] This was necessary since the West was constituted in its opposition to the Orient. To modernize, the Kemalists believed they had to Westernize; but, paradoxically, the very nature of Westernization meant Orientalization. For, given that the identity of the West was constituted vis-à-vis the Orient, they had to continue to articulate an identity of the Orient to constitute themselves as Western. The identity of the Orient could not be reduced to an aggregate of features and practices. The rejection had to be of that which unified all these elements into the Orient.

Thus, to be Western, one had to reject *more than* the Oriental; that is, one had to reject more than the use of the veil, the fasting in Ramadan, and so on. The rejection had to be 'superhard' as it involved a certain metaphorical surplus: the rejection of the impossibility of being the other. In this binary logic, representing the West meant the impossibility of being the Orient, an other which was not only the limit but also a threat to the West. Kemalism, by orienting itself towards the West, and embarking on the project of Westernization, necessarily (re)produced an Oriental subject. It did this precisely by imposing a bifurcation on Muslim societies between the modern and the traditional. What was involved in this system of oppositions was not just the contrast of two positive concepts, but the construction of the identity of the primary and privileged term through the presence of its other. The difference between the primary and secondary term not only separates and makes possible a hierarchy; at the same time it joins them and makes possible the subversion of that hierarchy.[21] Here, then, the secondary term cannot be outside the system, for the interval between the secondary and primary term is the very guarantee of the possibility of a system. It is this interval, this void between the West and Islam, that modernization is supposed to fill.[22]

But to fill this gap has meant constructing Muslim societies in terms of a spatial opposition between a modern metropolis and a traditional periphery. Modernization is constituted by constructing a bipolarized social space, and it is advocated as a means of closing this very same space. It is precisely this gap between the modernized and traditional, between the urban and the rural, between the West and Islam, that Kemalism articulated, and presented itself as the only means of suturing. Indeed, these binary divisions (so beloved of modernization theories) became the articulatory devices that grounded the coherence of Kemalism itself. We can see how Orientalist accounts of Islam find an echo in Kemalism. Muslim societies are seen in terms of a lack: the absence of technology, the absence of rationality, the absence of civil society, the absence of modernity. Conveniently, this lack can only be filled by imports from the West.

We find, then, with the Kemalist discourse, a curious fact. On the one hand, the Kemalists had to divide Muslim societies into modern ('Westernized') sector and traditional ('Islamic') sector; but, at the same time, they had to overcome this division. But this difference could not be resolved or settled – precisely because it was, itself, constitutive of the Kemalist discourse. Islam became the necessary constitutive outside of Kemalism, whose (differential) identity could only be fixed by reference to what opposed and undermined its unity.

As a consequence, the Kemalists followed a twin-track strategy with respect to Islam. On the one hand, they increasingly attempted to marginalize Islam as a public discourse, while simultaneously seeking to gain control of Islamic institutions. This was done either by absorbing the institutions into the secular mainstream educational system (for example, in Tunisia) and by introducing secular curriculum into Islamic institutes (for example, in Eygpt); or it was done by placing the head of the state at the head of the religious network (for example, Morocco) and establishing a parallel religious network (for example, Pahlavi Iran). In this way, Kemalism displaced Islam from the public arena controlled by the state.

And yet this act of displacement did not lead to the withering away of Islam; rather, it opened the possibility for its rearticulation in populist discourses (located in civil society) quite unencumbered by any association with state power.[23] It is in this light we should see Kemalism not as the secularization of Islam but as its politicization.

3. The Unevenness of the Available: Islam(ism) and Kemalism

The Kemalists' attempt to exclude and dominate Islam had the effect of disarticulating and unsettling it. What had been part of its unthought background became a subject of political intervention. It was not that Islam was 'out there' in Muslim societies, but rather that its political availability was inscribed within Kemalism. The rise of Islamism was only possible when the availability of Islamism could be articulated into a counter-hegemonic discourse.

But having said that, what is the weight we can assign to this category of *availability* of Islamism; that is, of a counter-hegemonic discourse? Is its accessibility sufficient to enable a discourse to become hegemonic? It would appear that Laclau seems to think so, especially when he suggests that on occasion availability is 'enough to ensure the victory of a particular discourse'.[24] This could be interpreted to mean that Islamism would emerge as the successor to Kemalism if the social order becomes so dislocated that Islamism remains as the *only* discourse of order. And while it is true that Laclau goes on to qualify this by adding that 'the acceptance of a discourse depends on its credibility',[25] still, at least in this account, 'availability' and 'credibility' seem to be nothing more than habitual metaphors (like 'tradition' or 'political culture') most political scientists grope for when their explanations begin to falter. In a move that would be uncharacteristically metaphysical (at least in the Rortyian sense), Laclau would appear to be suggesting that potentially hegemonic discourses are out there waiting to be discovered for the right kind of dislocation.[26] The problem arises because Laclau's main purpose in the section concerned is to make the case that there is no necessary correspondence between the content of a discourse and the organic crisis it tries to hegemonize.[27] But the difficulty remains precisely because he does not develop the argument far enough.

Let us try to further that argument. First, Laclau seems to be using 'available' in its more ordinary sense, while simultaneously hinting at more rigorous connotations. In conventional Heideggerese: what is available is what is ready-at-hand; and the ready-at-hand is determined by the task-at-hand. Now, there are many things 'standing by', all of which could potentially be put to some use. In a workshop, for example, a carpenter will have many tools: hammer, saw, chisel; but the availability of any of these tools does not depend simply on tools being there in the workshop, being there for the job she wants to do. Moreover or more to the point, it is the need for hammering, itself, that requires the hammer to be available for use. That is, the availability of something is a function of a task or project at hand.

The availability of a discourse for Laclau is not analogous to the presence of tools in a workshop in the above example. It is not the mere presence, for example, of the Nazi discourse that was decisive for the Nazi takeover. Nazi discourse was not lying around like an unopened book, which the frightened German middle class happened to stumble across during the dark moment of the Depression. Such an understanding of the available confuses it with the occurrent (presence-at-hand).[28] Or, to put this slightly differently, the availability of a discourse is not the same as the existence of a discourse. Something *becomes available* through its articulation.[29] That is, to keep with our example above, the articulation of the Nazi discourse contributed to the crisis of the Weimar republic, by helping to undermine the coherence of the Weimar order. In other words, then, the role of an available discourse is not simply to be the only form of order, but also one that contributes to the dislocation of the previous hegemony, precisely by undermining its co-herence. In short, available discourses are not merely phatic phenomena.

This leads to the second main source of confusion, that is, the relation *between* contingency, necessity and the available. To what extent, one might ask, can the construction of a hegemony ever be read as implying that there is no alternative to that hegemony? For a vital part of any hegemonic articulation is precisely the establishment of an interpretation that sees it as the only possible outcome. This involves the suppression of any other alternative. This retrospective construction of a 'no alternative' situation cannot be read as the confirmation of the availability of only what can later become the hegemonic discourse. The absence of an alternative is a reward for victory – not its cause. For example, communist discourse was also available in the Weimar Republic. However the Nazi hegemony was able to erase the memory of any alternative and represent itself as the only cure for Germany's crisis. It is clear from the context of the passage that Laclau is adamant that the formation of a hegemony is a contingent operation.[30] To argue that there is no alternative to a particular discourse would be to make a particular hegemony necessary. What is clear is that not all discourses are *equally* available in any social context. It is in this sense that one can better appreciate Laclau's comments on credibility. For the unevenness of the availability of discourses is constitutive of the social. This unevenness of availability limits the contingency of the link between the dislocation and the discourse that manages to suture that gap. Credibility is a reflection of that unevenness, but it is not a static screen acting as a filter external to the hegemonic struggle; rather, it is a part of that struggle. The unevenness of availability is a function of a sedimented power struggle rather than the epiphenomenon of some essence.[31]

Let us look at this development more closely with respect to Islamism. The mere discursive presence of Islam cannot account for Islamism. And since its availability is not only a function of its use, but also a function of the sedimented power struggle, Islamism cannot be thought of as the mere reflection of the essence of Islam. Rather, it is Kemalism itself which has politicized Islam, in its attempt to de-Islamize the public domain. At the same time, Islamism is a political discourse that makes Islam available as a means of undermining the Kemalist *anciens régimes*.

Let me put the question of availability in reverse: what makes possible the 'making available' of Islam by Islamists? What is broken that requires the Islamists to reach for a hammer? In other words, what makes possible the articulation of Islamism as a counter-hegemonic discourse? Often we find suggestions as to why this should be so taking the line 'the nationalists were in power, the communists were in jail, so by a process of elimination the mantle

of revolt fell upon the Islamists'. Even if we accept, for argument's sake, the
validity of this description, it is still not clear why the failure of Kemalist
regimes does not clear the ground for other discourses such as liberalism
and/or social democracy. What is clear is the way in which it opens up space
for theories like Khomeini's. For what is common to the discourses of
liberalism, social democracy, communism and Kemalism is that all these
discourses are founded upon modernity. What I want to do in the rest of the
chapter is to tell a story about the relationship between modernity, Kemalism,
the West and Islamism. I will show that it is by trying to understand this
relationship that we can make better sense of the rise of Islamism.

4. Westoxication:[32] Kemal Atatürk Meets Ayatollah Khomeini

The modernist character of Kemalist discourses has led many to assume that
the Islamist opposition to Kemalism is anti-modern. But is such a thing
possible? Can we Muslims reject modernity without our gesture of defiance
being recuperated as an example of a defiant gesture in modernity's repertory?
Is not modernity all-embracing?

Zubaida has shown why Khomeini's relationship to modernity cannot be
caricatured as a straightforward rejection. From Khomeini's political writings,
which Zubaida notes are not a literal recitation but a major reinterpretation of
traditional Shia doctrine, he focuses on some of the main preconditions
implicit in Khomeini's *Al-Hukumah Al-Islamiya* (Islamic Government).[33]
Zubaida demonstrates how Khomeini's radical reinterpretation is heavily
dependent on key modern notions.[34] Such dependence would appear
to confirm that it is impossible to position oneself outside modernity.[35]
If Khomeini, the 'arch-Anti-Modern' cannot escape modernity
then no one can. However, one of the most
interesting observations that Zubaida makes is
that despite Khomeini's dependency on modern
political concepts, his discourse is conducted
exclusively in the idiom of Islamic political

> 'Muslim Fundamentalism
> has no intellectual sub-
> stance to it, therefore it
> must collapse.'[36]

theory with hardly any reference to modern political doctrines.[37] This, as
Zubaida rightly points out, distinguishes Khomeini from all the recent
Muslim political theorists.[38] Khomeini does not feel it necessary to follow the
common strategy of Muslim apologists: he does not try and argue that Islam is
'real democracy', or that Islam anticipates socialism, and so on. There is no
attempt by Khomeini to try and locate Islam within a tradition of progressive
history in which major developments are redescribed as being originally
inspired by Islam. There is no obvious attempt to incorporate or even engage
with political concepts associated with the discourses of nationalism,

Marxism, liberalism. Indeed, Khomeini does not even examine the pros and cons of Western political theory. Rather, and in a move that Rorty replays, Khomeini simply presents his vocabulary as a challenge to the Kemalist hegemony.[39] As Zubaida points out, Khomeini writes as if Western thought did not exist.[40]

I think this paradoxical relationship between Khomeini and modern political thought is important. Let us be clear about what is at stake here. If the identity of a concept is a function of its usage, then clearly the use of a concept outside the context of its ignoble beginnings would imply the modification of the identity of the concept. Even though Khomeini makes no reference to European political theory, according to Zubaida his political writings only make sense in relation to a number of concepts which have come to be associated with the Western European political tradition.[41] I want to suggest that this non-reference to the West is significant and is a symptom of the crisis of modernity.

1. Modernity

There is much debate about whether modernity is over or is still going on. Those like Lyotard, who argue that it is over, argue that the history of modernity (the Holocaust, the corruptions of empires, mutually assured destruction, ecocide) has subverted the promises of its grand narratives (Reason, Enlightenment, Progress), thus putting them into question. This suspicion of grand narratives is what Lyotard calls 'post-modernity' and regards it as a new epoch. This going beyond modernity relies on a notion of modernity that has a certain uniformity, one which can be encapsulated and one that has important repercussions for our understanding of Kemalism. Kemalism, as has been noted, is structured around modernity. The weakening of the foundations of modernity itself would also involve the weakening of the certainties of Kemalism.

2. More modernity . . .

Now Rorty is unconvinced that such a global encapsulation is possible. He thinks that the attempts to be post-modern are a continuation of Heidegger's claim that the West has exhausted its possibilities.[42] In both cases a global picture is made up of a philosophical essence. Rorty would rather understand post-modernity as an attitude (or manifesto) than an epoch. He likes the idea of being suspicious of meta-narratives but he doesn't want to end up by saying that an age has come to an end.[43] This, he feels, is the conceit of philosophers who like to see clean beginnings and endings.[44] Pragmatists like him are more inclined to note that life is a little more messy than philosophers would allow for, and one just muddles along always in the middle of one thing or another.

There is a sense in which Rorty is right: all the concepts and descriptions used by people in the academic business tend to eradicate differences. When we talk about 'Europe' or 'South America' or 'bourgeois liberalism' or 'Islam', we are implicitly erasing the internal differences that constitute these entities. Modernity and post-modernity are no exceptions to this fuzziness. But Rorty is not saying that modernity is difficult to encapsulate because it is fuzzy. He is actually making a larger claim: modernity does not have any uniform theme from which we can abstract its logic.

If I have read Rorty fairly, I think he is wrong. I think it is possible to find a description of modernity which, though fuzzy as all descriptions tend to be, can allow us to speak about the end of modernity *as a hegemonic order* which opens up very different ways of understanding the issue of modernity and post-modernity. Rorty's account of modernity/post-modernity is limited because Rorty is better at philosophy than history. (This, in spite of his heroic attempts to devalorize the philosophical enterprise.) Even in his tangential comments regarding historical changes, he allows his parochialism to soften his pragmatism, so politics becomes an anodyne affair, in which nothing is staked and nothing is lost. Everything depends on what kind of books the bourgeois liberals are reading at the time. It is one thing to acknowledge the significance of *Uncle Tom's Cabin* in raising anti-slavery consciousness (among those who were not and had not been slaves), it is another to see in the reading of the book the end of slavery. This attitudinal approach to modernity/post-modernity leaves the dimension of power unaccounted for.[45]

3. Still more modernity . . .

Rorty's account of modernity is, like most accounts of modernity, structured around a gaze which goes from Europe towards the periphery. I want to suggest that there is a coherent way of seeing modernity which opens the way for understanding what comes beyond modernity. The description of post-modernity that I would favour is one that sees it as a 'decentring of the West'. This is the sense in which Young talks about post-structuralism: an awareness of the particularity of European culture.[46] Such a way of describing modernity/post-modernity allows us to bring together the aesthetic and philosophical discourses of modernity with its political and military discourses. What I like about *White Mythologies* is that the book attempts to include the role of other parts of the world in the generation of events in the West. This is important because, since the time of the Greeks, there has been a tendency to see the West as a product of autochthonous development: Athena-like, European culture bursts forth fully formed. The debates around post-modernity/modernity are no exception to this parochialism.

What I want to do is extend Young's analysis of the relations between

'Aquinas may be inconceivable without Aristotle via Averores: but it is perhaps pushing it a bit far to claim that we must trace the industrial revolution back to the Toledan translators. We are heirs of Greece not Baghdad.'[47]

European culture and imperialism and try to locate the emergence of post-modernity not exclusively in the centre (however qualified). I want to argue that it is the change in the relationship between periphery and centre which is constitutive of post-modernity. Then, I would like to suggest how it is that Islamism is implicated in this relationship.

Let me lay my cards on the table: I understand modernity as a fable about the exceptionality of the West. It is a fable cementing its legitimation and offering an explanation of its (Europe's) global domination. It defines itself as a ruptural moment which divides human history in two. It is built on a contrast with earlier epochs: 'which are darker, more superstitious, less free, less rational, less productive, less civilized, less comfortable, less democratic, less tolerant, less respectful of the individual, less scientific and less developed technically'.[48] The contrast between modernity and non-modernity is also a description of the contrast between what constitutes the West (Civilization, Democracy, Rationality, Freedom) and its Other (Barbarism, Irrationality, Despotism, Slavery). Thus these references to earlier periods are not purely temporal; modernity is also a spatial marker. The rupture that marks modernity also gives birth to the West and marks it off as being unique.

It is from the standpoint of modernity that we can raise a question so succinctly raised by Weber – the very same question with which Habermas begins his *Philosophical Discourse of Modernity*:

> A product of modern European civilisation, studying any problem of universal history, is bound to ask himself to what combination of circumstances the fact should be attributed that in Western civilisation only, cultural phenomena have appeared which . . . lie in a line of development having a universal significance and value.[49]

Modernity is a way of saying: 'only in the West' (as Weber goes on to say in the above quote). It may say many other things besides, but it always says this. Indeed, this intrinsic relation between modernity and the West is central to the way in which discourses of modernity situate Europe (and its *outre-mers*) vis-à-vis the rest of the planet. It is *only* Western civilization that is universal, though, interestingly enough; even when the West has been universalized, it still retains its identity as the West. The easy slippage between modernization and Westernization, the ease by which we can locate the central tenets of modernity back to their roots in 'our common European home', demonstrates the seamless way in which modernity just fades into the West and vice versa. Modernity, then, is not a type of discourse with a centre,

'The struggle of European liberals and revolutionaries from the Middle Ages onwards against clericalism and the Christian religion were necessary to remove the invocation of supernatural authority from political life and the same applies to Islam.'[50]

rather it is a discourse the centre of which is occupied by a particular identity.

Those people who think modernity has exhausted its possibilities are inspired by a very specific reading of Nietzsche's account of nihilism. But, as Warren reminds us, there are two distinct kinds of nihilism in Nietzsche: European nihilism and the original Ancient nihilism.[51] When Nietzsche is invoked it tends to be for the former nihilism; that is, the condition after the death of God, when nothing is true and everything is permitted. This nihilism arises from the interior of European culture, where the development of critical practices has undermined the ability to believe in any certainty. The parallels between Nietzsche's European nihilism and conventional accounts of post-modernity are clear.

But my interest lies more in Nietzsche's account of the original (political) nihilism: a nihilism that arises from the experience of political repression; a nihilism that contextualizes and historicizes the subordinated. This sense of nihilism, I think, captures closely the effect of European domination on the subjects of that domination. The experience of colonization brings forth the contingency of the world of those who have been colonized: their sacred narratives become (for the colonizer) just another collection of stories. The emergence of particularity as a particularity is related to the unevenness in the relations of power: only the powerful can articulate themselves as Masters of the Universe; while it is only the colonized, the defeated, who suspect the significance or the usefulness of their final vocabularies – the powerful are not called to do the same kind of questioning. This description would see 'post-modernity' emerging in the periphery and migrating to the centre via decolonization. Post-modernity, then, is not something that succeeds or eliminates modernity, but rather something that is found alongside modernity.[52]

Decolonization, coming in fits and starts (and, in many obvious ways, still incomplete), demonstrates the possibility of forcing a retreat of explicit Western power. In saying this, though, it is important to make two major qualifications. First, one should bear in mind that decolonization is not a homogeneous process; and, second, that the end of empire is not due to the West being overcome by a Hamletesque self-doubt or Rortyesque ironic liberalism. The retreat from empire is one of the main impetuses behind post-modernity and the revelation of the West's particularity behind its universalist facade.[53]

Much of the literature on post-modernity focuses on the centre, on, that is to say, advanced capitalist countries, and in particular, 'new forms of social and cultural movements' and the emergence of a politics of difference, that is, a political and cultural vision that emphasizes pluralism and heterogeneity (the much maligned multiculturalism). While we in the West play with the new possibilities created by the ending of the old certainties of modernity, others who cannot bear the world without foundations retreat into 'ancient' myths, search for a rock upon which they can base their identity. In contrast to the 'politics of difference' at the centre, a 'politics of authenticity' prevails at the periphery. To put it bluntly, just as we in the West are getting post-modern, the rest are still doing the things we gave up doing long ago.

5. The Politics of Authenticity

In spite of all the talk about contextualizing the West, post-modernity is still regarded as a Western experience, seen either as a political and ethical cul-de-sac or as 'There's a feeling I get the dawning of a new age. Whether the West is when I look to the West.'[54] rich (USA, EC) or poor (Poland, Czechoslovakia), it is privy to the experience of post-modernity. Let us talk cardinal points: how does, for example, decentring of the West fit in with the North/South divide?[55] What does it mean to talk about decentring in a hierarchical world? This seemingly apparent paradox illustrates some of the problems critics of post-modernity raise: how to account for the tremendous inequalities in military, political and economic dimensions of the world order (in terms of the so-called decentring of the West), when the West is itself the very expression of what it is to be 'centre'. In the next section of the chapter I will try and address in a very brief way some aspects of this issue. But first let us turn to the way in which the West has dealt with a politics of authenticity.

In the dim distant past we, in the West, also had a politics of authenticity. We would call people who practised that kind of politics Fascists or Communists. With the collapse of the Soviet empire, we have seen the marginalization of this politics based on foundation. True one may still find the politics of authenticity in isolated pockets or on the lunatic fringes, but not as a credible meta-narrative. We in the West seem to have grown out of the need to find an authentic identity; we know there 'Islam desperately needed to develop a secular face with Western assistance . . . if there is anywhere where secular Muslims have existed, it is in Bosnia. But fundamentalists have been in there preaching fundamentalism before they hand out the Kalashnikovs. Ten years from now you are going to have a fundamentalist state at the frontier of Europe and people will say: "Where did that come from?"'[56] is no such thing as authenticity or purity. Their world is hybrid, and their cities testify to their hybridity. You can eat Korean, Ethiopian, South Asian, Thai – world cuisine is only a phone call away. However, we know that 'out there' you can still find people who indulge in this politics of authenticity.[57] Islamists are such people – people who try and practise the politics of authenticity: they try and erase the hybrid, annihilate the playful for the rigour of orthodoxy. Islamism is the last of the meta-narratives.

Such descriptions are based on a set of assumptions whereby the politics of authenticity, in the context of the periphery, have the same logic as similar types of politics at the centre.

At the heart of this issue is a question: is either the form or the content of a discourse sufficient to allow us to characterize a meta-narrative *as such*? What makes a meta-narrative a meta-narrative: its unbending nature, its imperial ambition, or its place of enunciation?

I would argue that it is only possible to classify Islamism as a meta-narrative if we ignore the conditions of its enunciation; that is, forget its marginal status. In other words, by eradicating the hierarchical world order and focusing on the presumed content of Islamism we can describe it as one of the last foundationalist discourses. But having said this, is any attempt to constitute a centre, regardless of its context and its conditions of enunciation, sufficient to permit us to categorize that discourse as a meta-narrative? For isn't it precisely the impossibility of having discourses *without* centres that has led various post-modern thinkers to propose notions such as 'strategic essentialism' (Spivak) or 'weak thought' (Vattimo)?[58] What these notions try to do is to recognize that a meta-narrative is a meta-narrative not because it has a centre, but rather because its centre is strong. The solution they see is not to take on the strategy of 'infantile Leftism' (which would support the abolishing of centres) but, rather, to replace them with 'weak centres'.

But if it is the strength of the centre that makes the difference, then what makes the centre strong? One answer would be that a centre would be weak if its discourse recognizes its own indeterminate, contingent and provisional nature. Another way of answering the same question would be to see the strength of a centre as a function of power. By redescribing post-modernity from the perspective of the periphery we can perhaps see the limits of the peripheral politics of authenticity. Authenticity refers to an attempt to recover a pristine identity which has been suppressed. Thus, in the context of the discussion of Islamism, words like 'revival', 'resurgence', and 'return' are used. However, if Islam does not have an essence, its use is a reinterpretation, and any 'return' or 'recovery' is only that which is articulated as such.

This is to say, then, that one cannot understand a discourse by focusing only on its form and/or content; the conditions of its enunciation are vital.[59] But in the context of the periphery, the conditions of enunciation are, by definition, weak. This is why I think the discourse of Islamism cannot be read as another (pre)modernist meta-narrative. It may have the discursive economy of the grand narratives of the Enlightenment, but its conditions of enunciation are such that it cannot be confused with them.

An attempt to constitute a centre from a position of weakness, from the margins, cannot have the same hardness as a centre at the heart of a hierarchical world order. Islamism exists as a precarious alternative to Kemalism; it cannot but help engage with other traditions and discourses. It is constantly being asked to account for itself in the language that is not its own; it is always having to begin from a point it would not choose (for example, President Carter's description of intervention in Iran as being part of 'ancient history' – as though it had, apparently, no bearing on the anti-Americanism of the Iranian Revolution). In this sense too, then, the problem of the decentring of the West has to be understood in Gramscian rather than Spenglerian terms. For here the hegemonic order that naturalized and sedimented a certain narrative structure has broken down, even though tremendously unequal power structures are still in place. The West is being decentred to the extent that its claim that 'there is no alternative' no longer has the force it once did.

Interestingly, then, Islamism does not become the 'other' of post-modernity, but one of the possibilities of decentring of the West. Islamist movements are a *continuation and radicalization of the process of decolonization*. The Iranian revolution looked towards Islam, not France, Russia or China, as its inspiration and 'model'. To see Islamism as a continuation of decolonization in other contexts does not mean we can easily fit it within the framework of modernity. This is where Zubaida, by separating the content of Khomeini's theory from its conditions of enunciation, that is, by making the division between the text (form + content) and the context – concentrating, instead, on the content almost exclusively – fails to see that Khomeini is one of the possibilities of the post-modern condition. That is, Khomeini's political significance is only possible in the context of a decentred West. That is, until the Iranian revolution it was not possible to think beyond the great models of political modernity. Now one can say that Islamist discourses do not have to present themselves as products of, or as coming from, the terrain of Western political discourse.

'Islamic revivalist movements are not sweeping the Middle East and are not likely to be the wave of the future.'[60]

6. The End of History?

There are a number of objections one can make to the above arguments:

First objection

One could say that all this talk of post-modernity and decentring is all very well for philosophers and 'wannabe' philosophers, but in reality such descriptions have no influence on how a Muslim would lead her everyday life. Language games have their own communities, and not everyone will find descriptions of decentring interesting or useful.

But I would argue that the expression 'decentring of the West' is an abbreviation for a complex set of processes which have tangible effects, particularly in that these processes refer to the boundaries of a cognitive horizon. In a sense, what I am trying to describe is the transformation of a specialist language into a part of our background practices. For example, when they were first put forward, Darwin's theories of natural selection would require engagement in specialist discourses of biology/theology. But now the assumptions of Darwinism have come to form part of the final vocabulary of a large number of people who are not biologists or even academics.

Moreover, what I abbreviate as the 'decentring of the West' is the growing recognition (however hesitant and grudging) of the non-universal character of Western discourses. For, ultimately, the decentring of the West rests on the ability to think difference in a significant way; that is, to think difference beyond Western discourse's description of difference. From the October Revolution onwards, for example, the number of political subject positions available to Muslims would include Bolshevik, nationalist, and colonial subject. During the height of the Cold War one could be either with the 'Free World' or the Socialist Bloc – but the emergence of Islamist counter-hegemonic projects would be something not included in the political horizon.[61] The 'decentring of the West' has produced a situation in which the availability of Islam cannot be held back by projecting its opposition to reason and Western civilization. The Kemalist strategy in which a comparison was offered with the West – and Islam found lacking – is no longer that convincing. The weakening of the West has reduced its utility as model.

Second objection

Decentring of the West makes no sense in the context of the new world order. Rather than being decentred, the West is the only centre left standing. The fall of the Soviet empire confirms the hegemony of the West, and the state-of-the-art Western technology that blew Saddam out of Kuwait, the precision-guided munitions that shattered the so-called 'fourth largest army in the world', demonstrate that no new rival to the West is likely. There is no alternative to the West.[62]

But to what extent was Moscow an alternative to the West – as opposed to being an alternative to Washington? From outside the West, both socialism and capitalism were part of Western philosophical traditions. As Young writes: 'Marxism, as a body of knowledge, remains complicit with and even extends the system to which it is opposed.'[63] From the point of view of the Islamists, the collapse of socialism is not read as the failure of viable alternatives to the West. Socialism and capitalism are both considered to be part of the same Western civilization; they are both, to borrow Connolly's labels, 'civilisations of productivity'.[64] For the Islamist, the disintegration of one of the twin pillars of Western hegemony is confirmation of the decentring of the West.

The recent panic in the academy over multi-culturalism should also temper some of the post-Cold War triumphalism. After all, what kind of a triumph is it that requires the victors to fight tooth and nail to defend a cultural canon the victory of which is being so loudly proclaimed? The importance of Khomeini's style of intervention hints at a paradigmatic shift. The reason why the failures of the Kemalist regimes have not lead to a clearing for other political discourses – such as liberalism or social-democracy – is because these discourses were all centred on the idea of the West. The decentring of the West weakens not only Kemalism but also other discourses that are anchored in the figure of the West and were made possible by the expansion of the West. The 'entrenched vocabulary' of the Western political tradition is no longer strong enough to rule out of order the vague promises of an Islamist vocabulary.

Conclusion

Imagine L. is a Muslim student in an American university. She is sitting in front of Professor D. who teaches courses in Philosophy and in Business Studies. Professor D. is trying to convince her to take his course in Philosophy. L. is not wholly convinced; she says: 'I'm not sure, Professor; I'm not really into Western Philosophy.'

'But why not?' asks Professor D.

L. replies that it seems to her that philosophy is nothing more than the ideology of the Western ethos.

'Let me explain,' says Professor D., with a smile. 'Your statement is condemned to permanent incoherence; it is meaningless. What permits you to speak of ideology? For the distinction between ideology and philosophy is a philosophical distinction. Ideology means a particular discourse that has universalistic ambitions. Now, the opposition between the contingent particularity and the universally valid is a philosophical one. To criticize Western philosophy can only be done by using the weapons of Western philosophy itself. To speak outside Western metaphysics is impossible, for it has no outside. By saying that philosophy is an ideology of the West, you are already engaged in Western philosophy.'[65]

L. thinks for while, a haiku by Ishida Hayko comes to her mind, but she can't remember exactly how it goes: something about a caged eagle, feeling lonely, flapping its wings. L. begins to speak, the Professor stares out of his window, it will be October soon.

She says: 'I heard once that an ex-US army officer told General Giap that the Americans had never lost a battle in Vietnam. Giap replied that this was true, but it was also irrelevant.'

Notes

1. R. Rorty, *Contingency, Irony and Solidarity* (Cambridge University Press, Cambridge, 1989) p. 73.

2. Ibid.

3. G.W.F Hegel, *The Philosophy of History* (New York: Dover Publications, 1956) p. 360.

4. See, for example, E. Said, *Covering Islam* (London: Routledge, 1981) where he examines some of the aspects of the threat and confusion Islamist movements cause both politically and analytically.

5. My descriptions of 'Islamic Fundamentalism' have been mainly culled from the following: F. Ajami, *The Arab Predicament* (Cambridge: Cambridge University Press, 1981); M. Fisher, 'Islam and the Revolt of the Petty Bourgeoisie', in *Daedalus*, vol. III, Winter 1982, pp. 101–25; M. Gilesenan, *Recognizing Islam* (London: I.B. Tauris, 1982); F. Halliday and H. Alwai, eds, *State and Ideology in the Middle East and Pakistan* (London: Macmillan, 1988); and S. Hunter, ed., *The Politics of Islamic Revivalism* (Bloomington, Ill: Indiana University Press, 1988).

6. V.S. Naipaul, *Among the Believers* (London: André Deutsch, 1981) p. 398.

7. For an interpretative understanding of Heidegger's concept of culture as it relates to this point, see H. Dreyfus, *Being-in-the-World* (London/Cambridge: M.I.T. Press, 1990) pp. 15–25.

8. To what extent Islam was an important factor in the mobilization of the Iranian people, in opposition to the anti-Pahlavi regime, is a vexed question. Some, like Fred Halliday (*Iran: Dictatorship and Development* [Harmondsworth: Penguin, 1979]) feel it was the proletariat (in the form of the oil workers) 'flexing its muscles' that brought down the regime. Others, like Suroosh Irfani, *Revolutionary Islam in Iran* (London: Zed Books, 1983) acknowledge the importance of Islam in mobilization and organization of the Iranian Revolution.

9. Dislocation involves a certain loss of coherence when an event cannot be explained in the terms of the context of which it occurs. Therefore it reveals the fragility and the limits of that context.

10. E. Laclau, *New Reflections of the Revolution of Our Time* (London: Verso Books, 1990) pp. 43–60.

11. See S. Zubaida, *Islam, the People and the State* (London: Routledge, 1989) pp. 1–3 and 38–41; and E. Abrahamian, 'Khomeini: Fundamentalist or Populist?', *New Left Review* 186, March–April 1992, pp. 103–5. They both point to the inappropriateness of the label 'Islamic Fundamentalism' to describe various Islamic-orientated projects.

12. A. Ahady, 'The Decline of Islamic Fundamentalism', *Journal of Asian and African Studies*, vol. XXVII, no. 3–4, 1992, p. 231.

13. See R.A Hinnebach's comments on the social bases of the Syrian Islamists, and Norma Salem's observation on Islamists in Tunisia, in Hunter, *The Politics of Islamic Revivalism*, pp. 48 and 159–60 respectively. M. Moaddel finds that even in Iran almost 42 per cent of the members of the first parliament came from non-theological intellectual backgrounds; see his *Class, Politics and Ideology in the Iranian Revolution* (New York: Columbia University Press, 1993) p. 225.

14. If we use this criterion to describe Islamists, are we not also including the Gulf regimes, as well other Muslim regimes which use Islam as a marker of legitimacy? I would argue that all those regimes which use Islam as a marker of legitimacy are still trying to maintain a distinction between their identity and Islamic metaphors. That is, their vocabulary is implicitly or explicitly organized around a distinction between the ethical and the political. Thus, in this case, Islam acts as a marker of legitimacy because it remains an ethical signifier. It does not become a political signifier.

15. Zubaida, *Islam, the People and the State*, p. 42.

16. Mustapha Kemal Atatürk, *A Speech Delivered by Mustapha Kemal Atatürk, 1927* (Ankara: Basbakanlik Basimevi, 1983), p. 10.

17. See for example where Bryan Turner, in his *Marxism and the End of Orientalism* (London: Routledge, 1974), shows the importance in the work of Weber of Islam as a counterfactual model to the rise of capitalism. The counterfactuality of Islam resides in its cultural difference between it and Protestant Europe. As Turner argues, this difference is not as decisive or deep as is presented in the work of Weber and subsequent modernization theorists.

18. H. Enyat, *Modern Islamic Political Thought* (London: Macmillan Press, 1982) gives a

detailed account of the theoretical ferment that the abolition of the Caliphate caused amongst Muslim intellectuals.

19. There is much debate as to the extent to which Arab nationalism excludes Islam. Arab nationalists of various hues tend to push the 'Ummayadist' line about the indivisibility of Islam and Arabism. However, to the extent Islam is subsumed as either the 'first Arab revolution' or the 'genius of Arabism', it is clear that Arabist and other forms of Kemalism are willing to concede only a secondary (and private) role for Islam.

20. It is necessary to distinguish between the hegemonic logic of Kemalism, which made a very clear rejection of the Orient, and more hybridized (and more nuanced) positions in which the rejection of the Orient was more selective, emerging away from the state centres. In other words, Kemalism did not eliminate all previous associations and practices which involved Islam, even though it did have an impact upon many of them. Kemalism was hegemonic in articulating a central subject position of a de-Islamicized subject. However, this position opened the terrain of other possible subject positions articulated around it; ones that represented more hybridized subjectivities that were able to articulate, in different shapes and forms, Islamic and Kemalist elements.

21. J. Derrida, *Positions* (London: Athlone Press, 1987) pp. 48–52.

22. See L. Binder's *Islamic Liberalism* (Chicago: The University of Chicago Press, 1988) for a discussion of the link between Orientalism, modernization theory and Muslim societies.

23. A. al-Azmeh, 'Islam and Arab Nationalism', *Review of Middle East Studies*, vol. 8, 1988, makes a similar point regarding the split between Islamism and Arab Nationalism as being analogous to the division between state and civil society.

24. Laclau, *New Reflections*, p. 66.

25. Ibid.

26. Rorty makes the distinction between ironists and metaphysicians based on their different approaches to epistemology. See especially *Irony, Contingency, Solidarity*, pp. 73–8.

27. Laclau, *New Reflections*, pp. 65–6.

28. This use of 'occurrent' or 'presence-at-hand' is taken from Dreyfus's translation of Heidegger's *Vorhandenheit*, in Dreyfus, *Being-in-the-World*, p. xi.

29. See E. Laclau and C. Mouffe, 'Post-Marxism without Apologies', *New Left Review*, 166, November–December 1987 – a heroic effort to explain this to Geras – alas, to no avail.

30. Laclau, *New Reflections*, pp. 28–31.

31. See especially *Islam, the People and the State*, p. 161, where Zubaida comments how so much of the writing on the Muslim world suffers from slipping from the historically specific to the cultural essential.

32. This term is used by J.A. Ahmad, *Occidentosis* (Berkeley: Mizan Press, 1984) to describe the cultural policy of the Pahlavi regime.

33. This monograph can be found in Khomeini's *Islam and Revolution*, trans. H. Algar (Berkeley, Mizan Press, 1980).

34. See especially Zubaida, *Islam, the People and the State*, pp. 18–26.

35. On the impossibility of escaping modernity, see David Kolb, *The Critique of Pure Modernity* (Chicago: The University of Chicago Press, 1988) pp. 261–2. See also Laclau, *New Reflections*, pp. 187–8 for the impossibility of asserting Third World Identities in exclusive opposition to universalism. Interestingly, for Descombes, in his *Modern French Philosophy* (Cambridge: Cambridge University Press, 1980) pp. 136–40, one cannot even criticize Western metaphysics as being the ideology of the West, since the distinction between philosophy and ideology is itself a product of Western metaphysics.

36. V.S. Naipaul, as quoted in Said, *Covering Islam*, p. 7.

37. Zubaida, *Islam, the People and the State*, p. 13.

38. Ibid.

39. Rorty declares: 'Conforming to my own percepts, I am not going to offer arguments against the vocabulary I want to replace.' *Irony, Contingency, Solidarity*, p. 9. Alas, he forgets to cite Khomeini.

40. Zubaida, *Islam, the People and the State*, p. 13.

41. Ibid.

42. R. Rorty, *Essays on Heidegger and Others* (Cambridge: Cambridge University Press, 1991) p. 67.

43. Ibid., pp. 66–72.

44. Ibid., pp. 71–2.

45. In a similar light, see Connolly's remarks on the resignation of Rorty's politics, in his *Politics and Ambiguity* (Madison: The University of Wisconsin Press, 1987) pp. 120–22.

46. R. Young, *White Mythologies* (London: Routledge, 1990) pp. 19–20.

47. R. Carr, *The Spectator*, 11 May 1992, p. 27.

48. W. E. Connolly, *Political Theory and Modernity* (Oxford: Basil Blackwell, 1988) p. 1.

49. M. Weber, *The Protestant Ethic and the Spirit of Capitalism* (New York: Grove Press, 1957), p. 25; J. Habermas, *The Philosophical Discourse of Modernity* (Cambridge: Polity Press, 1987).

50. F. Halliday, 'The Iranian Revolution and its Implications', *New Left Review* 166, November–December 1987, p. 34.

51. M. Warren, *Nietzsche's Political Thought* (Cambridge, Mass.: M.I.T. Press, 1988) p. 14.

52. The experience of decolonization in the 'New World' (such as the American continent, Australia, New Zealand) illustrates the undecidable nature of its relation to modernity. In the case of Latin America, the independence movement started off as a loyalist reaction to the Spanish Crown in the face of the Napoleonic invasion of the Iberian peninsula. Here decolonization did not imply a questioning of the certainties of modernity; rather, it demonstrated its hegemonic character.

53. Young, *White Mythologies*, pp. 11–15.

54. Taken from Led Zeppelin's 'A Stairway to Heaven', this line was used as an epigraph by Bret Easton Elis for his novel *Less than Zero* (London: Pan Books, 1986).

55. Of course, such a description would be open to attack on the lines of: 'By enlarging the notion of post-modernity you make it meaningless.' Such an objection could only come from within the paradigm of referential language theory; i.e., that post-modernity has a specific positive content.

56. Salman Rushdie, *The Times*, 11 February 1993, p. 4.

57. See Aziz al-Azmeh's 'The Discourse of Cultural Authenticity: Islamist Revivalism and Enlightenment Universalism', in E. Deutsch, *Culture and Modernity* (Hawaii: Hawaii University Press, 1991). The curious thing about Azmeh's intervention is how he is able to criticize the essentialist logic of authenticity in the Arab world, but is unable or unwilling to overcome an equally essentialist notion of the universality of the West.

58. For 'strategic essentialism' see G. Spivik, *In Other Worlds* (New York: Methuen, 1991) p. 205. For 'weak thought' see G. Vattimo, 'Dialéctica, Diferencia y Pensamiento Débil', in G. Vattimo and P.A. Rovatti, eds, *El Pensamiento Débil* (Madrid: Catedra, 1990) pp. 31–6.

59. M. Foucault, *The Archaeology of Knowledge* (London: Tavistock, 1986) pp. 32–8, and 103–4.

60. Z. Brezinski, *Power and Principle* (Baltimore: Johns Hopkins University Press, 1981) p. 564.

61. For example, Fred Halliday writing on the eve of the Iranian Revolution discussed possible scenarios for a post-Pahlavi Iran. These included: a military dictatorship, a socialist revolution, a continuation of the dynasty. There is no indication of the possibility of an Islamist alternative. See his *Iran: Dictatorship and Development* (Middlesex: Penguin, 1979), pp. 300–309.

62. This thesis has been most sensationally advanced by Francis Fukiyama, *The End of History and the Last Man* (London: Hamish Hamilton, 1992).

63. Young, *White Mythologies*, pp. 2–3.

64. Connolly, *Politics and Ambiguity*, pp. 76–82.

65. This is the argument advanced by Descombes (1986), who reads the Foucault–Derrida debate as debate about the possibility of transcending the limits of Western reason, see pp. 136–9.

Notes on Contributors

Glenn Bowman is a social anthropologist teaching on the interdisciplinary Communications and Image Studies board at the University of Kent in Canterbury.

Rodolphe Gasché is Professor of Comparative Literature at the State University of New York, Buffalo.

Claudia Hilb is Associate Professor at the Faculty of Social Sciences, University of Buenos Aires.

Ernesto Laclau is Professor of Politics and Director for the Centre of Theoretical Studies in the Humanities and Social Sciences, University of Essex.

Aletta J. Norval is Lecturer in Politics, Department of Government, University of Essex.

Renata Salecl is a researcher at the Institute for Criminology, University of Ljubljana.

Bobby Sayyid is a Ph.D. student in the Ideology and Discourse Analysis Programme, Department of Government, University of Essex.

Anna Marie Smith is Assistant Professor, Department of Government, Cornell University.

Zoltán Szankay teaches at the Politics Department, University of Bremen, Germany.

Lilian Zac is a Ph.D. student in the Ideology and Discourse Analysis Programme, Department of Government, University of Essex.

Slavoj Žižek is Senior Researcher at the Institute for Social Sciences, Ljubljana.

Index